Reminiscer

Old Sheffield

Its streets and its people

Editor

Robert Eadon Leader

Alpha Editions

This edition published in 2020

ISBN : 9789354042355

Design and Setting By
Alpha Editions
www.alphaedis.com
email - alphaedis@gmail.com

REMINISCENCES

OF

OLD SHEFFIELD,

ITS STREETS AND ITS PEOPLE.

Edited by

ROBERT EADON LEADER, B.A.

SHEFFIELD :

LEADER AND SONS, INDEPENDENT OFFICE.

1875.

PREFACE.

This book does not claim to be anything so dignified as history. It is only a gathering together of the various threads out of which history is woven—threads which, if not seized and put into tangible shape, quickly escape altogether. Our local annals afford many illustrations of the loss that has been sustained through want of persons who would take the trouble carefully to chronicle small details, and no one can be fully conscious of that misfortune until he rises from the compilation of such a work as this. If each past generation for (say) a hundred and fifty years, had possessed its Cap'n Cuttle, who would not only have made a note of what he found, but have left that note where others could find it, my labours would have been greatly lightened.

I used the word "compilation" advisedly just now, for this book is nothing more ambitious. It had its origin in a very widely expressed wish that a number of articles and letters which appeared in *The Sheffield and Rotherham Independent* in 1872 and 1873, should, as contributions to our local folk-lore, be reproduced in a form more readily accessible, than scattered through the files of a newspaper.

My duty has thus been the modest one of collating, arranging, and (wherever that was possible) of verifying what more competent hands had written. To them, in the first instance, belongs any merit the book may possess. If I have thrown too flimsy a veil over the individuality of any member of this amicable confraternity, I must trust that the exigencies of editorship will form a sufficient excuse.

But Hallamshire men will feel that an additional value has been given to this gossip by the fact that most of the proof sheets have had the advantage of careful revision by the late Mr. William Swift, the one man best fitted to enrich by the suggestions, and to test by the resources, of his accurate mind. To his memory I venture to dedicate a volume, in whose progress he took a very lively interest.

I am quite conscious that not unfrequently events are mentioned in these pages which can hardly be considered properly to belong to "Old" Sheffield. Some of them have occurred within the memory of those amongst us who have not yet reached middle age. I have thought it better to err on this side rather than on the other; not to draw a line too hard and fast between the Sheffield of our own day and the Sheffield of our ancestors, conscious that each succeeding year will further remove any reproach that can be urged on this score.

R. E. LEADER.

ERRATA.

p. 27.—Isaac Barnes lived in the house at the corner of Campo lane and Hawley Croft, not of Lee Croft.

p. 31.—16 lines from bottom : dele the comma after " builder," and read "Joseph Oakes, the builder of Washington Works."

p. 31.—10 lines from bottom : for " assize," read "assay."

p. 44.—3 lines from bottom : for Sutcliffe, read Sutliffe.

p. 46.—line 22 : for Silvester, read Sylvester.

p. 71.—14 lines from bottom : for Younge and Rimington's, read Rimingtons and Younges'.

p. 87.—line 31 : for George Smith, read George Glanville Smith.

p. 98.—line 7 : for Peach, read Peech.

p. 103.—line 26 : for Laing, read Lang.

p. 110.—line 12 : for Rawmarsh, read Bramley.

p. 111.—line 6 : the name of Mr. Huntsman, as a steel converter, is omitted.

p. 192.—line 7 : for comparing, read confusing.

p. 202.—bottom line but one : for Riley, Carr & Co., read Riley Carr & Co.

REMINISCENCES OF OLD SHEFFIELD.

CHAPTER I.

PARADISE SQUARE, CAMPO LANE, HARTSHEAD, AND WATSON'S WALK.

Dramatis Personæ—Mr. WILLIAM WRAGG,⎫ *Ancient Citizens of*
            Mr. GEORGE LEIGHTON,⎬   *Sheffield.*
            Mr. SAMUEL EVERARD,⎭
            Mr. F. TWISS,   *The Antiquary.*
                       ⎧*a Modern Citizen of*
            Mr. RICHARD LEONARD,⎩   *Sheffield.*

Period—A.D. 1872-3.
Scene—A room in Leonard's house.

L EIGHTON : So the old steps in Paradise square have
    gone at last. Have you secured the top stone for your
collection, Mr. Twiss?

TWISS : No, it would have been rather too large ; but I
wish it could be preserved somewhere ; otherwise, like so
many other things that disappear, it will be consigned to
oblivion.

EVERARD : What eloquence has rung from that stone !

LEONARD : And what nonsense !

EVERARD : Brougham, Morpeth, Bethel, Milton, Elliott,
Dunn, Roebuck, and Mundella have thence charmed thousands of eager listeners.

LEONARD : And others have thence uttered rant enough
to cause the very stones to cry out.

LEIGHTON : There were few finer sights in Sheffield than
a great meeting in " t' Pot square," when the people were
really in earnest and the speaker a man of power.

LEONARD : The finest sight of all was when Mr. Henry
Hoole, flourishing his arms in a burst of exuberant eloquence, brought down his fist on Mr. Leader's hat and

B

knocked it over his eyes. That was a notable time, too, when Roebuck, sitting in his carriage at the bottom of the steps, listened to Campbell Foster's fulminations against him. There has seldom been so much use made of a white waistcoat and a loud voice. But this is not "Old Sheffield."

WRAGG : The eloquence from the steps has often been exceeded by the wit from the crowd, which always displayed a keen sense of the humorous and a quick perception of humbug.

LEONARD : Does anyone know when meetings were first held in the Square ?

TWISS : The first on record that I have found was in 1779, July 15, when Wesley preached "to the largest congregation he ever saw on a week-day." Then, in 1798, Rowland Hill came down and preached there one Sunday evening, after an afternoon service in Queen Street Chapel. He had an immense congregation, and confusion was caused towards the end by some fellow drawing his sword upon the people. Before that, out-door meetings were held on the Castle hill, or at the Church gates before the old Town Hall; sometimes on Crookes moor, or pieces of waste land—anywhere handy.

LEONARD : Pray spare us the old story about somebody who knew somebody else who remembered the Square as a corn-field.

WRAGG : Why should we ? There are people still living, or were not long ago, who remembered it a field of oats, entered from the top by Hicks' stile. An elderly lady, who died not many years ago, had gone with the maid to milk her father's cows, which were pastured there. There seems always to have been a footpath across, which was, indeed, the only thoroughfare from that side of the town. Pedestrians going up Silver street head (busier then, I believe, than High street) had to cross to Wheat's passage by Mr. Ryalls' office, if they were going to the Market; or if to the old Town Hall, they went over Hicks' stile, up St. James's row (or West row, or Virgin's row, for it has borne all three names)—there were steps at the bottom the whole width of the row—and then across the Churchyard.

EVERARD : The lamp in the centre of the Square has taken the place of the old cross shaft, removed there from Snig hill head ; but the steps up to it are, I should think, unchanged. The stocks were removed there from the Church gates.

WRAGG: And drunken men were placed in them on Sundays for punishment. The practice had to be dropped because of the disturbances it caused. The last instance of a drunken man being placed in the stocks was forty-three or forty-four years ago.

LEIGHTON: What became of the stocks in the Square?

WRAGG: When they got out of order, the two pieces of wood that confined the delinquents' feet became loose, and the late Mr. W. H. Clayton, the broker under the steps in the Square, removed them into his back yard for safety. There they remained for years, and no one ever inquired for them.

EVERARD: There were stocks also at Bridgehouses, opposite the end of the iron bridge; at Attercliffe; near Ecclesall Chapel; and near the old Sugar House, Sheffield moor.

WRAGG: Paradise square was the residence of notable men. I believe it was the first suburban place to which tradesmen retired away from their works.

LEONARD: Do you think so? There were surely suburban residences before that, and further out than that. I have been told by a gentleman still living, whose father resided there when he was a boy, that the Square has scarcely changed at all in appearance since very early in the century. It was then built all round as it is now, and with the same buildings, except a few which have been modernised on the east side.

WRAGG: Well, at any rate, many of the first families in the town lived there.

LEONARD: Dr. Gatty, in a note at p. 177 of his Edition of Hunter, says that "Thomas Broadbent took a lease of the field in 1776, and built the houses on the east side." Now, I happen to know that the lease to Thomas Broadbent—so far at least as concerns the land at the top of that side of the Square—is dated 1736. He had five daughters, and he built the five houses at the top—afterwards Bramley and Gainsford's offices and the adjoining ones—for them. On his death, they came into their possession. The date 1776 must be a clerical or a printer's error.

EVERARD: But that date suits better the corn-field recollections of the old inhabitants who have now passed away; unless, indeed, the Square remained a field after the houses on the east side were built. And this is very possible.

WRAGG: I have been told by a man who was in the service of her father, whose business was in Hollis croft,

that Miss Harrison was born in one of the houses at the top
side of the Square. Then Chantrey set up here, in what was
then No. 14, as an artist, and advertised that he took portraits in crayons. That was in 1802. Two years later he
made a step nearer his proper vocation, for he had commenced taking models from life.

EVERARD : It would be interesting to know if many of his
crayon portraits are extant.

LEONARD : Yes, numbers. You will find a long list of
them in Mr. John Holland's Memorials of Chantrey. The
whereabouts of most of them was known when that was published, in 1850.

EVERARD : You may see in the Old Church his first piece
of sculpture, the monument to Justice Wilkinson, which the
Iris, shrewd enough to predict the future celebrity of " the
young artist," praised as a " faithful and affecting resemblance." The bust of Dr. Browne, in the board-room of
the Infirmary, is also by Chantrey, executed in 1810—four
years after the Wilkinson monument.

LEIGHTON : Another worthy who lived in the Square up
to the time of his death, in 1817, was the Rev. George
Smith, curate of Ecclesall, and assistant-minister at the
Parish Church—the father of Mr. Albert Smith. He lived
near the bottom on the east side.

LEONARD : I see a window has been inserted in place of the
old door at the top of the steps, but the pillasters remain
to show where the door entered Mr. Hebblethwaite's school.

WRAGG : That room was originally built as a Freemasons'
lodge. It was afterwards put to various uses—a dancing-
school and a preaching-room. I remember hearing the notorious Robert Owen lecture there. At one time a considerable congregation of Independents assembled there, under
the ministry of the Rev. Mr. Parish. They contemplated
building a chapel, but they let the opportunity slip, and
much they regretted it afterwards. The last three survivors
of that congregation were Mr. Spear, of the firm of Spear
and Jackson ; Mr. Peter Spurr, tobacconist, father of Mr.
Spurr, chemist and druggist ; and the late Mr. Joseph Brit-
tlebank, scale-cutter. The leases have now fallen in, or are
falling in, so that possibly it may not remain long in its
old state.

TWISS : Yes ; the lease of part fell in two years ago (not
of the other part, for it is built on two leases), and that
shows that it is just over a century old, as the lease would

no doubt be a ninety-nine years' one. The room was built by Mr. Nowill, who had a shop in High street, opposite George street.

EVERARD : The pot market that was held in the Square on market days has quite disappeared, or is only represented by the crockery shops on the north side.

TWISS : There was a sort of pot market formerly by the Church gates.

WRAGG : The Square has been the scene of degrading transactions, as well as of honourable ones. Some brute once, for a wager, ate a live cat on the steps. I knew a person who bought his wife in the Square, whither she had been led in a halter.

LEIGHTON : "Q in the Corner" was an old public-house much frequented by fiddlers, since it was kept by Sam Goodlad, first fiddler on all important occasions.

WRAGG : The blind fiddlers were quite an institution. At one time there were six of them, several of whom were excellent performers on the violin. Their names were James Knight, Samuel Hawke, Thomas Booth, Alexander Clayton (brother of the late W. H. Clayton, broker), William Brumby, and Joseph Ward. They had their circuits, chiefly on the outskirts of the town, to which they went in pairs, playing firsts and seconds, and they kept to their own districts. At Christmas they went round " a Christmas-boxing," dropping into public-houses, and being liberally rewarded for the tunes they played.

LEONARD : There is a good story of a blind fiddler in John Wilson's edition of Mather's Songs, p. 55. This was " Blind Stephen," who was, I imagine, of earlier date than those you have mentioned.

EVERARD : The house at the top corner of Paradise square and Campo lane, now a dram-shop, was, sixty years ago, a respectable grocer's shop, kept by Mr. Newton (who was succeeded by Mr. Benjamin Ellis), and at that time was much celebrated amongst the grinders, both in town and country, for the quality of the articles of emery, crocus, and glue.

WRAGG : Yes, that shop had almost the monopoly of the trade.

TWISS : More recently the shop was occupied by Mr. Crossland, noted for his regular and punctual attendance to it the whole day long. His only recreation was a walk up Glossop road after his shop was closed at night.

EVERARD : Then came, as now, the barber's shop, at that

time occupied by the father and predecessor of the Mr. Copley who was recently burnt to death in a shocking manner by an explosion of gunpowder. The "Ball" Inn, next door, then the "Golden Ball," was kept in my youthful days by Antipas Stevens, a very intelligent and respectable man, who kept his house in proper order. I believe he took to it at the time Mr. Crich removed to the "Black Swan," Snighill. Mr. Stevens was by trade a silversmith; and I have an impression that he had been apprenticed to Ashforth, Ellis, and Co., or, at least, had worked for them. The Braziers' Sick Club met at his house, and the inn was, moreover, at that time, much frequented by country people on the market days, and more especially by the grinders from the neighbourhoods of Wadsley, Loxley, and Rivelin. After refreshing themselves there with the good "home-brewed," they would call at the adjoining shop of Mr. Ellis for their weekly supply of emery, and crocus, and groceries. In the watchmaker's shop a little further on, long occupied by Mr. David Johnson, and now by his son, was Mr. Zaccheus Dyson, whose active figure, dressed in a brown coat, drab small clothes, and broad-brimmed hat— for he belonged to the Society of Friends—still lives in the respectful remembrance of many of our townsmen. Mr. Dyson, it is related, once received a letter from a Quaker correspondent addressed "For Zaccheus Dyson, clock and watchmaker, Sheffield, near to a great heap of stones called a church."

TWISS: Mr. Dyson retired to Handsworth Woodhouse, and died there 4th June, 1861.

WRAGG: Narrow as Campo lane is, it was once still narrower, a slice having been taken from the Churchyard to widen it.

LEONARD: On the site of the offices of Burbeary and Smith, at the corner of North Church street, a worthy lady named Ward kept a school. She was much respected by her pupils and her friends, and she now enjoys a quiet old age in the Shrewsbury Hospital.

[Mrs. Ward died after this conversation took place, on the 31st December, 1872, aged 86. It is recorded that she enjoyed almost uninterrupted good health up to the hour of her death.]

EVERARD: The first shop past that was long occupied by the late Mr. John Innocent, bookseller. Before that it had been the lawyer's office of Mr. Brookfield, uncle of the late Mr. Charles Brookfield; and in 1839 Mr. Innocent there found the legal documents which were issued for the first prosecution of Montgomery in 1795.   Mr. Innocent placed in Montgomery's hands the papers he found, and from them he first learnt, and possessed certain proof, that he had been the victim of a state prosecution.   These documents stated, amongst other things, that "briefs were to be given to Counsel with the Attorney-General's compliments;" and "that this prosecution is carried on chiefly with a view to put a stop to the associated clubs in Sheffield; and it is to be hoped, if we are fortunate enough to succeed in convicting the prisoner, it will go a great way towards curbing the insolence they have uniformly manifested."   The papers, which were shown at an exhibition at the Music Hall, in 1848, were given to Mr. Innocent by Mrs. Brookfield, and he gave them to Montgomery, refusing all payment, although the poet offered any money for them.

LEONARD : I have heard that a third and still more bitter prosecution of Mr. Montgomery was threatened.

EVERARD : This was in 1806.   Montgomery actually received the legal notices for a prosecution, based on his strictures on the campaign in Germany, when General Mack and 39,000 Austrians laid down their arms.   He himself said, "I never knew how the blow missed me, for it was aimed with a cordiality that meant no repetition of the stroke.   The death of Nelson probably saved me, for in the next *Iris* I spoke of that event in a strain of such patriotism that my former disloyalty was perhaps overlooked."

TWISS : A fortunate escape.

EVERARD : A few doors further on the lane were the Scantleburys, worthy Quakers, who dealt in looking-glasses.   There was old Thomas Scantlebury, of The Hills; and he had three sons, John Barlow Scantlebury, Joseph Scantlebury, and Samuel Scantlebury.   Thomas Scantlebury and his eldest son, John Barlow, were very prominent opponents of Church rates.   Meetings used to be held in the Churchyard adjoining, and the speakers stood on the tombstones.   Some of the family emigrated to America.

LEONARD : Yes; the two younger sons, Joseph and Samuel. The latter is still living in Chicago, and retains his connection with the Society of Friends; as I see from a letter to the *Independent* respecting the opposition to the church rates. "Thomas Scantlebury," he says, "was the adviser, chiefly; while his son, John Barlow Scantlebury, took the more prominent part.   I well remember that, on one occasion, the opponents of the church rates would have fatally committed

themselves but for my father.   The momentous question had
been put and seconded in his absence, but the people refused
to vote on it until they had heard his views.   When he came
in, he very briefly stated his opposition to the motion, showing that it would form a very dangerous precedent.   The
motion was then withdrawn.   The people said that the Vicar
and his set could get on the blind side of everybody but old
Thomas Scantlebury.   I remember old Thomas Rawson was
at that meeting, as active as ever.   I believe I never saw him
afterwards."

TWISS : Mr. Thomas Scantlebury died at "The Hills,"
on the Grimesthorpe road, August 14, 1821 ; his son, John
Barlow Scantlebury, died April 28, 1837.   Old Mrs. Scantlebury was the daughter of John Barlow, the last of the family
that had carried on the old business of manufacturers of pen
and pocket cutlery on the premises in Campo lane, just beyond Mr. Scantlebury's, the east front of which looks down
the Hartshead.   They had been there as owners and occupiers of the property ever since the year 1679, "and I cannot tell how long previous," says Mr. Samuel Scantlebury
in the letter Mr. Leonard has just quoted.   It was Oba-
diah Barlow, the great-great-grandfather of Samuel Scantlebury, who had the premises in 1679.   Whether the Barlow
of Neepsend, who died in 1740, was of the same family or
not is doubtful.   John Barlow died in 1798, and one of the
best businesses in Sheffield died with him.   The trade mark
was the simple name thus—$\frac{BAR}{LOW}$

LEONARD : I have spoken of old Mrs. Ward.   Before her
time there was another lady of the same name, some six or
eight doors from the Barlow property.   She had been house-
keeper to the John Barlow who has been mentioned, and he
set her up in the grocery business.   Her shop looked more
like a greenhouse than a grocer's shop.   She always had her
window and every bit of spare room filled with some beautiful
flower or plant.   Mr. Samuel Scantlebury writes, " If I remember right she had a geranium that used nearly to fill her
front windows.   It was there I first saw the hydrangea.
There cannot be many who remember her ; she must have
been dead more than 65 years.   The dear old woman remembered me in her will.   She left me a guinea for pocket-money !"

WRAGG : Well, this brings us in our journey along the
lane to the Hartshead, and to the Broadbents' house fronting
York street, a few years ago occupied by Messrs. Pye-Smith
and Wightman, and now by Messrs. J. and G. Webster.

EVERARD : Before you tell us the history of that house, let me just say that in the workshops at the back of Mr. Scantlebury's premises yet another member of the Society of Friends, Mr. William Chapman, carried on for many years the business of an engraver.

TWISS : I well remember his burial (one of the last interments in the graveyard of the Friends' Meeting-house), and the solitary sentence uttered by Friend E. Baines—" After death the judgment."

EVERARD : He was a very amiable and intelligent man, highly esteemed in his denomination, and at one time he was actively engaged in promoting the welfare of its members by visiting the country districts. His grave and Christian deportment, combined with his kindly disposition and courteous manners, secured the confidence and respect of those who had any intercourse with him.

TWISS : We shall still keep among the Friends, for Joseph Broadbent, who died in 1684, was one of the first generation of the Society in the town. I believe it was his son Nicholas who built the house in the Hartshead. He died in 1736, and was father of Joseph Broadbent, merchant, said to have been the first banker in Sheffield, who died in 1761.

LEONARD : Is it worth while to go into matters that may be found by any of us in Gatty's " Hunter ?"

TWISS : No ; but the point I want to get at is, were the Broadbents the first bankers in the town ? I have been told that the first person who practised this profession in Sheffield was one of the fraternity of pawnbrokers. In the "Hallamshire," it is said, "In 1778, Messrs. J. and T. Broadbent opened a bank in Hartshead, on the failure of Mr. Roebuck's bank, which was the first known in Sheffield, and only lasted eight years ; and in 1780 the Broadbents failed."

LEONARD : If Joseph Broadbent died in 1761, how could he be a banker in 1778 ? Your information and Hunter's do not seem to agree.

TWISS : They were the sons of Joseph—Joseph and Thomas, who were the bankers of 1778; but had their father been a banker before them ? I saw the other day an early Sheffield bank note, of which I took a copy :

No. R t O 6

Sheffield Old Bank, January 24, 1783.

We promise to pay the bearer on demand Five Guineas. At Sheffield, value received.

HAN. HASLEHURST and SON.

£5. 5s.   R t O 6

Haslehurst and Son, it seems, became unfortunate ; for the note was endorsed with an exhibit under a commission in bankruptcy, 23rd June, 1785. But in the fact that it is called the Sheffield Old Bank, I am led to inquire : Did the bank, afterwards carried on by Messrs. Parker, Shore and Co., arise from the ashes of this one, for it bore the same name ?

WRAGG : Whether Mr. Joseph Broadbent was the first banker or not, he was, at any rate, the first merchant who traded with America. There is a good story told of one of the Broadbents, at the time of the suspension of the bank. That suspension took place on a Monday morning. On the preceding Sunday, some Derbyshire man came knocking at the bank door. A voice from within asked what he wanted. The countryman replied, " I have come to the bank." " We do not transact business on Sundays," was the answer. Then the countryman said, " I have not come for money, but I have brought some." The other replied, " That is quite a different thing." So the door was opened, and the Derbyshire man left his money.

LEONARD : That would be called by a hard name now-a-days.

WRAGG : The Messrs. Binney were afterwards in the Hartshead premises.

TWISS : Yes, but the first successor of the Broadbents was Mr. John Turner, a merchant, who died in 1796. He was uncle to Henry Longden and to Mrs. Binney ; and thus we see how the premises came into the occupation of the Binneys.

WRAGG : I have been told that the Binneys had at one time the best country trade in the town as merchants, and the largest steel furnaces (they have just been pulled down, and the bricks are in heaps in the yard). I believe they were the first steel manufacturers who had a tilt. One of their best travellers was the father of Mr. Joseph Haywood. I had the impression that the father of the late Mr. G. W. Hinchliffe, of Eyre street, was also a traveller for the Binneys, but that, I find, was a mistake.

LEONARD : So long ago as 1825, the building had been turned into lawyers' offices. In that year it was occupied by Mr. Copeland, solicitor.

WRAGG : While we are among the Friends, and so near their Meeting-house, permit me to say, one of them told me that, in his recollection, he can count more than a score who have left Sheffield and gone to America and become ministers, who, had they remained in the town, would never have been able to open their mouths.

LEONARD : I thought there were no ministers among the Quakers.

LEIGHTON : You must forgive the abrupt transition when I say—Now, hail to thee, old "Dove and Rainbow!" Sixty years ago, the drum and fife were scarcely ever absent from thy door, when Sergeant Kenyon and Sergeant Barber were on the look-out for recruits. Well do I remember seeing one of them come forth with his corporal, two or three rank and file, with drum and fife, and march boldly to Water lane, and there draw up his detachment in line. Then did the sergeant, with streamers flying in the air, sheathe his sword, and he and his men marched boldly into the public-house, and, like a gallant warrior as he was, called for his "tankard" of foaming ale. The sergeant had ready for each recruit a spade-ace guinea, with his Majesty's portrait impressed upon it, pigtail and all. The warlike song was—

> Roll up, so merrily, march away ;
> Soldier's glory lives in story :
> His laurels are green when his locks are grey,
> And it's heigh for the life of a soldier.

In my youth, I and others of my own age were in the habit of singing songs about "Lord Wellington in Spain," and Campo lane sent out its quota both for the navy and the army. I could mention names, were it necessary—John Dawson, himself the son of a soldier who died fighting in India, and Artilleryman Dixon, and others.

WRAGG : I have heard very old people say that the Dove and Rainbow was once on fire. The landlady had made her escape from the flames, but she turned back to rescue a considerable sum of money, and perished.

TWISS : That, I imagine, would be in 1782. The landlord's name was Thomas Oates, and a servant girl perished as well as his wife.

WRAGG : The old *Iris* office was at one time the largest shop in the town, and had the two largest windows—rounded so as to form the arc of a circle, like a few that are still to be seen, with small panes, unsupplanted as yet by big squares of plate glass.

EVERARD : Montgomery's last apprentice, Mr. Robert Leader, has spoken feelingly of the shutters which he had to put up and take down. They were "very many, very heavy, and had to be carried a considerable distance. When work in the office closed, at 6.30 or 7 p.m., the unfortunate apprentice had to return to the place at 8 or 9, to put up the shutters."

TWISS: Apprentices in newspaper offices have not to submit to such tasks now.

WRAGG: Before Mr. Gales's time this house was the residence of Dr. Buchan, who wrote there his celebrated work, *Domestic Medicine*. At one time the book was in the hands of almost every one on both sides of the Atlantic, wherever the English language is spoken.

TWISS: Another of Montgomery's apprentices, years earlier, was the eldest son of the Rev. George Smith. He was named Matthewman, after his maternal grandfather, and he became a partner of Montgomery's. He afterwards entered the East India Company's army and died in India.

LEONARD: I have heard Mr. Montgomery's sanctum described as an upper room behind the shop, over the office coal-place. It had a most depressing out-look upon back premises and dingy walls and roofs. The editor-poet had a standing office-desk in the room, but his favourite writing place was a round table which stood near the fire. At the time my informant best remembers the room, Montgomery was compiling his collection of hymns, and the table was covered with the books that he used in his work.

LEIGHTON: It has often been told how the poet sometimes served customers, but it was simply an accidental or exceptional thing. My feeling towards him when I was sent to make a purchase was one of fear—he was so curt. Then, of course, I was only young, and so great a man could not be expected to be civil to a boy!

LEONARD: Numbers of incidents connected with Montgomery's life might be mentioned, but most of them would be such as have already been published; and I take it the great object of our conversations is to gather together unwritten folk-lore.

WRAGG: I suppose there's no great harm if one does tell a story twice over?

EVERARD: At any rate, the subsequent history of the Gales family, which is second only in interest to that of Montgomery himself, has not often been told, and I should suggest that Mr. Leonard read it to us.

LEONARD: I've no objection whatever. This is it:—"When Mr. Joseph Gales, printer, bookseller, auctioneer, and editor of the then popular *Sheffield Register*, left the town in 1794, he went, as you all know, to America. The fact is, Mr. Gales had to flee. A meeting held on Castle hill in April of that year had passed strong resolutions and spoken fierce words against the Government, which led to a prosecution. Mr. Gales was present at that meeting, and appears to have sympathised with its objects, but he was not included in the prosecution. In June, a letter from a Sheffield printer to Hardy, the secretary of the London Corresponding Society, was seized, and Gales was suspected, though unjustly, of being the writer. A warrant was issued against him, and he only escaped arrest from the officers sent to execute it by a prompt flight. In the following week's *Register* Mr. Gales took a formal leave of his friends and readers, denying most distinctly that he had written, dictated, or been privy to the letter addressed to Hardy. If his imprisonment, or death, would serve the cause which he had espoused—the cause of peace, liberty, and justice, it would, he said, be cowardice to fly; 'but, convinced that by ruining my family and distressing my friends by risking either would only gratify the ignorant and the malignant, I shall seek that livelihood in another land which I cannot peaceably obtain in this.' Under such circumstances and with such feelings, Joseph Gales, after sundry concealments, got out of the country. After a short stay in Germany, he went to America and began life afresh. He was a clever, forcible writer and a keen politician, and his proclivities speedily drew him to his old profession. Arrived at Philadelphia, in August, 1795, he began business as a printer there. In about a year, judging from the numbering of one of his papers which is in our possession, dated June, 1797, he became the proprietor, by purchase from Mr. Oswald, of the *Independent Gazetteer* of that city. He called it ' *Gales's Independent Gazetteer*;' but he did not keep it long, re-selling it at the end of the first year to Mr. S. H. Smith, of whom we shall hear again. In September, 1799, Mr. Gales went to North Carolina, and there he established the *Raleigh Register*, which he published for forty years, only retiring from the concern a year or two before his death, which took place at Raleigh, on the 24th August, 1841, at the advanced age of eighty years. His youngest son, who was born in North Carolina, succeeded to the newspaper. When Mr. Gales arrived in America he had with him a son, also named Joseph Gales, then about nine years of age. This Joseph Gales, Junior, kept in the journalistic track. In 1806 he joined, as reporter, the *National Intelligencer*, a paper

that had been established in Washington, in 1800, by the
Samuel H. Smith previously mentioned, with the object of
maintaining a newspaper in the capital, Republican in politics, which should yield to the Administration a vigorous
support. In 1809 Gales was made a partner, and in 1810
he became sole proprietor of this journal. It lived until the
year 1869, when the *New York Evening Post*, noticing its
death, said :—' Mr. William W. Seaton, a brother-in-law of
Mr. Gales, and previously editor of the *Petersburg Republican*
and *North Carolina Register*, became associated with him in
the enterprise in 1812. The *Intelligencer* was a vigorous
supporter of the war with Great Britain, and enjoyed a high
reputation as a public journal. Messrs. Gales and Seaton
used to do their own reporting of debates in Congress, one
always sitting in the Senate and the other in the House of
Representatives, during the sessions. Their Register of Debates is regarded as a standard source of American history.
The tone of the paper under their management was firm,
moderate, and cautious. With a rearrangement of parties,
the *National Intelligencer* adhered to Mr. Clay, and was a
Conservative-Whig journal so long as the Whig party had an
existence. The proprietors stood high in public confidence,
and in 1840 Mr. Seaton was elected mayor of Washington, and
held the office for twelve consecutive years. Mr. Gales died
in 1860. The style of the *Intelligencer's* editorial management deserves a mention. There used to be often a sparse-
ness of leading articles, succeeded at intervals by the production of a paper covering a page or more, always written with
force and ability, but at the same time rather too solid for
the general reader.' Into the cause of the death of the *Intelligencer* we need not here inquire. It was prosperous
under the son of our old townsman, Mr. Gales, who, in the
free atmosphere of the New World, followed out the career
his father had begun here. After he ceased his labours and
went to his rest, the paper grew more and more out of harmony with the spirit of the times, and paid the penalty that
all newspapers so managed must pay—death. In the autumn
of 1868 an old contributor to the *Intelligencer* visited Sheffield, and being curious—as so many Americans are—to see
the place from which his former employer went forth, visited
the antique shop in the Hartshead where Gales commenced
and Montgomery continued the then dangerous trade of editor
and publisher. The poetic nine have long deserted the narrow alley. Where flowers of Parnassus once bloomed, the

votaries of Bacchus then revelled. In short, the building
had been turned into a beershop. Joiners were removing the
quaintly-carved door-case with the ancient fan-light, to replace
them with some more convenient structure in plain and vulgar deal. The stranger was horrified at the desecration, and,
inquiring, found that the old wood was being removed, with
some lumber, for lighting fires. His plea for mercy was admitted; triumphant, he carried off the old door-case, and out
of it had constructed a number of boxes, one of which is placed
in the National Museum at Washington, suitably inscribed,
and bearing a photograph of the premises rendered sacred by
the memory of Gales and Montgomery."

TWISS : It should be added that Montgomery's Hartshead
shop is, at the present time, not a beershop, but a grocer's.
The Gales family lived at Eckington for many years ; the
first of the name of whom there is record, Timothy, was appointed parish clerk in 1707. His son Timothy married
Sarah Clay, of Eckington, in 1735, and their eldest son,
Thomas, was the father of Joseph Gales, of the Hartshead,
the proprietor of the *Sheffield Register*. He was born February 4, 1761. I have here a copy of the inscription on the
tombstone of the family in Eckington churchyard :—

Under this Stone
Lie the Remains of three Daughters of
THOMAS and SARAH GALES, of Eckington,
and sisters of JOSEPH GALES, who died at Raleigh,
North Carolina, U.S., August 24, 1841, aged 80 years.
ELIZABETH GALES,
Departed this life, February 16, 1821,
Aged 49 years.
Farewell, beloved, we meet again.
ANNE GALES,
Died January 17, 1838, aged 70 years.
" Jesus saith unto her, I am the Resurrection and the Life."
SARAH GALES,
Died February 18, 1857, aged 84 years.
With these sisters, together and severally, lived for more than sixty
years (dying in the presence of the last-named, at Sheffield, April 30, 1854),
JAMES MONTGOMERY,
The Christian Poet, Patriot, and Philanthropist.
Requiescat in pace.

WRAGG : It was in the Hartshead and Watson's walk (so
called from Messrs. Watson's silversmiths' factory) that the
first eating-houses were established ; now there is not one left.

LEONARD : Yes, I understand the name of the proprietor
of one of the cook-shops there was Thornhill. He lived at
a house down Harvest lane, popularly called "T' hen hole,"

because there was a tradition that poultry feloniously obtained
was pushed through a hole into his cellar at night.

LEIGHTON: A little below, too, in Hartshead, Matthias
D'Amour kept a "cook-shop"—the first, I believe, in the
town.

LEONARD: D'Amour's "Autobiography" was written for
him by the late Mr. Paul Rodgers, if you will excuse the
bull, which is not mine, but theirs. It is an interesting story
of his adventures as a kind of confidential servant to various
gentlemen, and as valet to the Duchess of Gordon; but the
strangest part of all is that he should settle down at last in
the Hartshead, in Sheffield, as the keeper of "an eating-
house and poulterer's shop."

LEIGHTON: That is accounted for by his wife, who had
also been in the service of the Duchess of Gordon, having
connections in the neighbourhood.

LEONARD: In the course of the book we are not once told
what was her maiden name, but her mother lived at Wood-
hall, some eleven miles from Sheffield, and she had a brother
in Cheney row, whose name also is omitted. At first,
D'Amour set up a canal boat, and conveyed coal from Whittington and Norwood collieries to Retford; but jealousies
arising, he sold his boat. He came to Sheffield on the very
last day of the eighteenth century, began his eating-house at
4, Market street, did well there, and in four years removed to
the Hartshead, where he remained until 1826, when, "trade
being much depressed after the panic of 1825, he and his
wife willingly retired from all kind of business." In point
of fact, they seem to have lost their money. D'Amour was
a native of Antwerp, and was eighty-six years of age when
his life was published. He lived to the great age of ninety-
three, not dying until 1842.

LEIGHTON: In the Hartshead, some sixty years ago, the
late Mr. Thomas Pearson carried on business as a wine merchant, and there realised a large fortune.

WRAGG: It is said that on his late premises there are
two cellars cut out of the solid rock, one underneath the
other. They are now occupied by Messrs. J. S. and T.
Birks, grocers and wine dealers.

LEIGHTON: Then there was "T'oil i' 'Wall" (The Hole in
the Wall; and the house now occupied by Mr. Allcroft, with
entrances both from Hartshead and Watson's walk, was kept
by Mr. Sam Turner—"Gin Sam," as he was called, to distinguish him from "Flannel Sam," the draper. "Gin Sam"

was the most gentlemanly landlord I ever met with, both in manner and conduct. He was particularly good-looking, had a pleasant smile and a kind word for all about him, and took a pride in waiting upon his customers himself.

Twiss: And his customers included the most respectable business men in the town. There was more sociableness among the shopkeepers at that time than now, and the public-houses were so kept that orderly folk could go to them, without injury to themselves or to their reputation.

Wragg: The doorway of Sam Inner's public-house used to be almost blocked up on a Saturday night by men crowding to get in and by others trying to get out. Turner had formerly been a carpet weaver, and had worked for Mr. Wildsmith, of the Crofts. He got, however, by an accident, his arm broken, and during the period of enforced idleness which followed, he married a widow woman, whose name I forget, but who kept a public-house that was taken down to build the Town Hall. That would be about 1805.

Lamberton: Lower still in Watson's walk was Mrs. Kean's eating-house, once well known. On the opposite side, the premises now swallowed up by Messrs. Cockayne's carpet warehouse were occupied, though somewhat later than the time we have been speaking of, by a coffee-shop on the ground floor, the Mechanics' Library and a billiard-room up-stairs. In the corner now enriched in Messrs. Cockayne's shop were the offices to which Mr. B. J. Wake—a most honourable man, of whom I always think with respect and gratitude—removed from Norfolk street about the year 1816 or 1817. What is now the Waterloo Tavern was originally the manufactory of Messrs. Watson. They were, I believe, silver-smiths before plating on copper was invented, and the premises now occupied by Messrs. Birks and Mr. Atkinson formed their frontage.

Twiss: It was, if I am not mistaken, in one of the houses you have named that the amusing interview of Justice Wilkinson with the pugilists took place.

Leonard: What was that?

Twiss: Oh, you must know the story. The old Vicar was noted in his time as an amateur pugilist; and one day, when he was dining with some local officials at the house that is now the Turf Tavern, two strangers called and sent in an urgent request that he would see them. The Vicar, quietly leaving his companions, complied. What was it they wanted? With some apologies they told him how great a distance they had come in consequence of having heard of his fondness for boxing, and buoyed by the fond hope that he would not disdain, as a particular favour, to give them a display of his skill. Nothing could please the old Justice better. With great urbanity he at once assented, the gloves were procured, and were used with a " science " that convinced the visitors they had not taken their journey fruitlessly; and in the end they left well pleased with the success of their mission.

EVERARD : A good story, which I will cap with another, also appropriate to the locality, and also with a clerical flavour. About the middle of the last century there lived at Malin Bridge a working man, in humble circumstances, but who bore a good character amongst his neighbours for integrity and moral worth, and who was, moreover, a strict Churchman. He had a son named William, who had attained to an age suitable to receive the rite of confirmation, according to the ritual of the Church of England, and his father became very solicitous that this matter should be attended to without any unnecessary delay. On a certain day the Archbishop of York held a Confirmation service in the Parish Church, and this worthy man accompanied his son to Sheffield for the purpose of attending it. From some misunderstanding as to the time, it so happened that on their arrival at the Old Church, the Confirmation service was over, and the Archbishop, clergy, and congregation were dispersed. What was to be done ? A man of ordinary character would just have returned home. But, instead of doing so, he ascertained that the Archbishop had gone down to the house Mr. Leighton has spoken of, in Watson's walk, and thither the father and son followed him. The servants refused them access to the Archbishop, as he was just sitting down to dinner ; but, happening to overhear the altercation, his lordship came to the top of the stairs and asked what was the matter. The father explained the circumstances, and the Archbishop, after asking some questions, and hearing young William repeat the Lord's Prayer and the Creed, confirmed him on the stairhead of the public-house ! The father and the boy, we may well suppose, trudged home highly gratified with the enjoyment of so special a privilege. The son was afterwards the grandfather of a highly esteemed magistrate recently deceased.

LEONARD : I do not see why you should hesitate to add that the boy so confirmed was the grandfather of the late Mr. Thomas Dunn. He who had shown so much determina-

tion to get the rite administered to his son was the first of
the Dunns—the first also of the Thomas Dunns—resident in
this neighbourhood. He had come from Boston about the
year 1730, to be apprenticed to an ancestor of the late Col.
Fenton. His Malin Bridge house was a neat, substantial
cottage, with a pointed gable, covered with a fruit-tree. It
was swept away, along with adjacent buildings, by the great
flood of 1864. The son, William Dunn, the hero of the
confirmation story, was, as that sufficiently shows, brought
up a Churchman ; but, as he subsequently married a strict
Dissenter, his son Thomas, father of the late Mr. Dunn, was
educated as a holder of Nonconformist tenets, and, with his
family, he attended Queen Street Chapel for many years. He
was a self-taught man, of much natural ability, and his tastes
are indicated by the fact that he was the first person who lectured in Sheffield on electricity. His wife was a Holland, the
daughter of a resident at Shiregreen. She was eight months
old in 1745, when the Young Pretender and his followers
were marching south; and, as it was confidently affirmed and
implicitly believed that the rebels would impale every baby on
their swords, she was hidden in a holly bush. The rebels
are said to have been within a mile of her father's house at
that time, and every man in the hamlet had gone out to fight.

LEIGHTON : The fighting may be problematical.

LEONARD : Yes ; it is possible that curiosity, rather than
valour, had taken the men away, for we know, as a matter of
history, what an unopposed march the rebels had. This
story, however, reminds one of the tradition that, on his
return northwards, Prince Charles Edward visited Sheffield,
and was a guest of the Heatons, in the Pickle. I went into
that question once (as Mr. Brooke, in " Middlemarch," would
say), and I came to the conclusion that the evidence in support of the story was very feeble. It consisted chiefly of dim
remembrances of mysterious transactions, handed down by
old Mrs. Heaton, who was a little girl in 1745, to her descendants, and the cherished belief of the family that a harpsi-
chord, a sword, a wine-glass, and other articles were presents
from the Prince. On the other hand, the known facts of the
Young Pretender's progress and retreat lend no countenance
whatever to the legend.

EVERARD : Mr. Leighton has mentioned the Mechanics'
Library, and I think perhaps you may be interested in hearing some account of an institution very popular and useful in
its day, that has been drawn up by one who was intimately

associated with its management.   Do you care to hear it?

ALL : Much.

EVERARD (reads) : "Half a century has nearly elapsed
since the Mechanics' Library was first established, by resolutions passed at a public meeting, held in the Town Hall, on
December 27th, 1823.   Most of the individuals who took a
prominent part in that meeting have passed away, including
Montgomery, the Rev. Dr. Sutton, Sir Arnold Knight, Mr.
Edward Smith, Mr. Asline Ward, the Rev. Thos. Smith, and
others.

"From a small beginning the institution went steadily
forward, advancing year by year in public esteem, and strictly
adhering to its original intention of the purchase and circula-
tion of books, without allowing its funds to be diverted to any
other object.   In the course of thirty years it had accumulated 8,000 volumes, enrolled six hundred members, and had
a weekly issue of six hundred books.   Of the general character of these works Mr. Montgomery, who was from the first
the president, on a certain occasion bore this testimony :—
' I offer it as my deliberate opinion that there does not exist
in this kingdom a public library of miscellaneous literature in
which will be found a smaller proportion of objectionable
volumes than in this of the Sheffield Mechanics.   Without
meaning the smallest disparagement to what is called the
Gentlemen's Library here, the proportion of books not cal-
culated to be particularly profitable to the reader, or perma-
nently enhancing the value of the property itself, is far
greater ;' and which difference he attributed to the large admission of novels, romances, and plays.

"By a certain clause in the 24th rule of the Mechanics'
Library, ' novels and plays ' were excluded.   After things had
gone on quietly for some years, at length the abrogation of
this law became the subject of animated and even stormy debates at the annual meetings.   On the one side the ' Re-
pealers ' asserted that to exclude so large a portion of the
current and popular literature of the day was inconsistent
with the library being regarded as a public institution, and
also with the fact of the actual admission of works of ' fiction '
at all ; and that it was unfair towards those members who
possessed the taste for that kind of reading, and was opposed
to the entire spirit, freedom, and liberality of the age.   To
all this, on the other hand, the ' Constitutionalists ' stoutly
maintained that the clause in question was a fundamental
principle of the institution, and could not be repealed without

a breach of faith with the original donors of money and books, which had been solicited and given on that express understanding; that to make the change required would be to alter the entire character of the library, and to lessen it in public esteem and confidence; that the funds were much more wisely and profitably expended in solid standard works, which would tend to improve the intellectual and moral character much more effectually than the reading such ephemeral productions as ' novels ;' and that, whatever the library might happen to lose in subscriptions by adhering to the rule, it would be likely to lose much more by cancelling it.

" So the controversy went on at the annual meetings with more or less of acrimony, common sense, wit, and logic on both sides; but, on the whole, it was carried on in the spirit of fairness. This yearly breeze did the institution no harm, but rather good. It tended to purify the atmosphere and invigorate the life, and was not the occasion of anything worse than a very slight and temporary interruption of the general good feeling prevalent amongst the members.

" In 1853 a soirée was held in the Cutlers' Hall, on which occasion the Mayor, Francis Hoole, Esq., was in the chair, and the late Earl Fitzwilliam was present and made an excellent speech. The object in view in holding this meeting was of a strictly practical nature, namely, that of placing more prominently before the public the claims and privileges of the institution. One thing that especially commended it to favour was that it was not sectarian either in religion or politics. Its members consisted of every class of religion and all shades of politics.

" The Mechanics' Library thus went on year by year in its unostentatious course of practical usefulness, furnishing the means of self-improvement and intellectual gratification to hundreds who, without such provision, would not have entered on the course of life with the same advantages, and many of whom now, in middle life or advanced in years, look back upon the institution with no ordinary feelings of kindly regard and thankfulness.

" The Mechanics' Library had been established about seven years when Mr. Hebblethwaite was appointed secretary, which office he sustained, with only a brief interruption, for nearly thirty years. He had been a member from its commencement, and, in a speech delivered on the occasion of the presentation of a testimonial at the close of his services, he remarked :—' I was present at the origin of this library, at a meeting in the old Town Hall, on Saturday morning in Christmas week. It was an inauspicious time, but yet the room was crowded to excess. I have now before me the names of those who addressed the meeting. I was then a stripling, but I was intensely interested in the proceedings. I stood for three hours—for I could not get a seat—to hear the addresses, and none made a greater impression upon me than a speech of the late Rev. T. Smith, who was then at his best. It had a great influence on me at the time. He beautifully depicted the benefits such an institution might confer on the working men of Sheffield, and he mentioned the case of a working man of his acquaintance who, though spending forty years of his life in a cotton manufactory, had mastered Latin, Greek, and Hebrew, was well versed in mathematics, and had considerable knowledge of medicine. This man had had a wife and seven children to maintain by his own labour, but no family in the town was more respectable, no children were better fed, clothed, and educated, and several of them were reading Latin, Greek, and Hebrew with their father. This account of what a working man had done stimulated me to desire to do likewise, and renewed my ardour in the studies in which I was engaged. Thus the institution has imparted a bias to my life and character, and no doubt it has done the same thing for many others. It was no slight privilege as secretary of this institution to enjoy intercourse with its late president, Mr. Montgomery. I frequently saw him, and received from him such kindness as was most important to a young man in the position I was called to. The benefits that have resulted from this library, directly and indirectly, have been great. It has been the pioneer of some other institutions that have since flourished.'

"The office of secretary, to which Mr. Hebblethwaite was appointed and which he so long satisfactorily filled, was not one of honorary distinction, but required much time, thought, and work. These duties he discharged with a punctuality that seldom failed, and with uniform courtesy. One of his chief qualities was that of aptitude in matters of business. In fact, he may justly be said to have been a ' model ' secretary. All that he advised and did bore a certain impress of clear-sightedness, promptitude, and despatch. At the committee meetings (at which Montgomery, as long as he could, attended) there was scarcely ever a document wanting, an account incompleted, or minutes unentered, or any special business that he had engaged to do unattended to. All the matters to be considered and determined were clearly and orderly arranged. The discharge of these duties involved an amount of time and labour, cheerfully devoted to them, of which few can form any adequate conception. There can be no question that the institution was greatly indebted to his steady attentions and personal influence for the extent of its usefulness and the estimation in which it was held by the public. Besides his connection with the library, Mr. Hebblethwaite, for not less than thirty years, was the teacher of a large and efficient day school, and also, for more than the same period, the superintendent of a Sunday school ; so that it may be safely affirmed that few men—perhaps no man— ever exerted a greater or more beneficial influence on the minds of the youth in this town. Highly and generally esteemed by the members, as well as by the rest of the community, after a long course of honorary service, Mr. Hebblethwaite retired a short time before the institution was merged into the Free Library.

"On the formation of the Free Library it became quite evident that an institution supported by a public rate levied on all householders must seriously injure, and eventually destroy, one sustained by voluntary subscription. Such was the result. The Mechanics' Library became absorbed into the Free Library, and now only exists as a pleasant memory of the past.

"But as naturally identified and long connected with that institution, we now proceed to notice the librarian. Mr. Alfred Smith was as much a Sheffield notability, and in certain respects of a similar old-fashioned type, as the late Mr. John Holland. His father was a currier, for some time living in Queen street, but afterwards he removed to Fig Tree lane. Mr. Smith brought up his two sons, Alfred and Frederick, to the business ; and I have myself often seen Alfred with his apron on and shirt sleeves turned up above the elbows, standing at the shop-door. That shop was a stone building, apparently two centuries old, with small leaded window-panes, a little above Mr. Haxworth's surgery, in Fig Tree lane. Alfred's father was a respectable and shrewd man, possessing more than an ordinary share of information, and well known to the public men of that day. He greatly admired, and was intimately acquainted with, Montgomery, and stood by the poet on one of the occasions when he was examined and committed to prison by the magistrates, and went to fetch the persons who became his sureties.

" Mr. Smith, the father, was a stanch Liberal in politics, and the old 'currier shop' was a kind of meeting-place, where the most active local politicians of the time used frequently to resort for the purpose of learning the news and discussing public affairs. To that spot the late vicar, Dr. Sutton, used to repair to obtain information as to any event that was exciting public interest. It must be remembered that at that time there were no daily penny newspapers, or railway conveyance, or transmission of communications by telegraph. Young Alfred, as he listened to these discussions with attentive ears and eager interest, imbibed those political views and principles which, in a modified form, he ever afterwards held and believed in. He became in early life well known to Montgomery, and ever entertained for the poet a profound respect. He often spoke of Mr. Montgomery in such terms of high eulogy as seemed almost to amount to a kind of idolatry.

" For some time after the Mechanics' Library was first established, the work of librarian was done by voluntary services. Afterwards, Mr. Clegg was appointed to that office, and, on his resignation, Mr. Alfred Smith. On the occasion of the election Montgomery spoke of him in very kindly and favourable terms. On being duly installed into the office, his manners of old-fashioned politeness and efforts to oblige soon won the good-will and esteem of the generality of the members. With kindly feelings will many of them recall to memory his personal appearance. There was certainly something striking about it, including the bald head, high forehead, and long, pale, and unwhiskered face. His countenance, it will be remembered, was naturally grave, and on certain special occasions it was apt to assume that stronger expression of gravity that approached very nearly to the stolid and impassive.

" But, unlike this outward appearance, he was of a very cheerful, kind-hearted, and genial disposition. He had an extensive knowledge of books of a certain kind, and his ordinary conversation was rendered interesting by curious scraps and quaint conceits. His memory was very extraordinary, and, indeed, was the chief faculty of his mental constitution. He knew the greater part of Hudibras by heart, and could give citations to any length. Montgomery, of course, was a very favourite author ; and he often repeated passages both from his published poems and also from some others, which I suspect have escaped even the keen scrutinising search of the late Mr. Holland. In his younger days he had himself composed a considerable amount of poetry, which he could repeat to any extent. But it was in the doggerel style and Hudi-brastic vein ; and it is very doubtful whether he possessed the requisite literary taste and ability to have written anything that would at all have stood the critical ordeal if printed in a volume.

" Notwithstanding some manifest imperfections, he yet succeeded to a considerable extent in giving satisfaction ; and it may be questioned whether a more clever business man would, on the whole, have served the interests of the library better than the good-tempered, humorous, gossiping, and somewhat eccentric ' librarian.' He certainly had often to manifest a great deal of patience ; but, on the other hand, it is only fair to say he frequently required a large exercise of that said excellent quality towards himself. On certain occa-sions, whilst he was reciting poetry or telling some queer story, might be seen more than half-a-dozen youngsters wait-ing for an exchange of books, who, with eager looks were listening with delight to what he was saying; whilst amongst them might be a man who thought his time of some value, who would, with signs of anger and impatience, remonstrate against such delay. Instantly the tale would be cut short, and the applicant's wishes attended to, with many apologies and efforts to conciliate and oblige.

" On the occasion of Montgomery's funeral, with a large scarf around his hat, Alfred Smith was mounted on the box beside the driver of the carriage in which were the secretary, vice-president, and other officers of the Mechanics' Library leading up the procession. All along the road lined with spectators he was quietly recognised, and thus, by mere acci-dent, occupied a prominent position in paying his tribute of respect to the venerated poet. Soon after this event his health began visibly to fail, and he gradually sank into a debilitated condition ; but still, notwithstanding all persuasions to the contrary, he resolutely attended, to almost the last day of his life, at the library, thus finishing his twenty-five years of faithful and conscientious service. During that period it was the writer's privilege to enjoy very frequent and pleasant in-tercourse, and also at the end to follow him to his grave, and see his mortal remains interred in the Pitsmoor Churchyard.

" With his name the remembrance of the Sheffield Me-chanics' Library will ever remain closely associated—an insti-tution which may fairly claim to have fulfilled its original design for about forty years, by furnishing the means, at little cost, of reading valuable works on arts, science, literature, and religion, which were adapted to improve the intellect and to form and establish the moral and religious character."

WRAGG : Thank you. Our friend Leighton has, I see, fallen asleep, which is a reminder that we ought to be going home. *[Exeunt.]*

CHAPTER II.

CAMPO LANE, THE OLD GRAMMAR SCHOOL, THE TOWNHEAD.

Scene—The same.

Period—Two days later.

Present—EVERARD, WRAGG, LEIGHTON, TWISS, and LEONARD.

LEIGHTON : When last we met we mentally repeopled Campo lane with its old inhabitants, from the top of Paradise square to the bottom of the Hartshead and Watson's walk. Suppose we now go in the opposite direction, taking the Lane from Virgin's row to the Townhead.

WRAGG : Yes, that part is full of interest, though you moderns, Mr. Leonard, will scarcely credit it.

LEONARD : Well, it is difficult to find much romance there now, amid its dingy second-hand clothes shops and its squalid tenements. The only thing of interest about it I remember is a ghost story connected with the dreadful row of shops we come to first, going from St. James's row, on the left, that look as if they had started life with great pretensions, but the force of adverse circumstances has brought them to a worse plight than that of their older neighbours. The latter, if poor, have an air of decent poverty about them ; but these have nothing but a seedy look of decayed snobbishness.

TWISS : What you refer to was not really a ghost story, but only a great hoax, perpetrated by the aid of a magic lantern.

LEONARD : At any rate, a lot of people were well frightened, and one woman lost her life.

EVERARD : At the corner of St. James's row and Campo lane was a public-house. That part of the building which came to the front, forming a line with the Girls' Charity School, was, I believe, a comparatively modern projection, built of brick, and joined to the gable end of the old original house, which fronted Campo lane. The lower room of this new part was used as a " dram-shop," or kind of "bar," and the room over it was occupied as a store-room. The public-house proper was, I think, built of stone, or, if not, at all events with very old-looking bricks, and had small windows. The chief entrance then was in the very narrow part of Campo lane. I recollect that, when a youth, I went once or twice into this public-house, and noticed that the room in which we sat was very clean, the floor well rubbed and sanded, the ceiling low, and the window small. I do not remember what the sign was, or whether the old part of the house was "thatched." But it might have been so, and certainly was old enough to have been so at some previous period of its existence.

LEIGHTON : Let us get on. Among the low and dilapidated premises opposite is the cooper's shop where Mr. John Hall carried on the business of cooper, which Mr. Edward Hall has continued for so many years. At the corner of Lee croft, on the east side, now a broker's shop, is a fine old building with its grand staircase. It was, sixty years since, occupied by a retired merchant, a most respectable man— Mr. Parkin. On the opposite side of the lane, at the corner of St. James's hill, was his garden. I remember seeing gooseberry bushes in it. Now it is occupied as a sort of shed, used for storing horns, or something of the kind. I should like to know who changed St. James's hill into Vicar lane, and Virgin's walk into St. James's row. Whoever he was, he ought to have been whipped out of the town.

WRAGG : The house you speak of was afterwards the factory of Mr. Thomas Harrison, who had previously been burnt out of premises on the site of a portion of the Gas Works. At that time he was, I believe, a dealer in horns and hard woods ; but in Campo lane, where he was, I dare say, twenty years, he got up table knives. He removed into Holly street. He was a worthy and honourable man in all his dealings, but, I am sorry to add, he never recovered from the sad disaster connected with his fire.

TWISS : The house at the corner of Campo lane and Lee croft, now the Cup Inn, is an interesting old place.

WRAGG : Over the door it bears the date, 1726, and the initials, $_J{}^T{}_B$ or perhaps $_I{}^T{}_B$

LEIGHTON : That was the residence of Mr. Isaac Barnes, one of the old school of manufacturers. His workshops were just above. He was universally respected as an upright tradesman and an honest man.

LEONARD : The house was subsequently the residence of his son, Mr. George Barnes, who carried on this, one of the oldest cutlery trades in the town. Ultimately, however, the business was allowed to expire. Mr. George Barnes built himself a residence at Ranmoor, and the Campo lane house then reverted to what it is suspected to have been at first— a beershop.

LEIGHTON : Methinks I see old Isaac Barnes now, walking up to his old friend " Whit.," to smoke his pipe and enjoy his pint of strong ale at the " Warm Hearthstone," still, as of old, looking down the lane. Its then occupier and owner, Whittington Souter, bore a name renowned in the local annals. He was a good and charitable man, and highly respected by all.

EVERARD : When his customers called upon him for his song, he used to give these two lines :—

> There was a bee, and it lived in a wall,
> It just said " hum," and that's all.

LEIGHTON : Every Sunday forenoon he had a large piece of beef or mutton roasting, and his near customers were encouraged to bring their quarters of oatcake or slice of bread to dip in the capacious dripping-pan. He brewed the best ale in the county, a relative of mine being his maltster. They both got rich, and well they deserved it.

WRAGG : You only do justice to Mr. Souter's character. He was not only an upright, honourable man, but a sincere Christian. He attended Garden street Chapel, under the ministry of the Rev. Mark Docker, and when he died was its mortgagee. I believe he had purchased it from the Methodists when they removed to Carver street. He and his family are buried in the graveyard of Howard street Chapel.

LEIGHTON : He had a room in which tradesmen met for friendly chat, and they were served in silver pints.

WRAGG : Behind the public-house is a large door, and the yard is higher than the street. Mr. Souter had a carter, who had backed his cart towards this door, and was standing between the cart and the wall below the door, lifting something either into or out of the cart ; the horse moved backwards, and so the carter was killed, from the cart pressing against him. Some time after, the horse, being taken to Mr. Souter's field, near Mushroom Hall, fell into an old quarry and was killed. Mr. Souter was a kind and considerate man ; he did not close his connection with his carter's widow and family, but he continued their steadfast friend until his death.   There was a son whom he educated, and who obtained a situation in the office of Mr. Albert Smith, the magistrates' clerk.   After some years of faithful service he was articled to Mr. A. Smith, and became a solicitor.   He was the late George Wells, who was nicely established in Church street, next to the Sheffield and Rotherham Bank, when he died of an inflammation caught, if I remember rightly, from a cold taken in London while promoting, as solicitor to the Company, the passing of the Manchester and Sheffield Railway Bill.   He resided at the top of Cornhill, where the late Thomas Dunn previously resided.   Mr. Wells had made many friends, and died deeply regretted.

LEIGHTON : Well, here on our right, at the top of School croft, stood the old Grammar or Latin School.   In those days the presiding genius was the Rev. C. Chadwick, who, in 1800, " concerned to observe that persons are persuaded to consider the language and learning of the great models of antiquity of little use to boys not intended for a learned profession," advertised the commencement of classes for instruction in the English language.   The school had been built two hundred years, and well do I remember the rev. gentleman emerging from the steps (for the school was below the level of the lane), with his gold-headed cane and three-cornered hat, to the awe and admiration of the boys.   Part of the house he lived in is now the Burns Tavern, which stands at the western corner of School croft.   It was generally believed by us that the young gents had raised the devil in the old porch of the school, but had been so alarmed they never tried it again.   They were a bold and warlike race, and looked down with scorn on the schools below them, with which they were ever at war.   Their most determined enemies were from Figtree lane, where a school was conducted by Mr. Cowley. The contending hosts generally met about the top of Lee croft.   I have seen the " advance," the " charge," the " retreat," and the " rally," when, happily, the bell of the classicals was sounded, and a truce was made.

TWISS : Mr. Chadwick's son, the Rev. C. Chadwick, Jun., M.A., was for a short time—from November, 1801, to January, 1803, when he died—under master.   Mr. Chadwick was for many years the president of the Town Library.   In 1807, his old scholars presented him with a silver cup, bearing a Latin inscription.   He had been head master for more than

thirty years when he died, in 1809. Mr. Chadwick was also
vicar of Tinsley ; and it is he who is said to have given the
magistrates so deserved a rebuke when, coming out from their
duties in the old Cutlers' Hall one day, they were struck with
the horse on which he was just passing. "Here's Mr. Chadwick," said one, "riding a fine blood horse, while his Master
was contented with an ass." "Your worship," said the rider
to the speaker, "forgets that asses are scarcer now." "How
so?" asked the magistrate. "Government gets all it can to
make justices of," retorted Mr. Chadwick ; and no doubt he
rode on his way with the complacency of a man who has had
his revenge. The story is told in Wilson's edition of Mather.

LEONARD: The Grammar School was a low building, with
high pitched roof, lead-framed windows, and a porch. Its shape
was a capital L, the main part running from east to west, facing nearly southward, but being much below the street. This
part was occupied by the classes under the first and second
masters. The minor part of the building ran from the west
end northward, and was large enough for one long table, at
which perhaps twenty boys could sit on each side, under the
care of the writing master. The floor was of stone. The
furniture of the school consisted of low oak benches, three
to each class, forming three sides of a square, with a stool
for the præpositus.

TWISS : Before that, the boys' seats were more like stalls,
or the seats in cathedral choirs ; and against the walls was a
high wainscoting of dark oak, panelled. There was a second
row of stalls, with narrow desks before them, and in front a
broad way up the centre of the school from end to end. The
head master's seat, placed in the centre of the east end, was
composed of two massive oak sides, upwards of seven feet
high, and at least six inches thick, and terminating in
"Fleurs-de-lys" cut out of the solid. The boys' stalls ran
up to this seat on either hand. At the other end, the second
master's desk, among the junior boys, was the exact counter-
part of this ; and on the left of the junior school was the
projecting space towards the croft, where were the writing-
desks over which "Old Jacky"—as the venerable mathematician, John Eadon, was disrespectfully called—presided
every morning from eight o'clock to nine, before the classical
work of the day began. The front door, leading out into the
yard, was in the centre of one of the sides of the building.

LEONARD: The school was indifferently lighted, and owed
its warming to one large fire-place in the main building,

and another in the writing master's domain. The head master's house was at the west end of the building, facing the street. It was roomy, but dilapidated; and in the later years of the old school was unoccupied. The school building stood as much below the level of the street on one side as the Baptist Chapel stands above it on the other, the builders of the school having apparently dug its site out of the naturally steep hill-side at the head of the School croft, which sloped down the hill behind it to Tenter street.

TWISS: Among the boys who attended the school from 1808 to 1812 were the following, who have passed away:— John Staniforth, solicitor, and clerk to the Town Trustees; Frank Fenton, solicitor, London, (he obtained a celebrity in defending John Thurtell, who was executed for the murder of Weare, near St. Albans); Luke Palfreyman, solicitor, of considerable practice, and for many years of great influence; Francis Hoole, solicitor, Mayor 1853, Town Trustee; E. B. Tattershall, solicitor, London; John Dixon, solicitor, Sheffield; Broomhead Ward, M.A., beneficed clergyman in Wiltshire; Charles Brownill, J.P. West Riding, merchant, Liverpool; Samuel Mitchell, merchant, Sheffield, a distinguished antiquarian; Robert Naylor, accidentally killed at Roche Abbey, merchant; John Fenton, captain East India Service, brother to F. Fenton, and son of Colonel Fenton; Richard Ogle, nephew to R. Blakelock, Esq., died at Demerara; John Harwood, M.D., died in Sheffield; John Sterndale, M.D., died in East India Service; Samuel Staniforth, brother of John Staniforth, died in Paris; John Ward, merchant, Sheffield; Joseph Oakes, builder, of Washington Works, Sheffield. There are living at the present time:— Albert Smith, solicitor, and magistrates' clerk; Samuel Roberts, J.P. West Riding, Town Trustee; Charles Atkinson, J.P. West Riding, Mayor 1858, Master Cutler 1864; James Tillotson, J.P. West Riding; Thomas James Parker, solicitor, Sheffield; Lewis O. Sayles, late Assize Master, Leamington; Robert Younge, Church Burgess, wine merchant; Benjamin Vickers, merchant, Sheffield; Charles Radford, M.A., late Fellow of Brazennose College, now living at Bath; William Vickers, merchant, first chairman and principal promoter of Sheffield and Rotherham Railway. One of these survivors has said how well he remembers the tall figure of the Rev. Charles Chadwick, who held sway up to his death in the year 1809, entering the school from the centre door, with his clerical three-cornered cocked hat, and

walking with stately step to the cushioned throne whence, in
all the majesty of might and right, he looked around with
scrutinising eye for some delinquent,

> At Chadwick's frown all tremblingly alive,

on whom he contemplated bestowing his favourite "custard,"
that lay on the broad table before him, with these memorable
words deeply cut in the wood, "I forgot it," so frequently
impressed with biting effect on the open hand of many an
unlucky offender.   Over his chair were the emblems of scho-
lastic punishment—the rod, the cane, the ferrule with " custard " at the end—most artistically painted, with some memorable Latin lines.

"The second master," the same " Old Boy " goes on to
say, "was named Wheatcroft; we generally called him
" Little Widdy," a man of very small stature but of great
conceit.   During the time that intervened between the death
of Mr. Chadwick and the appointment of the Rev. Joseph
Wilson, he transferred the school to the house occupied by
the late master.   The school had got very small, and under
his management it grew beautifully less.   We had scarcely
twenty boys when the Rev. J. Wilson came into residence.
Mr. Wilson was a man of strong mind and determined character, being an excellent classical scholar, who had taken a
high degree at his college.   Under his system and method
of teaching the school soon recovered the ground it had lost,
and, ere twelve months had passed, had increased to more
than eighty boys—a sufficient number to claim and maintain
the supremacy over every other school in the town, both
mentally and physically, to which the numerous battles we
fought during the snowballing season can testify.   It was the
practice in those days to settle the disputes as to supremacy
in that practical manner.

"Mr. W. Wright was about that time appointed our
writing master, after the decease of Mr. Eadon, whose pupil
and assistant he had been.   Between him and Mr. Wilson
a very friendly feeling arose, which matured to the very ser-
viceable but unusual extent of the head master giving Mr.
Wright instruction in classical knowledge, which enabled him
to fill, to the satisfaction of all parties, the appointment of
second classical master, which he afterwards obtained on the
next vacancy in 1821 or 1822.   Mr. Wilson, although a man
above the ordinary stature, and firm in manner, was not
really so powerful as he looked, since he was incapacitated

from taking active exercise by having, either from accident or some other cause, had his left leg taken off below the knee, and a cork limb substituted. I believe he was the last person in Sheffield who used a sedan chair in visiting his friends. This was obtained from the Old Assembly Rooms, and had formerly been used by ladies only. At that period no hackney coach or cab was in existence. Among the few carriages kept in the town and immediate neighbourhood was one at Goddard Hall, by Philip Smilter, Esq., an old Catholic gentleman, who visited the town occasionally in a quaint old chaise, drawn by two light-brown, heavy, Flemish-bred horses with long manes and tails. Their speed was between a jog-trot and a walk. His postilion, in red, with bell-button, buckskins, and top boots, black velvet cap, and long straight whip ; the harness with breast collar and large square plated buckles, completed this unique set-out. The venerable man was a picture of the old squire in the costume of the early period of George III., so graphically delineated by Hogarth and other painters of his day. Poor Mr. Wilson had a sad end. One morning in 1818 Mr. Wright was hastily summoned from the school to the head master's house, and, on entering the library, found the unfortunate gentleman lying face downward on his secretaire, grasping a pistol just discharged. That terminated his life and position as head master of the Sheffield Grammar School. The Rev. W. White succeeded him."

LEONARD : At this point it is better that another former Grammar School boy, of somewhat later date than he whom you have been quoting, should take up the narrative :—

" In 1821, the Rev. William White, who had been elected in 1818, was head master, the Rev. G. Harrison second master, and Mr. William Wright writing master; but he succeeded Mr. Harrison in 1822, and was himself succeeded in the writing department by Mr. William Kirk. This school, as it was at that day, is especially interesting now, from the well-known men of later days who were then among the scholars. Indisputably, the first boy in the first or highest class was Thomas Goodison, who became an attorney, and practised in a very quiet way in George street. His signal abilities as a boy never developed themselves in his after career. Among his class-fellows was the late Wilson Overend, a fine youth, of great abilities and high spirit, but somewhat volatile, who became eminent as a surgeon, and was an important public man in the town.

Wm. Pashley Milner, now of Meersbrook, was another of this
class; as was also Robert C. Mather, who has passed many
years of his life as a missionary in India. In the second
class, at the same time, was William Overend, now Q.C., who
at over sixty years of age retains much of the countenance of
his boyhood. In the same class was Kay Fenton, youngest
son of Colonel Fenton, of Woodhill, on the Grimesthorpe
road, our first superintendent of police under the Act of
1818. The Colonel held office till his death, when he was
succeeded by Mr. Thomas Raynor, who was our first chief
constable, and the immediate predecessor of Mr. John Jackson. Urban Smith, the youngest brother of Mr. Albert
Smith, and now the vicar of Stoney Middleton, where he has
passed a quiet life in the discharge of the unostentatious
duties of a country clergyman, was in the second class. So
also were Astley Foulds, son of Mr. Samuel Foulds, surgeon,
Change alley, and himself the father of another generation of
surgeons; Nathaniel R. Philipps, of Broomhall, now recorder
of Pontefract; and Edward Hoyland, the elder son of a notable Quaker chemist, whose shop was next the Cutlers' Hall.
William Bell Mackenzie, lately deceased, for many years a
highly-popular clergyman at Holloway, London, was a Grammar School boy with some of the above, but had left the
school shortly before the period we speak of. The first and
second classes were under the especial charge of the head
master; but in his division of the school was also a junior
class, over which the boys of the first and second classes were
set as præpositi (Anglice, monitors). Here were Samuel
Eadon, now Dr. Eadon, the great-nephew of the fine old mathematician who, two generations before, was master of the
Free Writing School, and teacher of writing, arithmetic, &c.,
in the Grammar School. Among his class-mates were John
Crosland Milner, now of Thurlstone, J.P., brother of Mr.
W. P. Milner before mentioned; Robert Leader, who has
been connected with Sheffield journalism for nearly fifty years;
Thomas Hewitt, who achieved an unhappy notoriety and died
in his prime; Robert Stopford Taylor, surgeon, recently deceased. These names will show that the Grammar School
of those days contained a group of boys destined to be well
known in their manhood. Mr. White, the head master, is
worth preserving in one's memory. He was a little, lightly-
made, brisk man, quick and energetic in all his movements,
with a stern face, pitted by the small-pox, and with a sono-
rous and awful voice, never so terrible as in his sarcastic

moods. The exactest punctuality was his rule. In the first
portion of his mastership, Mr. White had acquired a name
for great severity in his punishments; but on one occasion he
so much overstepped the mark that there was a row, and the
result was that, at the time we speak of, his cane was almost
disused, though he was none the less formidable on that
account. Four or five boys who came from Attercliffe, and
generally arrived in a group, had fallen into the habit at one
time of being rather late. ' Here come the Attercliffians,' was
their sarcastic greeting from the head master one morning,
and the delinquents were cured. We never knew him to give
to any one the slightest mark of familiarity ; but, severe and
unbending as he was, the boys had a sort of love for him, as
was shown by the familiar name they had given to him—
' Daddy White.' Now and then he would summon a junior
class before him for a sharp *riva voce* examination, and these
occasions were very pleasant to boys who had done their work
well. The riddling of the brains of a class by the ' Daddy '
was a capital test of quality ; and it was fun to see how a big
hulking fellow, who ordinarily kept an unfairly high place,
would go tumbling down in stupid amazement, while others
went above him. And here it may be worth while to place on
record the sort of education given in the school. It was narrow, but thorough. Excepting an hour a day under the writing master, the classes going to him by turns, Latin and
Greek absorbed all the time of the higher classes, and Latin
only that of the lower. Each lesson was repeated and written
on slates in class. Incessant repetition was the order of the
day, till a boy knew all the declensions and conjugations,
regular and irregular, and all the rules of syntax with their
examples, as perfectly as his A B C. It was terrible drudgery
for a time ; but many a young mind which had revolted at it,
asking why he was to spend all his days over a dead language,
at last learned to like the sense of power and mastery it gave
him, when he looked on a page and there was not a word he
did not know in all its parts, all its relations, and its shades
of meaning. This system did not give boys much knowledge, but it gave mental tools, and taught a style of using
them for which many an one has honoured the memory of his
old master and his old school. In these days, when so much
is said of the imperative necessity of leavening all teaching
with religion, we may recall what was then the practice in a
school of which the vicar and the church burgesses are the
governors, and a clergyman was the head master. The only

religious book in the school was a Prayer-book, which lay on
the head master's desk. From it he read three or four brief
prayers at the opening of school in the morning, and then the
religious teaching of the day was done. Mr. Wright, whom
we knew both as writing and second master, was a remarkable
self-made man. He had been brought up in humble circumstances to one of the Sheffield trades ; but, by indomitable
study he attained to proficiency in mathematics, and very
respectable classical learning. About 1823 he gave up his
office in the Grammar School, and opened a school on his
own account in a yard in Bank street, where the office of Mr.
Smilter, high bailiff of the County Court, now is. A few
years later he built Howard Hill (afterwards purchased for the
Roman Catholic Reformatory for Girls), and there he conducted a successful school to the end of his life. He was
a rather heavy, ungainly man, with a hot temper and weighty
arm, but of genial disposition and kindly heart. Many Sheffield men have an honourable niche for the memory of William Wright. 'I like that ; it shows your head is at work;'
this is a sample of the encouraging remarks he would address
to a boy who showed an inclination to understand the reason
of things."

EVERARD : The Free Writing School down School croft
only takes us a little out of our way, and should be mentioned
here, not only as a kindred subject, but because he who was
its head master for so many years—Mr. John Eadon—also
taught writing daily in the Grammar School. The art of
writing was in those days an accomplishment, and not the
every-day commodity of the present time.

TWISS : I possess, and prize very highly, an old ex-
ercise-book written by Grammar School boys of the earlier
half of the last century. We sometimes hear writing described as being like copper-plate, but it is literally true of
this beautiful caligraphy. The exercises consist of Latin
verses, and are headed " Musæ Sheffieldienses, 1737." The
names of the writers may be interesting to you. First comes
"Geo. Steer," afterwards a mercer in the town, who is buried
in St. Paul's Church, near the communion rails. "Thomas
Younge," or as he variously spells his name, " Young," was
in the school 1737-39. He was born in 1721, and, after leav-
ng the Grammar School, took his M.A. at Cambridge, and
then went to study medicine at Edinburgh, where he took
his medical degree in 1752. He returned to Sheffield, where
he practised as a physician until his sudden death, in 1784.

He was the father of Dr. William Younge, who also was a physician of repute among us. A curious contemporary eulogy on Dr. Thomas Younge that I possess speaks of him as having a figure higher than middle stature, corpulent, sanguineous, and says "his countenance bespoke thought, sagacity, and penetration; his health appeared to be uninterrupted, either from a fortunate constitution or his great skill." The most beautiful writer in the book I am speaking of is "Daniel Boote," but of him I know nothing; nor can I trace "Geo. Ibotson." "Walter Oborne" was afterwards a magistrate. "Thomas Cawthorn, 1739," was probably the brother of James Cawthorn, the poet (also a Grammar School boy), whose memoir was written by the Rev. E. Goodwin.

WRAGG: Mr. John Eadon wrote the "Arithmetician's Guide," published in 1756, and he dedicated it to the trustees of the Writing School; and in 1793 and 1794 he published the first and second editions of the first volume of his "Arithmetical and Mathematical Repository." Had he published the other three volumes, which, he said, were nearly ready for the press, he would have taken his place in the front rank as a mathematician. He died in 1810, at the age of eighty. I should like to see some good account of him.

LEONARD: Should you? I can read to you, if you like, an account of him and his family, written by one of his descendants.

WRAGG: It will interest me exceedingly.

LEONARD (reads): "John Eadon, the mathematician, was the first of a family some of the members of which, without any intermission, have been instructing and educating the rising generation of Sheffield for nearly 120 years, and are doing so still. He lived, during his youth, at Ecclesfield, and was one of four brothers. Their father was a 'famous woodman of renown,' and his five sons, at all events for some time, followed the same occupation. Being tall and naturally muscular, strength and virtue—in its primitive meaning, viz., physical valour—were their characteristics. On these qualities they prided themselves, and, although kind in their natures, and tender in the extreme to protect the weak, woe be to him who offered an insult, or attempted to trample on the defenceless. In such circumstances they knew of no argument but the *argumentum ad pugnam*, and right skilfully was it brought into operation. One of them, in particular, was noted for his pugilistic tendencies. This was Matthias, afterwards known as Captain Eadon, the father of the late Mr.

John Eadon, who lived and died on his own freehold, at
Boston, in Lincolnshire.

"In those days the road from Sheffield to Ecclesfield was
infested by thieves. Every night robberies were committed,
and on that part called 'Sheffield lane,' after a certain hour,
no person escaped scot free. Strange to say, none of these
brothers were ever stopped. This Matthias courted attacks,
for he came home at all hours of the night for the very purpose—but in vain. This was to him a mystery, as people were
robbed half-an-hour before and an hour after he had passed
along. Having, however, a law-suit at York, the riddle was
solved. He there was told by one of the robbers, who had been
taken, that they dare not attack him, and they used to say,
'Here comes Matt Ayton ; we must let him pass, or he will
thrash us all together.' Being tall and powerful, and with
the spirit of a lion, these men acted wisely in making 'discretion the better part of valour.'

"These five brothers, it seems, followed the occupation
mentioned for some years, till circumstances broke in upon
the even tenor of their way. Being an out-door employment, the weather would often interfere and prevent them
from going on with their work. On one occasion the rain was
so heavy that, there being no likelihood of its abating that
day, the father and sons took shelter in a neighbouring inn ;
others had done the same, and the room was full. Whilst
drinking the 'nut-brown ale,' many were the topics of conversation. Some talked about themselves, others about their
children—how clever Susan was, and what a sharp chap
Tommy was ; and as for Bill, the village schoolmaster had
never had his like. Every man appeared to have a clever lad
in some way or other ; but old Ayton (Eden, now Eadon)
heard all this with a sorrowful heart, and at length, breaking
silence, he said, 'See,' pointing his finger, 'there is a thick-
head ; that lad of mine is nineteen years of age, and he does
not know A from B.' This was enough. The shame of
being exposed in a public company, and by his father, too,
raised the pride and kindled a spark in that young man's
breast which never went out till the spirit left the body.
Whilst he sat in that room abashed amid his compeers, he
determined that he would know not only A from B, but something more. He began next day, bought a penny primer,
found out an old woman who knew the letters—these he soon
mastered—made out little words, and soon he laid the foundation of all knowledge—the acquirement of the art of read-

ing. He found some one to assist him in writing and arithmetic ; and in this way his leisure time was spent, till he
began to think he knew more than most people about him.

"At this juncture the mastership of the Free Writing
School became vacant. He offered himself and was elected,
and held the post till his death. From the time of his publishing the ' Arithmetician's Guide,' in 1756, to his death in
1810, would make his tutorship of that school fifty years, at
least.

"It is evident from that there must have been natural
quickness of intellect and great aptitude in John Eadon, in
learning whatever came before him. It is said that when he
went to learn writing he imitated the copies so well that the
master said he must have come to make fun of him, as he
could copy them better than he could himself.

"Another story recorded of him is that, on one occasion,
when he was attending at the Grammar School in performance of his duties as writing master, a boy was brought up
for punishment before the rev. principal (Mr. Chadwick) for
having broken a pane. ' Well, sir,' said the master, ' I understand you have broken a pane.' ' No, I have not sir; I
only cracked it.' ' Well,' roared out the reverend divine,
' what's the difference between cracking a commandment and
breaking it ? Go to your seat, sir, and neither crack a pane
nor a commandment.' The time, the place, the tone, the
manner, and the silence of all present made such an impression on the mind of old John Eadon that, for a quarter of a
century, he was in the habit of telling the story of the lad
and the pane with great glee and gusto.

"He married Hannah Smith, of Tankersley, and had by
her three children, two sons and a daughter. His daughter
Mary married Mr. Joseph Bailey, one of the first merchants
in Sheffield who traded with America, and the late Samuel
Bailey was their youngest child. His sons were John and
George. John was a partner in the firm of Bailey and
Eadon, and became the father of Mr. Thomas Brownell
Eadon, of Western Bank. George died unmarried in the
house at the corner of Norfolk street and Charles street, now
used as a Turkish bath.

"Besides the two brothers, John and Matthias, of whom
we have spoken, there were Moses and William. From William spring the Eadons of Attercliffe, and the late Mr. George
Eadon, the carver and gilder, and his sons, the auctioneers.
The spelling of the name was altered from Eden into Eadon

about one hundred years ago, by John Eadon, the mathematician."

WRAGG : A most interesting account of a remarkable man. Ecclesfield was also the birthplace of Joseph Hunter, the historian of Hallamshire ; and Grenoside, in the same parish, was the birth-place of the Walkers, of Rotherham. In fact, many distinguished men have come from out-of-the-way places—as Chantrey from Norton, and George Wilson, of the Anti-Corn-Law League, from Hathersage. Some people would not think such villages likely to foster genius.

TWISS : John Eadon's brother William lived at Attercliffe, and was a joiner and lath-river. A very old gentleman is still living who remembers him, and who has said, " He and my father were very friendly, and had many an argument, for they were both fond of it, and were what was then considered scholars. William Eadon worked for my father, and often came to our house in Derbyshire lane. Smithy Wood was near, and while the work of enlarging Mr. William Shore's house at Tapton Grove was going on—it had been erected by a person named Badger as a speculation, and when Mr. Shore bought it he made considerable additions ; Mr. Edward Vickers afterwards rebuilt the house—some trees were felled in that wood. My father was anxious to buy one particularly fine oak, for the laundry over the stable at Tapton had to be laid with a plaster floor, and he wanted some good oak laths to lay it on. There were several people after this tree, and to decide the rivalry it was arranged that the one who could get first to the tree from a particular part of the wood should be the purchaser. My father knew the ground well, and laid his plans. When the signal to be off was given, his competitors plunged into the brushwood, while he slipped over a wall into a field, ran quickly down opposite to where the tree stood, and was back in the wood, standing by the trunk, while his rivals were struggling and scratching themselves among the brambles. He got the tree, and William Eadon rove it into laths, and those laths were laid down under the laundry floor at Tapton."

LEIGHTON : The site of the old Free Writing School is now occupied by a modern and substantially-built successor, erected in 1827, the old building, which had stood for 106 years, having fallen into decay. Mr. Worth was the architect. The yard or play-ground is, however, the same, though of less size than formerly. There used to be—for we are speaking of the time when the street called School croft was really a green field—a communication between the yards of the two schools. Job Cawood was the master in the days when I attended the Free Writing School. I think he must have been Mr. John Eadon's successor.

LEONARD : The late Mr. Samuel Bailey was a pupil at this school. It is said that, even in those days, there were observable in him all the elements of the after-man—reserve, reticence, and pride. He was not like any other boy. The pranks of lads had no charm for him. What would excite the merry giggle in others was looked down upon with silent indifference by him. He used to amuse himself in the play hours in riding on the back of a schoolfellow called Wilgous, who was always ready to play the horse for the boy-philosopher.

WRAGG : Several very old houses formerly stood about here, some on the site of the Baptist Chapel, and others were pulled down a year or two before the Temperance Hall was built. One of them bore a date early in the last century, and had a projecting window, with a second window at the side somewhat less than the former. A person looking through the latter could see the steps below, in Townhead street. I should not be surprised to learn that this was the first shop in the town having two windows. At the corner of Blind lane and Trippet lane was the shop of Mr. Brady, a respectable draper, whose daughters, members of the Society of Friends, will be remembered by you all. Trippet lane, as its width indicates, is greatly altered from the old days. Facing you, above the end of Blind lane, used to be Red croft, a *cul de sac*, with dwellings all round it. The "Brown Cow," and all the other houses on the left, up to Mr. Reynolds' mortar mill, were in Red croft.

LEONARD : In Gosling's plan, Red croft stands between a lane running on either side—the one following the course of the present street (then called Red lane), the other apparently being that narrow but ancient "twitchell," West Bank lane, by which you can get up into West street.

EVERARD : The street, from the top of Bailey field nearly to the end of Blind lane, was so narrow that two carts could not pass ; but, like a single-line railway, one of them had to wait until the other had come through. Hence this part of the way commonly went by the name of the "Narrow lane."

LEIGHTON : In Pinfold street there are yet remaining a few of the old cottage houses. Of such, I suppose, the streets used mainly to consist.

LEONARD : Yes ; when one looks at them it is impossible to help feeling that, interesting as are the reminiscences in which we are indulging, and tempted as we sometimes feel to long for power to sweep away innovations, it is just as well that we can't. Such houses show us to be far better off as we are.

TWISS : The original water-house of the Water Company is still standing, at the sharp angle between Pinfold street and Campo lane. It has just come into the possession of the Town Trustees, and will doubtless soon be sacrificed on the altar of street improvements. A comparison of this with the present handsome premises of the Company, in Barker Pool, exhibits very strikingly the contrast between the old order of things and the new.

LEIGHTON : In the angular space at the top of Townhead street, formed by the meeting of Church street, Bow street, Pinfold street, and Townhead street, stood formerly the Townhead cross. None of us can remember it—I doubt whether any of us know when it disappeared, or whither it went ; but that is no reason for passing it by without notice.

TWISS : The premises at the top of Townhead street now occupied by Mr. Jackson, pork-butcher, have a history. Here resided, more than a century ago, Mr. Matthewman, who was one of the originators of the Water Company. In 1744, he and Mr. Battie succeeded to the powers granted in 1713 to Messrs. Goodwin and Littlewood by the Lord of the Manor, and constructed the first works at Crookes moor. He was the maternal grandfather of Mr. Albert Smith.

EVERARD : This house was occupied for some years by Mr. Moorhouse, surgeon, who got killed by a fall from his horse. On his decease, Mr. James Ray, who had served his time with him, purchased the business of the widow ; and, after living and carrying on his profession on the premises for a considerable period, he built and removed to the house in Victoria street, Glossop road. At the time it was generally thought he was going too far out into the country. Mr. Ray was a tall and noble-looking man, more especially when on horseback.

WRAGG : Then Mr. John Turton practised here as a surgeon, and his son George also. The latter died in this house. They had both been cutlers in the employment of the Spurrs, in the neighbouring factory in Church street, the house which looks up Pinfold street. In Surrey street Chapel is a mural tablet to the memory of the late Mr.

George Turton. In the house looking up Bow street was Mr. James Wild. He was a presser. A more feeling, honourable, and upright man there never was ; but I am sorry to say he was not so successful in business as some of his neighbours. Later in life he was a dealer in horns in White croft. Near here, too, was Mr. Robert Brightmore, the maternal uncle of the late Mr. Samuel Mitchell. He had a large cutlery business, and was a merchant in the country trade. A portion of his business premises was cut through to make Bow street, when Glossop road was constructed. He built the large brick house on Brookhill, now surrounded by houses, part of which was the residence of the late Alderman Saunders. The father of Mr. S. Mitchell married the sister of Mr. Robert Brightmore ; and there was to have been a double marriage of Mr. Brightmore to Miss Mitchell, but it never came off. Mr. Mitchell lived in the old house some of you may remember, just above Mr. Brightmore's, on Brookhill, where Brightmore street now is, then a garden walk. There was a large weeping willow in front of the house, with a watch-box underneath, where watchmen retired for shelter on stormy nights.

LEONARD : Most of the streets that have been made around are called by the names of the Mitchell and Brightmore families—Mitchell street, Brightmore street, Robert street, Sarah street, Bolsover street, and so on.

EVERARD : The house, the garden, with the beautiful willow tree at the corner, and the entrance gate, were objects with which I was familiar from childhood, and will ever live as an interesting picture in my memory. The personal appearance and deportment of Mrs. Mitchell always struck me as affording the best idea of "a lady of quality" of the last century of any person I remember to have seen. She usually wore a black silk or satin gown, a white stomacher with an abundance of frills, and a remarkable turban cap or head-dress, which seemed to indicate somewhat of an Oriental taste. On a hot summer's day she might often be seen sitting in a latticed alcove partly screened by climbing plants and flowers, knitting or reading. This was the grandmother of the present Mr. Mitchell-Withers. His grandfather was a stout, good-looking man ; and his father, Mr. Brightmore Mitchell, was a schoolfellow of mine. Grosvenor terrace now fills the site then occupied by the old house and garden.

LEIGHTON (rising) :

"And so, without more circumstance at all,
I hold it fit that we shake hands and part." {Exeunt.

CHAPTER III.

Scene and Time—After supper at Mr. EVERARD'S.

Present—WRAGG, TWISS, LEIGHTON, EVERARD, and LEONARD.

WRAGG : Suppose from this hospitable board we get back to Church street?

LEONARD :—

> * * * Church lane, that poor narrow place,
> With wood buildings projecting ; 'twas quite a disgrace ;
> The roofs nearly meeting, a dark dreary street,
> Might justly be styled the " robbers' retreat,"
> Where shops were so darkened for want of true light,
> Appeared quite at noontide as though it were night.

LEIGHTON : Ah, you have got hold of James Wills's doggrel ; you should go on to quote his description of the street's improvement into " fine shops for each tradesman," and the " beautiful road into Bow street," where " coaches come down with the Manchester trade."

EVERARD : That widening took place in 1785, and was to the extent of about three yards.

TWISS : And it was still further widened in 1866-7 by another slice from the churchyard.

LEONARD : As we go down the street, we meet with various sites of much interest. There is, for instance, what was once the residence of Mr. Hall Overend, one of the most celebrated medical men of Sheffield in the early part of this century ; afterwards of his son, Mr. Wilson Overend ; and now the boot shop of Mr. Brown. Mr. Hall Overend died in May, 1831, at the age of fifty-nine. His medical knowledge had been acquired under the great disadvantages incident to that period. He served an apprenticeship to a noted druggist and apothecary, named Sutcliffe, who dispensed medicine and advice largely at a shop near the Bay Horse, on Sheffield Moor. Hall Overend was a diligent student,

and when he left Mr. Sutliffe, acquired a medical qualifica-
tion, and began practice in Broad lane. Thence he removed
to Church street, where his house and surgery occupied the
frontage from Orchard street to the corner of Smith street,
excepting the shop of North, the butcher. Mr. Hall Overend's skill, quickness, and diligence were rewarded by great
success. He had a most extensive and laborious, but profitable practice. At that time our medical men made their
rounds on horseback, and they began by degrees to seek
relief by the partial use of gigs. For some years Mr. Hall
Overend rode a mule—very handsome, fleet, and enduring,
but subject to fits of obstinacy, in which the animal would
fight long battles with his rider for the mastery. The urgency
of Mr. Overend's practice could not brook loss of time, and
the mule had to repair, by extra speed, the delay he had
occasioned. Mr. Hall Overend had felt so much the want of
facilities for a professional education, that he gave his eldest
son, John (who died early), and his second son, Wilson, the
highest training as physician and surgeon that the schools of
England and the Continent could afford. Mr. Overend also
established a school of anatomy and medicine for the medical
pupils of Sheffield. At that time the only human bodies
that could be legally dissected were those of people who had
been qualified by the hangman, and they were not obtainable
in Sheffield. Mr. Overend had to supply his school with
"subjects" by the agency of "resurrection men," and it was understood he did this at considerable personal risk, both from the
law and the populace. Mr. Hall Overend collected, at much
expense, a valuable museum of natural history, which his
family ultimately presented to the Literary and Philosophical
Society. Excessive labours had so much impaired Mr. Hall
Overend's health, that when Mr. Wilson Overend was prepared to assume the weight of the practice, his father with-
drew very much from it, and lived at Bolsover Hill, on the
Barnsley road, until his death. His surviving sons—of whom
we spoke in connection with the Grammar School—both
attained to eminence. Mr. Wilson Overend was a distinguished surgeon, and became an active magistrate and public
man. Mr. Wm. Overend, the youngest son, was a barrister,
and rose to the leadership of the circuit in Yorkshire. He
twice contested Sheffield, and once East Derbyshire, in the
Conservative interest. In 1859 he was returned for Pontefract, but had to resign his seat on petition. Mr. William
Overend has recently given up the practice of his profession

to enjoy the life of a country gentleman. Mr. Hall Overend was a Quaker—not very observant, however, of the rules of the "Society," though Mrs. Overend and her daughters wore the Quaker dress of the time and attended "meeting." The brother of Mr. Hall Overend was the founder of the great discount house in London, which acquired a degree of credit second only to the Bank of England. It was familiarly known in the City as the "Corner House." When, many years after the death of its founder, its management had passed into less honest and prudent hands, its failure shook the commercial world, and the day of its stoppage was called "Black Friday." Mr. Hall Overend's children acquired a considerable accession of fortune on the death of the widow of their uncle.

TWISS : A very few yards further down the street, on the other side—that is, at the corner of Vicar lane, where is now Mr. Thomas, surgeon, Mr. Jonathan Barber, the father of the present Mr. Jonathan Barber, surgeon, and of Mr. James Henry Barber, banker, learnt pharmacy with the same Mr. Richard Sutliffe whom Mr. Leonard has mentioned. Mr. Barber and Mr. Hall Overend married sisters. At this corner he and Mr. Silvester frequently met to carry on their scientific experiments, in the early days of the discovery of electricity, and they are even said to have invented an electric battery. Afterwards Mr. Barber commenced practice in Scarborough ; thence he removed to London, and subsequently he went to Montreal. Mr. Barber, in addition to his scientific attainments, was a man of great elocutionary power ; and a speech he made at Scarborough, in 1813, on behalf of the Bible Society, attracted so much attention that it was printed as a pamphlet. While in London, he was secretary to the Royal Humane Society, and distinguished himself by his eloquence at its annual banquets.

LEIGHTON: We must not linger round the most prominent object in the street, the Old Church and the churchyard, for Hunter, as to the former, and Mr. Holland's pamphlet, as to the latter, give us all information.

LEONARD : Yet I do not see in either of them a statement of the curious fact that when, in 1800, the Church was being repaired and altered, it was found that the east end stood on a vast bed of bones. This has been taken by some as a confirmation of the tradition that the Romans had a camp here—hence Campa or Campo lane ; but these philological guesses are very hazardous.

WRAGG : I fancy Campo lane means the lane leading to the country.

LEONARD : It is no use theorising about etymologies ; let us rather record that we do know. Mr. Samuel Roberts's Autobiography has fortunately perpetuated for us a graphic account of the Church before the improvements made at the beginning of this century. He wrote : " The Church itself was one of the most gloomy, irregularly-pewed places in the kingdom. It seemed as if, after the work of pewing had begun, every person who chose had formed a pew for himself in his own way, to his own size, height, and shape. There were several galleries, but all formed, as it seemed, in the same way as the pews—some of them on pillars, and some hung in chains. The Lord's closet was a gloomy structure. High under the lofty centre arch spanned from side to side the massive rood loft, behind which, filling up the apex of the arch, were the king's arms, painted most gloriously, and magnificently large. Under the clock, in a large glass case, yet scarcely perceptible in the gloom, was the pendulum, blazoned with an enormous staring gilt sun, solemnly and mysteriously moving from side to side with a loud, head-piercing tick or tack at each vibration. * * * Glad indeed was I always when the service was over ; when pattens began to clatter, and Johnny Lee, the clerk, was called to on all sides for a light to the lanterns."

EVERARD : One of the pews which Mr. Roberts speaks of as being " hung in chains " was fixed in the north gallery, over the stair head, and at the time went by the nickname of either the " coal cart," or the " coal barge," I forget which. Into this place my father, with other youngsters, used to climb ; and when perched up there, they could do very much as they pleased whilst looking down on the congregation below.

TWISS : You make no mention of the thirty fire-buckets which hung in the chancel ready (in the then primitive absence of engines) for use in the event of a fire breaking out in the town. The buckets and the hooks to hang them on were, as the inscription in the quire to his memory used to tell, given by Robert Rollinson, mercer, the maker of Barker pool. Perhaps you do not remember them or their successors (for Mr. Rollinson died in 1631), but they must have been there in the time spoken of by the late Mr. Roberts.

WRAGG : Mr. Roberts's mention of the great pendulum reminds me of a singular use to which it was once put.

Martha Wright, who afterwards became the wife of William Cutler Nadin, was a singer at the Parish Church, and on one occasion she fell asleep there during service. When she awoke, she found everybody gone, the church locked up and deserted. She tried in vain to make herself heard, when a very clever idea, suggested by the pendulum, struck her. She arrested its swing, and stopped the clock. The absence of the usual indications of the flight of time attracted the attention of the clerk. He went to ascertain the cause, and the girl obtained her liberation.

LEONARD: The present bells were put up in 1798, and the new clock, with its chimes, was erected in 1867. Sixty years hence our descendants will perhaps thank us for putting on record that the tunes played are: Sunday, "Easter Hymn;" Monday, "Home, sweet home;" Tuesday, "Blue bells of Scotland;" Wednesday, "The heavens are telling;" Thursday, "Life let us cherish;" Friday, The 104th Psalm; Saturday, "Caller Herring." You have no idea how difficult—indeed, impossible—I have found it to obtain a complete list of the old chimes. All I can get together are these: Sunday, 104th Psalm; Monday, "Blue bells of Scotland;" Wednesday, "See the conquering hero comes;" Saturday, "Happy clown," from Allan Ramsay's "Gentle Shepherd," a tune that was popularly known as "Tang Ends."

EVERARD: One of the tunes played was "There's nae luck about the house."

LEIGHTON: If old 'Siah Carr had been alive he could have told you not only the tunes of the late chimes, but of their predecessors, whose beauty he never ceased to lament. He was a great worshipper of them, and would sit on the "alablaster" stone listening to the airs most devoutly.

TWISS: Let us not forget to mention that the old clock turret in front of the steeple was removed when the new clock was erected, that being set into the steeple itself. In doing this a stone was found, which had evidently formed a portion of an arch in the Norman church. The pattern upon the stone fixes the date of the church as in the 12th century, and proves that this is not the original Norman tower.

EVERARD: I am sorry to see that our favourite Hallam-shire legend about the origin of the Tuesday evening's peal —that it was established in gratitude by a wanderer who, belated on the moors beyond Ringinglow, was saved by hearing their sound wafted to him through the still night air—is believed to be mythical.

Twiss : Yes, it is a beautiful story, but there is nothing to show that any legacy was ever left to defray the cost of ringing the bells on Tuesday evenings ; at least, neither the Town Trustees who pay for the ringing, nor the ringers who receive the payment, know anything of such a bequest.

Leonard : I fear this is another of your etymologies, Mr. Wragg. The story must have been concocted to fit the name of Ringinglow, which we know to have existed at least as long ago as 1574, when it was "a great heap of stones called Ringinglawe."* At any rate, the legend only shows that the bells were rung on Tuesday evenings before the legacy—if there was one.

Everard : This Tuesday ringing is only in the winter months. It begins on the Tuesday after Doncaster races—rather a curious calendar for church bells—and continues until Shrove Tuesday. It is no doubt an immemorial custom, connected possibly with the market day. The bells, by the way, are not now rung with the regularity or frequency that was formerly observed. We used always to have a bell at six in the morning, at noon, and at eight o'clock in the evening, on week-days ; and there was an early Sunday morning bell at seven o'clock, which was also the time on saints' days ; but these are dropped now. We only have the peals on "Queen's days" and special occasions—the three days following Christmas, the last day in the old year, and New Year's Day.

Leighton : It is a pity they should be discontinued ; but I think I remember business men complaining of the twelve o'clock peal as interrupting.

Wragg : Money-grubbers !

Leonard : I have been told by the ringers that the discontinuance of the bells arose thus : When Mrs. Sutton, the wife of the late vicar, was ill, they disturbed her, living as she did in the old Vicarage, so the Doctor ordered them to stop ; and as no one ever commanded them to be resumed, the custom fell into disuse. But I believe the eight o'clock curfew bell had been discontinued before that.

Twiss: Here is a contribution to our ringing recollections : "May 2, 1809, died, a few days ago, Mr. Richard Owen, much lamented, particularly by the Society of Change Ringers, to whom he had belonged nearly sixty years. They

---

* "Hunter's Hallamshire," new edition, p. 18.

E

will always bear in mind how cheerfully he led off the first peal that was ever rung of ten new bells, on the 29th April, 1799. He was interred at St. Peter's Church on the 29th April, 1809, being exactly ten years after the bells were first rung."

LEIGHTON: An interesting chapter might be written on the Old Church steeple. Here is a jotting for it, extracted from Mr. Gales's *Sheffield Register*, of July 18, 1789: "It has been judged expedient, from its being in a decayed state, to take down a few yards of the steeple of our parish church. The person employed for this purpose has fixed ladders to effect it, and on Thursday he took down the weathercock, amidst the acclamations of an immense concourse of spectators, who had assembled on the occasion. In the evening, after this had been effected, a slater, in a state of intoxication, ascended the ladders, to the terror of the spectators, who every moment expected he would be dashed to atoms. When he was within a few yards of the top, their fears were heightened by his hat blowing off; he, however, reached the summit, and came down again remarkably swift and perfectly safe, to the relief of those who witnessed the foolhardy attempt."

WRAGG: It is said that Mr. William Battie, who lived in Townhead street, in the house now occupied by Mr. Parkin, tailor, the James Wills who has been quoted lived, a door or two below, who once played a similar mad freak.

LEONARD: Yes; the story is that in his younger days he, for a wager, climbed up to the top of the old steeple by the projections, took hold of the weathercock, waved his hat, came down again by the same way, and reached the bottom in safety. "Billy Battie" was "quite a character."

EVERARD: I have sufficient evidence for believing it was not Mr. William Battie who did that piece of folly, but another man, who was, at the time he undertook it, half drunk. What Mr. Battie did was this: On the occasion when a certain portion of the church steeple was taken down and rebuilt (possibly the time referred to in that extract from the *Register*), several persons climbed up before the ladders were removed, as a sort of opening ceremony. Among them was Mr. Battie. As previously arranged, he stood upright upon the base, where the weathercock had to be fixed, with nothing to hold by, and played the National Anthem on his French horn. My father was present, and saw him thus standing, and heard this musical performance.

Twiss : I have heard Mr. Battie tell the story himself.

Wragg: That better accords with the character and position of Mr. Battie than the other story. He was a Town Trustee, and a person of considerable influence in that body. It was he who caused the opening to be made at the bottom of Broad lane and Townhead street, by the destruction of Radford row. In his younger days he was a cooper, but afterwards he was a successful ivory merchant.

Everard : I have forgotten the name of the man who actually accomplished the feat attributed to Mr. Battie, but he was a table-blade forger, and at the time was working for Messrs. Broomhead Ward and Thomas Asline Ward, brothers, who carried on business in Howard street, the latter living in the house adjoining, the whole now forming part of the premises of Messrs. Walker and Hall. This man (who, if I remember right, had been a sailor) was one evening drinking with his mates at a public-house, when the question of the possibility of climbing up to the top of the Old Church steeple by the projecting stones outside was mooted, discussed, and disputed. He thereupon laid a wager that he could do it, and started off, accompanied by some of his comrades. He successfully accomplished the feat ; but he told my mother, who knew the man and had the relation from his own lips, that though he did not experience much difficulty in getting to the top, yet, having arrived there, the extreme peril of his position so struck his mind as completely to sober him. When he reached the ground, without speaking to any one, he ran home half frightened out of his wits.

Leonard : I have always understood that the man's name was Thomas South. He was well known in the town. One version of the story says he turned the weathercock round.

Leighton : Let us take a glance into St. James's street, once the Vicarage croft, "a small field amidst gardens," with an old dry draw-well in it. You all remember the yellow Vicarage, now supplanted by the auction-room of Messrs. W. H. and J. A. Eadon, and the adjoining buildings.

Leonard : Yes, even I remember that unartistic building, with its plain rounded windows. I used to have a feeling of something like awe for the mysteries of the yard, entered from St. James's street by double doors, and to wonder how the space between the Vicarage itself and the high wall abutting on St. James's row was occupied.

Twiss : I have a rough drawing of the old place as it

appeared in process of demolition, in 1854. There was no upper story over the centre part—the oldest portion of the building—though it was long ago that the two ends had been added. Its combinations of lath, beams, plaster, and rubble were very antique. There is one relic of it still to be seen, but in an altered form and serving a new purpose. The large stone of the step leading into Messrs. Eadon's auction room by the door in St. James's street is the identical stone that served as mantel shelf in the oldest part of the Vicarage.

WRAGG : The street was long famous in another way— as the chosen home of the Scotch drapery business. Here, fifty years ago, Mr. John Brown, who subsequently built Columbia Works, first introduced that trade.

LEONARD: For good or for evil—a point on which opinions greatly vary.

LEIGHTON : It was here that the militia of the town used to be drilled and paraded. A soldierly-looking body of men they were, and they extended five or ten deep the whole length of the street.

EVERARD : In St. James's street was the house where Mr. Robert Hadfield lived, the warehouse being at the back. He had a family of four sons and two daughters : Robert, the youngest, died many years ago ; Joseph and Samuel were partners with the father ; Mr. George Hadfield, the present venerable M.P. for Sheffield, in early life removed to Manchester, where for many years he practised as an attorney. He, I am told, still signs cheques in the names of " Robert Hadfield and Sons." Mr. Robert Hadfield built the house at Crookes moor side for a country residence. Mr. Ray, surgeon, married one of the daughters, and the other died unmarried. Mr. Robert Hadfield's tombstone may be seen by passers-by in the yard of Howard street Chapel.

TWISS : There is an interesting point in connection with St. James's street. It is—from footpath to footpath, I believe—an exact proportion of a mile, and may thus be considered our Hallamshire standard of long measure.

LEONARD : Do you know anything, Mr. Twiss, of the history of the corner house to which inquirers after Sheffield folk-lore do much resort for interviews with that devoted and accurate antiquary, Mr. William Swift ?

TWISS : Now the Stamp office, you mean ? It was built by Mr. Stacey, who supplied the woodwork for the renovated Parish Church and for St. James's Church ; and it is fitted in a style similar to the latter. Mr. T. N. Bardwell, father of the present Mr. Frederick Bardwell, subsequently lived in it ; and after that, Mr. John Brown, of the firm of Parker, Brown and Parker, solicitors. When the firm dissolved, Mr. Brown, for many years stamp distributor, retained the premises, which are now occupied by his son, Mr. Walter Brown, attorney, and Major Fawkes, stamp distributor.

WRAGG: In St. James's row was Mr. Carr, staymaker, a nice elderly gentleman of the old style. He can still be remembered, clothed as well-to-do men were a century ago — in breeches and leggings. Sometimes he wore a spencer over his coat, or a top coat like those now worn by the inmates of the Shrewsbury Hospital.

TWISS: In the house adjoining the Stamp Office, the residence of that skilful surgeon, the late Mr. Henry Jackson, and now of his son, Mr. Arthur Jackson, formerly lived Mr. Brookfield, solicitor. Then at the corner of the row and Church street—now Mr. Wiltshire's, late Mr. Reedal's—was Dr. William Younge, the well-known physician, who died in 1838. I believe his father, Dr. Thomas Younge, to whom I made reference when we were speaking of the Grammar School, was there before him.

EVERARD : The premises in Church Street now occupied by the Bible Society were once the residence of Dr. Hodgson, father of Mr. John Hodgson, of Goddard Hall. Then Mr. Geo. Turton, surgeon, was their tenant; afterwards Mr. Aldam, Mr. Timothy Scott, and Mr. Algar. Dr. Hodgson entered into partnership with Mr. Joseph Waterhouse, and they built Portobello place, carrying on the silver plated manufacture there, under the firm of " Waterhouse, Hodgson, and Co." Mr. Waterhouse's son John married one of Dr. Hodgson's daughters, who is still living, having been a widow for many years. The Doctor built the house on Western Bank, the residence of the late Alderman W. A. Matthews; and he performed a still more notable building feat in the erection of Bell Hagg Inn, then and still popularly known as " Hodgson's Folly." He died in 1832.

WRAGG : The mention of Mr. Aldam reminds me of Mr. Daniel Wheeler, who was in partnership with him.

EVERARD : I question whether the partnership existed *here*. Daniel Wheeler had his porter vaults under the Quakers' Meeting House ; and, subsequently, Mr. Aldam had the same. I remember seeing the sign of " Daniel Wheeler" over the entry of what is now the Thatched House Tavern. That Mr. Aldam was in partnership with Daniel

Wheeler in some place is certain, but whether in Church street is uncertain. For my part, I do not believe he was.

WRAGG : At any rate, they were in partnership. I want, however, to mention Daniel Wheeler, not as Mr. Aldam's partner, but as the celebrated Quaker missionary, noticed by the poet Whittier. Just before the Russian war many people were quite astounded that " the three Quakers " should have had the presumption to visit the Emperor of Russia to endeavour to prevail on him not to go to war ; but had they known the close and intimate relations that had existed between the late Daniel Wheeler and the Czar Nicholas, and also the previous Emperor, they would not have been surprised at the visit of Messrs. Sturge, Peace, and Carleton. Mr. Wheeler " went about doing good."

EVERARD : Mr. Wheeler originally went out to Russia to manage a model farm for the Emperor Alexander, who, about the year 1824 or 1825 had visited England. He was a little, broad-built man, and he wore a grey Quakers' suit and broad-brimmed hat. He was away from England about ten years. Soon after his return, the Society sent him, with one or two others, to visit the mission stations in the South Seas, New Zealand, and other places. The journal he kept was not published, but it was handed round among the Friends for private perusal.

LEIGHTON : The site on which Mr. Aldam built the present wine and spirit establishment was previously a public-house, with the sign of the " Grapes." It was a respectable place of the kind, and was kept by a person of the name of Hall. The house front projected halfway across the causeway, beyond the line of the other buildings. It had three windows in the front, and also a window in each of the gable ends, one of them facing up the street and the other down. The Sheffield local band used to assemble here for practice. It included William Taylor, the French horn player, and his son John, the celebrated bugler ; together with the Cleggs, father and son, the trumpeters.

EVERARD : The Sheffield and Hallamshire Bank was built on the site of the house below the " Grapes." That was a well-built and respectable-looking house, with palisades in front.

TWISS : It was a house with a fine old staircase, and was at one time the property of the Fisher family, by whom it was sold to the Staceys, who, in turn, sold it for the purposes of the Bank.

LEONARD : The grandfather of the present Mr. William Fisher lived there. The house was an extremely good one. Behind it was a productive garden, in which, in addition to the commoner fruits, grapes were grown upon the walls. Then behind the garden were the horn-pressing works of Mr. Fisher—works still occupied by his descendants, though the trade has changed its character—in Orchard place. By the gates was, as I have been told, a very fine pear tree. After Mr. John Fisher, who died in 1820, his sons, Robert and William (the latter a fine old politician and reformer, remembered by all of us), occupied the house ; and then, as Mr. Twiss has said, it passed into other hands, although the works remained, and do still remain, the property of the Fisher family.

TWISS : There is a curious story about an old barber who had a shop about here. He was tall and spindle-shanked. His door was divided in the middle into two halves, and at night his window was lighted by a tallow candle stuck in a pint bottle. A number of mischievous youths—one of whom when an old man told me the story—fastened the lower half of the door on the outside, and then, through the upper half, threw in a number of lighted jumping crackers. They could see the poor barber sitting alone, and they watched the alarm and dismay with which he found himself suddenly in the midst of a fusillade. The antics of the tall and " ungain " barber, as he skipped about to avoid the crackers, and his futile attempts to open the door and so escape, amused his tormentors greatly.

LEIGHTON: Now we come to the old Cutlers' Hall, erected in 1726, demolished 1832, its predecessor dating as far back as 1638, when the Company built it on the site of some old " burbage houses." The second was a very unpretentious building compared with that which has now taken its place. It was a structure of three stories, with finished stone corners and a broad stone border round the windows, of which there were only two on the ground floor—between two doors, each of which was surmounted by a pediment. The two ground floor windows were protected by a low circular railing adorned with the cross-daggers ; while above, in the centre, between two upper rows of windows, four in number, was the coat of arms of the Company.

TWISS : Which still may be seen preserved in the wall at the back of the present edifice.

EVERARD : Adjoining the Hall was the " Bird in the Hand," kept by old Tommy Rose, the chief resort of the "chaps" who visited the town for trading purposes with their pack-horses.

TWISS : The ground floor of the old hall was used as a justice-room, and there for many years the magistrates sat. Some odd doings were enacted there in the days of Justice Wilkinson.

EVERARD : In that lower room one good thing, at any rate, was done, in the establishment of the Sheffield and Hallamshire Savings' Bank, in 1819. On that occasion I was a depositor of a small sum on the first day, and, I believe, the first hour of its opening. I have very distinctly before my mind's eye the countenances and figures of those who sat at the table covered with green baize, including the Rev. Thomas Sutton, Mr. Montgomery, Mr. George Bennet, Mr. Thomas Rawson, the Rev. Mark Docker, and others.

LEONARD : I have read in an old number of the *Courant* that there was a curious scene in 1795, when so much trouble occurred about the high price of flour. A relief committee had been formed to supply the poor with cheap flour, and they sold at so low a price that there were public rejoicings. A number of women with ribbons and cockades entered the room at the Cutlers' Hall, in which the gentlemen of the Corn Committee had assembled. After thanking them they marched in a body up to the head of the table, and told Dr. Browne, the chairman, that they had brought a chaise to the door, and begged leave to draw him through the principal streets of the town. The Doctor escaped by pleading that this would be inverting the order of things, and would be ungallant; and as he would not allow himself to be importuned into it, the women at length retired.

TWISS : That would be soon after the time when Dr. Browne wrote to Wilberforce the letter that appears in the "Life" of the latter, dated July, 1795 : "There was a numerous meeting at the Cutlers' Hall yesterday, when I opened business by reading your letters. They were so struck by the propriety of your recommendation, that they agreed to sign a resolution pledging themselves to the greatest economy in the use of flour. I was particularly desired by the whole meeting to reiterate their warmest thanks to you for your uniform attention to their interests. Price of wheat at Nottingham, 12s. per barrel."

LEIGHTON : A story has been told of a workman who could never agree with his strikers. He summoned his masters before the magistrates because they would find him neither single-hand work nor a striker. The man said the masters always found strikers; on the other side, evidence was given showing that they never found strikers; and Dr. Corbett, who heard the case (it was in the old justice-room of the Cutlers' Hall), said, "If men don't find strikers, and masters don't find strikers, who the devil does find strikers?"

EVERARD : A curious chapter might be written on the changes that have taken place in the Cutlers' feasts, as well as in the rooms in which those feasts have been held. The historian would find ample scope in tracing the gradual increase in sumptuousness from the days of good old George Smith, who was Master Cutler in 1749, when the total cost of the feast was £2. 2s. 9d., to the present day, when I should be afraid to say how much the feasts cost.

LEONARD : Even then the drink formed a very large proportion of the expense, though they were content with " ale and punch," instead of the champagne and hock of their degenerate descendants. Of the £2. 2s. 9d., almost one half, or 20s. 7d., went in ale and punch.

TWISS : How much one would like to know who were the guests there, and to have a description of the proceedings " from our own reporter."

LEONARD : We know that even then, or at any rate not long after, the feast was a great occasion, for in 1771, when Mr. Wm. Trickett was Master, there was a better show of dukes and earls and lords than can ever be attracted now. And in the town itself the occasion was a sort of fair; for we read in the *Courant* that " The Cutlers' feast was observed as a great holiday; the bells were kept constantly ringing during the three days it lasted, booths were erected in the Churchyard, High street, and Church street, for the sale of fruit, spices, &c., and all business was generally suspended."

EVERARD : At the feast this year (1872), Mr. William Overend complained that ladies were excluded from the tables. Why do they not in revenge revive the festival of the Mistress Cutler, which used to be held on the day following?

LEONARD : What! to eat up the broken victuals?

EVERARD : No, you cynic; I am sure the ladies' feast would be much more entertaining than the gentlemen's. There would be no unseemly manifestations of political feeling. If I were the Mistress Cutler, I would exclude reporters and every male person, and the revenge would be complete. The gentlemen would be racked with envy.

LEONARD : Pray when were these interesting ceremonials observed ?

EVERARD : Oh, in 1791 and other years.

TWISS : " The good old times !"

EVERARD : In 1807, Mrs. Brownell, the Mistress Cutler, "gave an elegant dinner to the ladies; and in the evening, an assembly at the rooms in Norfolk street." Mrs. Ebenezer Rhodes did the same in the following year ; but the year following that, Mr. Robert Brightmore being Master, times had become so bad that the Corporation announced that, "in consequence of the state of their finances, they suspend the annual feast and dine by tickets, 15s. each." Even earlier than that, in 1798, the feast had been paid for by tickets, 10s. 6d. each, for another reason, "the money usually applied to defray the expenses of the feast having by vote been appropriated to the subscription in aid of the exigencies of the Government."

LEONARD : We get a glimpse at the jolly doings at the old Cutlers' feasts from Mr. Holland's " Memorials of Chantrey." Speaking of Mr. Nicholas Jackson, the filemaker, of Shemeld croft, with one of whose daughters Chantrey had a love affair, he says, " Ancient guests at the Cutlers' feast will remember how his loyal songs formerly divided with those of another local worthy, Billy Battie " (of whom we have just been speaking), " the applause of the Corporation, when sung in the old Hall, in Church street." Fancy the manufacturers singing songs now-a-days on that grand occasion !

WRAGG : The handsome building of the Sheffield and Rotherham Bank, erected in 1866 in place of the plain brick structure, occupies the site of the premises once the residence and factory of the Roebucks. The history of Dr. Roebuck, the most distinguished member of the family, you all know.

TWISS : His brothers first opened correspondences with the Continent, and one of them was possibly the first Sheffield banker (1770) ; on whose failure, eight years afterwards, the Broadbents' bank was established.

LEONARD : When the Roebucks died, they had not a long journey to take. A tomb opposite the Sheffield and Rotherham Bank, dated 1752, bears the names of Roebuck and Fenton ; and Mr. Holland tells us that " in the month of May, 1785, Church lane was made wider by taking into it about three yards of the churchyard and removing a certain number of coffins, bodies, and gravestones, the last mostly bearing the name of Roebuck, and forming at present (1869) part of the floors in the cellars and kitchens of the houses opposite."

TWISS : In making that sweeping observation Mr. Holland did not display the accuracy that is desirable in such matters. The fact is, he has multiplied one single gravestone into a wholesale collection. The only basis for his statement is the following : When the Sheffield and Rotherham Bank made certain alterations in their premises, some years before the rebuilding, it was found necessary to remove the flooring in a cottage at the back, in which the bank messenger resided, and among the pavers so taken up was one which had been a gravestone, of which this is a copy : "Here was interred the Body of Rogger Robuck, late of Sheffield, joiner : he departed this life the 25th day of October, Anno Dom. 16 and in the 70th year of his age." The date is imperfect, only a portion of the third figure, which may be 0 or 6 or 9, remaining. The full date may be 1600, or any year between that and 1609 inclusive ; or it may be 1660, or any year between that and 1669 ; or it may be 1690, or any year between that and 1699. I have made a careful search in the parish register, but cannot find any entry of the burial of such a person. It probably belongs to the period between 1660 and 1669, if the following extract from " Depositions from York Castle," published by the Surtees Society, relates to the same person : "A true bill against Henry Bright, of Wharlow (Whirlow), gen., Stephen Bright, of the same, yeo., Roger Robuck, of the same, joiner, and Cornelius Clerk, of Cathorpe (Cutthorpe), co. Derby, gen., for breaking into the forest of Thomas Earle of Arundell, called Riveling Forrest, on 21 July, 1659, and killing a stag." I think it not impossible that the stone may have come from Nether Chapel, rather than from the Parish Churchyard.

LEIGHTON : Mr. Webb, a well-known Sheffield surgeon, lived from about 1813 to 1818, in a house on a part of the site now occupied by the Sheffield and Rotherham Bank. He was a stout-built, dapper little man, fond of dress, and he rode a good horse. He had removed to Church street from Norfolk street, and thence he went to Market street ; but he was not in the latter place long, for he died at Broomhall Mill, where he had gone for the benefit of his health, about 1820.

TWISS : I believe at one time he lived in Fargate, by "the Lord's house."

LEONARD : Mr. Webb was one of the first surgeons to the

Infirmary, and an amusing story has been told me of a quarrel he had with the Rev. Alex. Mackenzie, of St. Paul's. It was the custom in those days for the medical staff of the Infirmary to assemble for prayers before commencing their duties ; and Mr. Webb being invariably late, kept his colleagues waiting. At length this became so intolerable that Mr. Mackenzie took him to task, which the Doctor resented so warmly as to threaten to horse-whip "the black-coated scoundrel" for having the impudence to dictate to him. A few days afterwards, when about to mount his horse at his own door, Mr. Webb, seeing Mr. Mackenzie coming up the street, made a rush, and began to carry his threat into execution. The curate of St. Paul's ran for protection into the bank and sped upstairs, pursued by the irate doctor, both being followed by a number of clerks and others, astonished by this strange incursion. To appreciate fully the ridiculous sight, you must remember that Mr. Mackenzie was an excessively tall man—over six feet—and that his assailant was considerably under middle height. Mr. Mackenzie did not live long after that. He went up to London to undergo an operation for the stone, and he died there—in 1816. Mr. Webb had a garden at Harvest Grove, the end of Harvest lane, where Mr. Waterhouse afterwards built a house. He had a farm at Park Wood Springs, on land belonging to Parson Bland, of Bolsterstone, which was afterwards sold to the building society. Mr. Webb was accustomed to give lectures on surgery to medical students; and a list of his pupils would include such names as Wilson Overend, Jackson, France. But meetings of another kind were held at his house. Dr. Younge, Dr. Ernest, James Montgomery, Robert Hadfield, and others used to meet there to discuss politics. The Government of that day was very jealous of such meetings, and Mr. Webb's servants had instructions to represent to any callers at such times that he was engaged in lecturing upon surgery. Mr. Webb had himself been a pupil of his uncle, Mr. Charles Hawksley, whose surgery was in High street, near where Messrs. Foster, the tailors, are now ; and he was succeeded in practice by Mr. Nelson.

LEIGHTON : Mr. Webb has been credited with being the hero of a curious adventure among the colliers.

LEONARD : Yes ; but the assertion that the adventure happened to him is denied with much emphasis and some indignation by one who knew him well, and who asserts that he was not at all addicted to intemperance. I am told that it is more likely to have happened to his brother, Parson Webb, who was curate of Dore before the Rev. Frank Parker.

WRAGG : What is the story ?

LEONARD : Its hero, whoever he may have been, having been drinking in the neighbourhood of Intake, lay on the ground helplessly drunk. Some colliers going to work at a neighbouring pit, partly as a practical joke, and partly out of consideration for his safety, picked him up and took him down the pit with them. After some time the inebriate came to himself, and seeing a number of black visages around, and a place quite different from any he had ever seen, thought he was dead and in another world. The men had got with them a pitcher of ale, and gave their visitor some. He drank, and said it was very much like what he had the night before he died. This was likely enough, as it had come from the very public-house where he had been drinking. One of the men asked him who and what he was. He told what his name and profession had been in the former state of existence, but accommodatingly said he would there be anything the gentlemen pleased.

LEIGHTON : *Se non è vero è ben trovato.* And at any rate this brings us to the bottom of Church street, leaving us to contemplate the changed aspect of affairs where, on the one side, the big establishment of Messrs. Cole Brothers has sprung up—one hardly knows how many stories high; while on the other, the old Town Hall has long since disappeared.

EVERARD : I'm sorry to interrupt on the threshold of so interesting a theme, but had we not better reserve "the lobby" for our next meeting ?

OMNES : Agreed. *[Exeunt.*

CHAPTER IV.

The Old Town Hall, High Street.

Scene—The " Beehive." Host, Mr. Leighton.
Period—1873.
Present—Leighton, Twiss, Leonard, Everard and Wragg.

LEONARD : A very old gentleman of my acquaintance, aged 91, has given me an interesting account of the old Town Hall, at the Church gates. " I remember it," he said, " very well. It was not a large building. On the ground floor was the ' lobby, ' or gaol, called Sam Hall's parlour. There culprits used to be confined, and you could go and talk to them through a round hole in the door, such as you may now see in the doors of country pinfolds. Sam Hall was the gaoler, and he also sold pots and such like to make out his living. Above the lobby was the hall itself, approached by an external flight of steps facing down High street. I remember Wilberforce coming to address the electors of Yorkshire from those steps. A silly man, named Josiah, or ' Jesse,' from Grenoside, was among the crowd, and somebody put him on a great wig. This made a lot of fun, and caused some confusion ; and Tom Smith, the constable, who kept the ' Blue Boar,' down Westbar, ' nobbled ' the disorderly ones to keep them quiet."

Twiss : I have no doubt that speech of Wilberforce's was the one delivered on the 9th of May, 1807, when he was accompanied by Mr. Lascelles.

Everard : " Jesse," to whom Leonard refers, was a well-known and popular character in Sheffield in those days. His proper name was " Josiah," but he generally went by the soubriquet of " Jesse ;" and, from some of his unreasonable doings, the remark is still current and applicable to a person who has done any foolish thing, " What a Jesse he must needs be !" He was a tall, well-built, and powerful man, living at Grenoside, near Greno wood. His visits to Sheffield were very frequent. At that time the coaches to Huddersfield and Halifax ran that way ; and Jesse, on an evening, when tired with his day's rambles in the town, decidedly preferred riding home on the coach to walking. But then, there was the "fare," which he neither could nor would pay; so the coachman, until he learnt better, left him behind burning with indignation and threatening revenge. After such altercation, it was not unfrequently found that in the night time large stones had been placed on the road in the most awkward places, with the evident design of upsetting the coach. The act could never be traced to the perpetrator, but so shrewd a suspicion was entertained, that it was deemed a prudent thing to let Jesse ride home ; and as long as this was done, no large stones were found on the road, and the passengers were amused by his talk. One of his peculiarities was that he always carried a lengthy walking staff of some kind ; but he more especially preferred a long broom-handle. On coming to Sheffield without a staff, he would walk into some house, look out the sweeping-brush, and in an instant would be seen striding off at great pace with the " brush-steale," a number of women and children raising the hue and cry at his heels. Another of his eccentricities was his attendance on all the funerals he heard of. He was very impartial in paying this mark of respect, whether he happened to know the family or not. The attraction was the custom of giving to those invited to the funeral a "burial cake," being a large plum cake, before " biscuits " came into general use. This privilege of a " mourner " was always accorded to Jesse. One day, after attending a funeral in the neighbourhood of Broad lane, having one of these large cakes in each of his coat pockets, he asked a carter, who had just been delivering a load of coals, to allow him to ride in the cart. Jesse got in, and as he sat on the edge of the door, the man slyly uncottered it, so that he had not ridden far before the door came down, and Jesse fell on his back ; and whilst he was gathering up his cakes the man drove off. This little incident was related to me by one who witnessed it. Another of Jesse's peculiarities was his extreme fondness for singing and music. At that time the " oratorios " were often held in the Parish Church, on which occasions he was sure to put in an appearance and attempt to get into the place—of course without payment. On being repulsed by the doorkeepers, he would walk about in front of the church, and when the performance was fairly begun, with his very powerful voice he struck up at the church doors the chorus, "Lift up your heads, O ye gates; and be ye lift up, ye everlasting doors; and the King of Glory shall come in. Who is this King of Glory? The Lord of Hosts; He is the King of Glory." This had the effect of disturbing the audience and embarrassing the performers, so that the doorkeepers soon received orders to let poor "Jesse" come in; on which he at once became silent and absorbed, and seemed to enjoy the musical treat with great satisfaction. But I ought to apologise, my friends, for taking up so much of your time.

LEIGHTON: That old Town Hall was built in 1700, and was pulled down in 1808. It stood slightly within the churchyard, and projected right out into the middle of the way, where the open space at the entrance to East Parade now is.

LEONARD: Before it was "Sam Hall's parlour," it was "Sam Wibberley's." We get some idea of its limited dimensions from Nield's "Remarks on the prisons of Yorkshire" (*Gentleman's Mag.* lxxv. 301), which say: "The lobbies under the Town Hall are three dark cells, which open into a narrow passage, the largest eight feet square by six feet high. Each door has an aperture of six inches diameter. There is an offensive sewer in the corner of each cell." Since Nield adds that, although it was daylight when he went in, he needed a lighted candle, we may conclude that these were not very pleasant places in which to be confined.

LEIGHTON: Adjoining the Town Hall, facing down High street, were the stocks, afterwards removed to Paradise square; and the pillory.

TWISS: There was a curious illustration of the use of the stocks in 1790, when "nine men were put into them for tippling in a public-house during church time; and two boys were made to do penance in the church for playing at 'trip' during divine service, by standing in the midst of the church with their 'trip sticks' erect."

LEONARD: Well, we punish the former offence now, but in a different way. I'm not quite sure that we are wise in winking at the playing that goes off.

TWISS: There is another good story of the stocks, in connection with old Justice Wilkinson. A little girl in the street was incited by some mischievous fellow to go up to a gentleman walking along, and to say:

" They burnt his books,
And scar'd his rooks,
And set his stacks on fire "—

the well-known doggrel relating to the rioters' attack on
Broomhall. The child innocently went in front of the gentleman and, bobbing a curtsey, lisped out the lines. " What,
my dear ?" asked the Vicar—for it was none other. The
child repeated it. " Yes, my dear, " said he, " come along
with me ;" and leading her by the hand, took her to the
stocks, to her great distress.

LEIGHTON : Justice Wilkinson had a patriotic sympathy
with the fathers and mothers of illegitimate children, from an
idea that, considering the drain of the war, it was a public
benefit to add to the population. Some sayings of his, a
little too broad for reproduction in print, are yet told by the
choicest of our old story-tellers.

LEONARD : It was in 1791 that that attack on Broomhall
was made. The ringleader, one Bennett, was executed for it
at York.

EVERARD : I have always understood that the individual
executed was a poor, half-witted young man, whom the mob
purposely incited and pushed forward through the library
window, to commit the incendiary act of setting the books
and papers on fire. Had the event taken place now, the unfortunate lad, instead of being hanged, would in all proba-
bility have been sent to an asylum during her Majesty's
pleasure. This case, I have been told, produced at the time
such an impression on the public mind as led to the doing
away with the law, or custom, of giving " blood-money." I
say law or custom, because I have heard it denied that any
such law was ever enacted by the British Parliament. As
matter of fact, however, it must have possessed some shadow
of legal authority, as it was a thing practised in two instances, at least, in " Old Sheffield ;" and after the Broomhall riot the practice ceased to exist. My father was one of
those who, out of curiosity, went as an on-looker to that
scene of outrage, but, believing that the military would soon
put in an appearance, he began to make his way homewards.
In Black Lamb lane (now Broomhall street, but then a narrow country road), his retreat was, however, intercepted by
the approach, at full speed, with noise of jingling scab-
bards, mingled with oaths and curses, of a detachment of
cavalry. He jumped over the field wall and lay hidden until
they had passed. Then, concluding that there would certainly

F

be another troop soon following, he decided to go down the lane (now Hanover street) towards Sheffield moor, and by that roundabout way get home. He had not, however, gone far in that direction, before another party of soldiers made their appearance, headed by the colonel and Justice Wilkinson himself. He had then with agility again to perform the climbing and hiding feat, and thus managed to escape the dangers of his nocturnal ramble on that clear moonlight night.

LEONARD: It appears from the *Sheffield Register's* account of the affair that the cavalry in question consisted of a detachment of Light Dragoons, sent over from Nottingham "in consequence of an application to Government for them;" and it seems very probable that if the unwonted arrival of the soldiery had not suggested rioting to the mob, none would have taken place. At the Cutlers' Feast that year the guests "were almost frantic in their expressions of approbation of Mr. Wilkinson's conduct;" and the Mistress Cutler's party on the following day, "with that rapturous joy which females only elate in a cause worthy of their sex can express, not only drank his health · · · but nothing less than acclamations of applause would satisfy their ardour and zeal."

TWISS: There are other anecdotes about Justice Wilkinson's doings as a magistrate which may as well be mentioned in connection with the old Town Hall. Being called upon on one occasion to arbitrate between a quarrelsome husband and wife, he ordered that they should be locked up together until they could agree. The discipline proved efficacious, for, after a show of obstinacy, the refractory couple came to terms, and announced their contrition by knocking upon the walls, as had been arranged. Another is this: A lady, having quarrelled with her servant, was required to appear before the Justice. She refused to go before "Old Niddlety Nod" (a nickname given owing to a peculiar shaking of the head caused by paralysis), and had to be fetched by a constable. "So you refused to come before 'Old Niddlety Nod,' did you? You are here now, however, and 'Old Niddlety Nod' orders you to pay the servant her wages and the costs of the court."

LEONARD: That nickname reminds me of the description of Mr. Wilkinson given by one living who remembers him. "He was," said he, "a fine, venerable-looking old man; very stately, but rather palsied when I saw him. His head shook a little. He drove about in a large old family carriage with a pair of horses, and Joshua Gregory, his clerk, used to stand behind like a footman. I was at school at Chesterfield when the rioters went to Broomhall and 'burnt his books, and scared his rooks, and set his stacks on fire.' My father sent me word what mischief had been done at the Hall. After Justice Wilkinson died, Joshua Gregory went into a table-knife concern. The firm was Wostenholm and Gregory, but it did not continue long."

LEIGHTON: At the top of High street (now Pawson and Brailsford's, stationers) was the confectionery shop of Mr. Benjamin Walker, who was universally respected.

TWISS: You might go further back and speak of that corner when it was in the occupation of the Heatons. The inscription on their gravestone—which is the top slab of a tombstone—may still be read, near to the Vicarage. The most prominent member of the family mentioned upon it is "Thomas Heaton, late of this town, ironmonger, who died Dec. 19, 1734, in the 48th year of his age. He was easy and agreeable in every path of private life, and useful to the publick as a member of the three governing bodyes of the Town, the Church, and the Free School, and died generally lamented." Then follow the names of his wife and of a number of their daughters, ending in "Hellen, the last survivor of this truly Respectable Family, who departed this life, the 18th June, 1795." There were formerly, in front of the premises of which we are speaking, posts and chains, extending from below the church gates to the corner of York street.

LEIGHTON: There is a tragic history connected with the daughter of Benjamin Walker, of whom he was exceedingly fond. She was admired by all who knew her. It was "the old, old story"—she loved not wisely but too well. At the time when the South Devon Militia was quartered in the town the officers frequented the father's shop, and a broken heart was the end. On the premises next below, where Mr. Robinson and his father have been established as watch and clock makers for many years, was the post-office, Nathaniel Lister being Post Master. I cannot fix the date nearer than this—that it would be after 1810 and before 1815. At that time London letters were brought by horse mail round by Worksop, and the rider fired his pistol at the Market-place to notify his arrival. There was then only one letter-carrier for the whole town—a female who lived in Lee croft, and she carried the letters in a small hand basket, covered with a white napkin.

WRAGG : I think her name was Taylor. We must not
consider her duties to have been light simply from the small-
ness of the town. It was the price of the postage that was
the cause.

LEONARD : I find recorded, on the 17th December, 1819,
the death of Thos. Taylor, of Lee croft, aged 74. "He had
been for upwards of thirty years the principal letter-carrier
in this town;" and the obituary notice bestows on him a
warm eulogy. I presume your female letter-carrier would be
his daughter.

TWISS : Taylor was the publisher of the "Antiquities of
Sheffield," an early attempt at topography, to which is added
an account of the ceremony of laying the foundation stone of
the Infirmary. The imprint is, "Sheffield, printed for and
sold by T. Taylor, No. 7, Lee Croft, and may be had at the
Post Office; A. and E. Gales, in the Hart's-head; Slater,
Bacon and Co., Snig Hill." It has no date, but it must have
been published about the end of the last century. Taylor
was accustomed to go into the country with a newsman's horn,
selling newspapers.

WRAGG : At that time a letter to or from London cost
tenpence. Supposing the postage was to be raised to this
sum now, we should not see the present number of letter-
carriers. In travelling now, a person can go to London, or
anywhere else, whenever he thinks proper, by railway; not
so in coaching days. Then he would go to the coach-office a
few days or a week beforehand to bespeak a seat, and deposit
a part or the whole of the fare. When he went to London,
some person or persons invariably turned up to ask him, as a
particular favour, to take a letter to drop in the post-office at
the place of his destination. Many people discovered friends
they did not know of but for this. One manufacturer had
letters enclosed in his to other manufacturers, to save the
cost of postage. About a century back—nay, even less time
—it was considered more dangerous to reach London than
now Australia. At that time, a young man just out of his
time who bought a top coat would wear it as long as he
lived, and then one of his sons would wear it for years.
There was then no old cloth worked up into new—the stuff
was strong and durable.

EVERARD : Yes, things are greatly changed.

WRAGG : The other part of Mr. Robinson's shop was Mr.
Saunders' auction mart, before he removed into the premises
in East Parade now occupied by Mr. Bush. Mr. Saunders

lived at the corner of Wilkinson street until his flight to America. Then at the corner of York street, now Mr. Stacey's pianoforte warehouse, was Mr. Butcher's draper's shop. It would look strangely old-fashioned with its bowed windows, small panes, and steps leading up into it, now; but at that time it was the largest draper's shop in the town.

LEIGHTON : In those days there was no " selling off at an immense sacrifice;" no bankrupt stock amounting to "£2320. 17s. 6¾d.;" in fact, there was no humbug. Mr. Butcher knew that if his customers did not come one day they would another. He prospered, and died a rich man.

WRAGG : Mr. Vennor, one of the founders of Queen Street Chapel, and particular friend of the Rev. Jehoiada Brewer, was Mr. Butcher's predecessor in the shop.

LEONARD : I believe that, in 1828, the shops between East Parade and York street were occupied in the following order : Benjamin Walker, confectioner; Thomas Robinson, watchmaker; William Saxton, bookseller; and John Butcher, linen draper. With the exception of Mr. Saxton they had all been there many years before that. Mr. Saxton was succeeded by the late Mr. Samuel Harrison ; Mr. Walker (some time between 1833 and 1837) by John Clarbour, and Mr. Clarbour in turn by Samuel Thompson, so that the shop remained in the confectionery business for many years. In Mr. Thompson's time it was, however, divided, and the upper portion was occupied by Mrs. Lewis, hosier and staymaker. She was a daughter of the Mr. Outram, of whom we shall have to speak lower down.

TWISS : In a shop at the lower corner of York street, (on the site of that now occupied by Mr. Tomlinson, ironmonger), was, in 1787, Ezra Ridgard, the well-known bookseller. It was Ridgard and Bennet, in 1797.

LEIGHTON : Afterwards (in 1817) Mr. Polack, a jeweller, was there; but his end was very different from Mr. Butcher's, as he died in great poverty. Next below was a carver and gilder, named Robert Henderson, to whom old Mr. George Eadon was apprenticed. Henderson had himself been a fellow-apprentice with Chantrey, at Ramsay's, an earlier carver and gilder in High street. Chantrey painted Henderson's portrait. Ramsay's shop was lower down, where Rimington and Younge's bank was afterwards built ; but subsequently he occupied one higher up on the opposite side of the street. During his apprenticeship Chantrey rented and used as a studio a little chamber at the top of what is now Hutton's yard. Later he had a room at a **High street** confectioner's, named Botham.

WRAGG : And about here, too, earlier, was the shop of Nathan Andrews, the watchmaker, murdered by **Frank Fearn** in 1782. But I shall have more to say of this murderer when we get to another part of the town. There is some question, however, as to whether his victim's shop was in High street or in Church street.

EVERARD : I had the impression that it was at the top of the Old Haymarket, about the middle of the street by the new Post-office, running down to Sheaf street.

TWISS: And I have the belief that it was in Fargate, opposite the Old Red House.

LEIGHTON : Another High street worthy, who had his shop here, close to the thoroughfare into Hartshead, still called Hawksworth's yard, was Mr. George Hawksworth, quite a gentleman in position and manners. He was accustomed to lend his family plate for the adornment of the Cutlers' feasts of those days. He was one of the founders, and for many years one of the principal directors of the original gas company. The unlucky scheme for erecting the Commercial Buildings (now Messrs. Levy's) for a post-office, newsroom, and offices was of his origination. The building was sold by the mortgagee, and the shareholders got about 1s. 6d. for each £25 share. Mr. Hawksworth had "The Hills" on the Grimesthorpe road for his country house, and was distinguished for his successful gardening.

TWISS : Gosling's plan, 1736, is the chief authority for saying that High street was formerly called Prior gate ; and it is probable that hereabouts was the Priory. It was said in 1800, "There are no remains of the Priory, and its existence can only be known from old deeds, and the right side of High street, coming from the market, still retaining among the oldest inhabitants the name of Prior row."

LEONARD : Pretty nearly every yard branching out of High street has a history of its own ; and there are, or have been, quaint old places in them little heeded by the passer-by. There is the old "Grey Horse," for instance, which one of our local traditions represents as having been the resting-place of King John when once he passed through Sheffield.

TWISS : It is simply a tradition. The house was, perhaps is now, the property of the family of the Girdler's.

LEIGHTON : In Wilson's tobacco shop was the circulating library kept by Mr. Woollen—low and gloomy—which gave

Young Sheffield of those days the opportunity of reading the "Old English Baron," the "Mysteries of Udolpho," and the "Castle of Otranto," for free libraries were not.

TWISS : I have an idea that Hawksworth's yard was once called Trippet's yard. James Woollen, the stationer, who died in 1814, married Ann Trippet. His daughter, Mrs. Wade, afterwards had a circulating library in West street.

LEIGHTON : Next door lived Mr. Candow, the last leather-breeches maker. Then there was Mr. Colquhoun, tinner and brazier, who afterwards became engineer to the new Gas Company formed in 1834. Adjoining his workshops was the malthouse of Mr. Thomas Wreaks, whose sister kept a toy shop in front, which was then 35, High street. Opposite the end of George street was Mr. Nowill's, once Kippax and Nowill. He was the merchant and manufacturer who built the Freemasons' Hall in Paradise square; and he erected for himself a house at East Bank, and planted the line of tall poplar trees on each side the road still to be seen there. He was succeeded in his shop by Mr. James Crawshaw, father of Mr. Crawshaw, now registrar for the Sheffield West district.

LEIGHTON : The "Blue Bell" should not be passed without mentioning it as one of the old public houses of the town.

WRAGG : In the shop of Miss Fishbourne was Mr. Owen, the draper, a leading Wesleyan during many years. A daughter of his married the Rev. J. Rattenbury, afterwards President of the Wesleyan Conference. One of his sons was the first to attempt to trade as a merchant to Australia.

EVERARD : The jeweller's shop of Mr. Charles Younge was that above the "Star" Inn gateway. It has been in various hands lately, but its present occupant is Mr. Hyam, tailor. On the other side of the gateway was Younge and Rimington's bank. Then came the draper's shop of Cowen and Dixon.

WRAGG : Mr. Thos. Cowen was one of the early teachers of the Wicker Sunday School, afterwards in Andrew street; and Mr. Dixon married, firstly, one of the sisters of the late Mr. Robert Waterhouse, and secondly, Anne, daughter of Mr. Joseph Cowley, an eminent Wesleyan, who was a manufacturer in Pinstone street. Mr. Cowley's daughters Anne, Elizabeth and Sarah, are immortalised in many of the writings of Mr. John Holland, bachelor poet, recently deceased (December, 1872).

LEONARD : Next below, now part of Mr. Wheelan's cloth shop (No. 41), were the premises to which the *Iris* office was

removed, in 1825, by Mr. Blackwell, after he had purchased
that paper from Mr. Montgomery. In 1832, the late Mr. Robt.
Leader succeeded Mr. Blackwell in the occupation, removing
thither the office of the *Independent* from 30, Angel street.
The printing-office was afterwards in Mulberry street, in the
building that—originally a factor's warehouse—became the
preaching-room of the early Methodists, after their chapel in
Pinstone lane had been destroyed and their place of worship
in Union street abandoned.

EVERARD : Mr. Everitt, in his history of "Methodism in
Sheffield," gives an account of the persistent and ruffianly
persecution to which the persons who attended that chapel
were subjected. But that was a hundred years ago.

WRAGG : At the bottom of the street was Mr. Robert
Carver, woollen draper, one of the six tall men of the town.

LEIGHTON : Without touching the Market place for the
present, we now cross the street, and take the places of business on the left-hand side, going towards the Parish Church.
There we strike another post-office site, little changed since
the days when Mr. William Todd, the founder of the high
Tory *Sheffield Mercury*, presided over the arrival and despatch
of mails.

LEONARD : He had removed from Market street (where he
had begun the *Mercury* in 1807) in 1811 ; and he was appointed Post-master, May, 1815.

LEIGHTON : In the passage between Messrs. Cutts, Sutton
and Son's shop and that until lately Jackson's toy shop, we
used to wait for letters. Mr. Todd was a gentlemanly-looking
man, wore breeches and black silk stockings ; but he got
deeply into the books of Parker, Shore and Company's Bank,
and disappeared. Mr. George Ridge succeeded him in the
ownership of the *Mercury*, (1826) and removed it to his shop
in King street, then the third from the Angel street corner,
and Mr. Wreaks was at the same time appointed to the post-
mastership, and the Post-office was removed to the lower
corner of Norfolk street and Arundel street, now a tinner and
brazier's shop ; but thence it was in 1835 brought back into
High street, to the Commercial Buildings already mentioned.
The shop of Mr. Cooper, confectioner, was the next above
Todd's, a curious old gabled place, built with beams and
baulks, the upper story projecting right over the causeway.
I have seen the time when a load of hay has stuck fast and
been unable to pass the projecting gable. Mr. Cliff had a
rope and twine shop above Cooper's.

TWISS: His rope-walk was up West street, by the Hallamshire Hotel public house, and on the post of the yard adjoining that house might very recently be read the words " Cliff's Rope Walk." His daughter married Mr. Wm. Outram, cabinet maker, also of High street; and their daughters married into several well-known Sheffield families.

LEIGHTON: The present glass-fronted "Clarence" Hotel and Turnell's spirit stores have supplanted (for the worse, pictorially) the antique premises so long occupied as a dram shop, up to 1839 by Ward and Bawer, and then for many years by George Bawer alone. The enhanced rent required of Mr. Bawer was too much for his resources, and he ended his long tenancy unfortunately. It is a thousand pities that the frontage was not set back to the level of the " Stone House," in this, the narrowest part of the High street. It was not for want of efforts on the part of the Town Trustees that this was not done.

TWISS: When we were talking about the Old Churchyard, mention was made of the "alabaster" stone, or "t'alli," as it used to be called, and this part of High street reminds me of its history. There was, hereabouts, an inn, to which one night an unknown traveller came. The bedroom allotted to him had, besides the door communicating with the landing, an unused door which had formerly opened upon the yard behind, but at a considerable elevation above it. The traveller arose during the night and sought to leave his room, but he got to the wrong door, forced it open, stepped out, and falling to the ground was killed. All attempts to ascertain his name or to communicate with his friends failed; but he had a considerable sum of money in his possession, so a handsome tombstone was erected over his nameless grave— which unwritten tombstone you may see to this day near the chancel door. The top marble slab has, as you all know, been broken. It is a part of my story to add that the fracture was done in an attempt to rifle the tomb of the treasures that were popularly believed to have been buried with the unknown stranger.

WRAGG: The old Stone House, now occupied by Messrs. Prest, wine merchants, and as offices, must have a history. I should like to know it.

TWISS: It has a history, but who shall tell it? I, for one, have been unable to recover the clue. On the hopper of the spout at the back of the house are the initials and date $\begin{smallmatrix} & E & \\ I & & M \\ & 1727 & \end{smallmatrix}$ What do these signify, and how are they to be read? Elmsall? Marriott? I cannot tell. The house was at one time in the possession of the Greaves family (of Page Hall). To them it came through the Clays, who may have got it from the Elmsalls. Or one may speculate on its being a Marriott, through a connection between them and the Greaves family. Its builder must, however, remain a mystery until some further light is thrown upon the subject. In later, but still distant years, it was in the possession of the Watson family, who also had a public house in Watson's walk. They put into it the grandfather and grandmother of Mr. Stirling Howard, one of whom had, I think, been in their service.

EVERARD: This brings the Stone House within reach of my personal memory. When I was a little boy it was kept as a very respectable wine and spirit merchant's store, with a large country trade, by Mrs. Howard, her husband having died in 1785. Her son, the late Mr. Thomas Howard, succeeded his mother on her death in 1822. The other son, the late Mr. William Howard, was brought up to the silver-plating business, and his son, Mr. Stirling Howard, in due time joined him, until they retired from business. Mr. Thomas Howard will be remembered by you all in his later days, living in the little cottage near The Hills, and finishing his career in the Stamp Office. After him Mr. John Porter (father to Mr. John Taylor Porter, surgeon) took to the business in the old Stone House. Mr. Prest joined him as partner, succeeded to the business, and transferred it to his son, by whom it is now carried on.

LEONARD: Between Mulberry street and George street, but entered by a passage from High street, is the "Victoria" inn, formerly the "Bay Childers," which was kept by Thomas Amory, who died in 1772, and by his wife after him. There may be no better opportunity than this of noticing the recent stoppage of the old thoroughfare across the yard at the back of the "Victoria," leading from Mulberry street into George street. No doubt the name of the inn was changed about the time of Her Majesty's accession. There was a "Bay Childers" in Bridge street also, which disappeared about the same time.

TWISS: I am not sure that you are correct in saying that Mr. Amory kept the Bay Childers; I have always understood that it was the Blue Bell. However, in front of what is now the Victoria, where are the shops of Mr. Gray, saddler, and Mr. Travell, clothier, there was in the last century a saddler named Heald. His daughter married in 1776 a workman of her father's, Joseph Cecil, who afterwards, through some property left to him, became Lord of the Manor of Dronfield.

WRAGG : The shop at the lower corner of George street was occupied in 1797 by Mr. Cæsar Jones, druggist, a well known citizen of his day. Two doors above George street, Thomas Hardcastle published the *Sheffield Chronicle* in 1837-8. That shop was afterwards occupied by the late Alderman Saunders when he dealt in music and musical instruments, and it is now absorbed in the china shop of Messrs. Parkin, formerly for many years kept Mr. Riley, who had before that been a grocer at the corner of Meadow street and Allen street.

TWISS : Behind that was an old building where, in 1797, lived William Lee, a cordwainer. The yard was in those days called " Truelove's yard," no doubt from the fact of the Trueloves keeping a locksmith's shop there up to at least 1817, Maria Truelove being the last. Mr. Lee was a frequent visitor at the "Bay Childers" public house, and was much given to betting—so inveterate indeed was the habit that when, on his way to Doncaster races, he saw a vehicle in front, in which were his wife and only son, swaying violently, he called out " Five to four that our Jim's killed." The late Mr. William Ibbitt made a sketch of a very old fire-place in one of the buildings here—whether that in which Mr. Lee lived or not I cannot say—but doubtless it was one of the old High street houses, erected before uniformity of frontage was cared for. It is a large open brick fire-place, with large carved stone front, supported by pillars for jambs. I believe that in the old days there was, behind this place, a croft, extending to what is now Norfolk street, and that it belonged to the Waterhouses, who are buried in the Parish Church (Gatty's "Hunter," p. 251). Miss Ann Waterhouse, who died in 1787, was the last lady in the town who wore the once fashionable hoops. Her capacious skirts could not be steered into church without some difficulty, and the hoops which expanded them were destined to be the bender of the kite of Thomas Howard, then a boy. Her brother, the Rev. Robert Waterhouse, who died in 1778, left a small legacy to Marmaduke Wreaks, peruke maker, High street, and bequeathed some money in trust for Barbara Wreaks, the mother of Mrs. Holland. The father of the Ann and Robert Waterhouse mentioned was Henry Waterhouse, a solicitor in extensive practice in the town, who died in 1719.

LEIGHTON : A celebrated firm was that of Green and Pickslay, on the site referred to just now as subsequently the

Post-office, and more recently Levy's. They were, perhaps, the first and most extensive ironmongers in Yorkshire, and were noted for a peculiarly excellent cast steel, which they called "Peruvian." Mr. Green was a gentleman fond of field sports, and having the *entrée* of very good houses. But he had to give his great friends long credit, and was not the man to ask for payment, so that the inevitable end resulted, and Mr. Green came to poverty. He was a fine-looking man, and wore a wig. I remember him saying to me, "If ever you should become bald, Mr. Leighton, never wear a wig; I have regretted it ever since I began one." And well he might; for when he took off his wig I never saw a more splendid head than he displayed. The business was afterwards (in 1828) carried on by Pickslay, Appleby and Bertram. On the lower side of the entrance to Mr. Nicholson's (once Bardwell's) auction room, is the shop of Mr. Harrison, hosier. It was, in recent days, Mr. Joseph Pearce's, bookseller, and there he started the *Sheffield Daily Telegraph*, in 1855, afterwards removing to the other side of the street, where Littlewood's stay shop formerly was, and where the paper is still published.

TWISS : Hereabouts, at the close of the last century, was Mr. Geo. Brown, druggist, who was the owner of the premises in the Hartshead occupied by Montgomery and the Misses Gales.

LEONARD : We learn from one of Montgomery's letters, written from York Castle, that the annual rent of the premises was £27. 3s. ; and in another letter (May 9, 1796,) the poet suggests that Mr. Brown should be asked to fulfil a promise to paint the front of the shop and house before Sheffield Fair; adding, "I think if Miss Bessy [Gales] would call upon Brown, she could wheedle him" into it.

TWISS : Mr. Brown was the great-grandson of the Rev. Cuthbert Browne, curate of Attercliffe and assistant-minister at the Parish Church from 1662 to 1673. Mention is made of him by Hunter (Gatty's edition, p. 413) as having come to great poverty. The family is related to that of Revel, and its present representatives are claiming the Revel estates.

LEIGHTON : Above Bardwell's passage was Snidall, the watch-maker, well known not only in the town, but on the trout streams of Derbyshire. Then came Thos. Cooper, grocer, a Quaker, and the father of Mr. Cooper, of Neepsend, tanner.

WRAGG : He was specially celebrated for making the best candles in the town.

LEIGHTON : I have paid at his shop 4½d. for a pound of salt. There is an amusing story told of Mr. Cooper and Mr. Wm. Hoyland, a druggist in Church street. They both dealt in nutmegs, and Thos. Cooper getting to know that there was about to be a great advance in price, and that Mr. Hoyland had a large stock, paid a friendly visit to his neighbour. "I know thou hast a large stock of nutmegs, friend William," said he, "and I have an opportunity of selling them. If thou wilt let me have them, we can do business." Hoyland fell into the trap, and, discovering afterwards that he had been " done," he stood at Cooper's door and called to him in his shop, " Thomas, thou'rt a rogue." Thomas, in return, passing by Hoyland's shop, remarked to his friend from the door, " William, thou'rt a fool." The premises of Mr. Tinker were, many years since, a public-house, the " Spread Eagle." When I knew it, about 1821, it was kept by Thomas Pattinson, a nephew of Sam Turner, in Watson Walk.

WRAGG : After that William Clifton had it, but it was the lower shop of Messrs. Foster, tailors, not the shop of Mr. Tinker. When Mr. Foster, wished to enlarge his shop Clifton bought the " Sportsman's Group," at the top of Chapel walk, displacing one Roberts, and he carried the " Spread Eagle" sign with him. I cannot say how long the Fosters have had a tailor's shop in High street, but I believe the grandfather opened the first ready-made clothes shop in the town.

LEIGHTON : I believe there is now a George Foster of the fourth generation. Old Mr. Foster was a real man of business. At the close of the great French war, the Government advertised for sale a vast stock of old equipments given up by the soldiers when disbanded. Mr. Foster went up to London and bought large quantities of soldiers' jackets and belts, and I remember big crates of them standing in front of his door. There was hardly a grinder in Sheffield but bought one of the jackets, for they just suited their trade, and the wheels all looked as if a regiment of soldiers were at work. The belts were made of excellent leather, and they were largely used by the cutlers for buffing and for similar purposes. Mr. Foster realised a large sum of money by that transaction. He left his family wealthy. He was afflicted with a disease whose chief symptom was falling instantaneously asleep. I went once to him, as a boy, to be measured for a jacket. Standing behind, he made me hold my arm horizontally, with the elbow bent, and I thought he seemed very long in measuring it. A person on the other side of the street, at York street corner, was watching the operation, and, seeing him laughing, I looked round, and found that the old man had fallen fast asleep.

EVERARD : I, too, have seen Mr. Foster, who was a very stout man, fall asleep whilst seated on the hampers of soldiers' clothes. They stood on the edge of the pavement, and there Mr. Foster sold their contents, so long as he could keep awake.

WRAGG : There are various points about High street that need elucidating, if only some one could do it. Where, for instance, was the " Crooked Billet yard," said to have been the residence of Thos. Wild, who was credited with having made the knife which stabbed the Duke of Buckingham ? (Gatty's Hunter's Hallamshire, p. 166.)

TWISS : There can, I believe, be no doubt that the yard so called was that at the top of High street, running between Messrs. Cubley and Preston's druggist's shop and the " Thatched House Tavern." It is now called Foster's Court.

LEONARD : And where was the sign of the Cock, opposite which was the printing office of Revil Homfray, publisher of that early Sheffield newspaper, *Homfray's Sheffield Weekly Journal!*" Francis Lister, who began the *Sheffield Weekly Journal*, April 28, 1754, described his office as " near the Shambles," and " opposite the Cross Daggers," and we know that the Cross Daggers was on the site of or behind Mr. Colley's shop, in the Market place. In August, 1755, Revil Homfray, who in the previous year had circulated in Sheffield a newspaper printed in Doncaster and called the *Sheffield Weekly Register, or Doncaster Flying Post*, advertised that he had bought the *Journal* of Lister's widow ; and he continued to issue it from " his printing office opposite to the Cock in the High street." Where was this ?

TWISS : I do not know where the " Cock" was, but I think I can throw some light on the Mr. Simmons, bookseller, one of the persons of whom it is announced the *Journal* can be bought ; but that must be when we speak of the Market place.

EVERARD : Which let us postpone until our next meeting.

CHAPTER V.

THE MARKET PLACE, KING STREET, ANGEL STREET.

Scene—Messrs. TWISS, LEIGHTON and EVERARD are discovered as
    the guests of Mr. WRAGG. To them enters Mr. LEONARD,
    introducing a new member of the fellowship, Mr. JOHN-
    SON, a townsman of middle age.
Period—A.D. 1873.

WRAGG : Now for our old Market Place ; and first as to
 the shops facing the Shambles, from the bottom of
High street to the Hartshead passage.

 TWISS : I will attempt now to fulfil the promise I gave
when last we met. The property on the site now occupied by
Messrs. Richards and Son, tailors, was formerly—1607-1621
—in the hands of the Blythes, who were yeomen at Norton
Lees. Johan Blythe married Thos. Bright, yeoman, of Brad-
way, and surviving her husband, transferred this property to
her third son James, a mercer in Sheffield. (See Gatty's
Hunter, pp. 417 and 414, note.) Now, Thomas Bretland was
a grocer occupying a part of this property, and Nevill Simmons, or Symmonds, stationer and bookseller, was also a
tenant, and married Bretland's daughter. He has been
called "the father of Sheffield bibliography." The name
which he bore appears on publications in such different parts
of the country that it is impossible to avoid some confusion.
(See "Notes and Queries," 3rd s. Vol. iii. p. 93.) But it
seems probable that he was a native of Sheffield, since he was
married here and buried in the Parish Church (died 17th
July, 1735). But either he, or another man of the same
name, was a bookseller in London. One of his daughters,
Mary, married the Rev. Timothy Jollie, of the Upper Chapel
(1681-1714), and he had sons Nevill and Samuel. The former died before his father, but the latter was also a bookseller
in Sheffield, and possibly succeeded his father in the Market
place. I strongly believe that he was postmaster, and most
likely he was the "Mr. Simmons, bookseller, in Sheffield,"
one of the persons appointed to receive subscriptions and
advertisements for Homfray's newspaper.

LEONARD : And I have always understood that his was the business to which Mr. John Smith, bookseller, of Angel street, succeeded.

TWISS : At the same time that the Blythes held the property of which I have been speaking, the Rollinsons belonged to that next below it, where Mr. Jones is now. Robert Rollinson, he who improved Barker's Pool and who died in 1631, had his shop here ; his son Thomas Rollinson succeeded him, and the family continued in possession of the property throughout the greater part of the last century.

LEIGHTON: Seventy years ago and more Mr. Richards' shop was kept by a hatter, Samuel Daniels. James Daniels, his nephew, succeeded him, but he did not prosper in business. There was a well-known discounter here—Francis Wright Everitt. At that time the shop of Mr. Brookes, hosier, was a circulating library, kept by Thomas Cockburn. First above the Hartshead entrance were Thomas and John Willey, drapers (afterwards Willey and Judd).

WRAGG : In the shop of Mr. Jones, who removed there from King street, was another draper, named Cooper. I am sorry to say he failed in business ; and it was not a case of mere plastering and whitewashing, as bankruptcies are at present, for he was necessitated to enter the workhouse. He rose to be the governor, and was a kind and considerate man—not like many who, having had to endure adversity, try how harshly and cruelly they can treat others. There were a few old shops here that would perhaps resemble those still remaining at the top of High street, now occupied by Messrs. Foster, Cooper and Shilcock.

LEIGHTON : The " George " Inn is unchanged ; it is now just as it was fifty or sixty years ago, when kept by Mr. and Mrs. Lawton, whose property it was. They did well at it. At that time, too, the shop below, Mather's, was, as now, a hatter's, one of the very few hat shops in the town—Whiteley's. The druggist's shop below, now kept by Mr. Radley, is unchanged too. It was a druggist's then, kept by Mr. Gillatt. At the corner of Change Alley was Mr. Robert Wiley, father of the late proprietor of " Old No. 12." He died in 1825.

WRAGG : He was a draper. The son Thomas was, for some cause, discarded by the family ; but subsequently, after passing through many vicissitudes, he became a wealthy man, and a helper of those who had once despised him.

JOHNSON : What an institution " Wiley's window "— meaning " Old No. 12 "—was ! It was almost a substitute for the daily papers of the present time. All, or nearly all, the events of the day were chronicled there—the deaths from cholera, the debates in Parliament, the elections—anything out of the ordinary course. I remember going down daily, during the debates on the first Reform Bill, to get the names of the speakers for my father.

LEIGHTON : Mr. Wiley displayed great enterprise, and made wonderful exertions to get his news.

JOHNSON : Yes, when Earl Grey resigned, Mr. Wiley showed his public spirit by having the *Sun* newspaper express sent to him. The news travelled from London to Sheffield in 14½ hours—a great advance on 1806, when the news of the death of Mr. Pitt took three days to reach Sheffield. Mr. Wiley died October 14th, 1851.

TWISS : Change Alley, I believe, was formerly the site of a bowling green; and I somehow associate the name with the London Royal Exchange. The Websters, who had a house there and in the Park (with which they became connected through the marriage of Leonard Webster, cutler, with the widow of one of the Wrights of the Park), had relatives in London; and possibly in this may be found a glimmering of the origin of the name. The summer-house formerly standing on the ridge of the Park, was built by Leonard Webster as a study for his son, afterwards the Rev. John Webster, who was senior wrangler and senior chancellor's medalist in 1756.

LEIGHTON : Let us just take a peep into Change Alley in the lively days when coaches were coming to and going from the "King's Head," then kept by "Billy Wright." He was one of the old school of landlords, and had universally a good name. Mr. Wright drove the first coach from Sheffield to Glossop ; and I had the honour of sitting behind him. It was entering a country which had hitherto been sealed to all but a few sportsmen. The first view of Win Hill and the five miles of the Woodlands from Ashopton to the "Snake" is one of the most beautiful drives in England, and can never be forgotten. On that day, the sun shining brightly, the jovial coachman, the splendid greys, the cheery notes of the bugle, heard for the first time in those solitudes, caused the blood to dance merrily through the veins of all that goodly company, and was a portion of the sunshine of life.

> " How sweet in the woodlands, with fleet hound and horn,
> To waken dull echo and taste the fresh morn."

G

Another of my coaching experiences from the "King's Head" was taking my seat, more than fifty years ago, for London; and for years afterwards I could remember all the different towns on the route. But I will not dilate now on the pleasures of travelling by coach.

WRAGG : Your friend Mr. Wright was not such a model character as you think. About half a century ago, the coach was about to start, but was overloaded, and Wright ordered two additional horses to be put to, telling one of his men to get ready to ride postilion. When he was ready, Mr. Wright complained how long he had been, when the man replied he had been as quick as he could. The master, without more ado, began to horsewhip him. The passengers and lookers-on cried shame, and after more delay, another man was sent instead.

TWISS : We can trace back the occupiers of the "King's Head" for a long series of years. Samuel Tompson, who died in 1716, had held it. He, I think, had married the widow of Mr. Dickenson, a previous occupier, and father of the Rev. John Dickenson, an assistant minister at the Parish Church and curate of Ecclesall from 1752 to 1766. Mrs. Tompson took a third husband, Mr. Richard Yeomans, from Buxton, who, when he brought Derbyshire produce to market, had been accustomed to put up at the King's Head. He died in 1729; and the house in 1773 is described as occupied by Henry Hancocks. The next year we find it tenanted by James Kay, or Key, and he kept it for nearly the remainder of the century. After him came "Billy Wright," who retired from the management in 1824, and was succeeded by Mr. Wm. Woodhead, a name which brings us to modern times. He married the daughter of Mr. Wright.

EVERARD : The shop at the lower corner of Change Alley, until just now occupied by Mr. Stables, is, perhaps, the oldest in the town, and the only one now remaining with a projecting gabled front. When I was a boy, it was kept by Mr. Newton, brother to the Mr. Newton of the firm of Porter and Newton, in King street. On a certain occasion this building and its residents had a narrow escape from destruction. Mr. Newton had lately got a fresh apprentice out of the country, and one evening at dusk, the boy went to fetch some goods out of the storeroom, which was the garret, taking, instead of a lantern, a lighted candle in his hand. Observing that he returned without a light, Mr. Newton ascertained that not only had he committed this indiscretion, but that, to make the matter worse, having no candlestick, he had stuck the candle in what he called a barrel of "rape seed." "Rape seed," exclaimed Mr. Newton, "why there is none there." It then, in a moment, struck him that it must have been left burning in a barrel of gunpowder! As life or death and destruction hung on every moment's delay, Mr. Newton, with that prompt and decisive courage with which some men are inspired on perilous occasions, immediately, without saying another word, went up the stairs, and, on arriving in the garret, there saw the lighted candle stuck in a barrel of gunpowder containing sufficient in quantity to have blown down the house, and perhaps the adjoining property. Treading as softly on the floor as possible, in order to avoid any shake which might send a spark from the wick, he then very carefully got the candle between the second and third fingers of the one hand, and, placing the other hand beneath to catch any falling sparks, he slowly drew it out of the powder and carried it down-stairs. This hazardous feat was accomplished before the inmates below were aware of the extreme peril in which they had been placed. The courage, coolness, and presence of mind which had hitherto possessed him then gave way under a sense of the frightful danger that had been incurred and providentially escaped. No wonder that he swooned away. This account Mr. Newton gave to my grandfather with his own lips.

LEIGHTON : We must not forget to conjure up once more the different scene presented aforetime, when this now decorous triangle was really the Market Place, fenced round with posts and chains. The corn market was still held here up to 1830, when the present Corn Exchange was opened. All the vegetables were thrown in the middle of the street by loads. The corn market was held first—till twelve o'clock, I think ; then the market keeper rang a bell, and the vegetable market began. The Barkers—there were three of them, little men in top boots—and other shoemakers were accustomed to bring wooden shops and fix them up ; and other people used to have baskets of different things. Besides that, it was a regular market for fish and everything else. Old Mr. Cade, quite a celebrated man, kept a book stall by the right-hand gateway.

WRAGG : Yes ; James Cade was well known. He resided in the "King and Miller" yard, Norfolk street. In his lifetime he was always considered to be a man of some wealth, but it was not so ; he was one of those very good men that we hear of now and then in whom every person feels sure he could place implicit confidence, but on whose death the public and their friends find to their sorrow that they have been deceived. Not only did Cade not die a rich man, but he was worth "less than nothing," for his debts and liabilities were greater than his effects. I am sorry to say that his character for honesty was sadly impeached, as he mistook a sick club's money for his own. He died, I believe, about 1829.

LEONARD (reads) : "At the bottom of High street you might have been accommodated with a pair of 'leather dicks' (breeches), either for yourself or 'prentice lad, at Davenport's; or have gone for them to Ellis Grant's stall, at the top of the Market, within the chains. You would have found Old Milly Lowther's fish stall at the top of King street (Pudding lane), and Molly Rawson's fish stall facing Change Alley end; and Billy Wright, mending old buckles or matching an odd one, facing Hartshead. Then there were the old women with their meal tubs, with their great coats and leather pockets, selling meal by the peck; and now and then a lad saying, 'Dame, will yo gie me a bit o' meal, if you please?' 'Aye, lad, tak thee a bit.' New shoe stalls were plentifully arranged, facing the front shops at the top of the Shambles, the dealers crying, 'Naa, can oi suit yo wi' a pair? they're hoam-made uns—cum, try these on, oi think they'll abaat fit yo; they looken yore soize.' "

LEONARD : James Wills describes a similar scene, and contrasts the old Shambles, which formerly were "near the silk-draper's shop, now the Fruit Market," and which, most dismal, were then made of wood,

> " The sheds of the stalls almost closing amain,
> Formed an archway for customers out of the rain,"

with the time when

> " ———'Tis commodious, and forms a good square,
> With abundance of fruit and potatoes sold there."

He adds :—

> " Not fifty years since, at the Market Place head,
> Were the broad shallow tubs to sell oatmeal for bread ;
> And near them the slaughter-house stood in disgrace,
> Being a nuisance to all who passed by the place.
> *   *   *
> But now, who of shambles can make equal boast ? "

LEIGHTON : The shambles which excited his admiration (opened in 1786) were re-fronted, re-roofed, and altogether

renewed in the interior, about 1855, and it is no longer true
that

> " On the outside the figure of Justice doth stand,
>   With sword in the right, and scales in left hand."

What, I wonder, has become of her? The shopkeepers
around could hardly help being honest and honourable, for
they could not look from their shops, morning, noon, or
night, without seeing her to remind them of their duties between man and man. That beautiful statue was a silent
monitor to them, and was worth a hundred sermons. If the
figure was thrown on the lumber heap, it was the act of a
Vandal; if it was broken up, that of an Iconoclast. But
why not condone the deed by elevating our friend Ebenezer
Elliott to that higher sphere? Too long has he had his
lodgings " on the cold ground." The position he occupies is
degrading to his memory, and disgraceful to the town. Place
him on the site formerly occupied by Justice, and let his
figure be turned towards the three valleys which he loved so
well, and which he has immortalised by his verse. Then, in
imagination, will "the poet's eye, in fine frenzy rolling, glance
from earth to heaven" without interruption from the ground-
lings below him.

WRAGG : I do not know what has become of the figure of
Justice. I should have said it was over the Corn Exchange,
(which was completed in 1830) behind the New Market, but
I find that is a larger figure.

LEONARD : No, you would be quite right. I have the
authority of the Duke of Norfolk's architect for saying that
it is the identical figure which stands over the now doomed
Corn Exchange. I say doomed because that building is soon
to be swept away, its entire area to be thrown into the wholesale vegetable market, and a magnificent Corn Exchange to
be erected beyond it, on the site of the present Hay Market.
But even there a niche has been prepared in which "Justice"
is still to stand. She was executed by Waterworth, of Doncaster.

LEIGHTON : Below the figure, and under the cornice,
there used to be a Latin inscription which I have tried in
vain to recover. It began, " Hic forum, cum laniaris juxta
flumen —— " but I cannot get the rest.

LEONARD : Justice gave way to the Post-office, and the
Post-office has in turn once more given place to shops.

TWISS : Let us take this opportunity of recapitulating the
old Post-office sites and make the best list of postmasters

we can. It is not an easy task to get it complete, as anyone who tries will find.

George Carr, postmaster, as his gravestone in the Parish Churchyard tells us, "departed this life April ye 20th, 1701, in ye 68th yeare of his age."

The same stone (which would seem to indicate relationship) records the death of his successor, Jonathan Turner, postmaster, who died 12th January, 1713, aged 36 years.

Samuel Simmons was postmaster in 1742. His shop, as we have seen, was most probably in the Market Place, opposite the head of the Shambles. He had a salary of £43 per annum. He died at Pitsmoor, April 18, 1790, aged 87.

Francis Lister is the next name we find, and the dates render it quite possible that he was the same man who printed the *Sheffield Weekly Journal* (see ante p. 78). He died in 1755.

In 1787, Miss Lister was postmistress, and at that time the office was in a similar position to that which I suppose it to have occupied under Samuel Simmons—in the Market Place, opposite where is now Elliott's monument. In 1782, the salary of the postmaster had been raised to £50 per annum, and the single letter carrier had £12 a year as wages.

In 1791, Rice James was postmaster. The office was removed to Castle street, near the end of Castle green. James died May 3rd, 1800. He is buried in St. James's churchyard.

The period which follows is vague. A person named Hall, who died March 5th, 1813, was postmaster, I am told, at the Church Gates.

Nathaniel Lister, as I have good oral authority for saying, had the post office at the Church Gates, but I cannot give you the dates.

Richard Griffiths followed him, the office being in Church street, in the premises now occupied by the Religious Tract Society. Griffiths left to become agent for the Government packets at Holyhead, and was succeeded by

William Todd, May 6, 1815. The next week the Post-office was removed to Mr. Todd's premises in the Market Place, and there it remained until 1828. It is stated in the introduction to White's Sheffield Directory for 1833, that the office was, in Mr. Todd's time, worth £500 a year. Mr. Todd having left the town,

Mr. Joseph Wreaks was appointed Nov. 25th, 1826. He remained in the Market Place until Feb. 4th, 1828, when

he removed to the lower corner of Arundel street and
Norfolk street, opposite the Assembly Rooms. In 1833,
the premises of Pickslay and Co., in High street, were purchased for the erection of a Post-office, news room, &c.,
and thither Mr. Wreaks went in 1835. He died October
25th, 1843, and was succeeded by

Ellen Wreaks, his daughter. In 1845, the office was removed
to the bottom of Angel street, and from thence in 1850 to
the Market Place, the head of the Shambles. There it
remained until March 19, 1871, when it was removed to
the top of the Old Haymarket, and in July, 1872, Miss
Wreaks resigned, and was succeeded by Mr. T. Mawson,
the present postmaster.

LEIGHTON: Below Justice, at the top of the Shambles,
were four shops, two in the middle, under that figure, and
two at the corners. In one of the middle shops Messrs.
Thompson, of Westbar, sold books. One Burdon had the
other as a toy shop; and when he left it he went into the
shop which is now Mr. Roberts' carpet warehouse. He afterwards went to America.

EVERARD: Mr. Burdon was succeeded in the latter
shop by the Rev. James Everitt, at that time, on account
of his health, a supernumerary Methodist preacher. He
dealt more especially in old and curious books. He removed from Sheffield to Manchester, and kept a similar
shop there. On recovering his health, he resumed his
place in the Wesleyan body, and being eventually expelled,
was one of the chief instruments in establishing the
"Methodist Free Church." Below that shop, at the
corner of Market street, was a very respectable drapery
establishment, kept by Mr. George Smith, who, on account of
his diminutive stature, commonly went by the name of
"Little Smith." He often, in the summer time, wore nan-
keen trousers, white or light-coloured figured vest, and displayed a full ruffled shirt front as he very courteously showed
the ladies into the shop, he usually standing near the door.
At one time he had a partner, of the name of Mr. Joseph
Carr (brother to the late Mr. Riley Carr, of the Glossop
road), who in height was as much above the ordinary size as
Mr. Smith was below it. Afterwards, Mr. Ridal (who had
been his apprentice) became his partner; and for many years
the business was carried on under the firm of "Smith and
Ridal." They afterwards removed to the shop at the lower
corner of Market street, and the business is now carried on
by Messrs. Arnison and Co.

TWISS : There is a tradition that Mr. Smith was once actually apprehended, being mistaken for Napoleon Buonaparte. He died unmarried in 1846, aged 77. His grandfather, George Smith, died ten months after his marriage with Mary Greaves, and his grandmother was married for the second time, to Samuel Glanville, of whom we shall hear in connection with Angel street. But we are digressing.

JOHNSON : At the King street corner, on the site now occupied by Alderman Michael Beal, jeweller, was the flax shop of Mr. Wm. Cockayne, the grandfather of the present drapers in Angel street. Mr. Cockayne had a number of knowing friends who met to talk over monetary affairs, and chatted so much of the concerns of their neighbours, that his shop was called the "weigh-house." A cheesefactor, named Stoakes, occupied the premises after Mr. Cockayne's removal to a shop in Angel street, which was his own property. It is now occupied by Mr. Watson, druggist. At the Market street corner of the Shambles' head, was a butcher's shop. Much later, these two corners were occupied by Fisher, Holmes and Co., and Fisher Godwin, as seed shops.

LEONARD : Inside the Shambles the butchers were then, as now, in possession; but outside there were fruiterers' stalls running down the exterior, were there not?

LEIGHTON : Yes. Inside the Shambles, at the bottom, used to be the butter, egg and poultry market. There was a building above, at the back of Mr. Younge's spirit vaults, supported by pillars. Up the middle of the Shambles were two rows of wooden shops. In these the inferior kinds of meat were sold, and on both sides were other butchers' shops, as now. At the right-hand corner was a very respectable man, named Middleton.

WRAGG : Sixty years ago, there were butchers in the Shambles who could open their shops first thing on Saturday morning, and not have a bit of meat left by dinner time, when they would close their shops and go home. Then their shops were worth £100 goodwill; now the goodwill has quite vanished.

LEONARD : This description of the Shambles, as they existed from 1786 to 1855, gives as good an idea of them, both outside and in, as we could wish : " The Shambles are extensive and convenient, being 100 yards in length and 40 in breadth, and having covered walks in front of the various rows of butchers' stalls ; at the lower end a commodious market for butter, eggs and poultry ; and round its exterior shops for the sale of fruit, vegetables, &c. It is approached by several gateways, one of which opens into the market for shoes, tinware, &c., and another into the vegetable and fruit market on the opposite side of King street." When the last alterations were made, the whole interior area was cleared for the poultry, butter, and game dealers, the butchers' shops running all round.

LEIGHTON: The arrangement outside the Shambles was very different from now. Down Market place, or the fruit market, from the top to the bottom, outside, were sold fruit and such things. This lasted until the opening of the Market Hall on Christmas-eve, 1851, when the shops were closed. They were afterwards removed to widen the streets.

TWISS: A colonnade ran all round, the pillars supporting a projecting upper room, which at the same time afforded protection to the sellers and purchasers below.

LEIGHTON: Mr. Nicholson, market gardener, had the centre shop in the Fruit market; it corresponded with the market-keeper's house on the King street side; the others were little fruit shops. Opposite Nicholson's was the old-established "Cross Daggers." It is now converted into Mr. Colley's leather shop, new fronted, but with the old rooms behind still. The stabling was up the yard, with an exit into Norfolk street. Down King street were the market gardeners' and vegetable shops. At the bottom of the Shambles, in the Bull Stake, was Mr. Gregory, cheesemonger, father, I think, of the late Mr. James Gregory, surgeon, Eyre street.

JOHNSON: In the lower part of King street, where is now Mr. Hunt's flour shop, was formerly the father of Mr. John Jones, before he removed into the premises still occupied by his son in the Market Place.

LEONARD: I remember the square just above there, now represented by Garside and Shaw's timber yard and Castle court, where fruit and fish dealers congregated. It was called "The Green Market," and was disused after December, 1851.

EVERARD: Ah, that market was formed on the site of the old debtors' gaol, taken down in 1818. A curious place, indeed, according to our notions. It was a stone building, not very large, the gaoler being Godfrey Fox. People were incarcerated there for ridiculously small debts, and often for alehouse scores. The prisoners used to work at their trades, and you might hear cutlers and file-cutters hammering away as if they had been in their shops. Friends brought the work and took it back again, and also supplied the prisoners with food.

LEONARD : The debtors then made themselves tolerably comfortable ?

EVERARD : Oh dear yes. It was a queer kind of imprisonment. The gaol was often thronged with visitors until nine o'clock. There was a prisoner in each room, above and below, who solicited the passers-by to "remember the poor prisoners." The one above had a tin box suspended by a string ; and the other, in the lower room, with his hand through the window, held a similar box.

TWISS : In 1791, at the same time that Broomhall was attacked, the mob destroyed the doors and windows of the gaol and the house of Godfrey Fox, and liberated the prisoners. It was the prison for the liberty of Hallamshire, and the property of the Duke of Norfolk.

EVERARD : There were two classes of prisoners, the fees in what was called the "High Court" being 25s. ; in the "Low Court," only 6d. There was, in addition, "garnish," 2s. 6d. for the High Court, and 1s. 2d. for the Low, with which coals, candles and soap were bought for the common benefit of the prisoners. Nield, in his "Remarks on the Prisons of Yorkshire," describes his visits to the place in 1802. There was, he reported, no chaplain, nor any religious attention paid to the prisoners. Mr. Moorhouse, the surgeon to the overseers of the poor, attended to the sick. The High Court prisoners had a room about five yards square, which had two windows looking into the street. Up-stairs there were four rooms, two for men to sleep in, and one for women, the fourth being used as a workshop. The keeper furnished beds at 10½d. per week, two sleeping in a bed. The Low Court prisoners, or those detained for debts under 40s. (three months' imprisonment being held to release them from their debt and costs), had two rooms, about five yards by four, with a fire-place, and iron-grated windows looking into the court. In these they worked and slept, which made them "filthy beyond description." Four rooms had lately been added at the top of the house, one of which was used for the women at night.

TWISS : When Howard, the prison philanthropist, visited the place some time before, it would seem that these upper rooms were not in existence, for he reported that there were only two rooms, which were also used as night rooms for debtors of both sexes.

LEONARD : Nield adds that the Low Court prisoners found their own straw and firing. The courtyard had a damp earthen floor, and was about ten yards by six. Both sexes associated together in it ; and at his visit on Sunday, the 15th August, 1802, the Low Court prisoners were busy sifting cinders in it, the ashes of which they sold for three shillings a load.

EVERARD : After Godfrey Fox, Thomas Smith, constable, was gaoler, and at the same time kept the "Royal Oak," which was next to the gaol. On the gaol being pulled down, he and the prisoners removed to the premises in Scotland street, formerly a merchant's warehouse, with the house adjoining as his residence. Mr. Joseph Kirk succeeded him.

WRAGG : Thirty years ago, in one of the little market shops that then stood on the site of the old gaol, was Mrs. Horsfield, the mother of two Unitarian ministers, the Rev. T. W. Horsfield, the historian of Lewes, and the Rev. Frederick Horsfield.

LEIGHTON : Above this was the grocers' shop of Messrs. Porter and Newton, now carried on by the sons of the former, who have since removed one door lower down. Their assistants are credited with the perpetration of a practical joke, which became famous in local annals through a popular song with a jingling chorus being composed upon it. Opposite Mr. Porter's shop (about where is now the King street entrance to the Shambles) was the house of Joseph Eyre, constable and market-keeper, popularly known as "Buggy," or "Fussy." The lively young grocers contrived to tie a rope to the market bell, and one night when—the place being shut up—all was quiet, and "Fussy" was placidly enjoying the repose to which so great a dignitary was well entitled, he was startled and horrified to hear his bell—his own particular bell—begin ringing. With his dog "Turk," he went round the Shambles, breathing vengeance against the disturbers of his peace ; and when this was fruitless, he took up his station by the gate, assured that the ringers must be in, and must come out that way, so as to give him a chance of revenge. But he waited in vain. The bell went on tolling, to the great entertainment of the crowd that had by this time collected, until the string (which was stretched across the street) at length breaking, it fell among the bystanders, and they kept up the fun. Eyre at length discovered the trick, and breaking the cord short, stopped the game. "Hey, Turk," became a bye-word. It was written up in large letters

everywhere, and then the following song was heard in the
mouths of all the street boys at every corner :—

" One night of late, at ten o'clock, as I was sat reflecting
　On the sacks of wheat and bags of flour that I had been collecting,
　Toll goes the market bell, just as I was a-thinking
　I'd smoke my pipe and merry be, and end the night in drinking.
　　　　Hey, my dog Turk, go thee and lurk !
　　　　　He howl'd with joy to hear me ;
　　　　　For in such awe I have him now,
　　　　　　That he both loves and fears me.

" I'll fetch the lantern and candle out, and search where I suspect 'em,
　Amongst the stalls and on the walls, for there Turk may detect 'em ;
　I cried ' Hallo,' you're there I know, cannot I hear you prating ?
　I'll lock you up until the morn, for I am tired of waiting.
　　　　Hey, my dog Turk, go thee and lurk !
　　　　　For thou art very cunning ;
　　　　　I'll stop at the gates and break their pates
　　　　　　As fast as they come running.

" Since Buggy got me this place, each night I do undress me,
　So fat I'm grown, I can't bend down, my flesh does so oppress me.
　One night, when they'd put me to bed, arose a mighty squabble :
　They called me up again with speed to go and quell the rabble.
　　　　I called for Turk and bid him lurk,
　　　　　He howled with joy to hear me ;
　　　　　For in such awe I have him now,
　　　　　　That he both loves and fears me.

" I've beat thee, love, says Bet to Joe, and won thy guinea fairly,
　Thou ate too much pudding in thy youth, or thou'd have run most rarely.
　A barrel of porter we will have, and drink it at our leisure ;
　Fat Joe replies, ' Some ducks and peas,' as I was just a-thinking,
　Then we'll agree and merry be, and end the night in drinking.
　　　　I called for Turk and bid him lurk,
　　　　　He howled with joy to hear me ;
　　　　　For in such awe I have him now,
　　　　　　That he both loves and fears me."

LEONARD : I fail to find much sense in the last two verses,
and the lines limp so that there must be something wrong in
them. Another version runs :

" One night of late, at ten o'clock,
　　As I was sat inspecting
The bags of wheat and pecks of meal
　　That I had been collecting,
Toll goes the market bell just then,
　　And I was sore astounded,
I puffed and blew, but no one knew
　　That I was so confounded.
　　　I caught a Turk, and bid him lurk,
　　　　For he is very cunning,
　　　And I'd stop at the gates, and break their pates,
　　　　As soon as they came running."

TWISS : That song has been attributed to Mather, but his editor has not credited him with it. Mr. Wilson refers to the song as one which seemed lost, all but the second chorus, which he gives somewhat differently :—

> " Hey ! Turk, go catch that lurk,
>   For thou art very cunning ;
>   And I'll stand at the gate and crack his pate
>   As soon as he comes running."

The event to which the song refers took place in the days of the last Shambles but one, which used to be called " The Roundabout House." The perpetrator of the trick on " Buggy " Eyre, or, at least, its leader, was one Stephenson, who came into Mr. Porter's service from Grenoside, and I believe he also was the author of the song.

LEONARD : " I called for Turk" seems much better sense than " I caught a Turk," just as " Go thee and lurk" is more to the point than " Go catch that lurk." But oral tradition has evidently much corrupted the song.

EVERARD : Next above Mr. Porter's, in King street, came the bookseller's shop of Mr. George Ridge, where he published the *Sheffield Mercury*, after buying it on Mr. Todd's failure.

LEIGHTON : Yes ; but before that it was the shop of Mr. Pierson, also a bookseller and printer, grandfather of the present Mr. Pierson, solicitor. He died a rich man. It was a peculiarity of his always to wear a large ruffled shirt. His wife helped him in the shop, and he always called " Milly " when any difficulty occurred, leaving her to settle it. A story is told that on one occasion he invited an articled clerk of Mr. Robert Rodgers', named Froggatt, to take a glass of wine. The offer was accepted. Mr. Pierson, predicting that his friend would find the vintage good, placed the liquor before him. Froggatt tasted, and looked dismayed. " I think it is not quite right, Mr. Pierson," said he, as mildly as might be. " Oh," said the other, " it must be ; I gave such and such a price for it." Said Froggatt, " Well, just taste for yourself." He did so. " My ——," he cried, " it's Turkey rhubarb ; Milly ! "

EVERARD : That is the shop, now much changed, occupied by Messrs. G. and J. S. Burrell.

LEIGHTON : Yes ; it stood further back than the druggist's shop above, then Mr. Hodgkinson's ; afterwards, in succession, Mr. Fred. Machon's, Mr. Forrest's, and now Mr. Geo. Bennett's.

Twiss: Mr. Ralph Hodgkinson's father was, I imagine, the first Sheffield druggist. He was accustomed to go about from town to town on market days, selling his drugs, and he was in King street in 1775-1792, when he gave up business, and was succeeded by his son. The old man lived until 1810, in which year he died at Eckington.

Leighton: At the corner, now Mr. Muddiman's boot shop, was Mr. Gillott, the hatter, who has already been mentioned.

Twiss: But before this time, certainly in 1774, and even for some years earlier than that, Mr. Jonathan Whitham occupied that site with his watchmaker's shop, his wife also carrying on a millinery business there. Mr. Whitham died about the year 1808.

Johnson: Leaving King street we have now to cross the Shambles to Market street. It was here that Northall's *Courant*, that thorn in Montgomery's flesh, had its birth, June 10, 1793, but it was removed to King street, March 1, 1794, and expired there August 1, 1797. The *Mercury*—another great trouble to the editor-poet, was also started in this street, in May, 1807, by Mr. Wm. Todd, afterwards post-master in the Market Place, who had his shop here. His wife was a sister of the late Mr. Scholefield, M.P. for Birmingham; and Mr. Holland mentions that Chantrey executed his bust of the Rev. Jas. Wilkinson, now in the Parish Church, under Mr. Todd's roof, "the curiosity, the expectation, and the wonder of the public being largely excited during the important process of carving."[*]

Leonard: In Market street was the manufactory of Messrs. Proctor and Beilby, opticians, of whom I have compiled the following account from one of the late Mr. John Holland's numerous anonymous papers. The firm had been in Milk street, on the site of part of Messrs. Rodgers and Sons' premises now; but when the old butchers' shops were removed from Market street, the firm established themselves there, on the west side, with workrooms and dwelling-house in front, and workshops behind. The "Cup" inn is there still, unchanged; but everything else is altered. The principals in the firm were Luke and Charles Proctor, natives of the town, and originally makers, if not actually grinders, of lancets. Beilby was a Birmingham man, and was a teacher of drawing in Sheffield. "Luke Proctor was an agreeable man of fashion, an accomplished violinist, and

---

* "Memorial of Chantrey," p. 203.

he soon fiddled himself out of the firm. Charles, a lover of music too, was a quiet, assiduous and successful man of business," writes Mr. Holland, "and I remember how I used to look for his white wig opposite one of the windows in the old Cutlers' Hall, at the 'Feast,' where he sat 'above the salt.' He was a widower when first I knew him. His family consisted of himself, his three sons—Luke, George and William—his daughter, Deborah, and last, but not least, in those days, his sister, 'Miss Nancy'—a sharp little consequential woman, who did a great part of the familiar book-keeping of the concern, including especially the entering of the men's work and wages. Of the children, Luke died young ; George went to Birmingham, where he married and died ; William, of whom more hereafter, married Miss Deakin, a sister of the founder of the Deakin Institution ; Deborah married Thomas, a son of the original Beilby. He ultimately went to Birmingham, entered into the stationery business, and became the leading partner in the well-known firm of Beilby and Knott, publishers of *Aris's Gazette*. Charles Proctor, the head of the firm, died July 4th, 1808, and was carried by six faithful workmen to his grave in St. Paul's Church, where his wife was also buried. He left behind him, according to the 'Gossip's Gazette,' property to the amount of £30,000. The concern in Market street had now reached its culminating period of prosperity ; thenceforth its fortunes were downward. This was apparently due to several causes." At length the late Mr. Holland alone was left on the premises to make, as far as the brass work was concerned, whatever might be wanted in the entire range of the pattern book. "And although," says he, "it is long since I laid down, and shall never again take up, the tools of the optical instrument maker, I would not willingly lose the consciousness that I could still alternate the cutting of a fine screw with the using of a bad pen." Mr. Holland once gave an account of the more prominent workmen in this establishment. There were his father, also John Holland, and his uncle Amos, who made accurate imitations of the Dolland telescopes. Both lived in the country, and were not only bird fanciers, but bee farmers. The sycamore and mahogany outsides of the telescopes were made at a wheel on the Rivelin by William Chadburn, grandfather of Chadburn Brothers, the well-known opticians, of Nursery street, and it seems probable that his father had been there before him. Besides optical instruments, there were made tinder-boxes and inkpots in large quantities. "Excisemen's" inkbottles were made of brass, and were polished by old Daniel Vaughan, a Chelsea pensioner, who, after doing duty as a recruiting sergeant in Sheffield, went abroad and fought beside General Wolfe, at Quebec. "His extra-workboard forte was telling stories of soldier life, and especially a rehearsal of the loyal speech he used to make in our Market Place, while a handful of spade-ace guineas was kept dancing on the drum-head for the too successful temptation of many a mother's son." Then there was Ben Wright, another pensioner, who "treddled" his lathe with a wooden leg; and George Hadfield, not less remarkable as a toper than as a turner; old Billy Egginton, somewhat of a birdcatcher, who, living on the banks of the Don, had secured a crested grebe; John Taylor, a member of an old Sheffield musical family, his instrument being the French horn; little Jemmy Johnson, who beat the big drum in the Volunteer band. Then there was Dicky Hobson, a Birmingham man, in some way related to Mrs. Sally Booth, the actress, who used to visit Sheffield with Macready, and whose graceful performance with the skipping rope was so much admired. Another member of the Volunteer band was Johnny Coe, a little knock-kneed man, whose military status was to march before the leader with an open music sheet pinned on his back. He had been with the Proctors from the first, and was early employed by them in making ring dials, which some [though not Dr. Gatty—see his "Lecture to the Literary and Philosophical Society," Dec., 1872] think to have been Touchstone's dial. From Coe's account, these must have been common and cheap enough during the earlier half of the last century. They consisted of a brass ring, four inches in diameter. On being suspended from the hand by a string, the sun shone through a small hole in the rim, and indicated the time by a dot of light falling on the hour figure and its fractions inside. Two of the workmen, Clarke and Hancock, were members of the Volunteer force. William Padley was the brass caster, and Thomas Stovin the glass caster. Stovin's hobby was to keep cows, and he did it profitably. The chief of the spectacle makers was Thomas Bird, a brother of the well-known Bristol artist of that name. The bead-roll would be incomplete without the names of Ben Sayles and Grayson. "I regret," said Mr. Holland, whose words I have, for the most part, been adopting, "to be unable to recollect that religion was ever the subject of work-

day conversation, or, so far as I know, church-going the
Sunday habit of these men. I believe Jonathan Knight, a
glass grinder, and Thomas Wilson, a telescope hand, were
chapel-goers. They spoke of having seen, and had possibly
heard, John Wesley, during one of the latter visits of that
remarkable man to this town. Excessive drinking was then,
as now, the vice of the artisan.''

WRAGG : Proctor's firm erected the first steam-engine in
the town, in 1786. Boulton and Watt at that time let out
engines by way of bringing them into use ; but whether
Beilby and Proctor had theirs on loan, or bought it, I cannot
say. Their wheel has just been pulled down, and a wooden
circus occupies its site—adjoining Sheaf street. The late
Mr. I. P. Cutts served his time with them, and my impression of the issue of the firm is different from Mr. Holland's ;
for I have understood that he was taken into partnership, and
ultimately had the trade in his sole possession.

TWISS : Beilby and Proctor were not the first opticians in
the town. That honour is ascribed by the *Local Register* to
Mr. Samuel Froggatt, who died in 1787. His works were at
Royd's Mill ; and his son had a room at Walk Mills, now
the Albion Works, opposite the " Twelve o'Clock." His
grandson still carries on the business in the same neighbourhood.

LEONARD : I think we have now completed the circuit of
the Market Place, and are ready to descend Angel street.

WRAGG : In Angel street was Mr. Turner, draper, known
as " Flannel Sam," to distinguish him from his neighbour,
the publican, of the Hartshead, of whom mention has been
made before—" Gin Sam." He was the father of the late
Mr. S. W. Turner, solicitor.

TWISS : Both the grandfather and the father of Mr. S.
W. Turner were there. The former Samuel Turner, who
died in 1791, had no fewer than twenty-two children, one of
whom succeeded to the business, and afterwards resided at
Chesterfield, dying in 1832. He, I imagine, was the
" Flannel Sam " of whom you speak. There was another
Turner, who was a mercer, in Angel street, on the other side
of the way, where Mr. Heppenstall afterwards was, and where
Mr. Tasker is now. His Christian name was John, and he
was related to the Scholeys, of Coal Aston. He would be a
contemporary of the first Samuel Turner, if not even earlier
than that, as he died about the year 1796.

H

LEIGHTON: Down Angel street, where is now Mr. Carter's, shoemaker, there was an obstruction in the road. It was at the bottom of the "Angel" yard, and Mr. Wormall's shop is part of it. It formed the Volunteer rendezvous, or guard-room, and I have seen the men stand there to receive their loaves. It made a regular corner, or bend, in the street. After Mr. Peach, of the "Angel," died, Mr. Walker, tinman, altered it into its present form. He rebuilt, or new-fronted, the "Angel" inn.

WRAGG: Mr. Walker occupied the shop that was lately Messrs. Wilson and Sons, and is now a part of Mr. Hovey's drapery establishment. I think he was the first man who made coal gas, and it was to be seen in his shop—of course, very different in quality from what we see now, for it made great clouds of smoke. He had the contract for lighting the town with oil.

JOHNSON: Forty years ago gas had become common in saleshops, though there were many to be seen without it; but it was very rare in houses, and rarer still in workshops. We managed to see to read and write with only one candle, but how I cannot imagine, after being accustomed to gas.

WRAGG: I am speaking of longer ago than that, though it is only about that length of time since the old oil lamps, which used to make "darkness visible" in our miserably-paved streets, disappeared. The last, I believe, were in Hanover street and Broomspring lane. One night they were all smashed; their fragments must have been trampled upon, as there was not a piece left on the ground the size of a sixpence; so they were replaced with gas.

TWISS: I have met with a record that the first gas lamp lighted in Sheffield was at the corner of Benjamin Walker's shop, Church Gates, on September 19th, 1819. The same authority gives Howard Street Chapel credit for having been the first public place of worship lighted by gas in Sheffield. That took place on the 13th December, 1819. Queen Street Chapel was partly lighted on the same evening.

LEONARD: I recently spent some weeks in a small out-of-the-way German town, amusingly quaint and primitive in some of its habits. There was no gas, and the oil lamps hung from a cord swung across the narrow streets, and could be lowered by a pulley to be lighted. That experience enables me to imagine pretty clearly the state in which our English towns must have been before gas was invented.

EVERARD: Yes; one must go abroad to appreciate some of the inconveniences of the old days. The open gutter down the middle of the street, for both rain and sewage, can still be seen on the Continent; and the projecting spouts which, having no fall-pipes, discharged douches on the heads of passers-by, are only to be found in hidden nooks.

JOHNSON: As Wills sings—

> " You remember the sinks in the midst of the streets,
> When the rain poured in torrents; each passenger greets
> His fellow with ' What a wide channel is here,
> We all shall be drowned, I'm greatly in fear.'

> *   *   *   *   *

> " Yet, with all their good sense, still did none of them know
> How to light streets with gas lamps as we have them now;
> While that *ignis fatuus* that hung in our street
> Would scarcely discover the wretch we might meet."

LEONARD: And here is another quotation, as a contribution on the same point: " The town was then in a very rude state in every respect, it being only partially flagged, with many of the stones loose; there were very few lamps, and those feeble and far apart—often not lighted, or blown out. There were also projecting spouts from between the gutters of the roofs, from which, during rain, the water flowed in streams. Lanterns were dimly seen in the streets, like fire-flies, flitting about. Umbrellas were then unknown. A farthing candle was stuck in some of the shop windows, just serving to make darkness more dark."*

JOHNSON: Horace Walpole, in a letter dated 1760, speaks of Sheffield, through which he had passed, as " one of the foulest towns in England, in the most charming situation."

LEIGHTON: The mention of old Sam Peech, of the "Angel," reminds us again, like the " King's Head," how with the past coaching days has disappeared the lustre from these houses. Still, at the " Angel," the coaching department was carried on with great spirit by Mr. Wm. Bradley (of the Soho Brewery, lately deceased), up to the time that railways destroyed coaching. The arrival and departure of coaches running between Leeds and London, and on various other roads, made the neighbourhood of the " Angel " very lively.

WRAGG: Mr. Peech kept the " Angel " for about thirty years. In running opposition to other coach proprietors, he was known not only to take persons to London for nothing, but to give a bottle of wine into the bargain. He died in 1809. It was his predecessor, Mr. Samuel Glanville, who set up the first stage to London, in 1760, when pack-horses were

---

* " Autobiography of the late Samuel Roberts."

superseded.   The following announcement, relating to Mr.
Glanville's coaches, appeared in the *Sheffield Public Adver-
tiser*, of November 4th, 1760, and it may interest you :—
"Nov. 2 : Notice is hereby given, that the London, Leeds,
Wakefield, Chesterfield, Mansfield and Nottingham machines
on steel springs, in four days, sets off from the 'Swan with
Two Necks,' inn, in Lad lane, London, and from the 'Old
King's Arms' inn, in Leeds, every Monday and Wednesday
morning, at five o'clock ; breakfasts at the 'Angel' inn, in
St. Alban's ; dines at the 'White Horse' inn, in Hockley ;
and lies at the · Red Lion,' at Northampton, the first night ;
breakfasts at the 'Three Crowns,' in Market Harborough ;
dines at the 'Bull's Head,' in Loughborough ; and lies at
the 'Crown' inn, in the Long Row, Nottingham, the second
night; breakfasts at the 'Swan,' in Mansfield ; dines at the
'Falcon,' in Chesterfield ; and lies at the 'Angel,' in Sheffield, the third night ; breakfasts at the 'White Bear,' in
Barnsley ; dines at the 'Coach and Horses,' in Wakefield,
and lies at Leeds the fourth night.   And from Leeds to
London : Breakfasts at the 'Coach and Horses,' Wakefield ;
dines at the 'White Bear,' in Barnsley ; and lies in Sheffield
the first night ; breakfasts at the 'Falcon,' in Chesterfield ;
dines at the 'Swan,' in Mansfield ; and lies at the 'Blacka-
moor's Head,' in Nottingham, the second night ; breakfasts
at the 'Bull's Head,' in Loughborough ; dines at the 'Three
Crowns,' in Market Harborough ; and lies at the 'Red Lion,'
in Northampton, the third night; breakfasts at the 'Sara-
cen's Head,' in Newport; dines at the 'Angel,' in St. Albans ; and lies in London the fourth night.   Passengers and
parcels are taken in at the above places.   Two places reserved
in each coach for Nottingham.   Performed, if God permit, by
John Handforth, Samuel Glanville, and Wm. Richardson."

TWISS : Mr. Glanville died in 1803, in the Duke of Norfolk's Almshouse, at the age of 83.

EVERARD : There is a very interesting memorial of him—
one of the few heirlooms Sheffield possesses—in the Mayor's
Parlour, at the Council Hall.   This is his portrait, in crayon,
presented to the Mechanics' Library by Mr. B. Sayle, of
Brightside ; and beneath it his history is thus given :—
" Samuel Glanville, born at Exeter about the year 1720 ;
entered early into the army, and was present as a drummer
in the battle of Dettingen.   He afterwards came with a
recruiting party to Sheffield, and was billeted at the house of
Mrs. Smith, in Church street ; married her, and afterwards

kept the 'Angel' inn, to which house, about the year 1760, he worked the first stage coach from London. He died at Sheffield, in 1803."

TWISS : The artist was Raphael Smith. There is also another crayon portrait of Mr. Glanville in existence. It was in the possession of Mr. Charles Ridal, of the late firm of Smith and Ridal, already mentioned (see p. 87), until he left the town, when it was sold by auction. It was from the pencil of Chantrey.

LEONARD : At the time the portrait was presented by Mr. Sayle to the Mechanics' Library (would that more of our townsmen would follow his excellent example), Mr. Montgomery wrote, in the *Iris*, of Mr. Glanville as "no mean benefactor to the town;" and he quoted from the *Iris* of July 21, 1803, the following interesting sketch of his life :—
" He was born about 1720, near Exeter ; was apprenticed to a surgeon, but entered early in life into the army as a private. In 1741 he came to Sheffield, upon a recruiting party, and married Mrs. Smith, who kept a public-house in Church street. In a course of time he became master of the 'Angel' inn, and, about 1760, was a partner in the first stage coach from Leeds to London. After some years, he retired from the public line to a farm at the Edge, near this town, where he was noticed by Mr. Arthur Young as an excellent agriculturist. But, becoming at length weary of agriculture, he returned to his former occupation, and kept an inn at the 'Cross Keys,' in Wood street; and some time after removed to the 'Black Bull,' in Stamford. Here he buried his wife, and married a second. Business there, however, not answering his expectations, he came back to Sheffield, and opened a public-house at the Hermitage ; soon after buried his second wife ; and, not long after, was admitted into the Duke of Norfolk's Hospital, where he found a comfortable asylum during several years. In his early days, and in public life, he was steady, active [the writer of this memoir has seen him carry out three dishes at once upon his right arm from a public entertainment], attentive and obliging to his customers; cheerful, rational, and intelligent in private conversation; was looked up to with great respect by all his acquaintance, and closed his days with a constant serious attention to the duties of religion." I presume the " Wood street " mentioned would be in London.

TWISS: Mr. Samuel Peech also lived to be an old man. He was 70 when he died, in 1809, having kept the "Angel"

for thirty years. He had been succeeded by William Peech,
in the previous year. Samuel Peech is credited with being
the author of a large fund of shrewd sayings, and is the hero
of many quaint anecdotes. Reproached once with having
been originally only a stable-boy, he made the scathing
retort, " If thou hadst been a stable-boy, thou'd be a stable-
boy still."

JOHNSON : The last Sheffield mail coach, the " Halifax
Mail," performed the journey from London to Sheffield in
sixteen hours, arriving here at noon. After this was taken
off, a coach called the " Brilliant" started about 5 a.m.,
meeting the railroad at some point, and reaching London in,
I believe, about twelve hours.

LEONARD : The sculptor, Rossi, when a youth, lived with
his father, opposite the " Angel " inn. He executed that
" Angel," in terra cotta, which has been blowing so persistently on her brazen trumpet all these years, without producing a sound.

TWISS : In Angel street, too, was the druggist's shop of
Mrs. Mary Handley, one of whose daughters became the wife of
Mr. John Sterndale, surgeon, who lived in Norfolk street, in the
house now occupied by Miss Barry, dressmaker. Mrs. Handley lived, before the Sorbys' time, in the old house on Spital
hill, just beyond what was afterwards the Wicker Station,
called in the maps Hallcar. Mrs. Handley was succeeded in
the druggist's shop in Angel street by Benjamin Rose.

EVERARD : Amongst the earliest of the silver-plate manufacturers in the town, was the firm of Messrs. Ashforth, Ellis
and Co., whose works were in Angel street, up the passage
adjoining the shop now occupied by Mr. John Tasker, the
workshops extending so far back that some of the windows
overlooked what was, at a subsequent time, the fish and
vegetable market, situate between King street and Castle
street. This company carried on an extensive trade in various
parts of the kingdom. They had an establishment in Paris,
in common with the celebrated Wedgwoods, of Staffordshire,
their silver-plated goods being exhibited in one window, and
the china and porcelain in the other. At the first French
Revolution, the mob broke into the shop, and destroyed or
stole what was valuable, from which they sustained a heavy
loss. About the beginning of the present century, the premises in Angel street being found to be too small, the firm
built works at the top of Red hill.

WRAGG : Your mention of Mr. Tasker reminds me that we are indebted to the South Devon Militia for the presence of his family amongst us. Mr. Leighton mentioned the other day one of the bitter remembrances the Militia left behind them ; suppose we mention some of the sweet ones ? They were considered a very respectable class of men, not like the generality of militia regiments. They conducted themselves with propriety, and made themselves generally useful where they were billeted. One of the officers, Captain Toll, married the daughter of the Rev. Alex. Mackenzie, of St. Paul's, and so became possessed of the property at Sharrow-head, which he held until his death, when it was sold. His wife, on her death-bed, advised him to marry a friend of hers, and recommended her friend to marry him. Many of the men followed his example by marrying Sheffield women ; and when the regiment was broken up, not a few returned and settled in the town. The father of Mr. John Tasker was one ; and his brother, the father of Alderman Tasker, was another. William Melluish, who was also one of them, is the only survivor. He worked for George Addy and Son, in Pea croft, until their unfortunate failure.

LEIGHTON : The South Devon Militia came from that beautiful county, where " all the men are brave, and all the women fair," which produced the gallant sea kings, Drake, Raleigh, Gilbert, Frobisher, Winter, and a host of others renowned in history. The commander, Colonel Laing, was not a popular man. He pronounced the word " march " as " mairch," and was so often reminded of it that, on one occasion, he sent a file of his men into the gallery of the theatre to bring one or two of the culprits out. This resulted in the regiment being ordered elsewhere.

TWISS : Speaking of the Rev. Mr. Mackenzie, he had himself come into possession of the Sharrow-head estate through marriage with the niece of Mr. Batty, the former owner. You will remember that the narrow country lane surrounded by gardens, now supplanted by the Cemetery road, was called Mackenzie Walk.

LEIGHTON : Mr. Mackenzie was one of the six men in the town, fifty years ago, who were above six feet high. Mr. Carver, who lived at the bottom of High street, was another.

WRAGG : Mr. Hutchinson, the coachmaker, of Ladies' Walk (Porter street), would, I believe, be a third. He was so tall that he had a coach built expressly, with a recess for his legs. Waterfall, constable, would, I think, be the fourth.

He had the largest foot of any man in Sheffield. I knew a person who once put his own foot, shoe and all, inside the constable's shoe, and he could move it freely about inside. I cannot remember who the other two would be.

EVERARD : Mr. Holland, brother to the Doctor, certainly one of the best-proportioned men in Sheffield, was of later date. He kept the " Castle " inn, at the top of Snig hill and Water lane.

LEIGHTON : Besides being tall, Mr. Mackenzie was also very strong. It is said that, on one occasion, when painting at his house, the workmen went away to seek assistance in raising a ladder. When they got back, they found that Mr. Mackenzie had reared it himself.

LEONARD : In Angel street (now No. 30), nearly opposite the " Angel " inn, was the shop of John Smith, bookseller. He was a great dealer in old books ; but his misfortune as a tradesman was, that he loved his books too well to sell them. He was the father of Dr. John Pye-Smith, the celebrated Nonconformist scholar and divine, who was brought up in his father's place as a bookseller and bookbinder, but had such a greed for learning that, at an early age, he completed his education at Rotherham College, under Dr. Williams, and then became classical and mathematical tutor of Homerton College, where he spent more than fifty years of his life. John Pye-Smith was one of the young friends of James Montgomery, and edited the *Iris* for him when Mr. Montgomery was twice in prison for what were then called " seditious libels." John Smith (described by a gentleman still living, of the same surname—who sees a resemblance to him in one of his great-grandsons—as a tall, thin, grave man, wearing spectacles with a round horn rim) died in 1810, and was succeeded in the business by his son-in-law, Robert Leader, who in 1830 became proprietor and publisher of the *Independent*. After occupying the shop in Angel street for 22 years, Mr. Leader removed to High street to the shop now No. 41.

TWISS : John Pye-Smith, so called in memory of his great-uncle, the Rev. John Pye, minister of Nether Chapel from 1748 to 1773, was born lower down, in Snig hill, on premises we shall come to presently, adjoining the old Black Lion.

WRAGG : He was the most scholarly man Sheffield has produced. The preface to his Latin Grammar, published in 1814, is a most masterly production.

LEONARD : An old bookbinder, named James Brown, who had formerly worked for Mr. John Smith, used to tell how the young apprentice (the future Doctor) used to escape from his bookbinding and get away to his reading in a quiet corner where he was removed from any chance of disturbance.

EVERARD : In the Brocco, just below Edward street, through a gateway entrance, there was in my early recollection a day school, and here my father had the honour of having for a school-fellow John Pye Smith, who on that spot acquired the first rudiments of that learning for which in after life he became so distinguished. Dr. Pye Smith was esteemed alike for his erudition and his amiable and Christian character. The most important theological work he published was the " Scripture Testimony to the Messiah," which was adopted by one of the universities—I think Cambridge—as the text book on the subject. The late much respected Mr. John William Pye-Smith, who in 1856 occupied the position of Mayor of Sheffield, was his younger son.

LEONARD : Your mention, Twiss, of old Mr. Pye reminds me of his curious and systematic account-book, which is still in existence, and some extracts from which were published a few years ago. It is an instructive commentary on the cost of living in those days. Although Mr. Pye had an income of only £100, yet he kept a horse and saved considerable sums. Up to the year 1757, in which he was married, he paid the modest sum of £13 per annum for board and lodgings, and after his marriage his household expenses ranged from £2. 2s. to £4. 4s. per month. He appears to have paid his servant £2 per year in wages, and such entries as this occur : " For the keeping of my mare 6 weeks, 15s." Tea, however, is not the costly luxury it then was ; for 1½ lb. he paid 12s. 4d.

WRAGG : Another Angel street worthy was the first Sheffield poet—the Rev. James Cawthorn. He was killed in 1761 from the effects of a fall from his horse. I thought his father was a bookseller, but I see it stated that he was an upholsterer.

LEONARD : Yes, his grandfather was William Cawthorn, of Thurgoland, of whom his father was the second son. At the age of fourteen, James Cawthorn wrote a paraphrase on the 139th Psalm, some other poems at fifteen, and at the age of seventeen, his "Perjured Lover, or the Adventures of Alexis Brima." His works were collected and published in 1771, ten years after his death. The Rev. Edwd. Goodwin, perpetual curate of Attercliffe—1776 to 1817—married one of his sisters ; and Mr. Goodwin, his wife, their sons, and her

I

sister, are all interred at Hill top, Attercliffe. John, the eldest son of William Cawthorn, and uncle to the poet, was the first tenant of a farm in Sheffield Park, where he planted a row of crab trees, and sold the verjuice to the medical men of Sheffield. There may perhaps be still some old men living who remember filling their pockets with the crabs. The last tree was taken down about fifty years ago.

TWISS: The Rev. James Cawthorn does not appear to have held any living here. He is spoken of as a person whose "acquired knowledge is allowed to have been considerable; but his literary talents, it is said, bore but an insignificant proportion to his moral excellence."

WRAGG: I think we have almost exhausted the interest of Angel street—unless we recall the more modern name of Maugham, and are thereby reminded of a shocking accident which excited much commiseration. Mr. Maugham, draper, who occupied shops here, one of which is now Dick's shoe shop, was driving into town one morning with his wife, from Wadsley Park, when their horse took fright, and they were both thrown from the carriage and killed. This was on the 10th of May, 1848.

TWISS: Although we have previously (p. 87) spoken of the Post Office occupying, from 1845 to 1850, the site below that—in front of the Old Bank—we should not omit to mention it here. The one-storied shops which now stand there, occupy that Post Office site, and before the Post Office the triangular area was a vacant piece of ground, in front of the Bank, fenced off by an iron railing.

NOTE. Mr. C. Ridal, mentioned at pp. 87 and 101, died at Liverpool on the 10th February, 1874, aged 80.

CHAPTER VI.
Snig Hill and Westbar.

Present—Messrs. Twiss, Leighton, Everard, Wragg, Leonard
and Johnson.
Period—A.D. 1873.

LEONARD : In the space where Angel street, Snig hill,
Castle street, Bank street, and Water lane converge,
stood previously the Irish Cross. We have spoken of it before as having been removed—at least the shaft of it—into
Paradise square.

TWISS : I have reason to believe that the Irish Cross stood
rather within, or at any rate on the confines of the triangular
area we mentioned when last together—in fact just where Mr.
Dixon's shop now is, at the corner of Angel street and Bank
street.

LEONARD : Bank street was, of course, unmade at that
time.

TWISS : This locality possesses a very interesting association, as the site of one of Sheffield's earliest printing offices.
I prize highly a series of ballads, or as they are called on
one of the title-pages, "all sorts of new songs and penny
histories;" "Printed by John Garnet, at the Castle green
head, near the Irish Cross." They are not dated, but we
know from other sources that Garnet was there at any rate
between the years 1736, when he printed Cawthorn's "Perjured Lover," mentioned before, and 1745, when he printed a
"Covenant agreed on by Nether Chapel." He also issued
"A new Historical Catechism, by W. L., S. P., 1737." These
ballads of mine answer somewhat to our present street songs,
though more elaborate. They have such titles as these :—
"The Golden Bull, or the Crafty Princess, in four parts;"
"The Irish Stroller's Garland;" "The Petticoat loose Garland;" "The Extravagant Youth's Garland." Others are
religious publications. The dates I have given, 1736-1745,
are, you will remember, a few years earlier than the time
(1754) when Francis Lister had his printing office "near the
Shambles;" or 1755, when Revel Homfray had his "Opposite to the Cock in the High street." *

---

* See ante p. 78.

LEIGHTON : On the Castle street side of Water lane, in premises now destroyed for the erection of a new building, lived the Staniforths—father, son, and grandson. Both the latter were distinguished surgeons. Chantrey, who was a great friend of Mr. William Staniforth, of the middle generation, had to adopt a *ruse* in order to obtain a portrait for the family of the old gentleman, Mr. Samuel Staniforth. However, he produced an excellent likeness.*

WRAGG : Mr. William Staniforth was considered the best operative surgeon and oculist in the town. "Staniforth's eye ointment" was very celebrated. Mr. Cheney, Mr. C. H. Webb, and Mr. William Staniforth, senr., were the first Infirmary surgeons, and Mr. William Staniforth, junr., became a colleague of his father in that official capacity, on Mr. Cheney's retirement in 1812. William Staniforth, the elder, retired in 1819, and died, August 21st, 1833, aged 83 years. There is a marble medallion of him in the Board-room of the Infirmary.

EVERARD : He had a brother named Samuel, a linen-draper, in Castle street—in the shop, I believe, afterwards long occupied by Mr. Roebuck, currier. He lived in the house adjoining the shop; his brother, the surgeon, living next door to him, nearer Water lane. When I remember him after his retirement from business, he was a tall, thin, and sedate old gentleman, wearing a white cravat, full-ruffled shirt front, and a tail. In the drapery business he would be coeval with Mr. Vennor, of High street. He spent a large portion of his time in cultivating the flowers and fruits of his garden, which was a large piece of ground enclosed with high brick walls, opposite Mr. Bailey's gates at Burn Greave, in what was formerly Grimesthorpe road. He might often be met in the summer time in the Wicker, walking home, slow and stately, with a large bouquet of flowers, or a small basket of fruit, in his hand.

LEIGHTON : The Castle Inn still occupies its old position at the other corner of Water lane. O'Brien, the Irish Giant, had rooms there and received visitors. He used to light his pipe in the streets by taking off the top of the lamps. Joesy Eyre, the constable, insisted on entering O'Brien's room without payment, by virtue of his office, but when he wished to retire, O'Brien refused to allow him to do so, unless he paid, the alternative offered to him being an exit through the window. Fussy chose the more ignominious

---

* "Holland's Memorials of Chantrey," p. 168.

course of paying his money to be liberated. In Water lane, too, "Old Crownshaw" kept the "All Nations" public-house. The old politicians used to meet there. It was a most respectable part of the town then, but look at it now! Though it is improved since the Police Offices demolished a whole row of houses.

WRAGG: In Snig hill was Michael Raybould, the money-changer. At that time there was scarcely anything but copper money. Butchers and others took their copper to him for something more portable when they went to market, for which he charged 2d. per pound.

LEONARD: Just as you may see in Eastern towns now.

WRAGG: Besides this, other people went to him for change, and he charged them also 2d., so that he got 4d. each pound by the transactions. Mr. Stoakes, who has been mentioned as a cheese factor, at the top of King street, was the last person who changed money in this manner.

TWISS: It is recorded, on the 27th February, 1801, "The bellman has been crying that the inhabitants of Sheffield may be supplied with the best fine flour, at Michael Raybould's, Snig hill, at 10s. 6d. per stone of 14lbs." This was thought wonderfully cheap.

LEIGHTON: Opposite Michael Raybould's, the old Black Lion and another building, a shop, projected into the street, just below the gateway of the Black Swan. I remember a shoemaker and leather seller having the shop, and Mr. Twibell was there before he went to his late premises on the opposite side.

EVERARD: It was there that Dr. John Pye Smith was born. The premises were pulled down some years ago (1849) to widen the street.

LEONARD: A little below that, where is now Barker's shoe shop, the *Independent* first saw the light, for those were the premises occupied by Mr. H. A. Bacon, its originator. The printing office was in an attic, where a man could hardly stand upright, and the staff consisted of four apprentices and three or four journeymen, and the paper was printed on a small hand-press. The first copy was "pulled" by George Blythman, and was "flyed" by George Rogers, who has been intimately connected with the paper from that day to this. The first editor was an Irishman, named Fanning, the second Ebenezer Rhodes, the third Thomas Asline Ward; then the paper was bought by the late Robert Leader. Henry Andrew Bacon's father, Mr. Clay Bacon, had himself been a printer, but at that time he was a partner in the firm of Bower and Bacon, type-founders, in the Nursery, just by Messrs. Chadburn's wheel, in what is now Nursery street. They were the first type-founders in Sheffield, and one of the earliest firms in the provinces—at any rate, there was none other at that time nearer than London. Mr. H. A. Bacon married the niece of "Neddy Furniss," the shoemaker in Westbar green, and with her obtained a comfortable fortune. Mrs. Bacon survived him, changed her name a second time to that of Briggs, and is still living. One of her daughters married Mr. Atkinson, formerly a draper at the bottom of Angel street (now Mr. Hovey's), and the other Mr. Barlow, of Rawmarsh.

Twiss: We have now traced this newspaper to all its locations—Snig hill, Angel street, High street (with Mulberry street), corner of Bank street and Snig hill, and, lastly, Bank street. So that it has not wandered many hundred yards.

Leonard: The premises standing near the bottom of Snig hill, on the right, just before the street makes the gradual bend towards Newhall street, shame their neighbours by their antiquity. There we see again the gables, the small windows and inconvenient low rooms that used to be the characteristics of Sheffield architecture.

Twiss: You mean the house now divided in occupation between Mr. Jones, butcher, and Mr. Samuel Parker Hall, cutler?

Leonard: Yes, and the narrow gable above which is a fruiterer's, between them being the lower premises of a hairdresser.

Twiss: The house I speak of is the last before the street bends, and it must have a curious history, but I have not been able to get at it. There is a fine broad staircase going right up to the top. There is a tradition that it was once an inn—the Snigh or Snig, and hence the name. But you will say—what is a Snigh or Snig? It is an old Saxon name for the eel, and daring philologists connect this with the water at the bottom of Newhall street. Another derivation, you know, attempts to connect the name with the steepness of the declivity, which necessitated the application of a snag or brake to wheeled vehicles descending it.

Leighton: At the bottom of Snig hill, the uncle of Jonathan Marshall used to keep an iron and steel shop. He left his nephew a good sum of money, with which he set up the steel converting business in Millsands, and died enormously rich. He and Benjamin Rose, the druggist, of Angel street, were great companions. They both had plenty of money, but they walked to Doncaster races rather than hire a horse. Marshall had frequent losses, for hardly anybody ever failed but he was a creditor. It didn't matter, however, for he and the Walkers of Masbro' were the only people in the steel trade, so they had it and all its great profits to themselves.

EVERARD: It was in the service of Jonathan Marshall that the progenitor of the great firm of Thomas Firth and Sons acquired that practical skill as a steel converter which he handed down to his son, and which was the chief cause of the first success of the firm. His son besides being with Mr. Marshall was, before he started in business for himself, with the Sandersons.

LEIGHTON: Standing with its side to Newhall street and facing Millsands is Hollis's Hospital, or, as it used commonly to be called, Brown Hospital, built on the site of the first Dissenters' chapel in the town. Its history is to be found in Hunter's Hallamshire; but the inscription on the Newhall street-side, over a blocked up doorway, may be recorded here, for although there seems to be no present prospect of its obliteration, when such things do disappear there is no re-covering them :—

> "This Hospital,
> For sixteen poor aged Inhabitants of
> Sheffield or within two Miles round it,
> And School for fifty children, were founded by
> Thomas Hollis, of London, Cutler,
> 1703,
> And further endowed by his Sons,
> Thomas Hollis, 1724, and John Hollis, 1726,
> And rebuilt more commodiously by the Trustees,
> 1776."

EVERARD: While almost everything else round here has changed, this building remains the same, close to busy thoroughfares, and yet, as it were, removed from them. Stepping down here, only a few yards from the noisy streets, has to some extent the effect of getting into a Cathedral close.

LEONARD: At the bottom of Newhall street, are the offices erected some years ago by Naylor, Vickers & Co. They occupy the site of the old "horse dyke," in which lads used to bathe and paddle, and where the street watering carts were filled.

WRAGG : This part of Bridge street was called " Under the water" or " T'under watter," and " The Isle" was where Tennant's brewery now stands. In Water lane, were some troughs, or rather a well—hence the name.

LEONARD : Was it not hereabouts that the celebrated adventure of Tommy Hotbread took place ?

WRAGG : Yes. " Tommy Hotbread," took his name from calling hot cakes, " halfpenny rolls," on a morning. At that time, sixty years ago, all the spring-knife cutlers were knock-kneed from being underfed, and had long arms from the peculiar manner in which they worked; but Tommy was worst of all, and since he was a little feeble old man besides, it was as much as he could do to walk, let alone taking any one into custody. Besides, he had an impediment in his speech. One night he was fast asleep in his box, near Newhall street, when some fellows leaving a public-house, carried it and Tommy into the goit in Millsands. On Tommy awaking and observing the water in it, he said, " Be me thoul there's a thorn." He then cried out to his jokers, who were waiting to see the result, " Athihtance, gentlemen," and on discovering his true position he threatened, it is said, that if they did not get him out he would take them into " cuthdody."

LEONARD : The story is told in several different forms and with sundry variations. One account makes Tommy's watch box to have been near the Castle Inn, facing up Angel street. According to this version, the watchman did not wait to be in the water before he awoke, but as he was being carried down Snig hill, box and all, he roared out vigorously, "If yo doan't thet me doan, o'le tak yo all up." The grinders, however, went straight a-head and placed the box in the middle of the horse dyke, not the goit as Mr. Wragg said.

TWISS : The version given in a note in Mr. John Wilson's edition of Mather is, that the jokers were a party of scissor-grinders who had been at a trade meeting at Mr. Hinchliffe's, the Greyhound, Gibraltar, and they, on peeping into the box, at the bottom of Snig hill, found Tommy asleep. One of them went to " borrow" a clothes line which some good woman had left out at night, and with this cord they tied the watchman in his box and bore him off notwithstanding his shouts. This account agrees with Mr. Wragg in making the goit the scene of the immersion. Mr. Wilson tells another practical joke that was played on Hotbread by the workmen of Holy, Wilkinson and Co., when he was selling fruit in Mulberry street. They called to him out of the window for some apples, and made the coppers hot before throwing them out to him. On going up the stairs to complain to Mr. Holy, they poured a mixture of whiting and water on to his head.

LEIGHTON : The watchmen of those days would have presented a wonderful sight to a Government Inspector. The whole "*posse*" for the entire town did not exceed above half a score. Besides Tommy Hotbread, there were " Sammy Suck-thumb," "Neddy Jennings," and others. They were accustomed to announce the time and the state of the weather, and one great part of their duty was to call up people who had to rise early. Any lateness was sure to be excused on the ground that the watchman had forgotten his promise to rouse them. The watch boxes that protected the watchmen were put up by the Town Trustees.

WRAGG : Yes, we mentioned that under the willow tree, on Brookhill, once before.

JOHNSON : The Hotbreads and the Suck-thumbs, the Eyres, Woollens, Halls, and Hinchliffes, flourished about the end of the last century. But forty years ago we were still under the constable regime, for policemen had not yet reached us. There were Flather, Wild, Waterfall, and Bland for Sheffield, and Birks for Ecclesall. It was as common in those days to speak of fetching Bland, as it is now to go for a policeman. I saw Bland take past my father's shop, George Sandys, a butcher in Pinstone street, who had murdered his wife.

WRAGG : I fear you are not quite accurate in your facts. There never were more than three constables, but they had their " runners." Bland was first an assistant of Thomas Smith, to execute the warrants on debtors, and put them in gaol, in Scotland street. Nor was Birks a constable at first, he was " runner" to Marples, his wife's father, whom he subsequently succeeded. Wild had a runner named Wildgoose, " Jim Goose," and it was he who apprehended Sandys and took him to York. " Goose" and " Old Crookes," the watchman, generally did the work now assigned to detectives; but as Wildgoose couldn't read, he had no chance of becoming a constable, so he ceased to be a " runner" and worked at his trade—file cutting—until his death. In 1825, the constables were Thomas Smith, keeper of Scotland street Gaol; Thomas Flather and John Waterfall. The assistant-constables were John Waterfall, jun., James Wild and William Bland.

LEIGHTON : Wild, the constable, lived at one time in a house at the bottom of North Church street, opposite the old

Queen street chapel school-room; and subsequently in Queen street, opposite the chapel.

EVERARD: It is a little curious and very creditable that sons of both Wild and Waterfall became bank managers.

WRAGG: Tom Smith, whom I have named, subsequently kept the Blue Boar, in Westbar, and afterwards the Royal Oak, King street. He accumulated considerable wealth; but Hinchliffe, his senior, a fellow constable and fellow publican, the father of "Jemmy Queer," was not so successful. He ended his days in the Shrewsbury Hospital. His family appears to have been in the scissor trade for more than a century, one of them, Mr. Robert Hinchliffe, having produced the first pair of hand polished scissors in 1761.

LEONARD: The story is that he was induced to attempt to make them in order to ingratiate himself in the affections of the girl who afterwards became his wife.

JOHNSON: Smith and Hinchliffe were the proprietors of the bowling green further on, from which the present street takes its name.

LEIGHTON: The Blue Boar had been Mr. Hagger's house, with a coat of arms over it, and Smith new-fronted it. On the side nearest Snig hill—now the three shops between Woollen's and Raby's, was a grand house, belonging to Mr. Norris—Sammy Norris he was called. There were steps leading up to it, and the workshops of Norris, who was a razor maker, were up the yard behind. He was Master Cutler in 1777. Norris had two sons and one daughter, Catherine, who married Richard Ince, a solicitor at Wirksworth, of whom came the late Mr. T. N. Ince, of Wakefield. The elder son of Mr. Norris married the daughter of the Rev. James Dixon, vicar of Ecclesfield. The younger son, Thomas, became a clergyman, and was for some time chaplain to the Forces, and died at Chelsea in 1816.

WRAGG: The case of old Mr. Norris was a very sad one. He traded to Germany, and one year, by great exertions, took an unusually large stock of razors to Leipsic fair, expecting to reap the due reward of his efforts. Instead of customers to the fair came the French invading army, the city was fired, and Mr. Norris, it was said, had to secrete himself in a pig-stye. The disaster ruined him, for notwithstanding the commiseration of his creditors and the public, he never recovered his former position. He died an inmate of the Shrewsbury Hospital, July 16th, 1817.

LEONARD : I have just a shade of doubt whether it was the old gentleman or the son Thomas who went to Leipsic, for although afterwards a clergyman, the latter was at one time in his father's business. It is certain, however, that it was the old man who died in the Shrewsbury Hospital.

LEIGHTON : On the opposite side of Westbar, up a passage, the father of the late Peter Frith began business as an optician, 70 years ago. He prospered, devoting himself more to the fancy branches than his competitors, and saved a large sum of money. The father of old Mr. Oakes, the tobacconist, still living in Westbar three doors from the corner of Colson street, had a meal and flour shop on the same (south) side of the street, belonging to the late Benj. Withers' father. The rent was £9 per annum; it has since been re-fronted and is now occupied by Mr. Barlow, saddler, and a tobacconist, at a very much higher rental. At the corner of Colson style was Mr. Denton, grocer, of Fox hill. He was brother to the late William Denton, of Pitsmoor.

LEONARD : Old Mr. Oakes, who has been mentioned, is 86 years' old, yet he relates that Westbar has not greatly altered in his lifetime. In the part of it nearest to Snig hill, the buildings are much the same, though most of the shops have been refronted.

LEONARD : Westbar had the honour of producing the first Sheffield manufacturer who ventured to open direct business communication with London. The story is thus told :— About the middle of the last century, Mr. Fox, of Westbar— he who built the lofty houses near West court, in one of which he afterwards lived, and Mr. Samuel Fowler in the other—was the first person to undertake a journey to London for the purpose of selling his wares. It was necessary to go on foot, and before starting he made his will and gave a large farewell party to his friends. Nothing that his wife or friends could say to him could dissuade him from encountering all the fatigue, hazard, and difficulty of the journey. He started on foot, carrying his treasure on his back. The first day he walked as far as Mansfield, where he rested for the night. The next day he had to wait until a sufficient number of travellers met together to venture across Nottingham forest, on account of the numerous robberies that were committed on travellers there, and also because of the intricacies of the road. He reached Nottingham in safety, and ultimately he reached London, sold his goods to his satisfaction, and obtained plenty of orders for more. His example was soon followed by others, who went upon similar business, but this is believed to have been the first instance of personal intercourse with the metropolis.

EVERARD : Business journeys must have been made to London earlier than that, though doubtless they would be great and rare occasions. An ancestor of my own, in the cutlery trade, went up, I believe in the reign of Queen Anne, and I have a copper-plate, engraved by my great-grandfather, to perpetuate the memory of that event.

WRAGG : In New street, lived Spence Broughton, who was hung and gibbeted on Attercliffe Common in 1792, for robbing the mail-cart there. "He was," says Mr. Oakes, who remembers, as a boy six years old, seeing the gibbet-post being made by a man named Gregory, in the Nursery, " a fine fellow, standing six feet high." The Sunday after he was gibbeted, the road through Attercliffe was one mass of people going to see the wretched spectacle. It seemed as if everybody from Sheffield and Rotherham and all around had gone to visit the scene.

LEONARD : There is none of the uncertainty which attaches to Frank Fearn's gibbet-post in connection with the ultimate destination of Spence Broughton's. A few years ago—in May, 1867, large crowds were attracted to the Yellow Lion, in Clifton street, Attercliffe Common, to see an upright piece of solid black oak, 4ft. 6in. long and 18in. square, fixed in and passing through a massive framework, 10ft. long and 1ft. deep, firmly imbedded in the ground. The post was bolted to this latter. This relic was found by a person named Holroyd, while making excavations for cellars opposite the Yellow Lion, and I suppose there can be no doubt that they were the socket and lower part of the gibbet-post put up in 1792, the upper part having been cut away and removed some years before. I am not aware what became of them.

JOHNSON : The fragment of the post is still kept at the Yellow Lion.

TWISS : It was Mr. Henry Sorby, of Woodburn, who took down the gibbet when the land on which it was erected became his property. His chief motive was to put a stop to the injury done by trespassers visiting this relic of a barbarous custom. I suppose he must have cut it off instead of taking it up out of the ground. The gibbet was deposited in his coach-house, where I saw it. I am not clear what afterwards became of the post, but I am under the impression that it was used for a beam in a cottage, and that it was removed in consequence of the prejudice it caused against the house.

LEIGHTON : As an instance of the absurd stories that get abroad about such matters, I may say it has been solemnly affirmed, in print, that Spence Broughton's gibbet-post was set on fire and burned down by women who were collecting rubbish in the field. Solid oak like that would take more than casual burning.

EVERARD : I have seen an extract from the *Mercury*, of Oct. 6, 1827, which shows that Broughton's gibbet-post was removed on the 27th of September in that year. I visited it about 1817, when the clothes were fluttering rags, and the whitened bones could be seen.

LEONARD : Have you ever seen the touching letter which Spence Broughton is said to have addressed to his wife on the eve of his execution ? It is as follows :—

" My dear Eliza,—This is the last affectionate token thou will ever receive from my hand, a hand that trembles at my approaching dissolution, so soon, so soon, so very soon to ensue. Before thou wilt open this last epistle of thine unfortunate husband, these eyes, which overflow with tears of contrition, shall have ceased to weep, and this heart now fluttering on the very verge of eternity shall beat no more. I have prepared my mind to meet death without horror, and ah, how happy, had that death been the common visitation of nature. Be not discomfited ; God will be your friend. In the solitude of my cell, I have sought Him, His spirit hath supported me, hath assisted me in my prayers, and many a time in the moment of remorseful anguish hath whispered peace ; for, my dear Eliza, I never added cruelty to injustice. Yet, tho' I have resolved to meet death without fear, one part of my awful sentence, a sentence aggravated by being merited, chills me with horror when I reflect that my poor remains, the tokens of mortality, must not sleep in peace, but be buffeted about by the storms of heaven and parched by the summer's sun, while the traveller shrinks at the sight with disgust and terror. This consideration freezes my blood. This cell, this awful gloom, these irons, yea, death itself is not so grievous. Why will the laws continue to sport with the wretched after life is at an end ?

" My Eliza, my friend, my wife, the last sad scene approaches when I shall be no more ; leave the world and thee, my dear, to its mercy. Not only thee, but my unprotected children, the pledges of a love, through misfortune, through dissipation, through vice and infamy, on thy part unchanged. Ah, fool that I was to think friendship could exist but with virtue.

"Had I listened to the advice thou hast so often given me, we had been a family respectable and respected, but it is past. That advice hath been slighted. I am doomed to an ignominious death, and thou and my children, horrid thought! to infamy. To thee alone I trust the education of those ill-fated creatures, whom I now more than ever love and weep for. Warn them to avoid gaming of every description, that baneful vice which has caused their father to be suspended, a long and lasting spectacle to feed the eye of curiosity. Teach them the ways of religion in their early years. Cause them to learn some trade, that business and time may occupy the mind and leave no room for dissipation. When seated round your winter's fire, when the little innocents inquire after their unfortunate father, tell them gaming was his ruin ; he neglected all religious duties ; he never conversed with his heart in solitude ; he stilled the upbraidings of conscience in the company of the lewd and profligate, and is hung on high, a sad and dismal warning to after times. I see thee employed, while tears trickle down that face which I have so ill deserved.

"Adieu, my Eliza, adieu for ever, the morning appears for the last time to these sad eyes. Pleasant would death be on a sick bed after my soul had made her peace with God. With God I hope her peace is made. He is not a God of all terror, but a God of mercy. On that mercy I rely, and on the interposition of a Saviour. May my tears, my penitence, and deep contrition be acceptable to that Almighty Being before whom I am shortly to appear.

"Adieu, my Eliza, adieu, farewell ; the pen falls from my hand and slumber overtakes me, the next will be the sleep of death. Farewell.

"Yours in love.   SPENCE BROUGHTON."

TWISS : It is a touching letter and I see no reason to doubt its authenticity.

WRAGG : There used to be some little shops at the bottom of New street, which have been rebuilt. A great guinea buyer lived at the bottom of that street. He let in Walker's bank for a large amount, and as that was followed by the burning down of the cotton mill it was a bad year for them. At the top of Hicks' lane was Wilkinson, a tooth drawer. A miser named Smith lived near, the beginning of whose wealth was receiving compensation for a boy who was killed in a coalpit.   In North street was, 70 years ago, Daniel Hemming, who worked for Spurrs the cutlers.   He was the first man who invented oval shields for pen-knife handles.

JOHNSON : New street boasted the possession of one of the town pumps ; it still stands in the bend, up the street.

WRAGG : On a part of the site of the Surrey Music Hall (still standing in the ruin caused by the fire in 1865) was the uncle of the late Dr. G. C. Holland.   To his trade the Doctor was at first brought up, and as a youth he might be seen there making wigs.

EVERARD : George Calvert Holland was too remarkable a man to be passed over with a mere mention of that kind. The perseverance which enabled him to triumph over the disadvantages of a lowly origin, the scholarship which he snatched by his own hard industry, the romantic though painful vicissitudes of his life, and his genial personal presence alike point to him as an illustrious figure in the history of Sheffield during the earlier half of the present century.   I do not know that his physical bearing can be better hit off than in the appreciative biographical sketch which appeared in the *Independent* at the time of his death— March, 1865.   I should just like to read these sentences from among others :—

" The graceful courtesy of the man, the courtly kindliness of his greeting, and his never-failing refinement of thought, expression, and bearing marked him wherever he was as one who, despite his humble lineage, had received from Nature herself, and under her own hand and seal, the patent of a gentleman.   His great acquirements as a scholar were borne without any of the scholar's pedantry.   His arduous labours as an author, whose works are characterized by rare originality of thought, did not import into his manners any taint of the literary churl.   Reverses of fortune that would have crushed a man of less powerful and less active intellect had no power either to crush or to sour him.   His philosophic spirit stood by him through his declining health and ruined fortunes.   The sentient marble of which he was moulded was of all too fine a grain to receive any stain from extrinsic surroundings, and when his duties as a public man called him to sit in an assembly notorious for the irritating acrimony and offensive coarseness in which some of its members indulged, his unruffled urbanity and unaffected elegance never failed to exhibit him in admirable relief as one who could better brook insult than brook the idea that any word or action of his should be unworthy of a gentleman and a scholar. When circumstances were against him he rose superior to circumstances. Those even whose acquaintance with him was of the slightest, will think of him with most respectful regret. His full grey eye, and thin intellectual face that spoke, before his tongue could speak it, a cordial greeting, will live in the memory of hundreds who were privileged with his acquaintance, and who felt in his society that when a man is moulded and tempered and endowed like him, the advantages of worldly circumstances are but as the tinselled rags which the superstitious hang upon the images of the saints in a misjudged attempt to do them honour."

LEIGHTON : That is an admirable description of the man. I should like much to have my remembrance of the other parts of that notice revived.

EVERARD : Mr. Leonard showed it to me and I doubt not he will read it to us.

LEONARD : I will chiefly give you those parts which sketch Dr. Holland's personal history :—"Holland was born at Pitsmoor sixty-four years ago (this, you will remember, was written in 1865), when Pitsmoor was an outlying hamlet, and salmon were speared in the then clear waters of the Don. His father, a sawmaker, working with Kenyon and Co., gave the boy a fair education. The lad was not precocious. He was, happily for his future distinction, a child delighting in boyish sports, and manifesting no special aptitude either for learning or books. Nobody suspected him of superior ability, nor did he suspect it himself. At an early age he was apprenticed to an uncle, whose humble but honest business we need not indicate ; suffice it to mention that it was a business of small profits and quick returns, and one which gave young Holland a fine opportunity for the study of physiognomy and for observing the remarkable variety which exists in the size and formation of human heads. In the olden times the *perruquier* was often a little of the surgeon —in modern times even he sometimes lapses into the ancient trade—and the boy who was to become an accomplished physician, made his first approach to the profession through the antique gateway. At sixteen an accident led him to test his mental powers. One Sunday morning he was taking a walk with a companion, who told him he had composed a hymn, and who read the verses to him for the purpose of ob-

taining his opinion on their merits. Young Holland was
surprised at the talent of his youthful companion. The germ
of a worthy ambition was quickened within him, and partly
from curiosity as to his own qualifications and partly from a
dimly dawning consciousness of dormant power, he resolved
to try to write verses too. The result of this first essay in
composition astonished himself as much as it did his friends;
and from that time he became a regular contributor to the
Poet's Corner in one of those weekly journals which were at
that period the only newspapers published in the town. This
was the turning point in his life. New aspirations were
awakened within him, new tastes took posession of him. With
all the ardour of youth and all the vivid appreciation which
is felt by lads who are realising for the first time the flattering sense of superiority to their fellows, he became a reader.
But no reader of novels was he. The most ponderous tomes
of history, travel, and science were as novels to him, and he
ransacked libraries with the delighted eye of an explorer who
is meeting at every turn some new feature of what to him is
a new world. His love of the classics caused him often to
prolong his readings through the night. But he became
dissatisfied with translations; he burned to read Virgil and
Petrarch in their native tongue. Under difficulties which had
about them strange elements of the grotesque, he—the sawmaker's son—set himself to acquire Latin, French, and
Italian, and made such extraordinary progress as to become a
marvel amongst all his acquaintances. His was the faith
that worked miracles. He voyaged among strange fields of
knowledge in the spirit of a discoverer, and valued most the
acquisitions which at first seemed most remote. The uncle
was by no means pleased with the boy's bravery. The love
of knowledge had become an absorbing passion, and the plain
tradesman gravely shook his head, and uttered his fears that
no good would ever come of such a voracious consumption of
books. But the youth had wiser friends, who lent him books,
and frankly told him that he would wrong himself if he did
not seek employment in some worthier calling than in his
uncle's lowly trade. The first scheme of his friends was to
procure for him an admission to the Unitarian College, but
the want of the needful resources caused that project to break
down. Happily he had a relation, a surgeon, who took a
creditable interest in the splendid efforts at self-elevation that
were being made by so promising a youth. It was arranged
that the accomplished lad should go to Edinburgh and pre-

pare himself for taking his degree as Doctor of Medicine, and to Edinburgh he went. He spent three years in that city, making great progress in his studies, and becoming acquainted with and esteemed by the most rising men of the University. From the modern Athens he removed to Paris, where he diligently pursued his studies in anatomy, physiology, and pathology. Sensible of his vantage as a man of letters, he presented himself in Paris before the examiners for the degree of Bachelor of Letters, and was personally examined by the eminent Guizot, who bestowed on him special praise for his intimate acquaintance with the classics. After spending a year in Paris he returned to Edinburgh, where he completed his studies, and obtained his diploma as M.D. with great *éclat*. He then commenced practice in Manchester, became an active member of the learned bodies in that city, and made many friends among men of scientific and literary eminence. We have thus traced the sawmaker's son from the school to the shop—from the shop to the study—and from the study to the examination in which he earned the applause of the gifted professors of the Sorbonne, and we must now briefly sketch his professional life.

"Young G. C. Holland, now M.D. and Bachelor of Letters, did not remain long in Manchester. His youthful susceptibility was wounded by a malignant allusion in one of the local papers to his humble antecedents, and he moved for a while to Edinburgh, where he pursued his experiments and researches for his first physiological work, 'An Experimental Inquiry into the Laws of Life.' After committing this important work to the press, he came to Sheffield, and commenced practising in his native town. The flattering reception his book met with in the medical reviews and the public press raised him in the estimation of his townsmen, and in the course of a few years his practice brought him in about £1400 a year. During this time he was elected one of the physicians to the Infirmary—often lectured before the members of the Mechanics' Institution—was an active member of the Philosophical Society, and became its president. At the first borough election he was chairman for Mr. T. A. Ward; and at the second borough election he appeared on the hustings for Mr. S. Bailey, that gentleman having personally declined to contest the borough again. On all these occasions Dr. Holland displayed great activity of mind and often rose to a pitch of eloquence which surprised his contemporaries, and threw their oratorical efforts into the shade.

During the agitation for the repeal of the Corn Laws the Doctor made the serious mistake of joining the Protectionists. He became one of the lecturers, and had a discussion with Mr. Ackland, in the Theatre of this town. He had also a discussion with the veteran Free-trader, Mr. William Ibbotson, in the same place. This erratic course alienated the Doctor from many of his old friends, but the farmers around Doncaster acknowledged his brilliant services by presenting him with a purse containing 500 guineas.

"When the railway speculation commenced in 1843 the Doctor went into it with all the spirit of his sanguine nature, and with considerable success. He was chairman of several companies, and a director of many more. He was also a director in the Sheffield and Retford Bank, and of another at Leeds. Unlike some other speculators, he held his stock too long. The crash came, and with it a writ from the London and Westminster Bank for £54,000. He had then given up his practice, and was living at Wadsley Hall in the style of a country gentleman. He was driven into bankruptcy, and retired to a small cottage near Worksop until his affairs were settled. There, in poverty and distress, he wrote his 'Philosophy of Animated Nature,' a work which he always considered as his best. He then tried his fortune in the metropolis, and, although a gentleman in manners, an author whose works had received the highest compliments from the highest authorities on the questions of which he had treated, he was lost in the modern Babylon, and, mortified at his ill-success, he returned to Sheffield in 1851. On his return to his native town, it told against him that he countenanced and partially practised homœopathy. Homœopathy was heresy, and the orthodox in medicine, like the orthodox in divinity, look coldly on the heretically wicked. Indeed it is to be feared that an independence of mind which would not permit itself to be trammelled by routine, and a temperament which retained to the last the speculative and sanguine cast of his youth, did much to impede that practical recognition to which his extensive attainments and brilliant natural powers entitled him. Indeed a shade of sadness comes over us when we think of how much he has done for his age and how little the age has done for him We can count our doctors by the thousand, but when we are called upon to bury the author of ' The Philosophy of Animated Nature,' we are reminded that men so amiable, so learned, so gifted, and so passionately fond of curious research are public benefactors whose thoughts do not

perish with them, and whose labours entitle them to be regarded as the philanthropists who bequeath to the world—
not silver and gold indeed, but the mature fruits of the intellect with which they were endowed.   Dr. G. Calvert Holland, formerly President of the Hunterian and Royal Physical
Societies, Edinburgh, Bachelor of Letters of the University
of Paris, author of 'An Experimental Inquiry into the Laws
of Life,' 'Inquiry into the Principles and Practice of
Medicine,' 'The Physiology of the Liver and Spleen,' 'The
Vital Statistics of Sheffield,' 'The Philosophy of the Moving
Powers of the Blood,' 'The Philosophy of Animated Nature,'
and a little library of other works of the same high class,
was no ordinary man.   His address was worthy of his
appearance, his bearing became his reputation, his reputation
realized more than could even have been anticipated from his
youthful promise, and the only thing to be regretted is, that
when laden with honours and with years he did not reap a
greater material reward."

LEIGHTON : Thank you, I have enjoyed that much, for it
is all very true.

WRAGG : Robert Holland, the sawmaker, became at a late
period of his life, after the manner of so many Sheffield
artizans, the landlord of the Blue Boar, which has already
been mentioned.   George Holland, his brother, built the
property at the top of Hicks lane.

JOHNSON : In Hicks lane, lived a family that for several
reasons must be noticed—the Mellons.   Michael Mellon,
the chimney sweeper, was well known ; his grandson, Henry
Mellon, gave us a remarkable instance of a selfmade man ;
while the romantic story of one of the family becoming raised
to the peerage as Duchess of St. Albans is too good to be
lost.   Mr. Holland* tells us that he was unable to remember the street in which Michael Mellon's rhyming invitation to customers was hung out on a swinging sign-board,
but he fancied it was True Love's Gutter.   Whether Mellon
ever lived there or not he was certainly at one time a
" character " in Westbar, with his bow-legs and his habits
of insobriety, living, as I have said, in Hicks lane.   The
gravestone in the Churchyard, which Mr. Holland mentions,
is over his wife Sarah, who died the 6th October, 1807,
aged 42.   There is some little vagueness as to the relationship of Harriet, the actress, who is said to have risen
so high in the world, to this chimney-sweep, but the proba-

---

* "Our Old Churchyard," p. 18.

bility seems to be that she was his sister. It has been said she was his aunt, but that would make her too old to be the consort of the Duke of St. Albans, who was born in 1801.

TWISS : Is not the story altogether apocryphal ?

JOHNSON : I think not ; at all events it is a very curious one, none the less curious from the doubt that hangs over it. If by any means the identity of Harriet, Duchess of St. Albans, with Harriet Mellon, of Hicks lane, could have been tested by a law court, the case would certainly have been remarkable.

LEIGHTON : The Mellon family believed very firmly in the identity—though that, to be sure, is not much to go by.

TWISS : And it was repudiated by the " other side."

EVERARD : Mr. Holland, in the paper already mentioned, speaks of the relationship as an established fact, and the Rev. C. Collier in a " Notice of the Rev. Henry Mellon," in the *Reliquary* for January, 1872 (Vol. xii., p. 152), says that " of the relationship there can be but little doubt."

JOHNSON : He also speaks of the Duchess as Henry Mellon's great-aunt, which, since Michael was Henry's grandfather, confirms my belief that Harriet Mellon was Michael's sister. However, the story goes thus : Harriet Mellon went on the stage, and achieved a great success. A fine tribute to her acting is said to have occurred once at Liverpool. The character she was playing—that of a woman in the depths of poverty and distress—had to appeal for help against a remorseless bailiff. She acted the part with such feeling that a sailor in the audience rushed upon the stage to her assistance.

TWISS : Similar stories have been told of many actors.

LEONARD : What a sceptical mood you are in to-night !

JOHNSON : On the London boards Miss Mellon made a conquest of Thomas Coutts, the banker, grandfather of the present Baroness Burdett Coutts, and after his death she—

TWISS : (*aside*) Being no doubt very wealthy—

JOHNSON : —Formed a second alliance with William Aubrey de Vere Beauclerk, 9th Duke of St. Albans, the father of the present Duke.

EVERARD : Then was she the mother of the present Duke ?

JOHNSON : No. There was no issue. The Duchess died August 6th, 1837. The Duke married again, and the present Duke and Lady Diana Huddlestone are the result of the alliance.

LEONARD : I see Debrett describes the first Duchess as " daughter of *Matthew* Mellon, gent." The marriage took place 16th June, 1827.

EVERARD : It seems to me that Henry Mellon's career has something in it much worthier of family pride than this ill-matched alliance with the aristocracy, and this relative who would never acknowledge the pit from which she was digged, nor lend a helping hand to those who were still floundering in it. But Henry Mellon did without her, though her persistent refusal to notice his application for the help necessary to obtain a university training was a great disappointment to him.

TWISS : That he succeeded by self-help is all the more to his credit, and adds another to the eminent pupils who have conferred honour upon the Sheffield Boys' Charity School.

EVERARD : The source of the following sketch of Henry Mellon's career I have already acknowledged. Mr. Collier tells us that Michael, the wit and public character, begat John, and John, " a good steady man, who followed his father's trade," begat Henry in 1818. His father dying early, the boy was placed in the Charity School. His studiousness and love of learning made its mark, and he became the head boy. He was, on leaving, apprenticed as silversmith to Mr. Samuel Roberts, the great patron of that school, but during his apprenticeship he showed a strong ecclesiastical bent, teaching in Garden street Sunday School, and helping the clergymen at the Parish Church at the Sunday afternoon baptisms. What was of more importance, he studiously increased the knowledge already acquired, devoted himself to Hebrew, and ransacked the Mechanics' Library for works on poetry and history. Ultimately he became a student at the Church Missionary College, Islington ; passed through the course with diligence, and was ordained by the Bishop of London after a creditable examination. " What a strange transformation in a few years," says Mr. Collier—" a chimney sweeper's child —a poor charity boy, with his yellow stockings and leather breeches—an apprentice boy, with an apron tied round his waist—now the accomplished Rev. Henry Mellon. He was in every way worthy of his position. With an open, ruddy countenance, and a clear brow, he had a voice of fair compass, a graceful bearing, an entire absence of *patois* in his speech, an unassuming manner, and remarkable powers of conversation. I shall never forget when he occupied the pulpit in the church where he had sat as a charity boy, and where I heard his first sermon in his native town. Those who knew him as a boy, and many such were present, could hardly realise in the graceful preacher the poor lad born in the depths of obscurity and poverty." After a brief missionary career in India, where he lost his wife, the Rev. Henry Mellon returned to England, held curacies in Cornwall and Oxford, and eventually settled at Wadsley. "Poor fellow! His day was soon over. His sun set early. He died in his 32nd year (1849), and was buried in the churchyard of Wadsley." I have omitted Mr. Collier's estimate of his characteristics as a preacher, and the description of his keen appreciation of nature, since the work in which these occur is readily accessible.

WRAGG: It is hardly needful, I suppose, to recall the old Workhouse, standing out between the bottom of the croft or lane to which it gave a name, and Silver street. Yet one ought not to pass over that old and familiar landmark of byegone days, any more than we should omit to shed a tear in sympathy with the adjacent pump, bereft of all its utility, except as a preaching rostrum.

JOHNSON: It was put up by the Town Trustees, who wisely purchased the site of the old workhouse, to keep the space open.

WRAGG: "Neddy Furniss" was a Westbar worthy. He was a prosperous shoemaker, who left his property to his niece, already spoken of as the wife of Mr. H. A. Bacon, of Snig hill.

LEONARD: Near Furniss's shop was a celebrated gardener, named Thomas Burgin, who died in 1819.

WRAGG: He was, I believe, the father of the late Mr. William Burgin, the gardener, whose shop stood on the site of Mr. Sharman's grocery shop at the top of Corporation street. His was the garden near Brightside Vestry Hall, and his the orchard in Harvest lane that was such a grand sight when its fruit trees were in blossom. The Burgins were a family of gardeners. I have counted as many as four of them in the *Directory* published 1828. One of the buildings destroyed in making Corporation street was the shop of the late Mr. John Gaunt, grocer. On his retirement from business he removed to Darnall. He gave the site of St. Jude's Church, and afterwards paid largely towards its erection. He was from the neighbourhood of Penistone—I think Denby, where there are now some of the family. It is said one of the Gaunts at Denby can show the family descent from John of Gaunt, Duke of Lancaster. Mr. Joseph Gaunt, the scale cutter, of Pea croft, is a cousin of the late grocer, and I would also add, the Gaunts of Leeds, are of the same family.

JOHNSON: There are many other names well known in Sheffield that might be mentioned in connection with Westbar, though this would bring us to times more recent than we profess to take cognizance of. There was Mr. John Turton, the surgeon (see p. 42.); John Spink, the pawnbroker, who, marrying the niece of the owner of the property, turned Benjamin Fox out of the shop where the ruined Casino now stands; Benjamin Smilter, father of the present High Bailiff; Francis Cluley, the earliest surgical instrument maker, who was next door to the "Old Tankard," removing thence to Surrey street.

WRAGG : The "Old Tankard," by the way, was once kept by Jonathan Moore, one of the subjects of Mather's virulent songs.

TWISS : And it is pertinent to the locality to remark that Mather himself is said to have been born about the year 1737, in Cack Alley, a passage or "jennel" leading from Westbar green to Lambert street.

LEONARD : The house of Mr. Popplewell, currier, close to the "Old Tankard," bears date 1794.

JOHNSON : Then there was William Marshall, ironmonger and paper dealer, on the site of the Surrey Vaults, at the head of Workhouse lane ; the Dickensons and the Spurrs, connected by marriage with the Mellons ; Christopher Marshall, the pawnbroker ; George Shallcross, the miller, so long and honourably associated with Red Hill Sunday school. These and many others might be dwelt on were it not going too far out of the record.

LEIGHTON : You are all familiar with the palisaded house at the bottom of Lambert street, now occupied by Mr. Watts, clasp manufacturer—a business carried on there for many years. Long ago it was the residence of Capt. Chisholm. The workshops behind have been long used by coffin makers, and there is a story of an escaped debtor from Scotland street gaol finding secure refuge in one of those ghastly structures. And this reminds me of other whimsicalities of the neighbourhood—of the old lady living at the top of Bower spring, who had such a mania for storing farthings, that after her death they were found hidden about the house in barrows full ; or of "Sally Platts," the robust gardener's wife of 16 stone weight and 87 years of age, who began life as the only survivor of ten children produced at one birth, and who was currently reported to have been put into a quart pot in those days of innocent infancy. The name of her mother who achieved the feat of ten children at a birth was Ann Birch. Then there was Molly Revill, the celebrated oat-cake maker, on the site of the shops now occupied by Councillor Scarle and Mr. Miller, chemist.

EVERARD: George Harrison, a table-blade forger in Lambert street, was long a local preacher among the Independents—indeed he and "Bishop" Bower were the last of the old generation on the "plan." He was a member of Garden street chapel when the Rev. Mark Docker was there, and was one of the founders of Mount Zion chapel.

WRAGG: In Lambert street, or Lambert croft (Scotland street was formerly called Lambert Knott) the Tillotson family were located before they removed to Coalpit lane.

TWISS: There is a curious story told of the manner in which the further part of Westbar was raised to its present level. At one time, it is said, that portion between Westbar green and Gibraltar street was so low, that a person standing at the bottom of Furnace hill might with ease have leapt upon a load of hay passing down the street. There was then a converting furnace at the bottom of the hill, which was worked with only one box or pot. By some mismanagement the whole mass of iron was melted together in one huge solid block of steel, there being in the furnace at the time some ten tons of metal. Nothing could be done with this when it was cold, and after it had lain in the yard a great number of years, proceedings began to be taken for filling up the road below. The best employment that could be thought of for the mass of steel, was to let it go towards filling up the road. The tradition has been handed down by very old men, and if there be any truth in it the steel is still there, waiting to astonish some antiquaries of the future.

WRAGG: The Bower spring troughs were reputed to contain the best drinking water in the town. It came from Furnace hill, as was proved when Messrs. Hudson & Clarke erected their engine. That stopped the water, and Messrs. Gaunt & Turton's works were then built where the troughs had been.

JOHNSON: It was Mr. Turton who built the Bower spring works in the old Workhouse gardens, leaving Mr. Gaunt on Furnace hill. This would be between the years 1825-8. The history of Mr. Gaunt's business is worth tracing. It was sold to Richard Griffiths, who, having come to the town from his native Wales as a carter to Brittain and Wilkinson's, of Carver street, got initiated into the mysteries of steel converting, and ultimately became manager at Sanderson's. His son, for whom the business was intended, died; his son-in-law let it slip, and it was sold to Thomas Gatley, the son of a gardener at Attercliffe who had kept one of the stalls on the King street side of the market. Young Gatley was himself apprenticed to Isaac Deakin, penblade maker (son-in-law of George Merrill, fork maker, Harvest lane), and afterwards had a scrap shop in Gibraltar street, near " The Cherry Tree." Then he was at the bottom of Furnace hill, late Mr. Joshua Wortley's. Having acquired money he bought Gaunt's business, and subsequently sold it to Mr. Wm. Jackson, Sheaf Island Works. He acquired much of the property about here. Like so many other worthies whom we have had to notice, Mr. Gatley was connected with Queen street chapel—until 1834, when he seceded and was the means of establishing Mount Zion chapel, the congregation of which met in a room over a shop in Carver lane while the chapel was building.

LEIGHTON : Furnace hill was formerly called " t' Cock Tail ;" I haven't the remotest notion why. " The Cock Tail lady" was celebrated by Mather ; and " Buck Hathard," the son of a tailor, was also one of the "characters" it produced. Mr. Peech, a scissor manufacturer here, was the father-in-law of Henry Steel, who has made himself a name among the frequenters of the turf, and " t' Cocktail" had the honour of contributing a soldier to the Life Guards in the person of Samuel Wragg, who, and his son as well, was a cutler here.

WRAGG : The Quaker family, the Broadheads, have been associated with Westbar and the neighbourhood throughout the present century. Mr. John Broadhead, then a maltster, was in Scotland street, next door to the chapel. Then he came to the bottom of Furnace hill, subsequently crossing to the other side of Westbar, where the grocer's shop has been ever since. Mr. John Broadhead died in 1838. It is a little singular that not only did his son Alfred succeed to his own grocery business, but that four of his five daughters married grocers.

JOHNSON : Two trade notes may be made here. One is that " frame polishing" may be said to have had its birth in Furnace hill—that is polishing spring knives without the aid of steam or water power. It was originated by Mark Blackwell (landlord of " The Grapes") and his brother George, by way of resisting a strike of the grinders. And it succeeded too. The other is that the first nail cut in Sheffield is said to have been made down the yard by the " Dog and Part-ridge," the old public-house almost opposite to the bottom of the hill.

WRAGG : The Andrew family is closely identified with this locality. Old Joseph Andrew was a prosperous grocer and tallow chandler in Furnace hill before this century began. Three of his sons, Isaac, Matthew and Joseph, were grocers, the first-named in Westbar at the corner of Hicks lane, the second in Charles street, and the third, first (1825) in Paradise square and afterwards (1833) in Westbar green. Two other sons, twins, were William Henry and Albert George. They succeeded to the business of Messrs. George Butler and Co., spring knife cutlers, in Trinity street, which was afterwards removed to Trinity works, Eyre street, the old premises becoming Mr. Longden's foundry. Isaac Andrew was, in his later years, blind. His brother Joseph was the father of John Henry Andrew, steel manufacturer, a member of the present Corporation, and of Mrs. Crowther, Fargate. The Butlers employed a larger number of men than any other house in the trade when the " statements" of 1810 and 1814 were made.

TWISS : Towards the end of the last century all these streets running up the hill were thickly occupied by manufacturers. A familiar name among them is that of Daniel Doncaster, who, in 1787, was a filesmith in Copper street. In 1817 he was carrying on the same business in Allen street, while in 1821 the names of William and John take the place of that of Daniel, and in 1828 William alone. Then, in 1833 another Daniel had joined William, and in 1841 he carried on the business alone in Doncaster street and Copper street, and continued to do so until joined by his sons. It is said that Daniel Doncaster the elder bought a field opposite his Allen street works for a sum far below what one year's ground rents now amount to ; while you are no doubt aware that Daniel Doncaster the younger married the daughter of him who owned so much property in that neighbourhood that his name, Allen, was given to the street.

WRAGG : In Cross Smithfield was established, somewhere about the middle of last century, the business now carried on in Sycamore street by Mr. Thomas Wilson, the grandson of its founder. The germs of the business seem to have been laid by old Thomas Wilson at Ran Moor or Hallam. He was one of the enterprising men who first saw the possibility of dispensing with factors and of opening up connections of his own without the intervention of a middle-man. Determining to offer his knives—shoemakers' and butchers'—for sale himself, he packed up his goods and took them on his back into Lancashire. Wherever he sold any knives, he told the purchasers he should come again at a fixed period of time, and if the article did not suit he would return the money. On his next journey he had no complaints, but so much greater demand that some of the retail shops would have purchased the whole of his stock, but he kept to his promise to the others. He readily sold all he had taken, and soon returned home to manufacture more goods with which to complete his journey. This was the first time that the trade mark of the Four Peppercorns and a Diamond with the name " Wilson" went into the market ; now it is a guarantee of good quality in all the countries of the world.

LEIGHTON : Steadfast to their old localities in Snow hill are Richard Groves & Sons, perhaps the oldest saw manufacturers in the town. Mr. Groves, the grandfather of the present firm, always had an open Bible before him on his work-board.

JOHNSON : A very old workman for that firm was the father of the late Mr. Hebblethwaite, who survived his son and lived to a great age.

LEONARD : Talking of saw-makers reminds me that Spear and Jackson were in Gibraltar street—a few doors on the town side of the old Lancasterian schools—before they went into Saville street.

EVERARD : All book-worms will remember that favourite resort just by—Mr. Joseph Pearce's book shop. At one time it was on the premises now occupied by John Gartside Elliott, a son of Ebenezer Elliott, the druggist, who is famed for his prescriptions for children's disorders. Afterwards Mr. Pearce went into the shop which is now Hardy's furniture store.

LEONARD : The name of Ebenezer Elliott calls up remembrances of those days when he occupied the steel warehouse between the bottom of Snow hill and Trinity street. It was in 1833 that Elliott came to Gibraltar street, removing from Burgess street, where he had been in business as an iron and steel merchant since 1821. While here he built himself a house at Upperthorpe. In 1837, a commercial revulsion began, and Elliott used to say that he ought to have retired from business then, as he once intended. But being afraid of leading an idle life, "which being interpreted," said he, " means my unwillingness to resign the profits of business," he waited for the crash and " lost fully one-third of his savings, and after enabling his six sons to quit the nest, got out of the fracas with about £6000." However, as he pleasantly explained, he had his compensations, for " Had I built my house on my land at Foxley, three miles from Sheffield, as I proposed to do in 1836, I should now have been liable to be dragged into public meetings, subscriptions, &c., and deluged with the visits of casual strangers, as I was at Upperthorpe. Here, out of the way of great temptations, and visited only by persons who respect me (alas, by how few of them!) I can perhaps live within my reduced income." That was written from Argilt hill, Great Houghton, whither, as you all know, he had retired in 1841. He reckoned that he had paid about £18 per acre for his land, and that his rental did not stand at more than twenty guineas. In a letter to Mr. Tait, which shows the poet in one of his pleasantest moods, he gave a lively description of his household and his family. " My establishment is illustrious for a St. Bernard dog, and a Welsh pony, the observed of all observers, which, in its green old age of twenty years, draws a small gig, both untaxed. I also run my only Sheffield carriage, the wheelbarrow, besides a pony cart ; and I have set up a grindstone. Conceive of me, then, possessed of a mare, gig and harness, which with repairs cost altogether £8. 10s. 0d. ; a dog almost as big as the mare and much wiser than his master; a pony cart, a wheelbarrow, and a grindstone—and turn up your nose if you like !"

LEIGHTON : One sometimes thinks of Elliott as having retired rather early, since he was only twenty years in business in Sheffield. But that is because one forgets he was forty years of age when he came here.

JOHNSON : That was a very sad story that appeared some time ago about the death of one of his sons.

LEONARD : Yes, that was his second son, Benjamin Gartside, of whom, in the letter I have before quoted from, Elliott wrote : " My son Benjamin, unwarned by his father's losses, is carrying on a steel trade in Sheffield in my old premises, where (as he thinks, poor fellow ! for he is a great hoper) he has some prospect ; in any other country he would already have made an independency. He endures privations such as no man of his pretensions ought to endure anywhere, and such as no man will here endure if free-trade be obtained before all is lost. He is a fine young man, upwards of six feet high, of superior abilities and the highest moral worth— but, alas ! not unindebted to his grandmother !"

EVERARD : That last reference is to a nervous temperament and " body-consuming sensibilities" which Elliott himself always said he derived from his mother, whose life was " a continuous disease."

LEIGHTON : Do you remember the particulars of Benjamin Elliott's death ?

LEONARD : It occurred in December, 1867. Eleven years previously, on the death of his aunt Gartside, who left him her property, he gave up business and went to live in her house at Shiregreen—as charming a country retreat as could be desired. But it would seem his solitary life at the steel warehouse, where he had lived entirely by himself, had engendered in him misanthropic habits which he could not shake off—possibly he had no disposition to try. The garden was entirely neglected. Little by little every vestage of glass disappeared from the windows, the shutters were kept constantly closed, and Mr. Elliott lived in a small kitchen at the back, his only companion being a dog. His milk and other necessaries were handed in to him at the door, which he opened no further than to admit them. On two mornings in the winter of the year I have named, the door never opened for the reception of the milk, and on the night of the second the place was forced open, and there the recluse was found, stark and stiff, under the sinkstone, dressed only partially in trousers and shirt, his boots unlaced and without stockings. The room was covered in all directions with papers and memoranda. His seat had been a cast iron chair, his bed a sofa. An old printing press, some old arms, crockery, tools and other articles were strewn around in admired confusion, while on the mantelpiece was a memorandum, " That the Greeks were an intellectual but not a polite nation." Near the couch was a copy of Mrs. Shelley's " Frankenstein," so worn as to lead to the supposition that its gloomy fancies had been congenial to him. The other part of the house, with its books, its furniture and its paintings, was in good order and condition. It is said that Benjamin Elliott bore a strong resemblance to his celebrated father, and he had the reputation among his friends of being a man of superior attainments and some cultivation. Formerly he had been a contributor of both prose and poetry to a serial publication. An old friend who visited him a few months before his death, and who excited intense amazement among the neighbours by obtaining, after some delay, admission to the house, wrote : " If I had seen poor Ben in a forest I should have taken him to be a wild man—his hair and beard I should say had not come in contact with comb and scissors for years ; his apparel was a pair of very shabby trousers, destitute of buttons and fastened with twine, and a coloured woollen shirt. He wore no coat or waistcoat. I stayed with him a little over an hour, and was much surprised at his cheerful and jocular conversation. He told me many anecdotes of his father, such as how he thrashed a certain reverend gentleman who insulted him in his office in Gibraltar street, &c. I asked him how he passed his time ? He replied, chiefly in meditation, as his eyes were so bad he could not comfortably either read or write for long together. I told him I thought he was doing very wrong, both to himself and others, to shut himself from society in the way he did. He replied he was quite happy and comfortable, and he wished people to let him alone." I should add that he was sometimes heard humming cheerful airs or singing " Auld Lang Syne," and that he had not altogether lost interest in the affairs of the outer world, since he was a regular reader of newspapers, and he had journeyed to Sheffield at the county election of 1865 to vote for Milton and Beaumont.

LEIGHTON : The old Lancasterian school—before that a riding school, as its rough interior will enable you readily to believe—has broken out into shops since the new schools were built in Bowling green street. Some seventy or eighty years ago, or so, that building and the " Water-house" at the bottom of Allen lane, where the Burkinshaws were accustomed to preside over the sale of water by the bucketful, were the extremity of the town in this direction. On the premises last mentioned, the wooden water pipes, which may occasionally be seen when the Company is making repairs, were bored by hand. Some of them were taken up from Broad lane only a short time ago.

JOHNSON : That property was sold by the Duke of Norfolk to Mr. Matthewman and the original proprietors of the Water Company, and it was in their possession in 1741. It was afterwards sold to Lawyer Hoyle, and then to its present occupier, Mr. Laycock.

LEONARD : We have been traversing Westbar and the streets which run down the hill to the left, and have necessarily had to leave, for the time being, the district on the right, which includes Spring street and other places productive of much old-world gossip. Suppose, therefore, we now turn back to that ?

WRAGG : A prominent firm in Spring street was that of the Baileys. The late Mr. Samuel Bailey's father, Mr. Joseph Bailey, carried on business at the top of Workhouse lane, now the Surrey Vaults.

LEONARD : Suppose we go further back still—to the time of Mr. Samuel Bailey's grandfather—Matthias Bailey, who married Elizabeth Wood, at Ecclesfield, on Christmas day, 1733, and who, for many years afterwards lived at Masbro', and was employed in some responsible capacity in the works of the Messrs. Walker of that town. "They were" it has been written "plain, honest, hardworking people; their lasses went out to service, and the lad Joseph was put apprentice to a scissor-smith. When he had served his time he commenced business in Sands pavours, in Bow street, afterwards removed to the premises in Workhouse lane, and finally built the works in Spring street, the firm being then Bailey, Eadon and Bailey, factors and merchants." Joseph Bailey married Mary, the daughter of old John Eadon, of the Free Writing School, and Samuel Bailey was their youngest child. The Eadon in the firm was John, the elder son of the same John Eadon, and was consequently Joseph Bailey's brother-in-law.

WRAGG : The Spring street premises of the Baileys were at the corner of Love street. Spring street, once called Brick lane (1736), took its name from a well in Bailey's yard, and people used to fetch the water to boil greens, &c., as there was believed to be none like it. From little to more Joseph Bailey increased in wealth, built Burn Greave, and in the year 1801 was Master Cutler. He was one of the first merchants in Sheffield who traded with America. By thrift, economy, and industry, he amassed a fortune, which, with good using, has enabled his youngest son to leave £100,000 to his native town. It is not necessary to dwell on that son's achievements as a philosophical writer.

LEIGHTON : Nor on his poetic effusions !

EVERARD : How ? Samuel Bailey a poet ?

LEONARD : There is very good reason for believing that he was the author of "Maro," an anonymous poem published by Longmans, in 1845. It is a satire in verse, for it can hardly be called a poem. It has none of the imagination of poetry, as you may well suppose.

WRAGG : Samuel Bailey ought to have been the first parliamentary representative of Sheffield. I once asked a table blade forger, who was perhaps the most intelligent man in the trade, how he could account for Mr. Bailey having only 812 votes, instead of being, as he ought to have been, at the head of the poll, or close behind the late Thos. Asline Ward, with the distant candidates nowhere. He replied that he believed the circumstance of Mr. Bailey's having been a factor prejudiced the townsfolks' minds against him.

LEONARD: How could that be?

WRAGG: There had been a system, which was then just about dying out, of factors forcing stuff, that is to say goods, which they had themselves taken in exchange from manufacturers instead of payment in money. It was called "stuffing," or "taking up," and related chiefly to drapery and tea. The Baileys had, rightly or wrongly, the reputation of carrying the obnoxious system to a great extent.

LEIGHTON: The evil of the plan was the severity and injustice with which it pressed on the workmen. It was a system of "passing on" from one to another, and the people who could not "pass it on" any further were the victims.

JOHNSON: I see. The customers passed goods on to the factors, the factors to the manufacturers, and the manufacturers to the workmen.

WRAGG: Quite so.

LEONARD: The late Mr. John Holland has recorded, in one of his numerous anonymous papers, that the practice existed at Beilby and Proctor's, as well as at other firms. "Taking up," he explained, was obtaining on credit, with the employer's order, various articles of food, especially cheese and tea, and every description of clothing. This "stuffing" was not only compulsory, but the prices charged were generally exorbitant; of course they were paid for by a "setting-up," or weekly instalments, or stoppages on the cash side of the wages' book. This was convenient to the employer as a mode of barter between him and the merchant with whom he dealt, and both made an unfair profit by it, and it tethered the workman by a perpetual debt.

WRAGG: In those days merchants, or rather factors, for that was their name then, had signs on their premises stating that they held licences to sell tea or spirits. The last signs in the town were those of Hoult, Rowbotham, Wingfield and Wade, (it was over the archway), and on the premises of Mr. Lockwood, in Arundel street; and these were kept up long after the practice had fallen into abeyance. The firm of Harwood and Thomas, whose premises were in George street, now

L

the Sheffield Banking Co., had a room properly fitted up with shelves and counter like a regular draper's shop.

TWISS : I am sure nothing disreputable could be affirmed either of that firm, or of Hoult, Rowbotham and Co.

LEONARD : There were, I have been told, special circumstances connected with Harwood and Thomas's business—for instance, that Mr. Lewis Thomas, who was for many years a member of Queen street Church, was brought up as a draper. It is true that they had a large room (corresponding, I believe, in size with the principal business room of the Bank before it was enlarged—it used to be called the Old Coffee House) fitted up as a draper's shop.

WRAGG : My father has taken tea in this way at twelve shillings per pound.

LEONARD : No doubt there would be unscrupulous firms then as ever, and I do not defend the system, for it was open to the abuses we still see in districts where "truck" persists in surviving. It was well that it should be stopped, but it is only fair to show that something, as I heard from a friend a few days ago, can be said in defence, and that some of the houses were honourable enough to act fairly. My informant said, " The house in which I was an apprentice was in the country trade, as distinguished from the foreign merchants, and had a good share of the Sheffield trade with Belfast. To promote it they frequently had one or more hogsheads of hams or boxes of linen. We also kept black and green tea. All these were sold at fair prices, with very little pressure, if any, on the cutlers to buy them."

LEIGHTON : Bad as it was there is more to be said for this system than for the " swag-shops," whose operation was irredeemably evil. These were simply establishments that preyed on the misfortunes of others, their chief victims being " little mesters" in difficulties. When short of ready money, and without any immediate market for their goods, they sold them to the swag-shops at, of course, a large per centage of loss. But what was worse than this, unscrupulous factors' buyers or " devils," would make excuses to reject goods they had ordered when brought in, with the deliberate purpose of forcing the makers to the swag-shops, and of buying them thence themselves at a lower price.

EVERARD : The " stuffing" system was an abominable one, and it was carried out with a great amount of fraud and extortion ; but it may be said that commercial intercourse was not then out of swaddling clothes. The system was to some extent a natural result of the infancy of trade, and was an artificial attempt to overcome the difficulties of circulating goods. In these days it has been long superannuated.

JOHNSON : Our present complicated and wonderful trading system was not made in a day. It is going further back than the "stuffing" system, but let me read you this description of the infancy of the Sheffield trade :—" Formerly the manufacturers had no trade connections, but depended entirely upon persons coming to the town to purchase the articles manufactured. These traders were called ' chaps or chapmen,' and were mostly Scotch or Irish, with some English. Their chief resort was Tommy Rose's, The Bird-in-hand, Church lane. The house stood where the Cutlers' Hall in part now stands. They generally had with them two, three, or more packhorses for the conveyance of the goods purchased. When a ' chap' arrived, the ostler went round to each of the manufacturers to inform him of the fact, and each gave him a penny for his information and trouble. An old man said, ' Oive been raand wi' him mony a toime, when oi war a lad, aboon 70 year sin.' Sometimes there were two, three, or four ' chaps' in the house at one time, and each had a separate room for business. The cutlers waited until all was ready and then went upstairs ' i' their kales.' If they bargained they left the goods and took the money home with them. The house was sometimes quite crowded. There were other houses in the town which travellers or ' chaps' frequented upon the same business, but none was as popular as Tommy Rose's. This was a very precarious way of doing business. As the makers had the materials to find, as well as the labour, it put them to great inconvenience and caused many families to suffer great privations during the time they had the goods in hand. To remove this difficulty the Cutlers' Company frequently advanced money on goods deposited with them without any interest being charged. This was always thankfully accepted until the goods could find a market. In 1768, the Town Trustees let out £200 to twenty scissor-smiths, upon bond in small sums. In 1741, Sir Fras. Sitwell bequeathed £400 to the Cutlers' Company, to be let out in sums not exceeding £5 to any necessitous member or other inhabitant. It is remarkable there is no account of this in the Company's books, although there are persons now living who can remember their fathers having received money from this source. These benevolences assisted the trade a great deal, for if a person had a stock of goods he could not dispose of, he could take them to the Cutlers' Hall and deposit them there until he found a market. Tommy Rose's being next the Cutlers' Hall, where the 'chaps' usually put up, the goods were easily removed if wanted.

"In the year 1710, a person of the name of Wright introduced the first stage waggon. Before that all public travelling was equestrian, and the conveyance of all bulk and weight was effected by carriage as distinguished from draught. The burden was fitted to the animal's back—which not unfrequently was ill-fitted to bear it—and shambling along cross roads, fording rivers, and climbing steeps, the jaded brute day by day pursued his wearied route. In those days a busy street at dawn would present an appearance only now to be seen in Cairo, or some other Eastern city, when a caravan is preparing to start on its journey—only here, horses or mules, instead of camels or asses, were the beasts. Often a train of not fewer than fifty in number were being laden—the majority with the heavy produce of the manufactories, others with market stock, live and dead—grain and poultry, and vegetables, and even pigs. At last when all was ready, the bells tinkled, and human beings poured forth from the inn. These consisted of travellers and their friends, and merchants who, either accompanying their wares or on some other business, were journeying to the capital. Perched on high, amidst boxes and bundles, were children and women, old men and maidens, leaving amidst the tears of their acquaintance; whilst the more active of the men were either starting on foot, or more easily bestriding a beast which had some appearance of saddle and pillion on its back. The orders for march being given, onward they moved through the town, into the country, over roads on which a track was paved for the especial use of the pack-horse train; but lanes also had to be traversed, in which holes constantly occurred, producing violent shocks. Across swamps, where the sagacity of the animals had to be trusted, across swollen rivers where the women and the live stock were alike alarmed, the cavalcade at last reached its longed-for halting place for the night. Until 1747, or thereabouts, there was no travelling from hence to sell goods or solicit orders."

WRAGG : But we are wandering away from Spring street. It runs through what was once "Norris' field"—so called from the owner, Mr. Norris, who lived, as has been said, in Westbar. Old Mr. Oakes, who has been mentioned as still living, and keeping a tobacconists' shop in Westbar, was formerly a whitesmith, in Spring street, as was his father before him. Their shop was under Hirst's school, and from thence he can remember to have seen right across Norris' field and Colson crofts—then really fields, with a footpath through them—to the river, over which he could see persons crossing by a wooden bridge into the Bridgehouses, before the old iron bridge was erected. I have mentioned Hirst's school. It was opposite the bottom of Hicks lane, and was kept by the late Mr. Thomas Hirst, surveyor, who died in Fargate, and by his father. Between Hicks lane and Workhouse lane was Mr. Benjamin Vickers, who was Master Cutler in 1799. He was uncle to the then Mr. Vickers of Mill Sands, and grand-uncle to the late (1872-3) Master Cutler, Mr. T. E. Vickers.

LEIGHTON : The " Blue Pig," in Spring street, formerly the Boar, is an old public-house. It was kept many years ago by Mr. John Hawke, whom Mather attacked. Subsequently it was occupied by Mr. Webster and Mr. John Ellis.

LEONARD: It has been stated that at one time the late James Dixon, of Page Hall, lived in Spring street, next door to the Ball Inn, in a house the rent of which was £9 per annum. That was before he went into partnership with Mr. Smith—Smith and Dixon the firm was at first.

WRAGG : Spring street was the birthplace of a man whose history is a curious illustration of the vicissitudes of families—I mean the late Mr. William Stratford. He was born on the property of the Mr. Hirst already mentioned, in what is now the back part of the Bird-in-the-Hand beerhouse. He was the nineteenth in descent from John Stratford of the Parliament of Edward II., 1320, and the head of the pedigree ; and by a subsequent marriage of John Stratford, who died in 1533, with a lineal descendant of William de Traci, one of the four knights who murdered Thomas A'Becket, the late William Stratford was descended both from the Dukes of Normandy and the ancient Saxon Kings of England.

TWISS : How is that ?

WRAGG : William de Traci was a descendant of Ethelred the Unready, and of Queen Emma, daughter of the third Duke of Normandy, and by a series of strange events, the William Stratford in whom we are interested came to be the male representative of all the other Stratfords. The family decline began with Walter Stratford, of Farm Cote, Gloucester, William Stratford's great grandfather. There have been several causes assigned for his becoming reduced—as that he re-built the family mansion in a style too costly for his means, considering the largeness of his family, for by his first wife he had three children, and by the second ten. Only three of the thirteen children married, and of these the ninth and youngest son alone, George Stratford, continued the family line.

EVERARD : William Stratford's grandfather ?

WRAGG: Yes. Leaving the neighbourhood of his birth when his father got into straitened circumstances, he sold the estate, and, after living at various places, settled in Henley-in-Arden, where he had a corn-mill. But nothing prospered with him. He had two sons, Thomas and John, both of whom were apprenticed to the well-known Matthew Boulton, of the Soho, Birmingham. John served his legal apprenticeship, and was at the Soho when the celebrated James Watt joined Boulton, and it is said that John Stratford was the only person who could understand Watt's curious pronunciation of English. Boulton and Watt sent him to the Gregory Mine, Ashover, with one of their engines, to drain a lead mine on the estate of the late celebrated Sir Joseph Banks. This was in 1783, and after remaining at Ashover until 1800, he removed to London, and became the engineer to the New River Company.

LEONARD : But how about Spring street ?

WRAGG : I now come to that in the person of Thomas Stratford, the other apprentice of Boulton's, and with him our local interest in the family begins. Before his term of apprenticeship had expired he enlisted—not from dissipation, but because he was a man of lofty spirit and keen sensibilities. Mr. Boulton obtained his discharge, but he enlisted again in the artillery, and was discharged on the peace that resulted in the declaration of American Independence. He married a Birmingham woman, named Kelsey, and came to live in Sheffield—in Spring street, as already stated. From what I have heard, he and his wife would seem to have been the most singularly matched couple in the town. He was a well-formed man, 5 feet 10 inches, with red hair, and quite a gentleman in appearance, whilst his wife was a little, stumpy, thick-set woman, the darkest complexion ever seen not actually black, yet all their children were light complexioned. Mrs. Stratford, however, was very kind-hearted and amiable. Her husband worked for the firm of Barber and Genn, fender manufacturers, Spring street, and did jobs at home for Mr. George Oates, of the Wicker, and also for Mr. Linley, of Spring street, in ornamenting scissors, now done by grinders at the wheel. He was one of the first to join the Sheffield

Volunteers, at their original formation, and he was one of those who found their own clothes. Mr. Linley, for whom he worked at home, was Master Cutler in 1797. On the feast-day he remarked that Mr. Linley had not invited him to the feast. His wife replied, "Thee works for Mr. Linley, and as such thee't a working man." He sharply replied, "I'm as good as any man who will be there." His wife was accustomed to remark to her children that their father looked what he ought to be—a gentleman, and she seems to have cherished the hope that the family would be restored to its former position.

EVERARD : I should imagine that his family pride would keep him somewhat aloof from his fellow-workmen.

WRAGG : It did, and his respectable manner of conducting himself seems to have been specially offensive to some of them. In a very depressed state of trade, when Barber and Genn gave numbers of people warning, Thomas Stratford was amongst them. This discharge from employment sorely pinched him, and as a last resort, he undertook the menial work of assisting masons. Not being accustomed to the labour, and getting wet, he was seized with rheumatic fever, and never perfectly recovered. He died in 1808, in the 48th year of his age, and was buried in the Parish Churchyard, near to the Girls' Charity School.

EVERARD : It is a very sad history.

WRAGG : Now for the late William Stratford. He was the eldest son of this Thomas Stratford, and was brought up as a silver-smith. He served his time as a candlestick hand, but afterwards he was a spinner. He had a brother, Thomas, who, although he had lost a leg, was the leader of all kinds of rough play. He died a young man. Their sister married Mr. B. Hinchliffe, whose son, Mr. T. O. Hinchliffe, is now in Garden street. William Stratford married a daughter of William Gray, and had a son and a daughter; the son a silver-smith in New Church street ; the daughter married Frederick Withy Horsfield, the son of an apprentice of the late Robert Waterhouse's father, and the nephew of the historian of Lewes. The Horsfield family, which has been several times mentioned, is an old one. It was seated at Halifax, and had a grant of arms. I believe the Waterhouse family sprang from a person in Lincolnshire, and removed to Halifax. The present representative of the family is Major Waterhouse, of Well head, Halifax, the Tory M.P. for Pontefract. William Stratford was established in Bramall lane, but towards the end of his life he went to live at Mosborough. He died on the 18th of April, 1859, aged 72, and was interred at Eckington.

LEIGHTON: It is a little difficult to follow your description of the descent. One almost needs a genealogical table.

LEONARD: Beyond Bower spring, the footpath—Cottonmill walk—was the continuation of Spring street. It ran in the direction now taken by Russell street, across "Long croft," as the open space was called in 1771, towards Green lane. Of course it took its name from the cotton mill of Mr. Middleton. An open stream ran from the top of Cornish street, in front of Green lane, and emptied itself in the Don, below where Green lane works now stand. On the other side of the stream were cottage gardens. Middleton's silk mill—built in 1758, burnt down in 1792, and the cotton mill, re-erected on the same site only in turn to be burnt down in 1810, and again built only to become the Poor-house in 1829—stood alone in its glory, its nearest neighbour being Kelham Wheel, still there, as it had been at least as long before as in 1674, on the now covered-in "Goit." Across the river was the suburb of Bridgehouses, and all around was verdure. Those were the days when "The old cherry tree," whose name is now perpetuated only by the public-house and the yard where it stood, was still young, and when Allen "lane" and the Bowling green marked the extremity of the inhabited region of Gibraltar. Beyond, the road ran between fields—"Moorfields"—and on to the distant rural haunts of Philadelphia and Upperthorpe. There was Lawyer Hoyle's house up on the left; and the little barber's shop, just before you come to Roscoe place, near the junction of the Infirmary and Penistone roads, was alone in its glory until 1806, when Mr. Shaw built the stove-grate works just named, and with his partner, Mr. Jobson, laid the foundations of that trade which has obtained for Sheffield the manufacture of stoves and fenders previously claimed by Edinburgh and London. Two personal notes may be made as to Mr. Shaw and Mr. Jobson. The former was a Baptist, and he not only held service in his works on Sundays, but established a Sunday-school as well. Mr. Jobson was the last person in Sheffield who retained the old-fashioned *queue*, and a great scandal was occasioned by some officers cutting it off in St. Philip's Church, one Sunday.

JOHNSON: In Green lane, in the days we are speaking of, and even much later, the works had not become sufficiently numerous to interfere with bathing in the river. The Cleekham Inn and a grinding wheel occupied part of Messrs. Dixon's works at Cornish place, while Watery street was a rural lane with a stream running down it. Dr. Buchan, usually spoken of as living in the Hartshead, is said to have lodged at one time in a house at the bottom of Ball street.

LEIGHTON : We have had so long a talk to-night that we can hardly now enter upon the enticing suburban topics of which we are on the verge. Let us defer them.

CHAPTER VII.

OLD SHEFFIELD GARDENS.

Present—Messrs. TWISS, LEIGHTON, EVERARD, WRAGG, LEONARD and JOHNSON.

Period—A.D. 1873.

WE were all sitting, one charming and warm evening, in the cosy summer-house of our friend Twiss. It was not in the garden attached to his residence, for he dwelt in the recesses of a dingy town, with a melancholy grave-yard for his outlook. But he was old-fashioned enough and wise enough to stick to the traditional Hallamshire custom of keeping a small garden-plot out in the suburbs, to which he could retire in the intervals from business, in which he could delight his horticultural soul, and, above all, which gave him an object for a walk after the toils of the day. It was a treat to see him in the fading twilight of a summer night, wending his way back to his sooty brick dwelling, laden with rural spoils, with which to enliven it—a huge "posy" of lupines and sweet-williams, and pinks, of cabbage-roses and pansies, and other good old English flowers, now despised and rejected, in obedience to the "bedding out" mania, for masses of scarlet geraniums and yellow calceolarias. Nor was he above bearing through the crowded streets products of even a humbler kind—big-headed cauliflowers or juicy lettuces, or large-hearted cabbages—or some other palatable form of the much-embracing genus "greens." Of course, being in the country—so to speak, though we were by no means out of the reach or out of sight of the smoke—our talk was of country things. One told how his grandfather, a great garden-smith, used to delight to get away from his shop to his little plot down Bramall lane way—a walk among the hedges and through pleasant shady lanes; and another remembered being sent, in 1825, with a message to Montgomery, who had retired from his sanctum upstairs in the dingy Hartshead—over the coal place, and with depressing outlook on to brick walls and dilapidated roofs—to refresh himself for a time among the polyanthuses and daffodils of his garden, between Glossop road and Leavygreave. That is where Hounsfield road is now, for most of the space from Glossop road to Brook hill, belonging to the Water Company, was divided into these little plots.

The town in those days was literally surrounded with groups of neatly-partitioned gardens. The late Mr. Edward Baines (M.P. for Leeds from 1834 to 1841) was accustomed to remark that the multitude of small, nicely-kept gardens in its suburbs was a characteristic of Sheffield, in which it was in advance of any other large town he knew. Look which way you would, or go in what direction you would, there they were. Besides the celebrated gardens in the neighbourhood of Hanover street, there were similar gardens higher up Broomspring lane and Wilkinson street, and on the site of the Baptist Church on Glossop road, and up to Northumberland road and opposite Mushroom hall to Westbourne, Mr. Cadman's house, near which are a few remaining. From Glossop road the Water Company's land extended into Brook hill, and the gardens on this piece were always considered some of the best in the town. Near to and behind the late Ald. Saunders' house in Brook hill, were gardens, behind which were others, reaching down by Brightmore street, Bellefield street, Portmahon, Bedford street, and Waterloo houses (commenced building by the father of James Levick, the dahlia grower, and finished by his mother), to the river Don. Then on the opposite side of the river, the site of Neepsend brewery, and right up to the wood and Woodside lane; also on the opposite side of Woodside lane, under Pye bank, to the mouth of the railway tunnel. Harvest lane, and Green lane to Colson crofts were occupied in a similar way; and another plot of small gardens is now the site of the old Midland Station in the Wicker. These, as originally intended, were to have been the basin of the Sheffield canal. On the opposite side of the road, between Twelve o'Clock Wheel, or the Albion Ironworks, and the Norfolk bridge, was another lot of gardens, destroyed about 25 years ago. There were small gardens in the Park, part of which is St. John's churchyard. There were some others at Skye edge, down to Duke street, or the Intake road. At the end of Clough lane, down to the river Sheaf (Sheaf gardens), were gardens considered second to none in the neighbourhood, some containing good double houses, not like those in Club gardens, Sharrow lane. From these were others extending across Suffolk road, down to Harmer lane. There were also the gardens just destroyed at the end of Bramall lane, opposite Sheaf House, on the path to Highfield; and about 25 years ago was destroyed a plot of gardens that had extended from the top of Young street to Broomhall street. There were some others that have disappeared, to make room for buildings about the General Cemetery and Broomhall Mill.

"When all the above gardens were in existence," said Mr. WRAGG, "I believe one out of every three working men had a garden, which he cultivated more for pleasure than profit. This was far better than his present gambling propensities; but further, there were not a few instances in which the working man's garden assisted him to clothe his family, or to pay off debts, unavoidably contracted, by the sale of the fruit from his pear or apple trees. Now, there are no such places for a working man to resort to in his spare time, except for those who are members of some Land Society outside the town. It is said he may resort to the Library, or peruse his book at home; that he can amuse himself by holding communication with the great men of past ages; but all such talk is a delusion. Bodily toil and mental discipline will not go hand in hand, or blend. The garden plots remaining are, alas, but few; they may be almost counted on the fingers of one hand, some under the wood at Hillfoot, and some in Neepsend lane to the river; the Water Company's piece, Hanging bank, and in the flat below the site of the old dams, commonly called Upper and Lower Canada; some around Younge's Silver Rolling Mill; some, comparatively speaking recently made, between Hyde Park and the Manor. There are a few left in Ecclesall road. In Sharrow lane are the Club gardens, that have always been remarkable for the number of houses occupied by the tenants. Fenton Ville gardens and South View gardens, extending down into the Abbeydale road, are noted for the number of their florists,

the most successful of whom is William Allsebrook, famous
for rearing new kinds of polyanthuses. I am sorry to say I
believe all these gardens will soon be like the others mentioned—demolished."

LEONARD : Yes, they are fast being engulphed by the
omnivorous builders ; and the robberies to which they are
exposed are a great discouragement to the enthusiastic ama-
teurs who compete at pink shows, or dahlia contests, or who
strive to raise gigantic gooseberries, to be weighed at Florists'
Inns, and celebrated with a supper. Let us hope that this
annihilation of garden allotments does not indicate that the
healthy delight in floriculture that has always been a characteristic of Hallamshire is dying out. You may still see the
grinder returning from a pop visit to his little country delight,
laden with early spring rhubarb, or with roots of celery,
according to the season of the year ; and freehold building
societies have altered life so much as to give working men an
opportunity of having their homes standing in their own gardens, which is not only healthier but handier.

A member of our company mentioned the splendid bed of
ranunculuses which a resident in one of the houses still
standing opposite the top of Broomhall street, used to show,
and reminded us of the celebrated garden which the Staniforths, father and son, the eminent surgeons in Castle street,
had in the Grimesthorpe road, the present Gardeners' Arms
being their garden house. Mr. Wragg recalled that kind,
genial old man, Edward Middleton, baker, who kept the
Barleycorn Tavern, in Coalpit lane—the most obliging of
neighbours among amateur gardeners. The vicinity of
Hanover street used to be marked out like a chess board by
these gardens, and Middleton had one, near the corner of
Broomspring lane and Hanover street. The top part of it
forms now part of Hanover street, and the bottom extended
behind the houses of Mr. Owen, the draper, which face to
Broomspring lane. Afterwards, he showed his skill in one of
those previously spoken of, on Glossop road—where Charles
Thompson's cab premises are now, then belonging to the
Water Company—having gone there by reason of his neighbour, John Burton, the Quaker, buying a garden for him.
Mr. Wragg believed that the last possessor of Middleton's
garden, near Mr. Owen's houses, was the late Mr. Bennett,
grocer, Church street, elder brother of the present Mr.
Bennett, who succeeded him in his business. Joshua Wilkinson had the next garden above, and he sold it to William

Melluish, the last survivor among the many South Devon Militiamen who settled in Sheffield after the disbanding of the regiment. The garden above was Mr. Swift's, the father of Mr. G. E. Swift, in the steel trade, in Blonk street. At the front of Spring lane was Samuel Padley's (a Quaker), the father of Mr. Padley, of the firm of Padley, Parkin, & Co., silversmiths, in Watson's walk. The late Mr. Bramhall, one of the managers of Messrs. Rodgers and Sons, and Mr. Staniforth, grocer, of Broad lane, had gardens hereabouts. Mr. Roger Brown was the last who had Mr. Staniforth's. Just below, and behind Josh. Ingle's house, an old woman of the name of Savage had a garden, and did all the gardening herself. The late Mr. B. Hinchcliffe had a garden in this piece, and there is a tradition that the late Mr. John Holland occupied a garden here, but his nearest friends are incredulous about it. The story is that an old man, a relative, did the gardening for him, in which case it may possibly have been his uncle Amos. A file cutter, afterwards a silver stamper, named William Hague, had the first garden opposite old Mrs. Savage's. Being a frugal man he saved money, by means of which he built the houses at the bottom of Broomspring lane, and opened a grocer's shop at the corner. The last person who had Mr. Hague's garden was Mr. Worth, the joiner and builder. Mr. Turner, the Sheriff's officer in Campo lane, had also a garden; so had Mr. Taylor, of the Commercial Inn, Haymarket, now destroyed by the making of the new street into Norfolk street; and Mr. Theaker just by, for many years the only coffee-house keeper in the town, had two up to the time of their destruction.

James Levick, the ivory merchant, of Pinstone street, was a well-known dahlia grower. He raised from seed a dahlia which was named "Levick's Incomparable," the beauty of which was that the petals were tipped with white in so peculiar a manner that many persons supposed they were subjected to some chemical process. But this peculiarity was not at all of regular occurrence; and many growers, disappointed by obtaining flowers without the white tips, poured out their woes in the "Floricultural Cabinet," then published by Mr. Ridge, in King street, and conducted by Mr. Harrison, Lord Wharncliffe's gardener. They besought Mr. Levick to give them details of cultivation, and in reply, he could only say that the flowering was very eccentric, sometimes he produced the flowers with tips and sometimes without; and Mr. Paxton, having one year obtained most beautifully tipped blooms, set a large quantity the next year in most conspicuous places, and had not a single bloom tipped. The secret seemed to be to check a too luxuriant growth of the plant. Mr. Levick also produced a handsome crimson dahlia—Commander-in-Chief—which was honoured with a coloured engraving in the work named. Mr. Thomas Tyson, who kept the "Fountain,' in Coalpit lane, was a distinguished florist, and a man evidently much respected by his brethren, for "his funeral was attended by the florists of the town, who strewed his coffin with a profusion of most beautiful flowers."

Club Gardens, as has been said, were remarkable for the number of the houses occupied by the tenants. In one house resided the late Mr. Paul Smith, a well-to-do-man, said to have been worth six or eight thousand pounds ; but he was induced to enter into partnership with some firm which shortly afterwards failed. The creditors seized all the property of Mr. Smith to pay the debts of the firm, so he became a poor man, and died a recipient of the Iron and Hardware Pensions. Another resident in these gardens was the late Mr. Charles Unwin, of Westbar, the broker. Previously he had a garden in Brook hill, in the piece behind Mr. Brightmore's house. After the death of Mr. Thomas Nowill, Mr. Unwin bought his garden, and there he resided at the time of his disastrous fire, in which some thousands of pounds worth of his property and stock-in-trade was destroyed. It gave such a shock to his nervous system that soon after he died, about 16 or 18 years ago. Mr. Unwin was a native of Anston, and originally was a labouring man ; but he turned sawyer, and was a very hard worker. Another native of Anston was the late Mr. Henry Broomhead, the solicitor, whose father was a tanner.

Some of the best gardens in the neighbourhood were the Sheaf Gardens. About thirty years ago the late Mr. William Stratford had a garden that was remarkable for the neat manner in which it was kept by Mr. Stratford himself; and his tulip bed was the admiration of all beholders.

Hanging Bank Gardens, when in existence, were notable for the number of those tenants who exhibited gooseberries at shows (" berry showers",), the chief of whom, and the most successful, was the late Robert Green. He resided in one of the houses, probably built by himself or a former tenant, since it is not the work of a mason. He had another garden lower down, but one or two others intervened, and up a walk nearer where the stream of water ran from the Water Company's dams. From his success as an exhibitor of gooseberries, he obtained many copper kettles as prizes. When the time of exhibiting was about to take place, his garden had to be watched from the Saturday night to Monday morning to prevent his trees being stripped. Green was a spring-knife cutler, and worked for the late Mr. B. Micklethwaite, whose workmen were very respectable, honourable, and upright. Amongst them there were none of the coarse jokes, indecent conversation, or unmeaning, empty, and profane jests, so common among workmen in the workshops of the present day. They talked when they had something to say, and years after, when one would casually meet another in the street it was always with kindness and respect, something like one gentleman meeting another.

About 40 years ago, in one of the gardens near what is now the top of Fawcett street, just before Bellefield house, was a whitewashed house, with sash windows, in which resided the late John Milner, who in his day was said to have been one of the best, if not the best spring-knife cutler in the trade, and notable for his great powers of debate. He was born in Spring street or the immediate vicinity, and in his youth or childhood was a companion of the late Mr. Wm. Stratford. He was the last survivor of his early associates. When John Milner left the house it was not afterwards occupied. It dwindled away—lads first broke the windows, and next it gradually disappeared.

In Watery lane was a very good house standing back in a garden. For some time it was unoccupied, and from being untenanted it got into a dilapidated condition. A few years ago, a portion of one of its walls fell on some children, and one of them was killed. The last occupier was a person of the name of Ross, who left the town and afterwards died. Ross was a man who was going to get every one his fortune. People who believed they or their ancestors had been deprived or dispossessed of property flocked to him in crowds. Somewhere in the vicinity Ross had a rival, a woman, who had two strings to her bow, for in addition to being a fortune-hunter she was a fortune-teller.

The market gardeners' grounds ranged, for the most part, from Neepsend and the Old Park Wood to Hall Carr. There was George Stubbing, whose garden, kept before him by Mr. Thornhill, who had a cook shop in the Hartshead, extended from Woodside lane to Old Park Wood, being bounded on the north by Cook Wood. Part of his garden in Harvest lane is now the depôt of the Board of Health, while the

southern part, including the site of his original house, was
taken for the Manchester Railway. Before beginning a garden on his own account, Mr. Stubbing had been in the service
of Dr. Webb, of whose garden in Harvest lane he had charge.
There was James Andrews, who had an orchard at Neepsend,
where the Neepsend Nursery now is; and the orchard in
Harvest lane of William Burgin, now displaced by the various
works in Mowbray street, was one of the finest sights in the
town in spring time. Who does not remember, too, that
other orchard on the slope below Burn Greave, which everybody would stop and admire even so late as 1855-60 ? There
were two other Burgins besides William, but he was not related to them. They were brothers, George and Jonathan.
The former was the last inhabitant of the Clay's house, in
Bridgehouses; the latter had a fruit shop in Bower spring.
From Pitsmoor Church to Burn Greave, and to where the
Railway crosses Tom Cross lane, market gardeners had
their grounds, and a pleasant walk it was through them,
for the Burngreave road and Rock street were not made then.
The orchard and grounds between these two roads, where
Catherine street now is, were occupied long ago by John
Pearson. His family were table-knife cutlers at Neepsend,
but he was fonder of gardening than cutlering. Afterwards
the land was in the hands of Mr. John Garnett for many
years. Then it got into Chancery and was in a lost-looking
state until it was built upon. Mr. Garnett removed to the
land between the Wicker Congregational Church and Carlisle
street, Gower street having been made across it near to where
what was his house still stands. Gardens of similar kind
extended to Hall Carr lane, where, not many years ago, gyp-
sies might sometimes be seen. On the other side of the town
was Mr. Hatfield's nursery, on the Glossop road, adjoining
Wesley College, which often attracted passers by its beauty.

From gardens and gardening we got to talk generally of
the changes that have taken place in what may be called the
nearer suburban surroundings of the town. The youngest
member of our friendly group could, we found, call to mind
surprising changes; as for the eldest, the wondrous trans-
mutations to which he could bear witness were endless.
Within a very small radius of the Parish Church—say Carver
street Chapel—he had walked in green fields, or traversed
woods whose sites are now occupied by whole colonies of
houses, and it was told how tradition affirmed that a resident
at the top of Coalpit lane had shown his children Judge

Wilkinson's stacks burning at Broomhall from the field on which Carver street Chapel now stands, then called "Cadman's-in-the-fields." That was in 1791 ; a more recent story was that in 1817, two ears of wheat were plucked in a field at Roscoe place, each seven inches long. One of them contained 69 and the other 70 corns. Our old friend's description of Broomhall Spring, which he remembered when he was about 10 years old—in 1791—was very interesting. "I very well remember," said he, "coming with my father through the wood called Broomhall Spring. It extended from about Wilkinson street to Broomhall Park. It was full of very fine oak trees, with very little underwood, and the turf was soft like that of a park. I remember very well seeing the trees and the grass, and the sunlight gleaming among them. Not long afterwards the wood was cut down. The Government was then wanting a great deal of oak timber for ship-building, and the trees in Broomhall Spring were sold for that purpose. The roots were dug up, and the land turned into the gardens of which we have been speaking." The inscription on the stone over the trough was still there up to 1836. It ran :— "Spring Garden Well. To the public use, by the Rev. James Wilkinson and Philip Gell, Esq. Freely take—freely communicate—thank God ;" its site is now enclosed in the garden of the house at the corner of Gell street and Conway street. "Sheffield Moor," continued our nonagenarian friend, "was a shocking road for coaches. There was quite a steep hill from the Horse Dyke to the Moor head, and the heavy coaches had something to do to get up it. Very often two extra horses were sent as far as Heeley bridge to bring the coach up Goose green to Highfield, and then up Sheffield moor. The footpaths were a great deal higher than the road, which did not run straight as it does now, but turned rather towards the right. There were few houses about. One, I remember, in Button lane, was occupied by Mr. Kirkby, a retired butcher, a very nice man, who wore a wig. He was the father of James Kirkby, the silver plater, and Samuel Kirkby, the penknife manufacturer. Samuel had a large business, and was fond of horses. One day he was riding a spirited horse when he was thrown at the bottom of Waingate and killed. Near Sheffield Moor, William Jessop, father of Thomas Jessop, had a steel furnace. Porter street was a pleasant field-road called Ladies' Walk. There were trees on one side of it, and you crossed the Porter by a foot bridge. That led into Bramall lane and forward across fields to Heeley. The London road in those days, after passing Heeley, ran close to Meersbrook house, and up Derbyshire lane to Bolehill, then through what is now Norton Park to Little Norton, forward to Greenhill Moor. All goods leaving Sheffield southwards went that way. The only road westwards was up Sharrow lane and so to Ecclesall, Bent's green, and Ringinglowe. There was no Chesterfield turnpike, nor Abbeydale road, nor Ecclesall new road, nor Glossop road." Mr. Twiss reminded us of the fact that it was in 1821 that the new road to Glossop was opened for carriages; and LEONARD read a description which had been written in connection with the house of old Seth Cadman, the comb maker, in Young street. "From it there was a really charming outlook. Between Young street and the Moor head on the one side, up far beyond Broomhall street in front, and towards Sharrow lane in the other direction, there was little to be seen but well-kept gardens and equally well-tilled fields. Close to Fitzwilliam street I have seen growing as fine a crop of wheat as ever gladdened the heart of a Yorkshire farmer; and at that time Broomhall street, or 'Black Lamb's lane,' as it was called, was considered rather a dangerous place to go along at night. Seth's garden was opposite to his house, and over the footpath hung two splendid pear trees. At that time, as now, the neighbourhood of Young street was called 'Little Sheffield,' and gardens and fields divided it from 'Big Sheffield.'" Mr. EVERARD told us how he remembered a clear space between the bottom of Red hill and West street, including what was then Mr. Carr's house, now the Hospital and Dispensary. Said he, "The intervening space was occupied by the brickyard, and by 'Marsh's field' (in which Mr. Marsh's cows pastured, the cottage and cow-house being situate in one corner), together with the site on which Messrs. Sanderson Brothers' works now stand. Mr. Marsh did not bear at all a good name amongst us youngsters, for he very strictly maintained his 'manorial rights,' and hotly pursued and inflicted summary punishment on any of the youthful trespassers who had the ill-luck to fall into his hands. And so it was that whether engaged in playing at football, cricket, or kite-flying, as soon as 'Old Marsh' made his appearance, we knew it was high time to be off. At that period there were no houses on either side of 'Portobello' (with one exception) from the 'Britannia' public-house, opposite Messrs. Newton Bros., Portobello Works, up to Victoria street; but all was open space, including gardens, the brick-field, and the 'Burial Ground,' now

St. George's Church and churchyard. The exception referred to was the two houses, yet standing, about half-way between Charlotte street and Regent street, with a flight of stone steps out of 'Portobello lane.' In one of these houses lived a venerable man named Dr. Cheney, one of the 'old school' as to dress and wig, and who was totally blind. In the other house resided Mr. Mellor, the ropemaker. The gardens at the back reached down to a cross walk, now Glossop road, near the Bee Hive. Between these gardens there was a broad walk to their full extent, which Mr. Mellor used as a rope walk, where he spun his twine and ropes. Subsequently, in the lower of these two houses, not the uppermost as I once thought, resided for several years the late Mr. Leader, proprietor of the *Sheffield Independent*. In the upper one (now Mr. Joseph Kirk's) Dr. Cheney spent the last years of his life. From a house just above Sir John Brown made his start in the successful career he has run, his father building a number of houses on Dr. Cheney's land and occupying one of them.

"I well remember the time when the house, now enlarged and occupied as the Bee Hive public-house, was built in the cross garden walk just mentioned, which terminated at the top of Broomhall street. It was erected by a shoemaker, named Thomas Rose. He was a little man, wore top boots, and kept a hive of bees in the garden beside the house. He got a license for the house and called it the Bee Hive. His pear tree on the front yet retains enough vitality to show yearly a few leaves. With the exception of the old houses with gardens and palisades at the top of West street, and the large house in Broomhall street, beside which until lately the rooks have built, there were, I believe, no houses (except some garden cottages) from Portobello down to Holy Green, and the top of Bright, Gaol, and Young streets. All the intervening space was occupied with fields and gardens. Hanover street was then a narrow country lane, with fields on each side ; and I have myself pursued and tried to kill a weasel very near the spot where Hanover Chapel now stands. The 'burial ground,' so called years before it was enclosed and used, is now St. George's churchyard. This was a general play and cricket ground ; and on a summer's evening many groups of men and boys might be seen engaged in the game and enjoying the fresh air and the healthful exercise."

Mr. WRAGG added to these remembrances by a reference to Black Lamb's lane, now Broomhall street. If, said he, a person stood at the corner of Fitzwilliam street, with the hotel behind him, he could see the back of South street chapel on Sheffield Moor. The only shop in the neighbourhood, was kept by Mr. Hardcastle in Holly street—he who died sexton of St. George's Church. Mr. Sidebottom opened the next at the corner of Convent walk—now the Post Office. The oldest house on Glossop road is that above Mr. Sharman's, at the corner of Gell street, now occupied by Mr. Ward. For many years, indeed until his death, it was the residence of an old gentleman, Mr. Thomas Broadhurst. In the old days, Black Lamb's lane was quite a country walk.

LEIGHTON reminded us that the house at the corner, where Broomhall street and Devonshire street intersect, noted for the solitary ash tree in which the rooks persisted in building for so many years, was the residence of William Fairbank, one of the surveyors who planned Glossop road. His brother, Josiah Fairbank, lived in what is now the West End Hotel, at the bottom of Northumberland road—a house in those days with a charming garden both before and behind.

With such reminiscences as these the quiet evening slipped on, and we sat in silence for some time, lazily watching the smoke as it curled upwards from our pipes in the still air, as mentally we dwelt in the past. LEONARD broke upon our reverie with one of his abrupt speeches. The worst of it is, said he, that with all this much boasted extension and growth, the town is losing so much of its old beauty. Ten minutes' walk or so in any direction from the Old Church would have brought us, thirty or forty years ago, into charming country lanes. What a distance we have to go now before we get rid of the smoky blackness! Even Wincobank is losing its freshness, and is invaded by dull rows of houses. Heeley is repulsive, and as for Attercliffe, or Brightside, or Grimesthorpe, ugh! And how our woods have gone. Without going so far back as Clay Wood (so called from the Bridgehouses family) or Bamforth Wood, there were Cook Wood, and the Old Park Wood, and Hallcarr Wood, where such delightful rambles were to be had—"how fallen, how changed." Bamforth Wood reached from Hillfoot almost to Owlerton. It belonged to Madame Bamforth, and there was a well in it, the water of which it was pretended would cure every disease. People used to fetch the water from miles and miles.

LEIGHTON: Attercliffe has long been on the road to (pictorial) ruin, yet within the time you mention, though degenerating from country into town, it was not without its rural features. So late as 1836 it was still matter for remark that "Sheffield and Attercliffe appeared not unlikely soon to shake hands." Within a few years of that time two or three otters had been caught in the Don there—one of them in that very year; and it was then written by one who has but lately departed from amongst us, "From Brightside lane we have a pleasing view of the village; the houses appearing as if intermingled with the intervening trees.   *   *   *

There is a bridge over the Don, from the wall of which we look upon a short reach of the river, as it flows along the tree-fringed lawn in front of Newhall, which is not perhaps surpassed for its quiet, simple character. Here was formerly a pleasant walk along the river side—not yet quite obliterated —on this path the villager was once accustomed to meet a local poetess—Barbara Hoole, at the period referred to an interesting young widow, but subsequently much better known in the literary world as Mrs. Hofland, having become the wife of the painter of that name. While a resident at Attercliffe she published, in 1804, a volume of poems of a pleasing character, containing allusions to various persons, circumstances, and scenes well-known in the neighbourhood."

LEONARD : I see Mr. Holland, in the same book, speaks of the Attercliffe Parsonage, then occupied by the Rev. J. Blackburn, as "snug as a finch's nest in the adjoining trees." The trees are a melancholy spectacle now, all smoke-begrimed and a caution to finches.

TWISS : Catching otters in the Don at Attercliffe is almost as curious a notion as baptising converts at Neepsend, opposite Cornish place, yet that was done about the same time. "On these occasions the boats have been filled with spectators, while others crowded the banks—the singing of hymns, a sermon, and immersing the neophytes in the water in such a spot, forming, in connection with the scenery about Neepsend, a spectacle of a striking character."

EVERARD : This was rendered still more "striking" on one such occasion by an incident that occurred. The Minister and the intended subjects of baptism had the accommodation of the sheds of the public baths, partly open to the stream, for the purpose of making suitable preparations. Besides the banks being well lined several boats were filled with spectators. Just when the officiating Minister and the persons to be baptised were gone down into the water, and he was in the very act of pronouncing the sacred formula,— "I baptise thee, &c.," the occupants of one of the boats were so eager to witness that part of the ceremony that they pressed to one side, and lo ! the boat was instantly capsized, and they were plunged over-head into the river. They were, however, soon rescued without any particular harm beyond a great fright and a thorough soaking. An old friend of mine who witnessed the transaction, and possessed a vein of dry humour, used to delight in puzzling his Baptist acquaintances with the following query :—" That as the persons in the boat were voluntarily attending a religious service, the nature of which they understood, and that just at the moment and in the hearing of the Minister's scriptural words of consecration, *they were certainly immersed ;* the question was,—whether they did not as really receive ' Christian Baptism' on that occasion as the others ?"

LEONARD : It was at an earlier period that Mr. Wesley used to bathe in the Don at Walk Mill.

JOHNSON : William White, in his "Directory of Sheffield, 1833," has the following :—" Though the rivers of Sheffield afford ample means for the establishment of a large and commodious suite of cold baths, we have not yet such a desirable institution ; those who wish to enjoy the salubrious exercise of bathing being obliged either to immerse themselves in the open river near Green lane (where there are a number of dressing booths), or in the small and inconvenient baths in Bridge street, Younge street, Ball street, Pond street Gardens, and Upperthorpe." Can any one imagine for himself "a large and commodious suite of cold baths" in our Sheffield rivers as we know them ?

JOHNSON : The Upperthorpe baths were in what is now Addy street, and were kept by one Couldwell. The water that supplied them and adjacent troughs was splendidly clear and cold. It was used also by the Infirmary. The baths in Colson crofts were known as Brocksopp's. That was before the " Goit" was arched over, and I remember the sign informing the inhabitants that here were " baths in the running stream."

LEONARD : The extract I quoted just now shows what an immense deterioration our rivers have undergone. Forty years ago they were not the semi-sewers they are now. And the change is not only in the matter of cleanliness and purity, but in beauty also. In a small poem, published in 1838, by Frederick Horsfield, brother of the Rev. T. W. Horsfield, the historian of Lewes, entitled " A Rural Walk in June, in the neighbourhood of Sheffield," Mr. Horsfield having tracked the Don to " Sheffield, my birth-place and pride," says—

> " Here oft I've caught thy finny brood,
> And sail'd thy weir-bound waters o'er."

The " finny brood" is, I am afraid, not now oft caught here. One can scarcely imagine fish in connection with the foul stream, once a beautiful river. In a note, Mr. Horsfield says :—" The river Don in its course through Sheffield is, in many parts, adorned with gardens along its banks." We, who see the rivers of Sheffield in their present sad plight, are in danger of forgetting what they once were.

EVERARD : Yes; it was then, too, that Mr. Bailey's residence at Burn Greave, now so completely smothered by surrounding houses that it is absolutely invisible from the road, was spoken of as " a pleasant villa, standing on a gentle rise north of Sheffield, and about a mile from the town." There was no house between it and Mr. Sorby's on Spital hill.

TWISS : " The Hills" beyond Burn Greave, once the residence of old Thomas Scantlebury, the Quaker of Campo lane, was, in those days, a charming place. It has also been the residence of Mr. George Hawksworth, of High street, who was distinguished for his successful gardening. One of Mr. Scantlebury's sons once wrote :—"A. and E. Gales and James Montgomery used to call on us there. The poet generally preferred to sit on the rustic seat on the ' Common,' as it used to be called, to enjoy the beautiful view. And well he might. I once heard an enthusiastic Frenchman, who had travelled extensively in England, say it was the most beautiful prospect he had seen in the country."

LEIGHTON : It used to be said that there was no street in the town from which the country could not be seen. It was not, perhaps, strictly true, but it very closely approximated to the truth—and very pretty country peeps many of them were.

LEONARD : They were charming. " The scenery in the direction of Attercliffe," looking from High street, was noticed as " especially striking when the atmosphere happened to be more or less favourable, or even by moonlight." *

LEIGHTON : It is something that we still retain names indicating what many of our streets may once have been, and we should all most earnestly protest against the absurd mania for altering good old characteristic names. Harvest

---

* Holland's Tour of the Don.

lane and Daisy walk, Orchard street (Brinsworth's orchard), Nursery street and Cornhill, Mulberry street and Sycamore street (hill), Figtree lane, and many others, tell us what once was.

LEONARD : The idiots who change old names—Tom Cross lane to stupid Brunswick road, and Coalpit lane to Cambridge street—ought to be ostracised. They cannot have been native-born Sheffielders.

LEIGHTON : I am reminded of Elliott's lines :—

"Scenes rural once ! ye still retain sweet names,
    That tell of blossoms and the wandering bee :
In black Pea croft no lark its lone nest frames ;
    Balm green, the thrush hath ceased to visit thee.
When shall Bower spring her annual corncrake see,
    Or start the woodcock if the storm be near ?"

EVERARD : As to the outskirts we should have to make a complete circuit of the town to give even an idea of the changes. There is an article in the *Independent* which glances at something of this kind.

ALL : Read !

EVERARD : The writer has been speaking of the devoted loyalty of native Sheffielders to the town of their birth, and the charms that even its dingy streets have in their retrospective eyes. He has referred to the regrets one must feel " at the neglected opportunities almost all of us have had of recording and treasuring up our local folk-lore as it dropped from time to time from the lips of that generation now, alas, almost passed away, which was blossoming into manhood and womanhood when the Directorate had been abolished and Napoleon made Consul. Is there," asks the writer, " no Boswell in our midst who has made Sheffield his Johnson ; no local Crabbe Robinson or Mrs. Burney who has hordes of reminiscences and recollections that might be given to a grateful world ? Did Sheffield never possess some fertile letter writer whose correspondence would throw interesting light on the lives of our grandfathers and great-grandfathers ?" But the following is the part of the article I wish specially to quote : " In the absence of more systematic chronicles, we must be as satisfied as possible with what we can get, and we must see to it that those who are now children may not hereafter have to complain of any lack of material. And, indeed, it requires no great age to expatiate from personal recollection on changes that have taken place in Hallamshire, curious now and that will seem still more remarkable fifty years hence. A contemplation of the alterations in our town within the last (say) forty years, presents contrasts that are of striking interest, although 1832 is a point of time not sufficiently removed to enjoy the attractions of antiquity. It takes us back, at all events, to the pre-railroad era. In those days there was no difficulty in having your residence in the midst of charming rural scenes, and yet living within a quarter of an hour's walk of your business. Mr. Sorby's house on Spital hill was altogether free from the dinginess which set in some years later, and which was succeeded by a period of melancholy decrepitude preceding the now effected dissolution. Its gardens were still pleasant, for the smoke was not yet pronounced enough materially to injure vegetation. As for Burn Greave and The Hills, they were emphatically country residences, whose retirement was in no apparent danger of being infringed upon for years to come. Fields were where now stands the already deserted Midland Station, and Hallcarr, on the slope below the top corner of Spital hill, had its garden extending as far as Saville street. Saville street East and its long ranges of works were not, and it was only when Royds Mill was reached on the Attercliffe road that the pastoral character of the neighbourhood was disturbed by manufacturing industry. Newhall, built by Mr. Fell, was still an abode for a gentleman to desire, its grounds enjoying a stately seclusion that was the antipodes of rabbit coursing, pigeon shooting, and foot racing crowds ; and Hallcarr wood from the hill side looked down with its fresh waving trees upon a fertile valley, whose agricultural character was scarce broken. Attercliffe, Brightside, and Grimesthorpe were villages an excursion to which was a country ' out ;' even Pitsmoor was a rural retreat, still separated by a respectable fringe of hedge rows and meadows from the growing town. To it the only road was by Pyebank, or if you wanted a longer country walk by Harvest lane, or by the footpath from Tomcross lane; for the Burngreave road was unmade, and Rock street, beyond the old Brightside Workhouse, was a thing of the future. Pyebank could still sustain the country residences known as West Grove and Grove House ; Cook Wood was intact in its verdure, and as for the Old Park Wood, its sylvan recesses were endless and charming. The Infirmary enjoyed a delightful exemption from smoky neighbours, although there were indications of what was coming in projected streets behind it and in Roscoe place and Globe works, forerunners of the manufactories that have now seized upon the Penistone road. Beyond the

Infirmary, on the low side, was Philadelphia, and on the top side Upperthorpe, pleasant suburban colonies. The Nether Hallam Workhouse was alone in its glory in the lower part of the Crookes moor road, backed by the farmstead of Barber Nook, and looking down upon the four small reservoirs that occupied the valley below the Great Dam. Addy street, and the long rows of brick houses which are prolongations of it up the steep hill side, were as yet unimagined, but the upper part of Crookes Moor road—above Barber road, was much as it is now, though Butcher's dam had not become the neglected and grass-grown hollow it is, nor had the small, triangular sheet of water called Godfrey's Dam been as yet superseded by the large reservoir on the upper side of Dam road. Broomhill scorned houses that did not stand on their own grounds ; Broomfield had not yet been invaded by hordes of builders ; and as for Broomhall Park, the old Hall still stood alone in its glory, the only house within the domain, its nearest neighbours being the houses in Park lane. Broom Grove was not a road but a solitary house, the old footpath opposite the bottom of Newbould lane being still a thorough-fare to Ecclesall road. The Cemetery had not yet sprung into existence, but there were footpaths leading up to the remote region of Sharrow head. Across Sharrow lane, where Wostenholm road intersects it now, was still to be traced the old pack-horse road to Beauchieff. Mount Pleasant and the other residences at Highfield and Lowfield, together with Sheaf House, Clough House, East Bank, The Farm, and a number of others to the south-east of the town, enjoyed a delicious atmosphere and beautiful gardens. We need not remind our readers of the state of things now."

LEONARD : Rows upon rows of brick cottage houses !

LEIGHTON : Speaking of Newbould lane, the writer might have mentioned the old house of Benjamin Withers in Broom Park, with the magnificent weeping Willow in front, and the field sloping down to Clarkehouse lane. That ancient and decrepit-looking residence may well have been startled out of existence by the Congregational Church and the modern villas which have usurped its place.

TWISS : And as to Sharrow lane, the old house by the Pack-horse road, or " bridle sty," should not be omitted. It is a good specimen of the gentleman's house of the period, with an inscription over the doorway, G 1633 L—that is to say, George Lee. The family of Lee is very ancient in Little Sheffield, although no pedigree of it appears in the " Hallamshire." There was a Roger Lee, of Sheffield, butcher, who was living in the first year of Queen Elizabeth, and probably the same with a Roger Lee, who died about 1614. In the "Reliquary," vol. 2, there is printed a copy of "An inventorie of the goods and chattells, rights, and creditts of Roger Lee, late of Sheffield, deceased, priced by William Blith, William Bamford, John Quicksall, and Francis Barlow, the xvth daye of June, 1614." The amount is £307. 4s. 4d. Roger Lee was father to George Lee, who was dead in 1649, and left a widow, Anne, living in that year. In the same volume to which reference has just been made, there is also printed a copy of "The inventorie of the goodes, chattells, and creditts of George Lee, late of Little Sheffield, yeoman, deceased, taken and priced the three and twentieth daie of Aprill, Anno Dom., 1649, by Nicholas Stones, William Lee, Robert Bright, and George Ludlam." The amount in this case is £670. 13s. 4d. The next we meet with is Roger Lee, of Little Sheffield, gent., who seems to be referred to in one of the items in the last document. He was father to Jonathan Lee, of Little Sheffield, gent., living 1712, who had issue—George Lee, of Little Sheffield, Bachelor of Physic, identified in the initials on the old house, which was probably built by him. He died about 1719, leaving a widow and two sisters his co-heirs :—1. Elizabeth, married first to Daniel Gascoigne, of Sheffield, apothecary, and secondly (about 1721) to Christopher Cowley, of Sheffield, gent., and died without issue. 2. Ann, who married in 1715 John Fenton, of Little Sheffield, gent., and had issue a daughter, Elizabeth, who was wife to John Rotheram, of Dronfield, Esq., Sheriff of Derbyshire in 1750, by whom she had Samuel Rotheram, of Dronfield, Esq., Sheriff of Derbyshire 1773, who died unmarried in 1795; John Fenton Rotheram, who died unmarried in 1794; and an only daughter, Elizabeth, who also died unmarried in 1797. After her death the estate devolved to Mr. Joseph Cecil, in whose descendants it has continued to the present time.*

JOHNSON: About fifty yards higher up Sharrow lane is another house of less architectural pretensions, but still, in its decay, preserving some of the dignity of its former state. This appears to have been the house of some substantial yeoman at a time when the yeomanry were the strength of England. Over the door of one of the tenements into which

---

* See ante, pp. 74-75.

the house is now divided, appears the inscription, I D S 1638. Inside, the floors are still supported by oak beams and rafters, black with age. There is a fine oak staircase, and traces are distinct of a large open fireplace, extending along the entire breadth of the room.

TWISS : I do not know to whom that house belonged.

LEONARD : Our notice of the suburbs of Sheffield would be incomplete if we failed to glance at Page Hall in the days when Mr. George Bustard Greaves, with his bag-wig, and his portly person, did the honours of Sheffield to visitors of distinction, or rolled into the town in his yellow carriage (a phenomenon then) with sky blue liveries. It is just over one hundred years since Page Hall was built on land, described in the early deeds as " Page Field," and " Page Greave," by Thomas Broadbent, the banker of the Hartshead.* It was a notable place, for it was the first great outcome of the increasing wealth of the town. Many as have been the magnificent houses since built by our manufacturers, Page Hall stood alone then, and there were not wanting birds of ill-omen who, Cassandra like, prophesied a bad end to such unprecedented extravagance. There was some foundation for their gloomy views, for before the hall was finished, Thomas Broadbent, who must have been a man of large ideas, found that he had not sufficiently counted the cost, and that his plans were too grand for his purse ; so he curtailed the dimensions of the house in a way plainly to be seen in the entrance hall to this day. Nor was this all, for within a very few years (the house was built in 1773, and the event I now relate took place in 1780) the banking firm of the Hartshead had to suspend payment, and Page Hall was mortgaged to Mr. James Milnes, of Thornes House, Wakefield, the trustee under the bankruptcy. In 1786, it was conveyed to Mr. George Bustard Greaves, who had married the heiress of the Clays, of Bridgehouses. He, as I have said, kept high state there until his death in 1835, when Mr. James Dixon,† whose biography is one of the striking manufacturing episodes of the town, became the purchaser. It remained in the possession of his son, the late Mr. William Frederick Dixon, until his death, and the estate has just been sold (May, 1874) to Mr. Mark Firth, who intends to give a portion of it for the purposes of a public park.

LEIGHTON : Which reminds me that since we began these conversations, the lady of Weston Hall has laid down her

---

* Ante, pp. 9-10.　† Ante, p. 141.

benevolent life (May 3, 1873), and her property has been bought by the town for the recreation of the public.

TWISS: A word or two as to the earlier history of the "Page Greave" estate may not be uninteresting. Prior to 1717, it was in the possession of a family of Rawsons, and in that year James Rawson conveyed it to John Potter, of Beighton. It was in 1759 that the then representative of the Potters, described as a brushmaker of Pagefield, sold the estate to Joseph Broadbent, the father of Thomas, the builder of the Hall. Included in the estate recently sold, is Skinnerthorpe. Part of this formerly belonged to the Bournes, afterwards to the Mellands; the other part to the Barkers (of Bakewell) and the Lees, who, in 1775, assumed the name of Carril Worstley. I should not omit to mention that the Dixon family claims to have sprung from the immediate neighbourhood of the estate, the late Mr. James Dixon having been the grandson of William Dixon, of Shiregreen.

WRAGG: I do not know that, after the event Mr. Leighton has referred to, there is any impropriety in my telling the following anecdote of the father of the late Miss Harrison :— Mr. Harrison laid the foundation of his fame as a saw-maker thus. He sent a man, dressed like a working carpenter, in his shirt sleeves and apparently fresh from his work-bench, among the London shops, asking for "Harrison's saws." None of the shopkeepers had ever heard of such a maker. They had, of course, saws by this eminent firm and the other which they recommended to the customer, but he would have none of them, declaring that no saws were like Harrison's, and he must have them or none. This, from a practical man, made its due impression, and a few days afterwards, when Mr. Harrison *happened* to call soliciting orders, he found no difficulty in obtaining them. The story comes from an old workman of Mr. Harrison's and is, I am assured, authentic.

EVERARD: The night air gets chilly to old men. I shall go home.

LEIGHTON: And my pipe's out.

CHAPTER VIII.

Bank Street, The Crofts, Broad Lane.

Present—Messrs. Twiss, Leighton, Everard, Wragg, Leonard
and Johnson.
Period—A.D. 1874.

WRAGG : We might very well devote this evening's conversation to a tour in " low latitudes"—as they are now. They were not always so, as a glance at some of the houses will show. Any one can easily pick out the old residences of the old substantial manufacturers of the last century, many of them now turned into public houses.

LEONARD : Suppose we begin at Bank street and work our way onwards.

EVERARD : We shall, then, commence with the corner, which was the *Independent* office from 1846 to 1863.

LEONARD : These premises were built by Mr. Luke Palfreyman, hosier, Snig hill, father of the late Mr. Palfreyman, solicitor. Opposite is the Old Bank, now Mr. Waddy's auction room. It was here that Parker, Shores & Blakelock carried on business, and here that they failed in the year 1843, to the consternation of the town. One of the Shores lived in the house attached. Subsequently the premises were used for the Union Bank, until it was removed further on the street.

WRAGG : Proceeding, on the right we reach what was the leather-currier's shop of the late Mr. Elias Lowe—one which retained its old-fashioned character until the death of its long occupant, when it was turned into the offices now occupied by Mr. William Fretson. Mr. Lowe, as most of us remember him in his later days—portly, rosy-faced, and feeble, was far different from the Elias Lowe of the olden time. Then he was active and a busy public man. He was one of Sheffield's first Aldermen.

JOHNSON : His memory went far enough back to remember the figtrees, from which Figtree lane takes its name.

EVERARD : In confirmation of that fact, I myself well recollect, when a little boy, seeing the front of one of the houses covered with a figtree. It was either the same, or the next house to that in which "blind Jonathan," the fiddler, lived. He was a respectable man of that class in those days.

WRAGG : Mr. Lowe's brother, Isaac, was the keeper of a well-conducted beer-house in Bridge street.

TWISS : Next comes the *Independent* office of the present day. There formerly was a large garden, which must have had a terrace wall overlooking the precipitous hill side down to Snig hill. A part of the old wall was found during the building of Mr. Leader's present printing offices.

LEIGHTON : Opposite are the offices of Messrs. Smith and Hinde, the present partners being the sons of the original firm. What a profound impression the loss of Mr. Hinde, when crossing the Atlantic in the ill-fated Arctic, in 1854, made on the town ! Mr. James Sykes, late of the Victoria corn mill, was another Sheffield man on board.

WRAGG : The new Union Bank, on the left, was erected on the site of the Saynors' factory. They, prior to 1810, employed more hands than any other firm in the cutlery trade.

LEONARD : How completely workshops in this street have now given place to lawyers' offices.

JOHNSON : Thomas Saynor, lived at 14, Bank street, and carried on business at the back of Alderman Vickers' offices, The original Saynors were Samuel and John. They were both factors and manufacturers, their chief business being done in London in all kinds of knives, swords, shoe buckles, skates, scissors, and razors. The business subsequently came into the hands of Thomas Saynor, Scargill croft, who manufactured the sportsman's knife, scissors, razors, and pen machine knife. After the steel pen came into use, trade began to be bad. In sailing from London to Hull, a drunken sailor fell out of his hammock on to Mr. Saynor, and injured him for life. He lay for a long time in Hull, and after he came home he was unable to attend to his business. The mark which he struck was " Rainbow," and his eldest son strikes the same mark. At Whitby, Yorkshire, another brother, Jeremiah Saynor, was town beadle. John kept the Old Barrack Tavern Bowling Green, and another Saynor drove the coach to Doncaster and Thorne from Waingate. A branch of the family is still in Edward street and has been there for more than 50 years.

TWISS : We should not pass that old hostelry the George and Dragon without a mention.

JOHNSON : No, it was a noted market-house in the days when it was kept by John Cooper. I have seen on a Tuesday and Saturday a line of carts reaching from Figtree lane to the bottom of Bank street, and I believe the late Ald. Hoole was the cause of prohibiting their standing in the street.

TWISS : Let us take a peep up the adjoining lane at the Quakers' Meeting-house. It was re-built in 1806.

EVERARD : Either at the time when the Meeting-house was re-built, or during the period of some subsequent alterations, the Friends assembled in the large upper room of Mr. Hoyland's iron warehouse, now occupied by Mrs. G. Tucker, No. 7, York street.

TWISS : An important contribution to local biography would be an account of the worthy men who have been prominently connected with the Quakers' Meeting-house.

WRAGG : We have met with some already, and we shall yet meet with more.

LEONARD : On its site formerly were gardens, running down to and across what is now Bank street. The old Quakers' Meeting-house was, according to Gosling's plan, on the other side of Meeting-house lane, where are now the offices of the late Mr. Francis Hoole, formerly Mr. Tattershall's, and now again another Mr. Tattershall's.

EVERARD : Those offices were once of the school of the Rev. Matthew Preston, when he lived in the house in Figtree lane, now the Hospital for Women; and afterwards of Stephen Eversfield. Then on the other side of Figtree lane, occupying the site of the synagogue of the Jews that they have deserted recently (in 1872) in favour of a new one behind it with a frontage to North Church street, was Mr. William Cowley's English Grammar school.

JOHNSON : That room in the course of its existence has been put to very various uses, for it was the meeting place of the Chartists. Mr. Cowley's son married the daughter of John Cooper, of the George and Dragon. Bank street and Queen street fairly bristled with schoolmasters in those days. Besides those who have been mentioned, and Mr. John Eadon, of whom we shall have to speak presently, William Wright had a school in the room behind Mr. Smilter's office, before him occupied by John Addy, to say nothing of old Nanny Bashforth, who lived in the passage past Queen street chapel.

WRAGG : Mr. Addy was better known as a teacher of drawing. After Mr. Wright succeeded him in the room just spoken of, he lived and continued his profession in the house in front, now occupied by Mr. Barker, barrister.

LEONARD : It is rather a digression from Bank street, yet there may not be a better opportunity of adding that the Parish Churchyard used to be a common play-ground for all the boys who chose to use it. Numbers constantly availed themselves of the privilege and fraternized with the Charity School boys in all their youthful gambols. Their great amusement used to be vaulting over the tombstones. One feat in particular was to leap " o'er t'alli"—a so-called alabaster slab, but really of Derbyshire marble, forming the top of a tomb near the vestry door.* When the churchyard was closed to these pranks (1830), the late Mr. Samuel Roberts devised for the Charity boys the elevated playground high up above York street, where they may be heard romping any day.

TWISS : The Boys' Charity School would be a questionable "charity" in days written of by the gentleman whose name you have just mentioned, when its management was "farmed," and when the sleeping room of the poor little creatures was let for dancing parties and assemblies.

WRAGG : A past master of that school ought not to pass unmentioned—Mr. Joseph Youle, who published the " Arithmetical Preceptor," in 1813. As a tutor it has never been surpassed.

EVERARD : Returning to Bank street, one may remark that Meeting house lane and its precipitous continuation on the other side of Bank street, Scargill croft (at one time called Dover hill by some), and New street, the continuation of Figtree lane (once it was all Figtree lane), must be two of the oldest thoroughfares in the town. The cottages down there are very ancient.

TWISS : Scargill croft takes its name from the family of the Skargells (as it was then spelled), who were in possession of the property there some 250 years ago. I have seen the will of one of them, William, which distinctly referred to this property, distinguishing it into two parts, an upper and a lower. The will of Joshua Skargell, son of William, is dated February 12th, 1625, and he leaves in turn the property to his son William, together with " one cupboard with boxes and one iron deske which are in the chamber over the house wherein I now dwell, with all the writings in the same.

* Ante, p. 73.

N

And also all such goods as are in the said house and were given and bequeathed unto me by William Skargell, my late father, deceased." To his second son, Thomas, he left the Cow close and the Cow close head, two closes of land in Brightside "Bierley;" and " also those my ffoure cottages at or near the West-barr end, which I purchased of John Bayes, with one croft thereto adjoyneing." He had also land at Upperthorpe, which he bequeathed to his daughter, so that Joshua Skargell, yeoman, was quite a man of property.

LEONARD : There was still a representative of the family in the town towards the end of the last century, for, as we shall have to remark presently, Thomas Scargil, or Scargill, was an original member of Queen street Chapel, being one of the thirteen who left Nether Chapel to found it.

Twiss : New street must have been a very different place when houses were provided in it as residences for the assistant ministers of the Parish Church. The Rev. George Bayliffe was one who lived there up to the time of his death in 1804. He had been assistant minister for 44 years, holding also the curacy of Ecclesall for 34 of them ; and before that he had been curate to the Rev. W. Steer, of Ecclesfield, for 15 years. Born in 1721, he was, of course, a very old man when this century came in. Mr. Hunter has described him as low in stature, wearing a white curled wig and cocked hat, and accustomed to take early country walks before breakfast. The *Gentleman's Magazine*, in a notice probably written by his colleague, the Rev. Edward Goodwin, speaks of Mr. Bayliffe in his domestic relations in the highest terms, and says that " he was economical without parsimony, of the strictest integrity and ready to do every good work. In the discharge of his office as a clergyman he was piously regular and punctual on every occasion. His discourses were judicious and instructive, and accompanied with a proper degree of animation. In his clerical visits he was unwearied and diligent, and spared no pains to maintain that happy harmony which subsisted between him and his brethren."

LEIGHTON : Between New street and Scargill croft is now the County Court. To build it were removed the old houses where formerly was Mr. John Parker, solicitor, brother of Mr. Adamson Parker and of the Rev. Frank Parker, of Dore. Mr. Parker built the large house on the other side of New street, formerly the Highway office, now occupied as solicitors' chambers, where the celebrated Luke Palfreyman lived.

JOHNSON : William Wood, spirit merchant, lived at the top of Scargill croft. There was a large skittle alley attached to the house. Mr. Wood was one of the largest spirit merchants in the town. In this croft, too, were John Owen's malt kilns; and after him Mr. Parkin succeeded to them. His son now carries on the same business in Coulson street. William Walmsley, blacking manufacturer, was here also. He had a good trade, and at night he used to spend his time playing the dulcimer. He was a great favourite with the ladies, and he was in request at parties and balls along with blind Jonathan, the fiddler and wait, who lived in Figtree lane. Then there was Mrs. Binns, who kept the Nelson Inn, New street. It was one of the most respectable houses in Sheffield fifty years ago. When the notorious Peter Foden married and commenced business on his own account, he took the shop which then had a bow window in Bank street, since converted into offices, and now occupied by Mr. Henry Vickers. Patience Davy, the quakeress, kept a noted worsted shop next to the County Court, and a fine business she did. There was no knitting by machinery then, and no worsted like Patience Davy's. She was skilled in curing wounds and bruises, and people came from all parts of the town for her help. Her charge was " Thou art welcome." She retired with an independence to the better regions of Glossop road, where she died at a green old age. On the other side of the street, in one of " Lawyer Tattershall's houses," was William Nadin, stay maker, who lived and made his fortune in Fargate, opposite the Exchange drapery establishment, and retired to Bank street. His son William was apprenticed to the father of the late Joseph Woodcock, brushmaker. This son was a great politician and Jacobin. He married Martha Wright, of whom Mr. Wragg told us a curious anecdote in connection with the Parish Church, and Mr. Joseph Nadin, who represents St. Philip's Ward in the Town Council, is their son. John Bland, the late chief-constable of Rotherham, lived next door to Messrs. Clegg and Son's office. He was the son of William Bland, mentioned once before (p.113). Then in the house occupied by the firm of solicitors just mentioned, lived Samuel Broadhead—afterwards Broadhead and Atkin, Britannia metal and fine scissors manufacturers. The title deeds do not state how old this property is, but it was standing in 1787, when Henry Tudor bought it from John Nodder; and Mr. William Tattershall bought it from the trustee of Henry Tudor, in 1824. Then the late

Ald. Francis Hoole bought it from the executors of the late William Tattershall.

LEONARD : Before leaving Bank street we ought, at least, to mention the names of Robert Rodgers, solicitor, father of the present Mr. T. W. Rodgers, J.P. ; and John Watson, 3, Bank street, brother of Thomas Watson, silverplater, who educated eight poor boys at the charity school. He was one of the old Sheffield worthies. There was, too, the predecessor of the late Mr. Thomas Badger, as coroner, Andrew Allan Hardy, who lived at No. 19. Strange tales have been told of him when Lord Cochrane was wanted on a charge of high treason, but he was so much respected that the Secretary of State could not find any one who would give information as to his whereabouts.

WRAGG : At the corner of Figtree lane, is the beginning of Queen street, and the oldest house in the street, now occupied by Mr. Haxworth, surgeon. It was built in 1784 by one of the Hounsfields, of Pond hill.

TWISS : It has usually been said that Messrs. Rayner and Turner built the house. At that time the ground was covered with trees and was called Wade's Orchard. There seems to have been some hesitation whether to call the new street Queen street or Fig street.

WRAGG : It was in the same year that Queen street chapel was built by Thomas Vennor and John Read. As Mr. Twiss said of the Quakers' Meeting house so I might say of this— a biography of those who attended it would include some of the oldest and best families in the town.

EVERARD : This chapel, as no doubt most of you are aware, was founded by some members of the Nether or Lower Chapel, who "apprehended several things to be exceptionable in the ministry and conduct" of the Rev. John Harmer, its then pastor. As early as 1782 communications were exchanged between them and the Rev. Jehoiada Brewer, and eventually (March 26, 1783) he accepted their invitation. On the 28th of the same month, " Messrs. Vennor, Read and Smith agreed with Mr. Wheat, the attorney, for a piece of ground situate in Queen street, for the term of 99 years, at 1½d. per yard, for the purpose of erecting a place of worship thereon." Mr. Brewer came to Sheffield July 13, 1783, preached for a time in " the long room" in Norfolk street, and his first sermon in the new chapel (though not yet completed), December the 3rd. Meantime Mr. Harmer, declining to give the seceders their dismissal, expelled them from the communion of his church, and on the 26th November they made and signed a " Covenant" among themselves. There were thirteen of them and their names are of interest :

SAMUEL OSTLIFF,	THOMAS SCARGILL,
JONATHAN LOY,	JOSEPH BRADSHAW,
WILLIAM GRUBB,	JOHN SMITH,
LYDIA KERR,	MARTHA SMITH,
CHARLES CLAYTON,	WILLIAM BEARDSHAW,
MARY CLAYTON,	JOHN HOLLAND.
SARAH BROOMHEAD,	

Of these, Bradshaw and Beardshaw, as will be seen, by no means acted up to the spirit of their covenant. Two persons were appointed deacons in 1783, but the Church book does not give their names. A pamphlet, "printed by order of the church" in 1796, explains that owing to Mr. Read's position, as sole surviving lessee after the death of Mr. Vennor in 1787, and his determined " maintenance of power and sway," no formal separation of them took place. That pamphlet is entitled " A defence of the Principles and Conduct of the Independent Church assembling at Queen street Chapel, Sheffield, occasioned by the calumnious misrepresentations of a pamphlet called ' A Caution to all Independent Churches' "—which was issued under the name of the above William Beardshaw, who, with Mr. John Read, the lessee, Joseph Bradshaw, and others, fomented so much discord that they were expelled. Before this the property had been formally vested in trustees, and Mr. Read's power being thus ended, Samuel Ostliff, John Smith (the bookseller of Angel street), William Room, and Robert Marsden were elected deacons.

LEONARD : There is one circumstance that may be borne in mind to the credit of this chapel—the few changes that have been made in its ministry. The Rev. Peter Whyte is only the sixth pastor in ninety years. In this respect Queen street presents a marked contrast to Howard street Chapel, for example.

EVERARD : My father heard the Rev. Jehoiada Brewer preach his first sermon in the school-room in Milk street. After the chapel was opened, Mr. Brewer attracted large and overflowing congregations, for his vigorous preaching was something new in the town, and he exercised a powerful influence during the important years 1783 to 1796. There was at that time no evangelical preaching in connection with the Established Church ; and amongst the Evangelical Dissenters there were no indications of vigorous

spiritual life. The chief manifestation of the power of such
life existed amongst the Wesleyan Methodists. Howard
street, Garden street, Lee croft, and Attercliffe chapels were
non-existent—not to mention those that have been erected
during the present century. In fact, Nether Chapel and
Coalpit lane Chapel (then recently erected, in 1780, in consequence of a secession from the former on the appointment
of the Rev. John Harmer), were the only two Independent
places of worship in Sheffield. Mr. Brewer was a man of no
ordinary stamp. In person he was well built, possessing a
bodily constitution capable of sustaining a great amount of
physical labour and mental effort ; as the fact that he regularly preached six times a week, besides attending to his
other engagements, may sufficiently attest. He had a voice
of great compass, power, and flexibility ; and a countenance
indicative of energy and decision, deriving in part its expres-
siveness from a dark, piercing eye, which, as he gave utterance
to the stronger emotions of the soul, was wont to flash with
the fire of intense animation. As a preacher he was emi-
nently practical and searching. He was a man of action
rather than of speculation ; the popular preacher rather than
the profound metaphysician or learned divine. His *forte*
consisted in the clear comprehension and statement of scriptural truth. The interest and charm of his discourses chiefly
consisted in their being pervaded by the essential element of
strong common sense, rendered attractive by familiar illustrations, and enforced by a popular logic. As a pastor, he was
exemplary and faithful in the discharge of the duties of his
office. The theological system which he embraced and ex-
pounded was that which I may denominate as a scriptural
Calvinism. In political sentiment Mr. Brewer entertained
somewhat ultra Liberal opinions. His views and preferences
in this respect he boldly and openly declared, at a time when
such avowal rendered a man liable to be reproached with being
associated with infidels in the assertion of the necessity of
parliamentary reform ; and in the advocacy of the claims of
civil and religious liberty. Decided in all his views, he was
from principle and conviction a stanch Nonconformist. The
distinguishing characteristic of his ministry was its earnest-
ness. After a successful course of nearly thirteen years, some
unpleasant circumstances arose in the church, which eventually issued in Mr. Brewer's removal to Birmingham in
1796. He concluded his work in this town by preaching a
farewell sermon to a crowded and deeply impressed con-

gregation. On that special occasion he took for his text the words :—" Finally, brethren, farewell !" After giving out these words he burst into tears ; and although a man of great self-possession, he was so deeply affected that he had to sit down before he could sufficiently recover himself to be able to proceed. Mr. Brewer had laboured at Birmingham for about twenty years when a new and much larger chapel was begun. He was in feeble health when he laid the foundation stone of the building, and on that occasion remarked that when the chapel was opened they would have to walk over his grave! This proved to be the fact. He died on St. Bartholomew's-Day, the 24th August, 1817, aged sixty-six years ; and the late Rev. John Hammond, one of his converts at Sheffield, gave the funeral address.

LEONARD : Was there not some peculiar circumstance in connection with Mr. Brewer coming to Sheffield ?

EVERARD : Yes. His first settlement was at Rodborough, in Gloucestershire, and the event to which you refer happened there. It may be of much interest to any of you who are attracted by the philosophy of dreams. It is reported by most credible witnesses, who had it from Mr. Brewer's own lips. One Saturday night he dreamt it was the Sabbath ; and that after he had ascended the pulpit and commenced the service, he saw a stranger, whom he had never seen before, enter the chapel, and sit down in a certain pew. He thought that after the service, this person came into the vestry to speak to him, and gave him an invitation to Sheffield. That was his dream. The next day whilst engaged in the public service, he actually saw the gentleman whose likeness had been presented to him in his dream walk into the chapel, and take his seat in the identical pew. This proved to be no other person than Mr. John Read, who, at the conclusion of the service, went into the vestry and informed Mr. Brewer that his business was to propose to him a journey to Sheffield. It is certain that Mr. Brewer regarded this as an extraordinary circumstance, and it practically contributed to free his mind from all doubt or hesitation in accepting this "call."

LEONARD : The Rev. James Boden, who followed Mr. Brewer, was minister of the chapel from 1796 to 1839, with the Rev. Joseph Augustus Miller as co-pastor from 1836. Mr. Boden contented himself with keeping a mere list of members in the Church book during his time, so that we cannot trace the changes in the deacons more accurately than to say that Wm. Alsop, 1785-1830; Wm. Smith, 1803-1817;

William Andrews, 1803-1830 ; William Eagle, 1804-1820 ;
Lewis Thomas, 1805-1832 ; all filled the office somewhere
between the figures appended to each name, the first being
the year in which they joined the church, the second the
year of their death. In 1834, the list was : Robert Marsden, Pitsmoor hill side (the only survivor of the earliest
four) ; Thomas Dunn, Cornhill ; Robert Leader, Portobello ;
John Greaves, Glossop road ; George Merrill, Harvest lane ;
John Eadon, Broad lane ; Richard Thomas Taylor, Sheffield
Moor. Mr. Marsden died in 1834, and in 1844 (minister,
the Rev. John Hope Muir), Mr. Dunn and Mr. Taylor having
left the chapel, the places of these three had been supplied
by Edward Hall, Edward Hebblethwaite, and Robert Waterhouse. It is not worth while to bring down the record later
than this. With regard to Attercliffe Independent Chapel,
which Mr. Everard has mentioned, its origin dates from 1793,
when the Queen street people took an empty house at Attercliffe, and there Mr. Brewer preached every Wednesday evening. This was soon found too small, whereupon a chapel
was built, and opened in October of the same year.

LEIGHTON : Queen street Chapel is altered now. "I well
remember," wrote a minister who visited the town in 1859,
after many years absence, "when that chapel was fronted
with a dead brick wall, with a wooden gate ; no porch over
the doors, all within as plain as the simplest white-wash, a
narrow vestry at the lower end, and the Sabbath school conducted on the other side of the street, in the rooms where
Mr. John Eadon had his academy."

EVERARD : It was afterwards Farnsworth's, at the bottom
of North Church street. Mr. Eadon lived in the corner
house of that street and Queen street. But North Church
street was not opened through in those days. Below Wheat's
passage, leading from Paradise square, was a precipitous bank,
which had not then been cut away. Below that bank and immediately above the school, were the steps descending into
the wood-yard, as at this day. That yard belonged to Mr.
Fox, who lived at the house at the other end, facing Paradise
square. Projecting into the yard from Wheat's passage was
the house of Mr. Axe, round which the thoroughfare wound,
emerging into Wheat's passage by another flight of steps.
Below were the backs of the Queen street houses, in which
lived (next to Mr. Eadon's) William Knowles, then Quaker
Gurney, and at the corner, as now, was Mr. Bowman's, pawnbroker. The yard exists now just as it did then ; but it

has been superseded as a thoroughfare by the more direct route, since North Church street was opened through. The present Queen street school-rooms, behind the chapel, had not then been built.

JOHNSON: The school-room in North Church street was built by Mr. Knowles in 1779. The following lines are cut out in stone at the entrance of the door:—

> " Where grace and virtue mutually shine,
> Rich is the blossom, and the fruit Divine."

The school is and has been in the possession of Mr. Farnsworth for the last thirty years. William Evatt, dentist, lived where Mr. William Nodder's offices are, at the corner of North street. There was a large tooth hanging before the door, and I have seen both old and young when they have got to the door turn back again, the pain having ceased in fear of the dreadful operator. Mr. Evatt was a noted character, a member of the Society of Friends—

LEIGHTON: Whose house was a great gathering place for certain gossips.

JOHNSON: John Alcock, manufacturer of shot belts, powder flasks, and razor strops, removing from Pea croft, carried on his business where is now Mr. Hoyland, brush maker. Charles Alcock, who was formerly a member of the Town Council and an extreme Liberal, took to the business, and removed to Pond street, where it is still carried on by some member of the family. George Gurney, who belonged to the Society of Friends, kept the grocer's shop at the corner of Queen street, now a public-house; and next door below he kept a large store for cocoa and ebony woods; but he and his brothers emigrated to America.

WRAGG: Is there not some mistake here? It was Edmund Gurney who kept the corner shop, and he had a brother Joseph who dealt in ebony and ivory next door, and went to America. I am sorry to state that the last time I saw Edmund Gurney he was clerking a money club, or else it was in Mr. Watson's shop, in Fargate, where he assisted on Saturday nights. I believe he died in an asylum. I cannot say anything respecting his brother Joseph, the ivory merchant. The Gurney family is a very old one, and took the name from a place in France. The family pedigree begins in 912. There was a Hugh Gurney and his son at the battle of Mortimer in 1054, and also at the battle of Hastings. Another of the family was Sir Thomas de Gurney, one of the murderers of Edward II. A third son of one of the Gurneys became a Quaker under the preaching of George Fox, and the family has long been seated in Norfolk. The late Mrs. Fry was a Gurney. I am sorry I cannot show the connection of the Sheffield Gurneys with the Gurneys of Norwich, but, notwithstanding, they are of the same family.

LEONARD : Cousins, I believe.

WRAGG : Continuing along Queen street, we get into quite a new region, caused by the opening through of the street from Workhouse lane (Paradise street) to Westbar green, and Scotland street. On the right, near Silver street, have recently disappeared some old cottages that were below the level of the street. A few yards up Silver street is the Star inn, bearing the inscription—First house in Silver street, 1742, $_{J\,M}^{S}$ Fifty or sixty years ago, that was a good double house. In Silver street, too, the Messrs. Dixon carried on business before they removed to Cornish place. At that time a man who lived in Workhouse lane had his letters directed to Silver street, because it sounded more respectable. At the top corner of Silver street there was a grocer's shop which did a good business, its occupier being Mr. Thompson, who unfortunately failed about 37 years ago. Since then the house has gone through a variety of experiences, inclusive, of course, of a beerhouse. It is now occupied by a renovator of old shoes.

EVERARD : I have heard it said that this Mr. Thompson got his nickname of " Sponty Thompson," from having used the word " spontaneous" in a speech at some meeting. But I should rather think it was given to him as descriptive, in a single word, of his marvellous powers of speech and conversation. When very young I once spent an evening in his company, and was very much struck and interested by him. His words came in one continuous flow, and his language was far more pure and refined, and exempt from provincialisms, than it is usual to hear in the course of conversation.

LEONARD : Jonathan Watkinson, who was so unmercifully satirized by Mather that he is said to have died of a broken heart, was a Silver street resident. He was one of the principal manufacturers of the day, and was Master Cutler in 1787. His supposed offence was that he first exacted from workmen thirteen to the dozen; but it is doubtful whether he deserved the abuse he got, as may be seen from the notes in John Wilson's edition of Mather's Songs, pp. 63-67.

WRAGG: In Silver street head, near the Square, the grandfather of Mr. John Clayton, the auctioneer, changed his business from a leather breeches maker to a broker and auctioneer, and soon removed next door, to a much larger shop that was previously kept by a grocer, a well-known man, whose name I have forgotten. Mr. Clayton's second shop was the one lately occupied by Mr. Neal. He had not been in business more than ten years when he retired. He died in the house at the top of Convent walk, afterwards occupied by Mr. W. S. Brittain. Down at the corner was "Neddy" Maden, a shoemaker, who at his death had accumulated more than £30,000. He died on some of his property at the corner of Duke street and Porter street. In Westbar green, where is now the bottom of Scotland street (before it was opened through to Queen street, and when the only issue was through the crooked Grindle gate, opposite Silver street head), was the residence and manufactory of Mr. Ellis, file manufacturer. The house stood backward, with palisades, and occupied the breadth of the now street. He was a very respectable man, but I am sorry to say one of his apprentices was Frank Fearn, who was gibbeted on Loxley chase for the murder of Nathan Andrews. Frank Fearn was naturally of a depraved disposition, and Mr. Ellis often predicted he would die with his shoes on. A story is told, that when on the scaffold he said : "My master has often told me I should die with my shoes on, so I shall pull them off and make him a liar."

LEONARD : Mather, in his song on Frank Fearn, makes him penitent on the scaffold, but possibly with more poetical licence than historical truth.

TWISS : There has been a good deal of speculation as to what became of Frank Fearn's gibbet post. It is commonly believed that it was used as a foot bridge over the Rivelin or the Loxley ; and it has been stated that, having been washed down to Sheffield by a flood, it came into the possession of a builder, and was used by him, along with a quantity of other old material obtained by the removal of the Shrewsbury Hospital, in erecting a row of cottages which stand in a street that still bears the builder's name.

WRAGG : In Grindle gate lived the grandfather of the late Mr. Thomas Dunn.

LEIGHTON : At the corner of Westbar green and Grindle gate was the grocer's shop of Joseph Haywood, father of the late lawyer and magistrate. It is still in the same trade.

EVERARD : When I went to school with Thomas Haywood, the younger son of the grocer mentioned, the family kept and lived at a shop in Scotland street, opposite Nowill and Son's warehouse.

WRAGG : In Scotland street was Mr. Benjamin Parkin, a large spring knife manufacturer. He turned the front of the premises into a dram shop and carried on the business of a spirit merchant. The place is now Messrs. Mower and Pearson's. Near where is the pawnbroker's shop of Mr. Hides was, 60 or 70 years ago, Mr. Samuel Peace, grocer. He afterwards became a saw-manufacturer and acquired an ample competency. He was father of the late Mr. Charles Peace, one of our early aldermen.

LEIGHTON : One improvement here is that the " Scotland street feast," which had degenerated into an excuse for drinking and immorality, is a thing of the past, but it died hard, and has not long since disappeared.

EVERARD : At the bottom of Pea croft was (and is) a baker's shop, kept by Goodison, the father of Mr. Goodison, the attorney.

LEONARD : The house is still standing in Pea croft that was built by the grandfather of Mr. Albert Smith—George Smith, who was Master Cutler in 1749, and whose feast, as already told, cost £2. 2s. 9d. That was in the days when the apprentices lived in the house with their masters; and as Mr. Smith had besides a large family of children, he used to lead rather a long procession when he went, wearing his cocked hat, down the Croft, up Silver street head, and across Hick's stile field to the Parish Church, of which one of his sons was afterwards to be assistant-minister. There they occupied two pews. It is a family tradition that on a Sunday to be remembered, one of the apprentices ventured to complain about the pudding. Mrs. Smith got up and boxed his ears, saying : " Thou grumbles at such pudding as this ! Better flour and better watter were never put together."

LEIGHTON : We have changed all that by the modern system of apprentices. The alteration was beginning at the close of the last century and attracted the attention of Wilberforce, who remarked, in his diary, " An increasing evil at Sheffield is that the apprentices used to live with the masters and be of the family ; now wives are grown too fine ladies to like it ; they lodge out, and are much less orderly."

LEONARD : But under the old system, apprentices, if not left so much to themselves, had very hard times of it. There is a wonderful difference between the duties they have to perform now and those of the old times. The last apprentice of Montgomery has said: "Mr. Montgomery's apprentices used to take down and put up the shutters of the Misses Gales' shop, which were very many, very heavy, and had to be carried a considerable distance. When work in the office closed at 6.30 or 7 p.m., the unfortunate apprentice had to return to the place at 8 or 9 to put up the shutters." And I have heard one who was an apprentice in another printing office—that of Mr. Bacon, the founder of the *Independent*, and who helped to pull the first copy of that journal, contrast his duties with those of printers' apprentices in these days. When his work at the office was done, he was a sort of body-servant to his master's wife, running her errands or weeding her garden.

LEIGHTON: Those were cases in which the apprentices were non-resident. Some amazing stories are told of the treatment the apprentices in the staple trades met with, in the shape of board and lodging, at the hands of their mistresses. This story was told by an old man named Dawson, who worked at Scythe wheel, Loxley bottom, and who was apprenticed to "Johnny Jackson," the keeper of a public-house in the middle of Crookes. He was the youngest apprentice of four. He related that they never had anything to their supper but grout porridge—which was made from the refuse of brewings, and may be described as the essence of grains—and were allowed neither fire nor light. One night, when they were going home from the wheel in the Rivelin valley, the oldest apprentice, whose name was Uckler, said to his companions, "Now my lads, if it is grout porridge to-night, I tell you what I shall do. I shall throw my piggin (a wooden vessel with a handle holding about a quart) under the ass-nook, and you must all follow the same tack." This was agreed to, and when they got home, sure enough there was the inevitable grout porridge in a large "piggin," with a wooden spoon. Uckler seized his piggin and threw it away; and the three others did the same and ran up stairs. The master came, armed with a stout stick, and gave each a good "hiding;" but the result was porridge. They were never offered grout again.

WRAGG: Talking of apprentices, there was a man in Allen street who had sixteen. He was a cutler of the name of Barber, and he belonged to the property opposite Radford street. Oat-cake was then the constant fare, and people with apprentices always had a batch beforehand, that the lads might eat less. It is not therefore, specially surprising, that when they had an opportunity they snatched a cake from the bakestone. One lad was known to put an oat-cake in a coal basket, with the coal over it, while another concealed one under his shirt, and though instantly missed it was devoured before recovery was possible. On one occasion they had brewis or brewes for dinner. One of the lads, thought to be somewhat deficient in intellect, was seen to be pulling off his jacket. When asked what he was going to do he replied, "I'm going to jump into the pancheon to fetch that big piece of cake out on the other side." Barber, with all his parsimony, died in the Workhouse.

LEONARD : What is brewis ?

WRAGG : Oat-cakes, mixed with dripping and hot water poured on, seasoned with salt and pepper.

EVERARD : It is the traditional dish when the Cutlers' Company lunch together before the annual swearing in of the Master Cutler. It is an old Saxon dish. In "Gareth and Lynette" we read : "He had not beef and brewis enow."

LEONARD : A Sheffield rhymster, named Senior, has sung the woes of the apprentices :—

> " When t' prentice lad ate green wort cake,
>   Ta milk an' porridge blue,
> An' if at neet he dar'd ta rake,
>   Theze turn'd a darker hue.
>
> E t' morn be t'larum clock struck six,
>   If t' Rosco bell 'ad dun,
> E Lord Mayor shoes an' leather dicks,
>   E t' smithy he were fun,
>
> A wurkin fur his daily bread,
>   That came at braikfast time,
> Grac'd wi' a fringe, az green a tinge
>   Aż t' faantin o' this rhyme."

TWISS : Another Sheffield man, in describing the former condition of apprentices, said that the bad treatment to which they were subjected originated the saying, " He's treated as bad as ony 'prentice lad." " They were," said this writer, " indifferently fed and worse clothed, but it must be admitted that some good old ' dames' behaved well to them. The masters, however, kept them in the smithy all the time possible from early in the morning till almost bed time. This confinement was very injurious to young lads, and from standing in awkward positions to do their work a great number of them became knock or 'knocker'-kneed. The growing 'prentice in his smithy attire was a picture. Tall and thin, with looks that bespoke hard work and poor feeding, he would be encased in leather breeches that had been big enough three or four years before, but with which now he was on bad terms, they having run in and he having run out. The consequence was garments that did not cover to the knees, ludicrously tight, and shining with oil and grease. Or if they were of fustian, they were less constraining than the leather, and consequently needed a constant 'hitch' to keep them from slipping down altogether—for braces were not. On his head he would have an old hat crown, or a brown paper cap; his shirt sleeves doubled up would probably reveal a pair of old stocking legs on his arms. Sometimes, but not always, he enjoyed the luxury of stockings on their proper members, with a pair of old shoes of the 'mester's' or 'dame's,' by way of saving his own for Sundays. Add to these things a shirt unbuttoned at the neck, and a leather apron, and you have a picture of a cutler's 'prentice of former days. The regular diet of the lads was, in the morning a quarter of 'what (oat) cake,' and milk porridge, with not too much milk. To dinner there would be broth and meat from fat mutton or coarse parts of beef. A quarter of oat-cake to 'drinking' at four o'clock, and supper as breakfast. It was considered the height of extravagance to eat oat-cakes that were not a week old. Monday was baking day, and a week's batch was done at a time, so that by the time they were eaten they were quite mouldy, and before the batch was finished they were nearly a fortnight old. The lads then called them biscuit. It used to be said that to let the lads eat new bread would ruin a man with a hundred a year. After supper, the 'prentices had to fetch, on their heads, water for the house supply (sometimes from a considerable distance) ; to feed the pigs ; and then, if there were no errands to run, they might play till bed time. Before a lad was bound he generally 'went a liking' to his proposed master, and if this led to satisfaction on both sides he was taken to the Cutlers' Hall, where he was bound apprentice until he had attained the full age of twenty-one, the binding fee being half a crown, which was paid by the lad's friends or the master. His seven years' service was no pleasant thing to look forward to, but there was the encouraging prospect of having a good trade in his fingers at the end of the time. That over he had to take out his mark and

freedom before he could begin working as a journeyman with
safety. His mark was registered by the Cutlers' Company
for a fee of 2s. 6d., with 2d. annually as 'mark rent.' If he
neglected paying this for seven years any other person might
take the mark. Otherwise it was piracy for any person to
strike a mark without the consent of the owner. Sometimes
a mark was let for a sort of royalty—say 1s. per gross if it
were a profitable one. There have been instances of the
right of mark being sold for as much as £150, when it was
in good repute."

LEONARD : I do not think we ought to dismiss the subject
of apprentices without a glance at the " Dames," who had
so much to do with them. There used to be a saying that
there have been no good doings in Sheffield since so many
fine mistresses came into fashion and the good old dames
were supplanted. Dames were always looked upon as matrons,
and claimed respect. The 'prentice lad regarded his dame
as a mother, and she acted a motherly part to him. Dames
had all the management of the affairs of the house and family,
" t'mester" never interfering in them. " There were," said
a writer now dead, " a great many dames when I was a boy,
and they would have taken offence if any one had given them
title of mistress, since that word was then used only in its bad
meaning. Ladies of higher rank were ' Madams,' as Madams
Shore, Fell, Bamforth, Hutton, &c. Some of these madams
wore hoops of cane near the bottom of their gowns, 40 inches
or more in diameter, and to enter a door they had to pull
their gown bottoms aslant to obtain entrance. Nothing so
ridiculous had ever been seen until crinolines came into vogue
a few years ago. There was a wonderful difference in the
appearance of these madams and the dames. The latter, on
a working day, had a linsey-wolsey or checked bed-gown, in
which to do her household work; a woollen or blue apron before her, and her plain cap fitting close to her head. The
house was a model of brightness and order. Everything in its
proper place, ' clean as a new pin,' the pewter and pewter-case
a credit to her care. The trenchers as clean, the fire-irons,
candlesticks, brasses, coppers, &c., as bright as hands could
make them. In the evening you would see her daughter and
the servant girl—should one be kept—at a spinning wheel.
All the dame's bed and table linen had been spun thus : each
had her task of spinning to accomplish by the end of the
week, and the noise was such as would not now be tolerated
by the male members of the family. On a Sunday, the dame

was a model of cleanliness and neatness. Not a pin out of its proper place; her gown-body and sleeves as tight as her skin, the gown skirt (open in front) displaying an excellent quilted petticoat, three or four thicknesses of calamanca. Nor was she ashamed of a fine Irish linen apron, as white as the driven snow. On her head she would have her best mob-cap, neatly plaited and tied close under her chin. Her gown came up to her neck, and then appeared a white muslin kerchief. Her hair was turned up in front over a roll an inch and a half broad, and behind her head her hair was turned up close. No flowing ringlets about *her* face, and nothing to hide a full view of it. Her stockings were of white thread, knitted by herself in intervals of leisure ; her shoe heels an inch high, her shoe fronts adorned with a pair of bright buckles. In fine weather she would wear a short silk cloak, with lace upon the cape and bottom, two inches broad ; in wet weather, an oil-case hood and tippet. A pair of good pattens were necessary to keep her out of the dirt, and she took care to hold her petticoats up to the calves of her legs, to prevent any chance of them being ' drabbled.' When umbrellas came into vogue she wondered how people could have the pride and assurance to walk under them. She wore no preposterous stays that laced behind, but a pair of good ' jumps,' with three or four buckles and straps in front—which were invariably slackened upon the hearthstone, and the stomacher taken out a little time before going to bed. Then was the time when, with garters also taken off her stockings, the good dame unbent. ' Mester' and dame would have their pipes upon the hearth, with a quiet talk over family matters. The good dame was noted throughout the neighbourhood of her house for her good and charitable disposition ; she was always ready to give help to those in sickness or distress. Dame Hoult, who lived at the sign of the Parrot for many years, was, perhaps, the last person who went by the old name. That was 70 years ago."

TWISS : So much for the 'prentices' natural task-mistress. Now for the shops in which they worked :—" Smithy, in Sheffield, is becoming an obsolete term; instead of speaking of ' ahr smithy,' our cutlery makers have ' my factory,' or ' warehouse,' or ' workshops.' To realise the Old Sheffield smithy you must picture to yourself a stone building, of similar workmanship to common field walls, seven or eight yards long by four wide, and seven feet high to the rise of the roof. It is open to the slates or thatch. The door is in the

middle of one side, with the fireplace facing it; and at either
end is a hearth, with the bellows in the corner, and the
' stithy stocks' in their proper situations. The walls are
plastered over with clay or ' wheel swarf,' to keep the wind out
of the crevices ; sometimes the luxury of a rough coat of lime
may even be indulged in. The floor is of mud, the windows,
about half a yard wide and a yard long, have white paper,
well saturated in boiled oil, instead of glass, or in summer
are open to the air. In one corner is a place partitioned off
' for t'mester' as a warehouse or store room, and on each side
are the work-boards with vices for hafters, putters together,
&c. Over the fireplace is a paddywack almanack, and the
walls are covered with last dying speeches and confessions,
' Death and the Lady,' wilful murders, Christmas carols, lists
of all the running horses, and so forth. Hens use the smithy
for their roosting place, and some times other live stock have
a harbour there—as rabbits, guinea pigs, or ducks, while the
walls are not destitute of singing birds' cages. There are
odorous out-offices close adjoining, and it is essential that the
whole should be within easy call from the back door of
't' mester's' house.''

WRAGG : We must not pass Pea croft without a mention
of that old and respectable firm, Matthias Spencer and Son.
In 1787, it was simply Matthias Spencer, file smith; but
later the son was added to the firm, and they became steel
converters and refiners ; and, instead of the simple '' file
smith,'' they were '' manufacturers of files, edge tools, saws,
&c.'' The descendants of the original firm are still there,
and old Mr. John Spencer, who lives at Rotherham and has
not discarded breeches for such new-fangled things as trousers, is the senior past Master of the Cutlers' Company. He
held the office in 1835.

LEIGHTON : Another Master Cutler of Pea croft fame was
George Wood, scissors maker. His was the house with the
palisades, now a beer-house. His year of office was 1791,
and the previous year having been distinguished by a dispute
between the masters and their workmen, in which Mr. Wood
took a prominent part, he came in for a share of Mather's un-
sparing abuse.

WRAGG : In Hawley croft were located the Messrs. Rodgers,
now of Norfolk street. In the same street is a stone building,
with quoins and string courses, and two bow windows—
having evidently been shops. The date of this is 1724, with
the initials $_T^M{}_M$. The door above is a very large house ; when

it was built it would perhaps be the largest house in the town. It was a beer-house for a number of years.

EVERARD : The house consists of 24 rooms, one of which is built up, and it is now used as a lodging house. Over the fire place is a sort of shield bearing the date of 1721 and the initials $_D^T_S$; (the S is somewhat doubtful—it may be some other letter). My father has often told me that when he was a little boy and lived in the neighbourhood, " Squire Bright," as he was then called, lived in this house. He was described as a goodly-looking personage, with powdered wig, cocked-hat, golden-headed cane, and silver shoe-buckles, who might often be seen standing at the entrance ; whilst the young urchins were wont to gaze upon him with admiration and wonder, and would occasionally get a peep at his flock of beautiful pigeons, and at the green grass-plot at the back of the house, together with the gardens. These comprised the land extending to " Lee croft," and, I believe, included the site on which Lee croft Chapel now stands.

LEONARD : Mr. Holland has it that one of these Hawley croft houses—probably he means that of 1724, was built and occupied by Jonathan Watkinson, of whom we spoke in connection with Silver street. I do not know on what evidence.

LEIGHTON : In Hawley croft, too, was Jonathan Beardshaw. He kept an inn, the very house above described, with the passage that leads into Lee croft, and he made much money there.

WRAGG : Yes, it was the Ball he kept, and he did it with profit and credit to himself. He was the father of the late Alderman Beardshaw, and the grandfather of the present Messrs. Beardshaw, of Baltic Works, Attercliffe.

LEIGHTON : He was by trade a silversmith, but on his only surviving son, George, coming of age, he set him up, and entered into partnership in the saw trade.

WRAGG : In White croft were Mr. James Wild (of whom I spoke in connection with his residence at the top of Town-head street) and the Jervises, descended from the Dutch cutlers who were amongst the artisans that quitted the Nether-lands to avoid the cruelty of the Duke of Alva, and who came to Sheffield through the instrumentality of the Earl of Shrewsbury.

EVERARD : "Lawyer Jervis," the Rev. Mr. Jervis, formerly of the Collegiate School, and Mr. Jervis, late druggist in Glossop road (who had been apprenticed to Messrs. Carr, Woodhouse, and Carr), were of this family.

WRAGG: In Sims croft—No. 6—the grandfather of the late Mr. Rowbotham, grocer, carried on business before he removed into Tenter street, opposite the bottom of Sims croft, about 80 years ago. It is easy in all these streets still to spot out the houses of the old manufacturers. They are mostly now public or beer houses. At the top of Sims croft, for instance, there is one. Formerly it was occupied by a person named Bee, in the brace-bit line. In his day, it was said, he was making money fast by possessing a valuable secret in gilding. There, 60 years ago, one of his sons kept a hunter, which was considered a wonderful thing at that time. In Hollis croft, on the premises now occupied by the Messrs. Elliot, were the Greaveses, before they removed into Division street (now I. P. Cutts, Sutton and Co.'s premises) prior to building Sheaf works. Higher up in the street were Messrs. Kenyon's file works, afterwards occupied by Charles Burgin; and at the top, at the corner of Red hill, was the residence of Mr. Gardner, a partner in the firm. It was near to Mr. Dunn's, and was as good a house.

WRAGG: Next to the Kenyons' works, in Hollis croft, were those of the Harrison family, of whom Miss Harrison, of Weston, was the last representative. There, too, were fixed the Shepherds, razor manufacturers. The last survivor died on Crookes moor, late the residence of Mr. Edwin Hunter. Higher up resided John Knott, who claimed to be a poet. I never saw him but once. He was a poor old man, with somewhat curious features, dressed in a Hanby's Charity coat. When I saw him he had one of his productions, which he appeared to be offering for sale. The price, he said, was twopence; and he boasted that it was equal to any of Montgomery's. He wrote two nautical songs that possessed fire equal to Dibden's. I should like to see his effusions printed in a collected form, as Mather's have been. If I am not mistaken he married the sister of Thomas Smith, the constable, —at any rate there was some relationship. He was by trade a working hatter—now, I believe, there is not a hat made in Sheffield—but one of the eccentricities of genius he possessed was a love of drink, and he ended his days in the Kelham street Workhouse. At the top of Hollis croft was an extensive table-knife manufacturer, named Brownhill, who had the premises now occupied by Mr. Stephen Bacon. He had the character of being ready to second anything at the meetings of the Masters' committee; so on one occasion it was moved that all the table-blade grinders should be hung. Mr. Brownhill, either unintentionally or for the sake of the joke, maintained his character by seconding it, and he got in consequence a cognomen of "Second-the-motion-Brownhill," to distinguish him from his brother Jonathan, at the Red hill works. That name stuck to him until his death. On the opposite side were Makin and Sanderson, fork manufacturers, the latter of whom was subsequently in business lower down in the same street. Mr. Makin, better known as "Makin in the Brick-hole" (Carr lane), died on the 10th of March in the present year, in his 91st year, having become a recipient of the pensions of the Iron and Hardware Charity, as was also his partner, Mr. Sanderson. He was one of the Makins of the Pickle, and I have heard him say that he believed he was the only one living in the town or neighbourhood who heard John Wesley preach on his last visit to Sheffield in 1788.

LEONARD: I fancy he may have been mistaken, for a venerable friend to whom I have had previously to refer, Mr. William Ash, remembers to have heard Wesley—though possibly not at his last visit. It was when he preached in old Garden street Chapel, which then belonged to the Methodists. The women sat on one side, and the men on the other. The same old man once heard Dr. Coke preach in Carver street Chapel, and the celebrated Mr. Benson, the contemporary of Wesley, preach at his grandfather's house at Heeley.

TWISS: And up to a few years ago—1867—there was an old lady living who not only heard Wesley preach, but had his hand laid on her head, and who received sixpence from him. It is appropriate to mention the story here (you will find its details in Gatty's Hunter's Hallamshire, p. 302), since she married in 1791, Richard Howlden, a cutler in this Hollis croft we are speaking of. He died in 1807. She remained his widow, and died not long after Dr. Gatty saw her, aged near 100.

WRAGG: The mention of Mr. John Hawksley, dealer in stag horns, another Hollis croft worthy, should not be omitted. Messrs. G. and J. W. Hawksley, until lately powder flask manufacturers, Carver street, are his relatives.

LEIGHTON: An old Hollis croft public-house was "The Cock."

WRAGG: Yes, it was once kept by the father of the Mr. Jonathan Beardshaw, who has been mentioned as landlord of the Ball, Hawley croft. His widow and his daughter's husband, named Henderson, also kept it.

LEIGHTON: Passing down the street, a few days ago, I

found myself standing opposite to the house. I was sorry to see that the cock had lost some of the gay plumage which adorned him so well 40 or 50 years ago; yet he still holds up his crest as proud as ever, and is ready to do battle as in the days of yore against all who shall presume to poach upon his domestic domain. I thought of the days that are long gone by, and of the old song :—

> " Bright Chanticleer proclaims the dawn,
> And spangles deck the sky."

Again,

> " My Lord, the early village cock hath thrice
> Bid salutation to the morn."

And again, that it was St. Thomas's Day. All hail to the founders of the Hollis Hospital, from whom the croft takes its name. They are to be found recorded within the grounds at the bottom of Snig hill, and a full history is given in Hunter's Hallamshire. The trustees in their wisdom, and no doubt with the best intentions, let the ground in Hollis croft on building leases for 900 years, the front at 1s. per yard, and large pieces of ground at the back for nothing. That they were generous souls is sufficiently proved by their allowing three guineas to the tenantry to enable them to enjoy a good old English dinner. It was held at the " Cock," on St. Thomas's Day, and these are the names of some of those who took a delight in attending. There were three brothers of the name of Shepherd, two of whom I knew. They were invariably together, one of them walking about a yard in advance of the other. Other two brothers were Samuel and Benjamin Marples. I had the pleasure of knowing them well—honesty and truth were in them, and when one died the other could not live; he did not long survive his friend, his companion, his brother. Now, whatever I have said in praise of the above applies equally to those I shall mention below—Mr. Philip Law, Mr. John Spencer (Matthias Spencer and Son, Pea croft) ; and oh, what delight I feel when I meet his venerable figure, and look upon his cheerful countenance. He will long be remembered. Mr. Jonathan Beardshaw, of whom more anon; Mr. John Hawksley, Mr. James Wild (of whom you have heard before), Messrs. Shirtcliffe, Skinner, Barraclough (Messrs. Wingfield and Rowbotham), Benjamin Leathley, Thomas Makin, Charles Sanderson, and various others. Their descendants are still amongst us, keeping up the good names of their families. The dinner is over, the usual loyal toasts are given, the landlord is ordered; the spirits, the lemons, the sugar, &c., are brought in, and Mr. Beardshaw, in accordance with the time-honoured custom, is called to mix the punch. He consults his friends. A little more lemon, says Mr. Wild; a little more sugar, says another; and the mirth begins. Mr. Beard-shaw is called upon to sing his song of the " Flat Backs ":—

" To mak 'em we are willin,
A basket full for a shillin,
Red herrins and potatoes
Our bellies to be fillin."

But though times were bad with them, they could still be generous with the ale, and " Pray the' gie Steen (Stephen) a sup, for he is varry dry, his throat is full of smithy sleck, the wind has been so high." Other songs followed. The old warlike ones were not forgotten.

" Let the song go round, let the shouts resound,
Let the trumpet sound on Spanish ground;
Let the cymbals bang, with a merry, merry clang,
To the joys of the next campaign—
To the joys of the next campaign."

Amidst all the mirth and jollity which prevailed, one thing was never forgotten, a subscription for the poor widows of the street. It was always a liberal one, and I have no doubt carried comfort and consolation along with it. It is not always a pleasure to recall the past, but in the course of a pretty long life I have experienced a full share of bright sunshine, to which I can look back with pleasure; and some of the moments I passed on St. Thomas's Day, at the sign of the " Cock," are among these. Several of those whom I have named above could well afford to ride in their own carriages, but they were plain men, and would have felt ashamed to have been seen in them; but in these days, when wealth is accumulated by leaps and bounds,

" Some drive along with four in hand,
While others drive at random,
In wisky-buggy, gig or dog-cart,
Curricle or tandem."

Twiss : When speaking of fraternal affection of Samuel and Benjamin Marples you might have added that, inseparable as they were, it was the rarest thing in the world to see them without their wives. The four were always together, and formed a most harmonious quartette.

Wragg : In Bailey street we may again see what I have noticed before—the houses of substantial manufacturers turned into taverns. Behind they had their workshops. The top house, No. 12, until recently a beer-house, was the residence of one of the Wing family, who carried on a good file trade in the yard. In this street, about 50 years ago, resided "Jemmy Frith," the first money-club defaulter in the town ; and his relative, John Wright, "Honest John," who followed his example in 1833, was born here.

LEONARD : You are certainily comparing the father with the son. It was James Frith, the son of Jemmy, who defrauded the money clubs. The original Jemmy Frith was for many years leader of singing in Carver street Chapel—indeed from the opening of the chapel until his death. He gathered together a large company of vocal and instrumental performers for Christmas Day, nearly filling the whole front part of the gallery. For many years this was at five o'clock in the morning, but subsequently it was held at six o'clock, in Norfolk street Chapel ; and at half-past ten, and six in the evening, in Carver street. Occasionally he secured the services of his cousins—I think they were—Sam and Tom Frith, both of whom were accustomed to discourse sweet sounds in Queen street Chapel. If I recollect aright, all three had almost unsurpassed voices and capacity of modulation.

WRAGG : At any rate, the Frith I mean slipped away to America to evade the consequences of his delinquencies, but Wright was transported from Pontefract sessions (1833). He was defended by counsel, but he made a speech of so much ability in defence, that it was noticed by the first Lord Wharncliffe in passing sentence. His Lordship told him that he appeared to be a person of no ordinary abilities, and a man of some considerable education, but on that very account he was all the more dangerous. None of the learned counsel present, could, his Lordship added, have made a better speech. His clubs were held at 56, Orchard street. A few years after his transportation, a memorial was got up to the Government, which enabled his wife and family to rejoin him. They were residing at No. 32 in this street—the door below James Frith's residence. The men who were members of "Honest John's" clubs are now very few. Out of the 36 witnesses who appeared against him at Pontefract I believe there is only one left—a gentleman who has been Mayor and who is still an Alderman. It was on Mr. B. Hinchliffe's case that Wright was convicted. Hinchliffe paid Wright five pounds, two shillings and a penny. Wright scratched out the five and put the money in his pocket. On his trial he put forth the plea of ill health, which had placed him under the necessity of engaging other clerks, and this might be the cause of the irregularities or deficiencies. At the time it was always thought other people also had a finger in the pie.

TWISS: So far as Broad lane is concerned, I don't think we can improve upon the interesting and exhaustive account of it that has appeared lately under the title of "Personal Recollections of Broad lane and its Vicinity;" and fancy I am not far wrong in imputing its authorship to our friend, Mr. Everard; so I think he cannot do better than read it to us.

EVERARD: I decline to plead either guilty or not guilty to the imputation, but I have no objection to read the "Recollections," premising only that they are by one who is a native of the place. (Reads)

"About the beginning of the present century, Messrs. Ashforth, Ellis and Co., silver-plate manufacturers, having found their works situated behind Angel street too small, they built and removed to the manufactory now belonging to Messrs. Horrabin Brothers, at the top of Red hill. One of the partners, Mr. Samuel Ellis, had a number of years previously built and resided in the house in Broad lane, the garden and orchard extending to the top of Red hill, and which is now occupied as a Roman Catholic presbytery. He was somewhat remarkable in his personal appearance, being tall, with a nose and profile not unlike the Duke of Wellington's. He wore a brown wig, Quaker-shaped coat, white cravat, and shoes with large buckles. He was so exceedingly fond of flowers that he was scarcely ever seen abroad without having a flower or sprig in his button-hole; and was known by scores of people only as 'the old gentleman with a flower in his coat.' Mr. Ellis afterwards sold the house and land in question to Mr. Henry Longden (grandfather to the present Mr. Longden, of the Phœnix foundry), who was one of the original Methodists; and an account of his life and labours was published many years ago by his son. The Orchard was the plot of ground on which Red hill terrace now stands, and which was built by Mr. John Vickers, who bought the property of the late Mr. Henry Longden, and for many years resided there.

"Mr. Vickers was the first, I believe, who began the Britannia metal teapot manufacture in Sheffield. His works were in Garden street, or 'Garden Walk,' as it was at that time named. This trade he had for a while to himself, and was celebrated for the excellence of his wares ; until at length others, amongst whom were Messrs. Dixon and Smith, established in Silver street up to the time of their removal to ' Cornish place,' began to rival him."

LEIGHTON: Excuse the interruption, but is that statement that Mr. Vickers was the first manufacturer of Britannia metal teapots quite correct ? I have heard the honour claimed for Mr. Constantine, then carrying on business in Scotland street, who was uncle to Mr. Edwin Smith, sculptor, Cemetery road.

EVERARD: I know that the question, "Who was the first?" is a disputed point, but it is my conviction (in the absence of stronger evidence to the contrary than I have yet seen), that to Mr. John Vickers, in partnership with his father Mr. James Vickers, the honour is due. As a boy I knew him as far back as 1814, when his father was dead, and he was carrying on the business probably at the period of its greatest success. Mr. Rogers Broadhead, the successor of his father's firm, has confirmed me in my opinion, and has fully admitted the priority of the Messrs. Vickers to Messrs. Broadhead and Co. As for Mr. James Dixon, he was an apprentice, I believe, with Messrs. Broadhead and Co., and afterwards worked as a journeyman both for them and for Mr. Constantine.

TWISS: I have an account of the origin of the manufacture from the pen of an elderly gentleman, now deceased, which quite confirms your view; and since his father had something to do with the matter, he had good opportunity for forming an opinion. This is his story :—" I have heard it said that Mr. Nathaniel Gower was the first person who began the Britannia, or white metal trade, but I differ in opinion, because of circumstances which have been known to me from childhood, and from proof in my father's memoranda. Mr. Nathaniel Gower was an early manufacturer, and a very respectable person in the trade in its infancy [he was in partnership with Mr. Georgius Smith, and died in 1813, aged 83] ; but Mr. James Vickers, of Garden street, was the first person who began manufacturing white metal articles in Sheffield. About the year 1769, a person was taken very ill, and Mr. Vickers visited him in his sickness. This man was in possession of the recipe for making white metal. Mr. Vickers bid him 5s. for the recipe, and the offer was accepted. Having experimented and found the metal to be of very good colour, Mr. Vickers purchased some spoon moulds, and began casting spoons. Getting them well finished, he obtained a tolerable sale for them. He then got moulds made of vegetable forks, and these assisted the variety on the market. My father was visiting him in a friendly manner one night, when Vickers said, 'Well, Charles, if I had but £10, I would get up a stock of goods and go to Lunnon with them.' My father lent him the money, and a short time afterwards, in another conversation, Vickers says, 'Well, Charles, I thought if I was in possession of £10 I could have done anything, but now I find myself as fast as ever I was.' My father replied, 'Well, James, I can lend thee another £10, if thou thinks it will do thee any good.' He did so. Vickers went to London, and his journey was successful. He sold his articles, and got orders in excess of the material he could obtain to execute them with. He kept the money until after his second journey, when he repaid my father. He then began making a different kind of article, as tobacco boxes, beakers, tea and coffee pots, sugar basins, cream jugs, &c., and got on rapidly in business. Froggatt, Coldwell, and Co., Spoiles and Gurney, and Parkins, in Campo lane, were all old houses in that line."

EVERARD : During this break off, permit me just to remark that Messrs. Broadhead, Gurney, Spoiles and Co., were established as manufacturers in Bank street, in 1789. I will now proceed with the reading of the paper :

"At the top of Red hill, some years subsequently, lived Mr. Morton, who had formerly carried on a large silver-plated business, and was the grandfather of the late Mr. Thomas Dunn. The celebrated Independent preacher, the Reverend William Thorpe, of Bristol, had been one of his apprentices ; and never came to Sheffield without visiting his old master. In the large house in Solly street, or Corn hill, fronting Red hill, lived for many years Mr. Thomas Dunn, senior : and this was the home in which our late highly esteemed and able magistrate was brought up.

"The ground on which Red hill School now stands was a garden, in which, as a child, I have gathered flowers. It was then occupied, and I believe owned, by Mr. Binney, the father of Mr. Binney, the attorney. In 1811, this school was built as a Methodist Sunday School ; the upper rooms being let off as a day school. The first schoolmaster was M. Guion, a person of French extraction, who was an able teacher, and carried on for many years this respectable commercial academy. At this school were educated, as my schoolfellows, the late W. F. Dixon, Esq., of Page Hall ; the late Mr. Brightmore Mitchell ; Mr. Henry Elliot Hoole, of Green lane Works ;

the late Messrs. Morgan and Henry Armitage, of the Mouse-
hole Forge ; Mr. Henry Pickford, 'the learned grinder,' who
acquired a knowledge of French, Latin, Greek, and Hebrew,
by nearly his unaided efforts, and who died in early life ; and
Mr. William Ibbitt, who at one time represented the St.
George's Ward in the Town Council, and was well known by
the publication of a series of coloured prints, being 'Views of
Sheffield and the neighbourhood.'

"The school in question was afterwards kept for a number of years by the late Mr. John Eadon (who had previously
occupied the school belonging to Queen street Chapel), the
nephew and assistant of the celebrated John Eadon, the
mathematician.

"A few yards from Red hill, down Broad lane, there is
a blank space enclosed with a high and substantial wall. Few
persons of the present generation will be aware of that spot
having been a Cemetery. At the commencement of this
century it was the only Quakers' burial ground in the town ;
though they had several places in the country. I myself have
seen two persons interred in this plot, both of them adult
females.

"The next building below was a large and respectable
house, with a clock in front of it. This was the residence
of Mr. Samuel Hill, who was much celebrated in his day for
his proficiency in clock making and repairing. Many of his
clocks may be seen in the town, but more especially in the
neighbouring villages, with his name on the face. He was
a tall man, wearing a broad-brimmed hat, long coat, with
breeches and leggings. He kept a stout pony on which to go
his rounds in the country, with his case of tools ; and at their
own houses cleaned and repaired the clocks of the farmers
and villagers. He was a respectable man, and very widely
and generally esteemed.

"Although at a period earlier than my recollection, yet
the late Samuel Hadfield, Esq., told me that his parents had
at one time resided in one of the three houses at the corner
of Red hill and Broad lane (I forget which), when himself
and his brother George—afterwards M.P. for Sheffield—were
young boys.

"The Broad lane of my early days was very different in
appearance to what it is now. At that time the lane proper
was the highway, but sunk lower than the present causeway
by four or five feet, from St. Thomas street to Newcastle
street—and to some extent to Rockingham street. The

opposite side was a rough bank of red earth (from whence the name) partially covered with grass, with footpaths from the lower to the higher ground. After remaining a number of years in that state, the late Mr. James Dixon, being appointed overseer of the highways, lowered the Red hill from top to bottom, and with the soil filled up the road to its present level, and sloped the bank to its actual state.

"In the neighbourhood of Broad lane there lived a man, whom I well knew, named Michael Davenport, by trade a table-knife cutler, but possessing great genius for mechanical inventions. He got a boat about three feet long, and fitted it up with a little steam-engine which he himself had made. When he thought the thing was complete, one day at noon he brought it to Mr. Harrison's brick pond, to put it to the practical test. He had a fair number of spectators, young and old; but in consequence of something the matter with the engine, or the fixings, the boat would not move. After trying for some time to remedy this defect, certain of the young rascals present added to poor Michael's chagrin at the failure by mockingly advising him to give the boat a good push, and then it would swim over the pond right enough, at the same time well knowing that it was not for that mode of sailing he had brought it there. But notwithstanding the failure of this experiment, Michael was perfectly right in his idea and in his firm belief, that boats and ships might, and certainly would, be so constructed as to be propelled by steam power. Since that time what progress has been made in this respect, what thousands of steam vessels have been built, and what numbers are now ploughing the ocean in every part of the world!

"At the commencement of the present century, in the bottom house in Red hill, now occupied by Mr. Skinner, surgeon, there lived the Rev. Benjamin Naylor, the assistant minister of the Upper Chapel, and at one time partner with Montgomery in the *Sheffield Iris*. The son of that gentleman was the first inoculated for the cow pox in Sheffield; and the late Offley Shore, Esq., of Meersbrook, was the first in the immediate neighbourhood. In the former of these cases the vaccine matter, enclosed in a quill, was obtained direct from Dr. Jenner, the celebrated discoverer of this preventive of that dreadful disease, the small-pox, which at that time made very fearful and extensive ravages throughout the kingdom. The operation in both instances was performed by Mr. William Staniforth, of Castle street, at that time in full medical practice.

"On the opposite side of Broad lane, in the first house above St. Thomas's street, lived Mr. Ibbotson, the father of the late Mr. William Ibbotson, who married his cousin Mary. Mr. William Ibbotson was consequently brother-in-law as well as cousin to Mr. Henry; and they took to the old gentleman's business, which I believe was the saw trade, and entered into partnership as 'Ibbotson Brothers.' As is generally known, they built the Globe Works; and were one of the first firms in Sheffield which established an extensive trade in saws and cutlery with America.

"During that dreadful time of bad trade, about 1812 or 1814, when flour was six and seven shillings per stone, and even at that price much of it so unsound as to run out of the oven bottom in baking, there were some twelve hundred able-bodied men on the parish, who were sent to the 'burial ground' (now St. George's churchyard) to get clay and to level it. They all wore wooden clogs, partly as a badge of receiving parish relief; and this, I believe, was the first introduction of the wear of wooden clogs in Sheffield, the custom being imported from Lancashire. Many of these men were honest, industrious, and respectable artizans; and the sound of their daily tramp in wooden clogs up and down Broad lane was very sad and ominous; more especially in the ears of such as were themselves expecting soon to be reduced to the like deplorable condition. I believe the spirit and feeling prevalent amongst this mass of working men, at that time, was discontent with the Government, and despondency as to future prospects. They were as men almost driven by the force of circumstances to the verge of despair and revolution. Never in my memory has there been in Sheffield so bad and distressing a time.

"The burial ground above referred to, at length actually became what its name indicated it had been reserved and intended for, by the erection, in 1821, of St. George's Church, at the laying of the foundation of which I was present. It honoured the day of the coronation of George IV. On this occasion there was a triumphal arch erected from the old church gates to the opposite side, illuminated by the lately introduced light of gas.

"In my school-days I have had the honour of playing at cricket, on the burial ground, with the late Mr. Thomas Dunn, being at that time boys residing in the same neighbourhood.

" Let me now add a brief description of what was at the time generally known as the 'Brickholes.' This comprised the large brickfield that extended from St. John's street, nearly to Bailey lane. This was the property of the late Mr. Thomas Harrison, of Weston. The chief manager of this brickyard was old Joseph Marsden, the father of Tom Marsden, afterwards the celebrated cricket player, but who then worked with his father at making bricks.

" A large space out of which the clay had been dug became, by supplies from various sources, filled with water, so as to form a pond extending from Newcastle street to a little beyond Rockingham street. In the winter seasons this was a noted place for sliding and skating. In one part the water was of such a depth that I once saw a person have a very narrow escape from drowning. It was a winter's day, the ice being of great thickness, when, just at dusk, a man who was coming from Trippet lane to Broad lane, in crossing over did not happen to see that there was a hole broken in the ice, and in he went over head! With his hands grasping the edge of the ice he cried out loudly and piteously for help, when a tall young man, snatching a knur stick out of my hand, and another similarly provided, rushed to his aid, and rescued the poor fellow from his extreme peril. The part of Rockingham street where this occurrence took place is, of course, made ground across the 'Brickhole;' and certain portions of Newcastle street and St. Thomas's street are the same.

" It may, perhaps, be a fact interesting to some to know, that the said 'Brickhole' was the spot from whence Sir Francis Chantrey got the clay with which he made his first attempts at modelling busts and figures. He lodged for some time with Mr. Outram, (father of the late Mr. Outram of High street), who carried on the business of cabinet-maker and joiner, living in the house next to the Sovereign inn, the yard and workshops occupying the space now filled up by the said inn, and the houses in Rockingham street extending down to the narrow lane. There was a shop window fronting Trippet lane, in which he exhibited his furniture for sale. One of the first attempts, I believe, of Chantrey at crayon portraits, was the execution of a likeness of old Mr. Outram. This was framed and hung up, and I have often examined it with great interest when a boy. The fact of the great sculptor, who acquired a reputation in that department of art second to none in the kingdom, or perhaps in the world, having dug the materials for his first efforts of plastic skill out

of this spot, is, I think, quite enough to make it interesting,
at least to the minds of some old enough to remember the
place as it then existed, and who admire the genius of Chantrey.

"It will hardly do to conclude these personal recollections
of Broad lane without some brief reference to its annual
festival—an event long anticipated and much enjoyed, especially by the young folks. It was held on Holy Thursday,
and was regarded as a general holiday. In preparation for it
during the previous week, there was a great stir of whitewashing and cleaning, so as to put on the very best appearance.
On that day the Sunday clothes were worn. The best thing
about that festival, as it *now* appears to me, was that it
partook very much of the spirit and character of a social
gathering of relatives and friends—when the married daughter
came to her former home with her children to see 'grandmother,' and aunts and uncles, while youthful cousins of both
sexes, met in kindly association, indulged in joke and laughter,
keenly enjoying ball-play and all other innocent amusements.
Such, at least, was my home experience; and, from all I saw,
my impression was that the experience of our neighbours was
of a similar kind.

"But the great attraction for us youngsters was the gin-
gerbread stalls, the crankies, the swings, the puppet shows,
and the races. The open space, not so large then as now, at
the bottom of Townhead street and Broad lane was just like
a fair. Amidst all this life and animation, restless activity,
din, and turmoil, in perfect contrast might be seen the
'blacksmith,' with pipe in his mouth, and bare brawny arms
resting on the smithy door, looking on the busy scene, with
countenance calm and complacent.

"But the grand expectation and sight were the races.
These were run by donkeys and ponies; the jockeys being
generally milk boys out of the country, who, disencumber-
ing their asses of saddles and milk barrels, prepared for the
contest. The prizes usually were a hat, a smock-frock, or a
teapot; and the courses Bailey-field, Bailey-lane, and Broad
lane. How the riders managed to rush up and down the
steepness of Bailey-field, and the narrowness of Bailey-lane
without some breaking of the necks or limbs, either of themselves or the spectators, is to me up to this day a mystery.
Wearing the new hat, adorned with flying colours, his ruddy
face and bright eyes beaming with conscious triumph, the
victor, after re-saddling his ass, was then accompanied a short

distance homeward, amidst shrill and loud, and hearty acclamations. Such, in 'auld lang syne,' was Broad lane Feast."

LEONARD : Those town feasts, innocent and desirable as they no doubt were when originally instituted as convenient opportunities for family gatherings and so forth, degenerated into mere occasions for drinking; just as fairs, necessary once for business as feasts for social purposes, have outlived their day and are now simply nuisances to all but a few shopkeepers and showmen.

TWISS : Crookes feast is still kept up and should perhaps rank as a village, as distinguished from a town feast. It came usually earlier in the year than any other held in the neighbourhood; but it is recorded that in 1818, through some peculiarity of the calendar into which I have not dived, Broad lane took precedence, being held on the 30th April, while Crookes followed on the 1st May—its usual day. Scotland street feast was held on the 29th of May.

LEONARD : The explanation of the circumstance you mention is that Crookes is a feast fixed on the 1st of May, and Broad lane feast was on the moveable festival of Ascension-day or Holy Thursday. In 1818, Easter was remarkably early (March 22,) and Holy Thursday fell that year on the 29th of April. Easter had not been so early since 1761, and it will not again fall so early for many more than the 100 years mentioned—not until beyond the year 1999.

TWISS : The other town feasts were the Wicker, held on the second Sunday in July ; Little Sheffield, September 29 ; and Attercliffe, on the Sunday nearest to St. James's day.

LEONARD : The old fixtures for Sheffield Fair were the Tuesday after Trinity Sunday and the 28th November. Since 1849, the summer fair has been held a week sooner— that is in Whit-week, so as to kill two holidays with one stone. You are aware that an attempt to combine the winter fair with the Christmas holiday has lately been revived.

LEIGHTON : The village feasts and wakes were very popular about half a century ago, and in many places they were kept up with remarkable spirit. They became, however, a great tax upon those who resided in villages near towns, for on such occasions they were sure to be visited by nearly all, if not all of their relatives, friends, and acquaintances, who seldom omitted availing themselves of a jaunt into the country. And they always took care to be at the village in time for dinner on the feast day. It was formerly a maxim that Sheffielders would go a dozen miles, at least, to see their country cousins for a bellyful of meat. There were no small numbers, however, who went solely for recreation, or to see the stirrings at the place or in the public-houses.

EVERARD: Were the town feasts instituted to give an opportunity of returning the hospitality of the country people?

TWISS: I do not know. Wakes were, in the Catholic times, a dedication of a church, which was kept by watching all night, or what was better known in those days by the appellation of "the vigil." Feasts were originally instituted when there was but a small population in the country, and so on an appointed day the relatives and friends by common consent met together; and at parting an invitation was given to them to return the visit on a fixed day at their respective residences, which might then be in some new formed village. This was called the village feast-day, and caused a great influx of visitors; and being repeated periodically, eventually obtained a degree of notoriety. The parties who thus assembled generally required something to amuse them. The fiddler was engaged for the dancing of the young people, who, with juvenile hilarity, "tripped it on the light fantastic toe," whilst the bull or bear was obtained by the landlord of the public-house (if there was one in the village) for the trial of dogs—a good dog being of considerable value. Matches at football, too, not unfrequently took place, as well as other athletic games. Family affairs were, for the most part, talked over on Sunday. On the following day the sports began. The feast dinner did not consist so much of the delicacies of the season as in the quantity of good, substantial food. The poorest person took care to brew a met of malt ready for the wakes or feast; and it was a practice the night before the feast for neighbours to go to each other's houses to taste their respective "taps" of home-brewed.

WRAGG: There are one or two points not touched on in Mr. Everard's account of Broad lane that I should like to add. The George and Dragon was the residence of the late Rev. Mark Docker's father-in-law, Mr. Brammer, and behind were his pressing shops. When Sanderson Brothers and Co. were in one of the lanes behind the National School, Carver street, they got up more table-knives than any one else in the town, and cut their own bone hafts and scales. The nog ends of the bones were led away as rubbish, and innumerable cart loads of them were thrown into the river at Green lane, and in the brickholes—between Messrs. Riley, Carr and Co.'s works and Rockingham street. Great quantities of them have been dug up in making and enlarging the common sewer. The house mentioned as the residence of Mr. Ibbotson (first above St. Thomas' street), was afterwards occupied by Mr. Guion, the schoolmaster. The door above, now part of the Florist inn, was built by one of the sons-in-law of the late Mr. John Nicholson, of Darnall, who had, before his marriage, been coachman to Mr. Read, of Attercliffe, but who was, when in Broad lane, a scale presser. He attended Howard street Chapel, and an amusing story was told to me about him by a person who was with him on the occasion. The minister, in the course of his discourse, remarked that the time was getting on faster than his sermon. Mr. Nicholson's son-in-law called out from beneath one of the galleries, "Oh, never mind the time; go on." Mr. Boothroyd, who died a few months ago in an accidental manner, was one of his apprentices. Close on the Brickhole was Newton's band-spinning walk. He was better known as "Old Packthread;" and having, by rigid industry and frugality, amassed a competency for each of his children, he went to reside in the bottom house but one in Wilkinson street. With reference to Tom Marsden, the cricketer, he lived in the Jericho, and it was there, and in the Brocco, that he was to be seen, whenever he could get any one to join him at cricket. His wife, when a girl, attended the Garden street Independent Sunday School: her parents lived in the yard above the Florist inn. The father's name was James Garside, who was for many years employed at Younge's spirit vaults, and from that occupation obtained the soubriquet of "Brandy Jemmy." In the yard below St. Thomas' street, Mr. George Bowden had some workshops. He got up table-knives, and, travelling on foot, he visited gentlemen's houses and small country towns, and on his return brought back bones and stag horns, being also in the horn and stag cutting line. In this humble way he acquired a competency, and lived for many years at Ranmoor, where he died not long ago.

EVERARD : There is a resident of Broad lane, once somewhat prominent, who has not been noticed—I mean Joseph Barker, then a New Connexion minister stationed in Sheffield, who resided in Red hill terrace. I understand he gave out the hymns when the first stone of Mount Zion Chapel was laid. He was afterwards excluded from the New Connexion, and was the occasion of a great deal of trouble and some disruption in that body. He then went about the country as an infidel lecturer, and passed through a strange and miserable course of life in England and America. He was eventually reclaimed, and publicly renouncing infidelity in all its forms, he has tried to undo, as far as possible, the mischief he had done. He published an interesting book, with the title of "Teachings of Experience," in which he gave a very striking account of the phases of doubt, scepticism and atheism, through which he had passed ; together with the means and process by which he had been restored to his "right mind" and to the Christian faith.

WRAGG : There was also William Gray, boot and shoe maker, the great "jumper," who lived in Broad lane, the fourth door below Rockingham street. He was, perhaps, the most celebrated jumper that ever travelled with equestrians. One of his feats was to jump over a stage mail coach, with the passengers seated on the top. The way in which he became connected with the horse-riders was that his friend, John Milner, was in the fair when there were two equestrian establishments, namely, Ryan's and Adam's. One of these persons had a leaper, called the "Flying Hussar," from his having been in the army, and the proprietor challenged the production of his equal. John Milner went up to him and said that he could find a man that would surpass him. The proprietor replied that he could not be bothered with him or his application. This circumstance got to the ear of the rival proprietor, who sought out William Gray and engaged him. This, of course, made his establishment the most popular ; people flocked in crowds to see a man jump who was a native of the town. Wherever the establishment with the "Flying Hussar" went, the other invariably followed. At one of the towns in Lancashire, of which the "Flying Hussar" was a native, it was arranged they should contest their jumping powers. Twelve horses were set side by side ; the "Flying Hussar" had the first jump, when he alighted on the back of the sixth horse ; but Gray went over them all. The Lancashire people were so exasperated at the defeat of their townsman, that they used threats of violence against Gray, and it was feared they would carry them out. He got away from the booth in some unusual manner—I forget how. He was not only one of the best and quickest makers of boots and shoes, but, had he been disposed, he might have equally distinguished himself as a pugilist, or race runner; but he possessed more respect for himself than to enter on such a course. That he was a man of great muscular power the following simple instance may be sufficient to show. His wife having complained that she could not use a large maidening pot because it leaked, he told her to fill it with water. She having done so, he lifted the pot over his head, to see where the leakage was, with the greatest ease, and then replaced it on the floor. He possessed considerable conversational powers, and was a good debater. He lived in Broad lane about fifty years. He was a native of Cottingham, near Hull, and his father, I believe, was a market gardener.

LEONARD : Your account of Gray's marvellous jumping powers, reminds one of the still more wonderful doings of Ireland, a Yorkshireman, who exhibited in Sheffield in 1802. An old gentleman of my acquaintance has seen him kick a distended bladder suspended on a pole exceeding twenty feet in height. He also saw him jump over a coach, with four volunteers, having their guns and fixed bayonets in their arms, on the top ; but my informant has some diffidence in telling what seems so incredible.

TWISS : Oh, things quite as extraordinary and difficult of belief are told. As for instance, that he leapt over three men seated on horseback ; over a corn waggon ; that he hopped, and kicked with the same foot, the sign-board of the Greyhound public-house, in Westbar; and that he thought nothing of clearing a turnpike gate, if it happened to come in his way, as easier than going through a turnstile. One peculiarity with him, indeed, seems to have been that he did not treasure up his powers for the circus and the spring-board, but delighted to do them on all occasions for the fun of the thing. He was a Driffield man, and his "mates" used to win many wagers from strangers by backing him to leap over their gigs or carts. In Tickhill, once, he is said to have leaped over a horse at a stand, and then to have cleared it back again without turning round. At Hull he sprang over a number of soldiers standing with fixed bayonets, and to prove his strength of arm, it is related that he has lifted up a chair with a man sitting in it, and has held them out at arm's length. His sister is said to have possessed similar powers, and often amused herself by leaping gates and hedges.

EVERARD : It is probable that some of those stories may be just a shade overdrawn, "distance lending enchantment to the view." But my father witnessed most of the feats now described, performed by Ireland in the Lancasterian school.

TWISS : The Brocco, in this part of the town, alone now remains to claim our attention, and we cannot do better than again trouble our friend Everard for his account of it.

EVERARD (reads): "The Brocco of my early boyhood was a wide and steep declivity, not very easy to describe. Whatever features of beauty the scene might possess, lay in the landscape beyond it. What those were one of the late Mr. Ibbitt's published views, entitled 'The Valley of the Don,' will convey a clearer idea than any verbal description. Standing by the house occupied by the late Mr. H. A. Bacon (the first publisher of the *Sheffield Independent*), at the top of Garden street (Garden walk it was formerly called) the Brocco consisted of a steep and very rugged bankside. It reached in its steepness as far as Edward street, and then extended in a slope and a comparative flat as far as Allen street. The ground was red earth and stones; from whence the boys used to dig 'raddle,' with which they often transformed their faces into a resemblance of the war-painted Red Indians, or the mountebank harlequin. There was a thin covering of grass on the flats; but only in certain parts sufficient depth of soil to form sod. The appearance, as seen from the bottom, was that of a number of little hillocks and knolls of red earth of various shapes, partially green. There was a footpath from the top of Garden street down the steep incline to Edward street, East; and another sloping road, now built upon, as a cross street. Allen street, at the point of it that crossed the Brocco, was only a highway without any houses, so that there was a clear space and view from the top of Garden street to the Jericho.

"This view included Mr. Hoyle's house (Hoyle street), which then stood enclosed in what, perhaps, might be described as a small park. At the back of this house was a row of high trees, serving as a rookery, where the birds built their nests, and around which they might be seen taking their aërial flights. The narrow lane, now called Burnt Tree lane, was then the road from Allen street to Portmahon, in which there was a white painted pair of gates, with the carriage way running in a straight line to the front door of the house. In the same lane stood an oak tree, which, during a severe thunderstorm, was struck and scathed by the lightning. Hence the name it acquired."

WRAGG: From Radford street downwards was, sixty years ago, quite in the country, there being only the houses of Mr. Hoyle and of several cowkeepers—well-to-do men, of some property.

LEIGHTON: Old lawyer Hoyle was a great man, with his cocked hat.

WRAGG : There was in Radford street Mr. Dounes, the first Baptist minister in the town ; also Mr. Dixon, a cutler, the father of James Dixon, the founder of Cornish place, and of the Rev. Francis Dixon, for many years the consistent · minister of Lee Croft Chapel, who, besides, was said to be the best auditor of accounts in Sheffield. It is reported of the late Mr. Robert Rodgers, solicitor, that he often declared there would never be another " Frankey Dixon" at accounts. It is said that the late Hugh Parker was a sleeping partner in some colliery, and when the firm was dissolved, Mr. Parker was not satisfied with what he had to receive, so he suggested that Mr. Dixon should audit the accounts, to which it was agreed, the result to be final. A cart load of books was taken to him, and this is said to have been the greatest job Mr. Dixon ever had, and he had many. As the result of Mr. Dixon's labours, it appeared Mr. Parker, as he had firmly anticipated, had a large sum to receive. Mr. Dixon was paid what he charged, and Mr. Parker gave him, in addition, one hundred pounds. Mr. Dixon was the maternal grandfather of Mr. Alfred Allott. At the corner of Radford street and Allen street, was Mr. Beardshaw, cutler, the grandfather of Mr. Beardshaw, the engraver. Out of his shop was an un-interrupted view of the Cotton Mill, and when that building was on fire, one of his apprentices saw the flames. Running down the yard to a scale and spring maker, who was working there, he cried that the Cotton Mill was on fire, would he go ? The man could have seen the conflagration from his window, by simply raising his head, but he quietly went on with his work without taking the trouble to look, as he answered : " No, lad, there will be now't put down for it on Saturday neet." In more modern times, in the same neighbourhood, were Messrs. Richard and William Jessop, whose parents were in Pond street. They lived next door to each other, in what is now 245 and 247, Western Bank. In their business they were both together in one room, and for years did not speak to each other. When one wanted the other's opinion, he wrote a question on a bit of paper and passed it over to his brother, who wrote a reply underneath. They said they were of the family of Jessops, of Broomhall, and when the Rev. James Wilkinson died, advertisements appeared for claimants to his property. I have heard Mr. William say they sent in a claim among others.

LEONARD : You remind me of a story of two other brothers, named Glossop, who lived at Stumperlowe Hall.

They were bachelors, and their nephew gave himself the airs
of their heir-at-law.   One day as they sat smoking their
pipes over the fire, Tom, after much musing, spoke : " I say,
John, there's ahr Fred been saying what he'll do when he
gets ahr money, as he's ahr heir."   " Well," asked John,
after a long pause, " what's to be done ?"   " Why," replied
Tom, " one on us must get married."   " Which shall it be ?"
faltered John, conscious of impending misery.   " Don't
know," said his brother, " let's toss up."   They tossed up,
and matrimony fell to John's lot.   Putting his finger in his
eye, he whined, " Thah's bet me again, Tom.   There's never
anything nasty to do but thou maks me do it."   However, he
pocketed his chagrin, took a wife, and there was issue one
daughter, who married a solicitor, named Sargeant.

EVERARD (severely): The prospect from the top of Brocco,
about which I was speaking when interrupted, embraced a
sight of the Infirmary, then standing amidst fields and gardens ; the old Barracks, rendered conspicuous by their whitewashed walls ; the Club Mill, ensconced in the valley beside
the stream of the Don ; the house at Wardsend, on the mar-
gin of the wood ; and above all, the Old Park Wood and
Cook Wood, then existing in much of their primeval beauty ;
their sylvan solitudes undisturbed by the shriek of the railway whistle, as the trains now, by day and night, rush and
thunder through.

LEONARD : I have seen a water-colour drawing in the
possession of Mr. Samuel Gardner, taken from his father's
house at the top of Red hill in 1802, which embraces just
such a view as you describe.   Anything more completely rural
could not be imagined.

EVERARD (continuing to read): " On a dark November
night, in the year 1817, I remember standing with my father
on the top of the Brocco, from eleven o'clock until midnight.
It was on the occasion, and at the very time, of the interment of the lamented Princess Charlotte.   The hillside was
partially covered with groups of spectators, who stood to
watch the firing of the minute guns in the Barrack yard during
the hour of the funeral procession.   The flash of each discharge illuminated for an instant the entire valley, succeeded
by a sense of deeper darkness, as the sound boomed up to
where we stood and reverberated amongst the woods and
hills.   This midnight darkness and the firing, together with
the solemn ' dumb peal' that fell upon the ear from the bells

of the Parish Church, produced on my mind a lasting impression.

"In 1819, there was assembled in the Brocco one of the largest public meetings—certainly the largest I ever saw—held in Sheffield. The occasion was what was then termed the 'Manchester Massacre,' where a public meeting, met to petition Parliament, was, by order of the magistrates, attacked and dispersed by a troop of Yeomanry. Many persons were wounded, and some lives lost. This violation of English liberty roused such a feeling of indignation throughout the country that numerous town and county meetings were held to enter solemn and emphatic protests against it. The meeting in the Brocco was for the purpose of addressing the Prince Regent, and petitioning parliament to institute an inquiry into this outrage on constitutional law and order. The procession was formed in the Wicker, and included almost all the clubs and friendly societies in the town and neighbourhood, with their respective banners and bands of music. On arriving at the ground they were marshalled in their appointed order. The platform was erected on the flat part near Allen street. The late venerable Samuel Shore, Esq., was the chairman, and the late Earl Fitzwilliam was one of the speakers. That vast assemblage, numbering many thousands, and standing rank above rank on the slopes of that natural amphitheatre, together with the display of flags and symbols, presented a magnificent and deeply impressive spectacle. The resolutions having been passed with unanimity, the great meeting dispersed peaceably and in order. More than half a century has passed away since that day; and during this period what changes in the way of improvement have taken place in our political, social, and commercial condition as a nation !

"Adjacent to the Brocco, and almost forming a part of it, was a vacant space much used as a play and cricket ground, named Jericho. On that spot I once witnessed an assemblage met for the purpose of either taking an active part in, or looking on at the cruel and barbarous old English sport of ' bullbaiting.' At that time a man had lately been imported into this neighbourhood, whose proper name I have forgotten, but who went by that of Runcorn, the place from whence he came. He was a strong-built, broad-chested man, with a somewhat surly countenance. He was accompanied and assisted in his vocation by his wife, who at that time was a handsome young woman, but after a very decided type of

rustic beauty. With cheeks like roses, and her strong red
arms, bare above the elbows, she was dressed in a gown of
showy pattern, and on her head she wore a white cap, adorned
with ribbons. Perched on a high wall, and full of boyish
curiosity, I had a perfect view of the whole scene and proceedings. The crowd assembled included some of the choicest
specimens of blackguardism to be found in the town and
neighbourhood. Amidst noise and clamour, passing jibes,
and cursings, together with the yelpings of impatient dogs,
the ring was at length formed, and the sport began. 'Mistress Runcorn,' armed with a hedgestake, which she wielded
with effect, kept the ring, and received the toll for the dogs
at the rate of threepence a slip; whilst her husband attended
to the bull, to see that he had fair play. The animal thus
brought to the stake to torture was a fine, young, and active
one; being, in the current slang of the ring, 'good game.'
There he stood at bay, moving his head from side to side, and
watching the point of attack. The dogs, one after another,
were then slipped, and flew at him. Some of them the bull
managed at the first rush to catch with his horns, and either
gored or tossed them high into the air. Certain of their
masters, on seeing their dogs thus flung, ran to catch them
in their aprons or arms; whilst others allowed them unaided
to run the risk of crippled limbs, or broken backs. The high-
trained dogs appeared generally to aim at the nose or throat
of the animal. One of them fastened and hung on the poor
brute's nether lip, whilst he ramped about in agony and rage,
as far as the tether would allow. And as the climax, at
length a savage dog seized the bull's nose, causing the blood
to flow, and kept his hold until the noble, ill-used creature
was brought down upon his knees to the ground. The event
of the bull being pinned was immediately hailed with a shout
of ferocious delight and triumph, and with loud expressions
of brutal merriment. So the cruel and degrading 'sport'
went on to the end.

"This, I believe, was the last bull-bait in Sheffield. As
a sad, though fitting sequel, I may add that this man, Runcorn, was eventually (May, 1824), so fearfully worried by his
own bear, in a field on the Intake road, that he died in consequence, in the Sheffield Infirmary."

LEIGHTON: Runcorn's real name was William Ladsley.
I believe the circumstances of his death were these. He had
unmuzzled the bear, which was usually a very peaceable
animal, and set it at liberty by way of a treat, on "Bellows

plain," near his residence in the Park. In some way, never explained, the bear becoming suddenly enraged against its master, turned upon him, knocked him down, and worried him on the spot. The poor man's body was taken up in a shockingly mutilated state, though it was with difficulty it could be liberated by slipping dogs at the bear. The murderer was shortly afterwards shot; the hind paws of the animal were fourteen inches long.

LEONARD: Bears seem subject to these fits of anger. A similar case, most of you will remember as occurring within the last few months at the "Welsh Harp," Hendon.

TWISS: Another local case happened at or near Ecclesfield. A bear, kept by a person there, got at liberty and worried the owner's wife.

WRAGG: A noted Sheffield bear-ward was old Arnold Kirk. Like Ladsley he was accustomed to take his bear to the different wakes, for the purpose of baiting. The following is one of his adventures:—Going with his bear to the Derwent wakes, he had reached the middle of the moors, when bruin turned sulky and would proceed no further. At last, when it was quite dark he got into motion again, and Kirk, guided by a light, managed to conduct him to a cottage. The old couple who dwelt there were quite willing to give Kirk a lodging; but how about his unwieldly companion? If they had only, said the old woman, sold their calf, which was to be fetched next morning by the butcher, a day before, bruin might have occupied the shed. Arnold was equal to the occasion, and it was arranged that the calf should be brought into the kitchen, the bear to take its place in the "crib." This was done, and sleep fell upon the mixed household. About midnight Arnold was disturbed by Dick, the bear, making a great noise and growling. Going to investigate the cause, he found that bruin had got a man under him. Arnold called out, "Hold him fast, Dick." He went and informed the old people, who came immediately; and as soon as the old woman saw the man she exclaimed, "Way, Lord bless me, if it is'nt t' butcher we seld t'coaf to 'en he wor to a fetched it and paid for it it mornin'." Arnold says, "So th'art cum'd a coaf stealing, art thou, and thou's getting a fine 'un there; squeeze him again, Dick." The bear did as he was told, and roared out "boukh," again. "Now then, rascal," said Arnold, "if thou does not agree to pay 't price of t' coaf, I will unmuzzle him, and he shall worry thee." He had to purchase liberty from his awkward antagonist by paying his money and receiving no calf in return. The inhabitants of the cottage thus made a good thing out of their hospitality.

JOHNSON : Let me cap that with a bull-baiting story. On one occasion a bull had been procured at Bradwell wakes for the purpose of baiting, but no stake to fasten him to had been provided. Old Mr. Bagshawe, of the Hazlebadge pastures, so far entered into the spirit of the sport that he exclaimed, " Tey him to mey, tey him to mey. We'll neer loost' beit for t'wont on a steck"—supposing, no doubt, that he was sufficiently strong to hold the bull. They did so, and upon the first dog being slipped at the bull, he set off and took Mr. Bagshawe with him at the rope's end through the adjacent brook, and it was with great difficulty that he escaped with his life.

LEONARD : The following " nomine" or proclamation by the bull or bear ward when the ring was formed may, perhaps, wind up our gossip on these obsolete cruelties : " O yes, O yes, O yes ; one dog one bull, or one bitch one bull. Three rebukes and a wind. Everybody keep twenty feet from t' stake or take what comes. Now for t' first dog."

LEIGHTON : Well, we have had a long but very interesting sitting. Good night. *(Exeunt.)*

CHAPTER IX.

THE OLD HAYMARKET—THE WICKER—THE NURSERY—
BRIDGEHOUSES.

Present—Messrs. TWISS, LEIGHTON, EVERARD, WRAGG, LEONARD
and JOHNSON.

Period—A. D. 1874.

LEIGHTON : Before the Old Haymarket was used for the purpose that its name denotes, a cattle market was held there. That, in 1786, was removed into the Wicker. There it remained until 1830, when it went to its present site between the river and the Victoria Station road.

LEONARD : Wonderful changes have taken place during the last few years at the top of the Old Haymarket, in the way of opening it out, first by way of Jehu lane (Commercial street) to the bottom of Norfolk street, and then by demolishing the buildings in the corner to make the new road to the Midland Station. And here we come upon the newest and latest location of the General Post Office. We have found its changes to be many.

WRAGG : Yes, the Nag's Head is an old hostelry that has disappeared to make way for these improvements. It was once kept by the Heatons, one of whom became a barrister. He was employed in Harwood and Thomas's warehouse, as a clerk or manager. Some dispute arose, and, regarding him as their servant, they gave him his dismissal. But he claimed to be a partner, and he had so well studied law and had secured for himself so strong a legal position, that in a law-suit the firm lost, and had to compromise the matter for a large sum.

LEONARD : Do you know what is said to be the origin of the name Jehu lane ? The tradition is, that when Mary Queen of Scots arrived in Sheffield for imprisonment at the Manor, this lane was the main road, and through it she had to pass. The streets had not been planned in expectation of such things as coaches rolling through them, and the lane astonished the Queen's coachman to such an extent that he ejaculated "Jehu!"—by way, I suppose, of invoking the tutelary genius of drivers in his difficulty.

EVERARD: *Credat Judæus!*

LEIGHTON: How the glories of the Old Haymarket have departed since the suppression of the fine old Tontine, and since the rattle of coaches and the galloping of post chaises, and the cracking of postilions' whips gave way to "Waterloos," which, in turn, have been supplanted by ignominious omnibuses and innovating tramways.

WRAGG: The Tontine, built on the site of the Castle barns, was finished in 1785, James Watson being the first landlord, and James Bickley the last. People stared with amazement at the erection of such an hotel and considered its promoters dreaming, but the year after it was acknowledged to be the first in the kingdom.

LEIGHTON: O, why was it pulled down? How well I remember the older Charles Clegg, trumpet-major to the Yeomanry Cavalry, being ordered by the magistrates to sound "the call" for the corps to assemble. Like a brave man as he was he mounted and sounded, first at the front of the Tontine, and then on the flat above the Commercial inn, at that time the vegetable market. There a potato, thrown with great force and unerring aim, entered the mouth of the trumpet, knocked out two of his upper teeth, and he ceased sounding for ever. My old friend had blown his last blast, and never more did he at early morn sound the reveillé, or the tattoo at dewy eve.

EVERARD: At this same Potato riot, or at one about the same time, the following incident was witnessed by my father. The mob was standing near the Yellow Lion inn, and the late Justice Parker, with the constables, stood opposite the Tontine, when a large potato was thrown with great force by an athletic man, wearing a leathern apron, as if by trade a blacksmith or blade forger. The missile struck the magistrate on the chest, and he, lifting his hand to his breast, staggered back. It would appear that as soon as the man saw what he had done his heart smote him (for the justice was a favourite magistrate), and, standing forth a space in front of the mob, he shouted out—"Mester Parker, I didn't intend that to hit yo; I meant it to hit Tom Smith." Thomas Smith, the constable, was standing near Mr. Parker at the moment, and thus escaped being the victim of this very sincere, if not good, intention.

Twiss : The Tontine's history is so well known that we need not go through the old story. Dr. Gatty gives a good description of what it was in its glory, when " twenty horses and five postboys were always ready when the yard bell rang," and how suddenly it collapsed on the opening of the Midland railway. " Twenty pairs of horses were wanted one day; on the morrow the road was forsaken. Thus one of the fine old English inns, in the court-yard of which a carriage and pair could be easily driven round, came to-grief." It was in 1850 that the Duke of Norfolk purchased the hotel for the erection of the New Market Hall.

Leonard : I don't know what Wills means by—

" The old Laiths [barns] in Bullstake, that dismal retreat,
Where hearses and stalls very often did meet,
Is now a large Tontine—the length of a street."

Leonard : The site of the Royal hotel has been occupied for the purposes of a public-house for great numbers of years. It was as long ago as 1779 that " Mr. Godfrey Fox purchased of Mr. Barlow the old public-house and black-smith's shop, and on the ground whereon they stood, built the Rein Deer tavern."

Wragg : Ah, Godfrey Fox occupied that house something like fifty years, and then he went into New Church street. He seems to have been a man of education, for I have a book of his. It consists of a number of pamphlets bound to-gether—comprising Burke's Speech in 1780, and his Reflec-tions on the French Revolution ; also a letter to a Noble Lord (Earl Fitzwilliam), and a reply to this by Mr. C. Browne. On the leaf of the book is written, " From the Author to his friend Godfrey Fox," and on the fly-leaf is written, in a good, clear hand, " Godfrey Fox, Sheffield."

Leighton : We have previously spoken of " Old No. 12" and its spirited proprietor, Mr. Thomas Wiley.

Leonard : I remember that for many years, in the wood-work below one of the windows, was preserved the hole made by a bullet fired by the soldiers during the riot at the first borough election, in 1832. Mr. Wiley had the date painted round the hole.

Wragg : A passing glance at the Town Hall, erected on the Castle hill, the foundation of which was laid in 1808 (altered and enlarged in 1833, and again in 1867), must suffice. Many Sheffielders, indeed, have been glad enough to fight shy of the unpleasant holes " under t' clock," in the days when the new police offices were yet unbuilt.

LEONARD : Some day, perhaps, it may be of interest to remember that the deserted drinking fountain inserted in the wall of the Town Hall, facing Castle street, was the first erected in Sheffield when the fashion arose for supplying these useful places for quenching the thirst. It was erected by the Town Trustees, and was opened by the late Mr. Wm. Fisher, in 1859.

LEIGHTON : These drinking fountains were not a brilliant success here. They were put up by various patriotic individuals, at the Church gates, the bottom of Spital hill, the Moor head, Broad lane, and Gibraltar street, but there soon arose a difficulty about a constant supply of water; the stream stopped and the fountains were abominably disfigured by mischievous boys and roughs. In fact they became nuisances.

LEONARD : Here is Castle street, or True Lovers' gutter:—

> " For lately two lovers were sat on a rail,
> On the edge of the sink, fondly telling their tale,
> When the flood washed them down in each other's embrace,
> For no longer the lovers could sit in that place ;
> And hence, True Lovers' gutter, the name that was given,
> Because by the flood these two lovers were driven."

WRAGG : At the top of Castle green was Mr. Samuel Horsley's shoe shop. He married the sister of the late Mrs. John Nicholson, of Darnall, and one of his nieces lived with him, as he had no children. Mr. Horsley had a nephew on his side, named Glossop, who also lived with him. From this circumstance an attachment was formed between the two, but the young man died, and was buried at Queen street chapel. Mr. Nicholson's daughter became chambermaid at Page Hall, and married Mr. Greaves's coachman. Two of their children, if not three, died in their infancy, and were buried at the old Chapel of Ease at Attercliffe. Then the husband died, and was buried with the children. When the widow (Mr. Nicholson's daughter) died, she requested to be buried with her uncle Horsley, and asked that a walking stick that belonged to the young man Glossop, her uncle's nephew, might be put in her coffin, and buried with her. This shows how strong was her attachment. Mr. Horsley, although a Baptist, attended Queen street chapel, and greatly resembled old Joshua Stephenson. There was a curious circumstance in connection with Mr. Horsley's will. When in his death-illness it was being written, he desired that what he had to leave should be equally divided among the children of his wife's sister. His wife then put in, "excepting John and Elizabeth;" so these two had nothing, although the niece was the one

whom they had brought up, and the John was the grandfather
of the Messrs. Nicholson, of Mowbray street. Perhaps some
particulars of John Nicholson, of Darnall, may not be out of
place here. You will remember the brook on coming out of
the fields by the pathway to Darnall? Instead of turning up
the lane to the village, pedestrians cross it and follow the
course of the brook. There is a row of houses in front, and
at the far end, somewhat detached, is an old shop—there
Mr. Nicholson carried on business, and in one of the houses
he lived. He was descended from the widow Nicholson, mentioned by Hunter in his Hallamshire, as being at the formation of the Nonconformist Church at Attercliffe. His wife
was one of the Wadsworths, whose name is mentioned in the
same way by Hunter. Mrs. Nicholson, previous to her marriage, was lady's maid to Lady Bute, at Wharncliffe Lodge.
They had one son and five daughters. The son was father of
Mr. William Nicholson, late of Sycamore street, and grandfather of the Messrs. Nicholson, of Mowbray street. Of the
daughters, it was said there were not five finer young women in
the neighbourhood. Four out of the five married. One has
been already spoken of as chambermaid at Page Hall, and as
having married Mr. Greaves's coachman. Another was servant at Mr. Read's, Attercliffe, and she married the coachman of Mr. Read. All Mr. Nicholson's daughters married
men who, after their marriage, learnt the trade of a presser.
Two were coachmen, as I have said, one a collier, the fourth
—I don't know what. The collier soon left pressing, and
turned butcher. He opened the second butcher's shop in
Attercliffe (the first butcher in Attercliffe was named Fawley),
and was also the constable. Now as no one could then be
connected with any branch in the cutlery trade except he had
served a legal apprenticeship, these sons-in-law of Mr. Nicholson must have been bound after their marriage. I know for
a fact that one of them was bound to Mr. Nicholson, as the
indenture still exists. It states that he was to learn the
trade of a maker of knives, and bears the date of 10th
January, 1784. It is signed John Nicholson, the attesting
witnesses being Ben Broomhead, the then Master Cutler, and
George Wood. There must be some irregularity in the indenture, as it does not contain the signature of the man apprenticed. What the Master Cutler was I do not know, but
George Wood we noticed in connection with Pea croft. He
writes a beautiful hand; not so Ben Broomhead. Mr. Nicholson's son-in-law (apprentice) took out his freedom on the 25th

day of March, in 1791, and it bears the signature of Joseph
Ward, the Master Cutler, whom I presume would be the
father of Thomas Asline Ward. At that time this mature
apprentice was the father of four children. Mrs. Nicholson
used to taunt or joke her three married daughters for marrying men who had to learn a trade after their marriage, and
told them there was a gentleman who courted one of the
other two. They wondered who he could be, and desired to
see him ; when, lo and behold, he turned out to be a collier,
and turned presser like the other three, but only for a time.
In those days the trade of a presser was a good one. We
came across one of these sons-in-law as residing in Broad
lane. Mr. Nicholson removed to Sheffield to be near his
children, and lived at the top of Broad street, between New
street and the street above, where he died. The property is
destroyed by the railway. His son or grandsons carried on
in Pond street, now 129, lately occupied by Mr. Allcock. In
1804, William Nicholson was Master Cutler. He was a file
maker in Pond street, but he was not son of the foregoing.

TWISS : Passing on to Waingate we stand on classic
ground, but it is a little foreign to the tenor of our usual conversation to go so far back as to try to conjure up an imagi-
nary picture of what the old Castle used to be. The materials
for such a picture are very scanty, and all that remains to us
above ground is the name. " We know that the Castle stood
on rather more than four acres of land, in the angle formed
by the confluence of the Sheaf and the Don, that it was fairly
built of stone and very spacious, and stood around an inward
court and an outward court. Antiquaries may show a stone
in their museums that once formed part of its fabric. Men
who work in what we now call Castle Folds, tell a somewhat
doubtful story of the ground sounding hollow beneath their
hammers, an indication of the existence of cellars. But the
castle itself is nowhere to be seen. Its site is defiled with
killing shambles; its court-yards, barns, stables, and servants'
rooms, its state apartments and its great dining hall, have
given place to shops and works, public-houses, cottages, and
stables. Sheffield Castle, once so massive and strong, has
become a tradition and nothing more."*

LEONARD : That hollow sound beneath the hammers is
not so apochryphal as might be supposed. Some interesting
results could be obtained if only we could carry out such ex-
plorations as the Palestine Fund has been engaged upon in

---

* " Sheffield Castle and Manor Lodge in 1582," by J. D. LEADER.

Jerusalem; but instead of that we actually have opportunities for investigation, when they are thrown in our way, hidden from us. Take, for instance, the narrative that was laid before the Sheffield Archæological Society, in October, 1872, of an interesting discovery and an absurd concealment.

WRAGG: Let us get down into the Wicker, and among the things and people within the memory of living men.

TWISS: What! without even a passing mention of the four alms-houses for poor widows, that were at the foot of the Lady's bridge until 1767 ?

WRAGG: At the old tilt, across the Lady's bridge, which has been so long at work in hammering out the glowing metal, once worked and lived the father of the late Alderman Edwin Unwin. Mr. Unwin was once himself with a man of very different character, Joseph Dewsnap, better known as "Pimpey," who lived in the house now occupied in part by Mr. Leeds, surgeon, and in part by Mr. Aitchison. Dewsnap was originally a razor blade striker, but he became a rent and debt collector, and was the first defaulter in that line. He reigned about seven years, his career being short but "merry," for he made a grand flourish. There are many stories of his extravagance. You may remember that in his latter days he was employed to go round to the grocers, telling them when to raise the price of flour.

LEONARD: Quoting from a notice of Mr. Unwin, which appeared at the time of his death, it may be truly said that great responsibilities were thrown upon him by this default of his employer, but "his genius for figures, his strong good sense and his integrity enabled him so to bear this ordeal that he early established a high character, and laid the foundations for success in life. Mr. Unwin first came into public life as one of the Improvement Commissioners, a body constituted under a local Act in 1818, for lighting, cleansing, watching, &c., the town within a circle of three-quarters of a mile from the Parish Church." Mr. Unwin was elected a commissioner, in August, 1830, and he continued in the office, acting as auditor to the Commissioners, until 1865, until the powers of the body were transferred to the Corporation. In July, 1830, Mr. Unwin became one of the directors of the New Gas Company, and three years later he accepted the office of managing director, retiring from his profession as accountant. When, in 1844, the two companies amalgamated, Mr. Unwin assumed the management of the united concern. Under his control the company was highly efficient and very successful. Mr.

Unwin was a very useful and consistent member of the Town Council. He was first elected in 1845, for Ecclesall Ward; afterwards he represented Upper Hallam, and he was an Alderman from 1856 to his decease. In 1868, a flattering requisition was presented to him by a large majority of the council, requesting him to stand for the mayoralty, but in deference to his medical adviser he was compelled to decline. Mr. Unwin died in London, on the 7th of February, 1870.

WRAGG : Near the bridge was Ebenezer Rhodes, the graphic author of "Peak Scenery," the best literateur Sheffield has yet produced. He was a man of consequence, as he was Master Cutler in 1808 ; but I am sorry so say he was not successful in business. The firm was Rhodes and Champion. Mr. Rhodes died December 16th, 1839, in Victoria street. At the far end of Stanley street, opposite Clay gardens, was John Skinner, who, 40 years ago, had the best steel pen trade in the country, but somehow or other the family let the trade slip out of their hands, and it seems to have taken flight and settled in Birmingham, and enriched the late Joseph Gillott, once a pen blade grinder at the Kelham wheel, now Mr. Crossland's corn mill. In connection with this neighbourhood, it would not be right to pass over the late Edward Smith, for he came of an old Wicker family. His grandfather, Stephen Smith, who died in 1809, at the age of 78, was established in the Wicker. Edward Smith was a man of sterling abilities, but of no ambition, as he might have entered Parliament when he thought proper, under the auspices of the Anti-Corn Law League. As chairman of a meeting, Sheffield never had his equal. He was a man whom a lawyer would call the League's chamber council, as they resorted to him for advice in any doubt or difficulty, and he always encouraged them never to despair, as he had no doubt of the ultimate issue—that success would sooner or later crown their efforts. There are people who can remember Mr. Smith as a lad at home with his parents, at 66, Wicker, then at 114, now the shop of Mr. Simmons ; and finally at Fir vale, with a flower garden second to none in Yorkshire.

EVERARD : Edward Smith took lessons in drawing and water colours, of the same master and at the same time as myself.

WRAGG : The " Station inn," at the corner of Stanley street, was the manufactory of fine scissors and the residence of Mr. Francis Oates (whose family, I believe, came from Stannington), father of the late Mr. Thomas Oates, who became master of the Lancasterian school, and was for many years an Alderman of the town. Another son, George, commenced the Wicker Sunday school—one of the most successful institutions of the kind the town has ever seen, and with which many memorable men among the Independents have been connected. Its beginning was extremely humble, for George Oates began it with only one scholar, an apprentice of his father. He then induced about half a dozen of his neighbours to send their lads, and they met in his father's kitchen. That becoming too small, they removed into the late Mr. Brelsforth's day-school, up the lane, close by. Brelsforth was a diminutive man, quite a cripple, for he could neither stand nor walk without crutches. Under one part of the room was a "midden," and under the other a bear was kept. What with the stench and what with the grunting of the bear, you may well conceive that it was school-keeping under difficulties; but, after great efforts and self-denial, the school in Andrew street was erected (now an omnibus shed for the Carriage Company), and more recently, in 1855, it culminated in the church and schools erected near Burngreave, but keeping the old name of "Wicker." Connected with this school was Joseph Whittington, penblade grinder, an honourable, upright man without any ostentation; the late Edward Hebblethwaite who, Mr. Sissons the president of the Sunday-school Union was not afraid to say, was the best superintendent in Sheffield, Samuel Biggin, Christopher Hyde, James Taylor, Robert Waterhouse, George Tucker, and his brother-in-law, Thomas Birks, who was Mayor in 1849, and Joshua Biggin— the last five were all members of the Corporation. Mr. Joshua Biggin died on the 7th of January, 1873, and Mr. Christopher Hyde is the only survivor.

LEIGHTON: The Bull inn, Wicker, was, if tradition does wrong them, a favourite meeting place of Ebenezer Rhodes, Joseph Gales, James Montgomery, and such men. It was known as "Billy Hill's parlour."

TWISS: That must have been the old 'Sembly house, for in 1775 it is recorded, that it was kept by Hill as a public-house, and that "there were no houses beyond, excepting Mr. Smelter's, between that and the Occupation road, then a foot-path. The ground was open to Tomcross lane, where was a large pasture, kept by a person named Handley, of Old Carr, who took in a great many cows; hither the lasses came in great numbers every night to milk them."

EVERARD: I think it was not the "Bull inn," but the "White Lion inn," on the opposite side of the street, a short distance before you come to Stanley street, which was the favourite meeting place of Montgomery and his friends. It was next door to Ebenezer Rhodes' premises, and, I believe, was kept by a person of the name of Wood, whose son married the eldest daughter of Mr. Rhodes. John Holland (Life of Montgomery) gives an account of the evening when Montgomery suddenly "dropt" going. He had got on his top coat, and was just about to set of, when he asked himself —why he might not just as well stop at home as go? He decided to stay at home, and never went again. It is my impression, that Montgomery had been subject to certain doubts and qualms of conscience, at least as to the waste of time and probably dissipating influence of such convivial meetings.

LEONARD: We have on a previous occasion had some talk about the manner in which the neighbourhood beyond this has changed, within far more recent times than that—within forty years, indeed.

WRAGG: The date when the cattle market was brought down here has already been mentioned. Some of the posts, remnants of the old pens, were remaining up to the time the Manchester, Sheffield and Lincolnshire railway viaduct was built, between the Falstaff inn and the public-house below.

LEIGHTON: We must not forget to mention the old residence of the Heatons, in The Pickle—where, the family tradition says, the Young Pretender once came. Pickle house, which still stood within the memory of persons yet living, was where Mr. John Hobson's steel works are now, the Pickle being the name for the district from the entrance to the old Midland station to the Twelve o'clock. The district near the latter, on the town side, was called Jerusalem. Beyond, all was open country, including what were at the beginning of this century called the Local Fields—where the local Militia was reviewed. These extended towards Royds Mill. Colonel Fenton, the first commissioner of police, living at Wood hill house, on the Grimesthorpe road, could thus have a good view of his review ground in the valley below.

EVERARD: In the Pickle were the silver refining works of the father of the present Mr. Joseph Dixon, afterwards removed to Mowbray street.

WRAGG: We should not leave the neighbourhood of the Wicker without remarking on the learned attempts that have been made to arrive at the correct etymology of the name.

There seems to be little doubt, however, that it was once a marshy place, and that the osiers growing there, and used in basket making, gave it the name.*

LEONARD : The branches of trees, hazel twigs, and so forth, have been found in digging in various places in the neighbourhood of the White Rails, and the sandy deposits tend to show that in these parts the river was once very apt to overflow its possibly not very accurately defined banks. The whole vicinity of the Nursery and the Wicker would, in early times, be swampy.

WRAGG : At the Bridgehouses end of Nursery street, near the Iron bridge and destroyed by the railway, was the Bridgehouse, the residence of the Clay family. Robert Clay, who died in 1737, came from Chesterfield to Sheffield, and for some time resided at Walkley. His granddaughter married Mr. George Bustard Greaves, of Page Hall—

LEIGHTON : Who was extremely wealthy, since the property of the two families was joined by his marriage with the heiress of the Clays.

WRAGG : Mr. Greaves had a warehouse and town residence in Norfolk street, and, previous to his purchase of Page Hall, he lived, I believe, in a large house on Oaks green, Attercliffe. He was the only person in the town who kept a carriage with coachman and footman. Hunter's pedigree represents the Clay family as having expired in an heiress, as a genealogist would say, but this is not so, as Joseph Clay, the father of Mr. Greaves's wife, was twice married. By his first wife, Elizabeth Speight, he had a son, who went to America. From some cause Mr. Clay discarded him, and left him only £10, all his property going to Mrs. Greaves. This disinherited son, however, left issue in America, one of whom was the founder of the Clays of Kentucky, from whom descended the celebrated American senator, Henry Clay. His head, according to phrenologists, was the best developed or most equally balanced on record.

LEONARD : Mr. Clay was the only gentleman in the neighbourhood who was eulogised by Mather—all the rest he satirised or vilified. But this must have been Joseph Clay, not Robert Clay, his father, with whom Mr. John Wilson has confused him. Robert Clay died in the year in which Mather was born.

---

* Hunter's derivation is quite different, but equally doubtful. See for this and other particulars respecting the Wicker, Hunter's Hallamshire, Gatty's edition, 403.

WRAGG : The last inhabitant of the Clays' house was George Burgin, who had entered Mr. Clay's service in boyhood. His son was a printer.

LEIGHTON : The Brightside Bierlow stocks were formerly on the Bridgehouses side of the old Iron bridge.

EVERARD : I well recollect them.

LEONARD : Yes, even I call to mind the remnant of them, and old Mr. Oakes, still living in Westbar,* remembers being incarcerated in them—as he told me with much amusement one day. His offence, I grieve to add, was playing at pitch and toss on a Sunday. Sam Hall, the constable, caught him, and kept him there for an hour. " My mother," said the old man, " came to see me, and didn't she call the fellow for putting me in." He remembers, too, to have seen a man (Bill Jones) tied in a cart and flogged by the beadle on its progress from Castle street to the Town Hall. At Rotherham he saw a man put in the pillory, and subjected to the operation of being pelted with rotten eggs. That was Dick Crown.

WRAGG : As to Bill Jones, there must be some mistake there—he was the whipper, not the whipped, for he was the beadle at the Town Hall; so that instead of receiving, he inflicted the punishment. This Bill Jones took persons to Wakefield House of Correction after their commitment by the magistrates. Hence arose a very common saying at one time in the town, when one person saw another deviating from the path of rectitude—"Bill Jones will soon have thee, without thou mindest." From the road to Wakefield being then up Pye bank, one person would threaten another he would " Send him up Pye bank." The prisoners had to walk, fastened together by a long chain, like a slave gang.

LEIGHTON : Bridgehouses was, in 1789, associated with a tragedy which caused much excitement at the time. The story has been variously told, and it is difficult to get at its exact merits now. A leg of mutton had been taken from a man's basket as he went over Lady's bridge, and one version is that the thieves asked the person who carried it to go with them and get it cooked for supper. One of the men turned King's evidence, for there was £100 (blood money it was called) given to anybody who got a man hanged. The people would have torn him in pieces, but he escaped—it was from

---

* Mr. Oakes (see also pp. 115, 116) has died while these sheets have been passing through the press (Sept. 2, 1874), aged 88.

that butcher's shop at the corner of Chapel street, Bridge-houses—by putting on women's clothes.

EVERARD : I think it must have been the prosecutor who had to escape from the anger of the people, as it was against him that public anger was chiefly directed. His name was Wharton, and the story, as I have heard my father tell it, was that the men did the act as a rough and foolish joke, the prosecutor well knowing them and they him. When they saw that he took the matter seriously, they went and tried to persuade him to take back the leg of mutton, but he positively refused, probably having an eye to the "blood money." Instead of taking the mutton to a constable or a magistrate, the jokers foolishly took it to a public-house and had it cooked for supper. It has been said that Wharton himself partook of that supper, but I never heard that before, and I do not believe it.

LEONARD : The *Sheffield Register*, in April, 1790, in which month the unfortunate men were executed, said—"The behaviour of these unhappy men, since their condemnation, manifested a hearty contrition for their crimes and a becoming resignation to their ignominious fate. * * * Much disturbance has arisen in this town since the execution of Stevens and Lastley, from an idea that the prosecutor swore to aggravated circumstances which really did not happen. This suspicion has gathered strength from the solemn asseverations of the two unfortunate men, communicated in a letter to their shopmates, dated the evening previous to the execution. The populace have several times beset Wharton's house, and hung the figure of a man on a gibbet before his door, but yesterday they were so violent as to break every window, and otherwise so much damage the house as to render it scarcely habitable. The current report when our paper went to press, was that Wharton had escaped in woman's clothes." The popular sentiment is reflected in Mather's song on the execution of the men, and his denunciation of Wharton—"Thou villain, most base, thy name must eternally rot."

JOHNSON : The neighbourhood of Bridgehouses reminds me of " Silly Luke," whom I often used to see there ; and he, in turn, calls to my remembrance how many eccentrics we had formerly about the town ; now any that we have seem to be hidden. Besides " Silly Luke" there used to be " Mr. Bowman," " Jack Burton," " Soft Charley" and his brother George, " Belper Joe," and others.

EVERARD : It was a very painful thing to see the poor creatures pursued by a crowd of thoughtless boys, "making game" of them, as they called it. But we had no Idiot Asylums then in which they might have been trained to more usefulness.

LEIGHTON : There was an earlier eccentric than these— Thomas Calver, an inmate of the Brightside workhouse, whom the children dubbed "Billy Red-waistcoat."

JOHNSON : "Silly Luke" had a solid substratum of sense beneath his folly; he was quite shrewd where shirking work or getting food were concerned. Many of his sayings have been handed down. He told the workhouse officials they might make him work, but they couldn't make him like it. He said also "that he liked neither nuts nor nut-shells, but real-down, good-eating roast beef and plum pudding." When teased by the grinders who, in those days, worked with water power instead of steam, and were consequently dependent on rain for the means of working, Luke wished we had a "sow-metal" sky, with a round hole for the sun to peep through—for he wanted to keep the rain from his enemies but not to lose the sun for himself.

LEIGHTON : Luke gave Dr. Sutton, the vicar, the name of "Old Jog-my-eye," because he would not give him money or pudding; of the latter he was very fond. The vicar had a cast in his eye, and Luke followed him about saying, "If thou won't give me pudding I'll call thee Old Jog-my-eye." The Doctor got Luke's liberty somewhat restricted after that. Nothing frightened Luke so much as to be told he should be a grinder—for the grinders had ground his fingers.

JOHNSON : Mr. Bowman's peculiarity was an affected style of walking, varied every few yards with a skip, and "Soft Charley," when told by the boys to "walk proud," put on a ridiculous strut. Miss Hall, the miser, was a very familiar figure in our streets and about the market at one time, in her search for dirty scraps with which to make a cheap dinner. It used to be said that her bonnet was renewed by being rubbed over with coal-tar, or "oily-coil" as the vulgate hath it. She was quite wealthy, and her will greatly disappointed some who had diligently paid court to her for it. Among the eccentrics of about forty years ago, two of the most prominent were Edward Price, known as "Lord John Russell," and John Shaw, known as "Magnet Jack." "Lord John Russell" was a working brush maker. His speciality was going about making political Reform speeches to a large following of boys, and he always rounded off his address with some word ending in "ation," which he pronounced *ore rotundo*. Magnet Jack, too, was fond of spouting when in his cups, and was a well-known maker of magnets and fireworks. Both these men in their sober moments were men of high intelligence. They were very well-meaning men, doing most harm to themselves. I believe Price, in his latter days, became a reformed character.

LEIGHTON : "Jack Burton" was still in the workhouse a few years ago. One of his favourite antics was to stare through the windows of the houses in St. James's row. He generally chose dinner time for his appearance, and Jack's long face, suddenly pressed against the window when Mr. Reedall had a dinner party, has often frightened the ladies.

TWISS : I believe the late Mr. Henry Jackson cured him of that trick.

CHAPTER X.

THE PONDS—NORFOLK STREET—SHEFFIELD MOOR— BARKER POOL—FARGATE.

Present—Messrs. TWISS, LEIGHTON, EVERARD, WRAGG, LEONARD and JOHNSON.

Period—A. D. 1874.

LEIGHTON : Old townsmen, revisiting Sheffield after an absence of some fifty years, are as much struck by the changes in the Corn Exchange and New Haymarket as anything else. The old Hospital Chapel was then just over the Sheaf bridge, with its adjacent rows of tenements for decayed tradesmen or their widows, which were reached by a descending flight of steps.

LEONARD : They will be still more struck in a few years more, should the plans that have been prepared for sweeping away the present Corn Exchange and throwing its area into the wholesale vegetable market, and erecting a new Exchange that will occupy the larger part of the new Haymarket, be carried out. Though there does not seem much chance of that.

TWISS : It was in 1827 that the New Hospital was opened. When the old Hospital Chapel was taken down, in 1829, the foundation stone was found to contain this inscription : "This foundation stone to the Hospitals of Gilbert, Earl of Shrewsbury, laid this 20th Oct., 1774, by Henry Howard, Esq." That part was not, therefore, very old; possibly it represented the re-building after the flood, caused by the rapid rising of the Sheaf, had destroyed part of the Hospital and drowned four inmates.

EVERARD : Turning towards Pond street we come upon Shemeld croft, the site of the old file manufactory of Nicholas Jackson, who has been mentioned as giving evidence of his vocal powers at the old Cutlers' Feasts. His ancestors were Norton men, and at his residence young Chantrey was a frequent and intimate visitor. The practical jokes which he and the young ladies played upon one another led not unnaturally to an *affair de cœur* between him and Susanna Jackson. She seems to have been one of his first sitters for a crayon portrait, which was still in the family a few years ago, and may be yet.

TWISS : The poet Mather worked for Nicholas Jackson.

LEONARD : On Bakers' hill a dame's school was kept by Mrs. White, a Wesleyan, who is still remembered by some old inhabitants. One of her former scholars wrote a few years ago with much gratitude for her early instruction, and he added that the house was still standing. "I went down," he also wrote, "to Barrel yard dam, because, when a boy, I almost lost my life there one winter, through the breaking of the ice. I found it a dirty ditch in comparison with the lake-like dimensions and appearance which it had in my early imagination. I had not a few reminiscences of Pond street, and of the localities down Harmer lane, and along by the Lead mill and Burton bridge fields. But how changed are they ! The hill where the coke fires blazed covered with houses; Balmforth dam, where in my youth I once suffered inexpressible agony at the sight of a drowning man, dwindled almost to the insignificance of its neighbour of the Barrel yard; and a ducal residence planted where, in my earliest days, I had gathered daisies and acorns."

WRAGG : At the Lead works lived and died the celebrated Dr. Browne ; a man of a kind heart, and a general benefactor to the poor : when he died (in 1810) they felt they had lost their best friend.

TWISS: I am unable to give the exact date of the commencement of the Sheffield Lead Works, but they were in active operation on the 2nd February, 1763, when the stock was valued at £5278, and the buildings at £2600. At that time the partners were Dennis Browne, James De la Pryme, Samuel Turner, William Cooper, and James Allott, and the works were situated in Shude hill. During that year Mr. De la Pryme left the firm, and Mr. James Greatrex took his place. During 1768, Messrs. Allott and Turner acquired Wm. Cooper's share of the business, and in the stock-taking of January 14th, 1769, Dennis Browne's executors take the place of Dennis Browne. During that year James Greatrex also died, leaving Messrs. Allott and Turner the only surviving partners; but the representatives of the deceased partners retained their interest in the business until the end of 1774, when a new arrangement was entered into. The new firm carried on business under the style of Allott, Gunning and Co., and the partners were James Allott, [Doctor] John Browne, Wm. Harrison, Thos. Gunning, Thos. Rawson, Jas. Wheat, John Shirecliffe, and Wm. Bullock. Before the stock-taking of March, 1781, Mr. Bullock had disposed of his interest in the business to Messrs. Gunning, Rawson, Wheat and Browne, who, with Messrs. Allott and Shirecliffe, then comprised the firm. In 1782, a partnership for 21 years was entered into, which continued by agreement until 25th November, 1811, when Dr. Browne's executors sold their interest, and on the coming of age of Carlos Wheat, the Wheat family sold their shares to Thomas Rawson and John Barker, so that at this date the only partners were Messrs. Rawson and Barker and Elizabeth Gunning. On the 1st May, 1821, Thos. Rawson and John Barker purchased of Captain and Mrs. Gunning all their interest in the works.

LEONARD: Dr. Browne never held the office of physician to the Infirmary, but he took a very active part in establishing it, and was the first chairman of its weekly Board. He was a man who played a very prominent and useful part in the affairs of the town. Like Justice Wilkinson, he had the honour of a public funeral, and his features too, were perpetuated in marble by the hand of Chantrey.

EVERARD: At the establishment of the Infirmary a warm discussion arose, as to whether the benefits of the institution should be limited to the ordinary inhabitants of the town, or be extended to persons coming from other places. Doctor Browne, on that occasion, took a very decided part in advo-

cating the latter; and it was through his influence, in a great
measure, that the institution took the name of "The Sheffield
General Infirmary," affording help to whomsoever might need
it, coming from what quarter of the world they might.   Mr.
Job Fretson, the grandfather of Mr. Wm. Fretson, the solicitor, being well aware of the worthy Doctor's strong feelings on
this subject, on presenting a request for an order of admission
for some poor person, took care to head the paper in a distinct
hand, " To the Board of the Sheffield *General* Infirmary."
The Doctor, on taking the paper and seeing the heading,
marched about the room repeating the words, "The Sheffield
General Infirmary ; yes, Sir, perfectly correct, the *General*
Infirmary—I have great pleasure indeed in giving the person
a recommendation."

TWISS : Dr. Browne is spoken of in Hunter's Hallamshire
as " a gentleman of no great depth, but he had good address,
very plausible manners, and withal a very generous and
bountiful disposition."   He is satirized in a political squib,
written at the time of the great Yorkshire election of 1807,
in the following lines :—

> " For shame, Dr. Browne,
> So soon to disown
> All the friendly but fulsome professions,
> Which to Lascelles you made
> But to break, I'm afraid,
> And to increase your small store of transgressions,
>   John Browne."

The town went into mourning for Dr. Browne for one day ;
and Miss Seward has preserved his memory in one of her
published letters:—" Dr. Browne, of Sheffield, who lives to
promote the good and the pleasure of others, brought us for
one day the two younger and twin sisters of Miss Rogers."
This was said in 1783. Possibly a few particulars as to the
other partners named may not be uninteresting to you.

EVERARD : Most acceptable.

TWISS : Dennis Browne was a surgeon, a relation of Dr.
Browne.   He died in 1767, and was buried in the chancel of
the Parish Church.   Samuel Turner was most probably the
mercer in Angel street, who was the father of 22 children, and
died in 1791.[*]   James Allott, who became the principal partner in the firm, was the son of James Allott, of Chrigleston,
near Wakefield, by Margaret Clay, of Bridgehouses.   He resided at Attercliffe, and married Esther, daughter of William
Burton, of Royds Mill, and died without issue, 30th August,

---

* See ante p. 97.

1783, when the bulk of his property passed to the Greaveses, of Page Hall and Banner Cross. Thomas Gunning was the son of John Gunning, of Turney's court, Cold Ashton, Gloucestershire. He married Mary Shirecliffe, by whom he left an only daughter, Elizabeth, who married her cousin, Capt. Matthew Gunning. It was this Captain and Mrs. Gunning who sold their share in the lead works to Messrs. Rawson and Barker in 1821. John Shirecliffe lived at Whitley Hall, was father of Mrs. Gunning, and died 13th May, 1789. The pedigree of the family is given in Gatty's edition of Hunter, p. 446. Thomas Rawson, of Wardsend, married for his first wife a daughter of John Barker, of Bakewell, and died without issue 24th March, 1826. He was also the founder of Pond street Brewery, and was commemorated in the political squib already referred to in a coarse verse beginning—

"Tom Rawson, Tom Rawson,
Thou mash tub, Tom Rawson."

His position in the Rawson pedigree will be seen on reference to Gatty's Hunter, p. 451. James Wheat was a solicitor, clerk to the Church Burgesses and Town Trustees, and the first member of the Wheat family who settled in Sheffield. Mr. John James Wheat, of Norwood, is his grandson. Carlos Wheat, on whose coming of age the Wheat family sold their interest in the business, was the youngest son of James Wheat, and became the Rev. Carlos Coney Wheat, vicar of Timberland, near Sleaford. He was born in 1792.

WRAGG : In Paternoster row were the Messrs. Creswicks, the silversmiths. A person in their employment was formerly one of the unfortunate people who, in a time of very bad trade, were employed by the parish authorities in levelling the " berrin' ground," now the site of St. George's Church. Fortunately, better times came, and some of those persons were prosperous. The one I have mentioned opened the first pawnbroker's shop in Rotherham. Of several others who afterwards held up their heads in the town, only one is surviving. Mr. William Holmes, an old gentleman, then over 70, who, in 1836, said he could remember corn growing in Paradise square, carried on business as a table-knife manufacturer at 154, Pond street. He remembered the walk across the field. The Holmes's were previously in Broad street, Park. At 173, Pond street, was a cutler named Micklethwaite, who left two sons. One opened a shop in London, and soon lost what his father left him. He then went to Hamburg, and prepared some razors, which he sold

with a few other things. He made his boxes to hold a pair
of razors. Having previously cut up the wood into proper
lengths, breadths, and thicknesses, they were glued together,
and their corners rubbed down on the sinkstone ; and then
the boxes were lined by his wife. He carried on in this way
until he returned to Sheffield; and at one time he had a
good German trade conducted in several different places in
the town. He died in Glossop road, on the premises which
he built, now occupied by Mr. Alexander Patteson. At one
time, George Crookes, the watchman, was his scale and spring
maker, at Crookes. In Pond street, too, is the celebrated
brewery of Thomas Rawson and Co., established in 1780.
Thomas Rawson, of whom Mr. Twiss was just speaking in
connection with the lead works, may be called the father of
the radical reformers in Sheffield. At the corner of Pond hill
is the warehouse of Messrs. Stephenson and Mawwood, late
Hounsfield's. One of that family, the Doctor, with whom Mr.
Haxworth was apprenticed, built the first house in Queen
street, in 1784, now occupied by Mr. Haxworth, the surgeon.

TWISS: A small portion of the old "Hawle at the
Poandes" may still be seen between Pond street and the road
to the new Midland station. The inventory, found among
the Talbot papers, of Lord Shrewsbury's possessions at
Sheffield (1582), mentions painted canvas hangings for windows and chimneys, boards, stools, flagons and so forth, but
the enumeration does not throw much light on the use to
which this building was applied, or help to prove or disprove
the tradition that it was a laundry.

LEIGHTON: The road to the new Midland railway station
has wrought great changes in the neighbourhood of "The
Ponds."

LEONARD: The streets lying between the further end of
Pond street and Norfolk street are striking, after many of the
old localities we have been speaking of, for their symmetry.
It is evident, at a glance, that they must have been carried
out on a definite plan.

WRAGG: Yes. They were already projected so early as
1771.

EVERARD: Towards the close of the last century that district, now so sooty and grimy, was quite suburban. The late
Mr. Samuel Roberts cut down a field of corn to build his
silver-plating manufactory in Eyre street, on the premises
now occupied by Messrs. W. Sissons and Sons, his successors
in business.

LEONARD : The Rev. Jehoiada Brewer lived in Eyre street, just below the Howard street crossing. The Rev. George Bennet, so well known for his benevolence and his missionary travels, occupied the house at the corner of Eyre street and Charles street, and the Rev. James Boden, Mr. Brewer's successor at Queen street Chapel, lived in the same street, as did also the Rev. James Knight, for so long a period the incumbent of St. Paul's Church.

WRAGG : In Eyre street were the silver shops of Messrs. Gainsford, Fenton and Nicholson. Mr. Robert Gainsford was the father of the late Mr. Robert John Gainsford, solicitor.

LEONARD : Who died at Rome, where he was spending the winter, on the 6th February, 1870. He was educated at the Roman Catholic College, of Oscott, near Birmingham, and was articled to the late Mr. Henry Owen, solicitor, of Worksop. He commenced the practice of his profession in Sheffield, in 1831, in the midst of the popular agitation to support the Reform Bill of Earl Grey. Mr. Gainsford ever took a lively interest in Liberal politics, and a prominent part in our local elections. In 1844, he became a partner in the firm of Haywood, Bramley and Gainsford, and he went through enormous labours in the legal and parliamentary business connected with the railway mania. Mr. Gainsford was a frequent writer on social and political topics, and the education controversy largely occupied his time and thoughts. He was a regular contributor to the *Dublin Review* and the *Tablet,* and other organs of his own (the Roman Catholic) church, and many letters from him also appeared in the *Independent.*

WRAGG : Lower down Eyre street was Mr. Sykes, the powder-flask manufacturer, a somewhat singular man. The Messrs. Fenton have the works now. In Furnival street, at the corner of Eyre street, was Mr. Samuel Mitchell, who carried on the edge tool and file trades, besides being a merchant. He was also, though not very successfully, at Whiteley Wood works, erected by his relative, Mr. Thos. Bolsover, to whom is usually credited the invention of silver-plating. At those works was the first rolling mill erected here, and Mr. Mitchell used to tell of Mr. Bolsover saying that when he began to build, people said he had a purse with a long neck, but when he finished it was all neck. As an antiquary and genealogist Mr. Mitchell had not his equal in this part of the country. He issued the prospectus of a History of the Hun-

R

dred of Scarsdale, or North Derbyshire; but the work was never brought out.

LEONARD : In his later years Mr. Mitchell was carrying on works at Woodhouse Mill, near Handsworth.

WRAGG : In Furnival street, too, is the warehouse of Messrs. Parkin and Marshall, but previously of Messrs. Smith, Moorhouse, and Smith. One of the Messrs. Smith has attended Carver street Chapel for so long a period that a singer, who visited it after an absence of forty years, said Mr. Smith was the only person he recognized. Lower down are the works of Messrs. Roberts and Belk, the silversmiths. This place was first occupied by Messrs. Furniss, Poles and Furniss. Mr. Henry Furniss, of the firm of Sanderson Brothers and Co., who recently died, was one of the sons. In Charles street was Mr. Broadhurst, table-knife manufacturer, whose life contains an incident of splendid devotion, worthy of comparison with the noblest self-sacrifices history chronicles. Forty years ago, in a passage from Liverpool to the Isle of Man, the vessel on which he and his daughters were crossing was wrecked, from the drunken stupidity of the captain. He and two of his daughters had clung to some vestige of the vessel, when on observing it would not hold all three, the daughters voluntarily stepped off to save their father, that he might be spared to the younger children. Mr. Broadhurst had been Master Cutler in 1842.

JOHNSON : One of my earliest recollections is standing in Howard street on a summer's night, and seeing the funerals of cholera victims in the Cholera Ground at Clay Wood in 1832, and I recollect few things that seemed more appalling than this, and the sight of the " Cholera Basket," as the conveyance used to transport patients to the hospital, was called.

WRAGG : The premises now occupied by Walker and Hall, were the warehouse of the late Thomas Asline Ward, who was a candidate for the representation of Sheffield in Parliament, in 1832. He was Master Cutler in 1816, and was one of Sheffield's most prominent men for many years.

EVERARD : He was a fast and early friend of Chantrey, and a member of the circle of refined men of literary and scientific tastes, which Sheffield then could boast.

WRAGG : Joseph Ward, Master Cutler in 1790, and Samuel Broomhead Ward, his son, in 1798, were of the same family. Messrs. Cammell and Johnson, afterwards of Cyclops works, first commenced business in this street. You know that the congregation of Howard street Chapel removed from Coalpit lane in 1790. The Chapel was attended by the Tillotson family, the late W. and S. Butcher, when young men, the Mappin families, Samuel and Joseph Hadfield, also by George Hadfield, when young. Mr. Hadfield's father is buried here; and the father of Mr. George Wostenholm, one of its deacons, is also interred in the Chapel yard. One of its most talented ministers was the late Rev. R. S. Bayley, who established the People's College, to give not only a sound, but a higher education to those who toil for their living. There are many who have derived great benefit from the College.

LEONARD: Mr. Bayley was so noteworthy a man that possibly you may like to hear an extract or two from a biographical sketch published at the time of his death—November 15th, 1859. He was born at Lichfield, and was an instance of what may be accomplished by resolution in the pursuit of knowledge. He was a man of indomitable self-will, and he carried into all his objects the same resolution that he showed in self-culture. But he was not always judicious in the choice of his objects; and while his talents procured him many friends, his inflexible self-will often broke his friendships and interfered with his usefulness. Though always well-meaning he was often imprudent, and not sufficiently careful of his ministerial standing and character. This brought him into collision with the members of his church, and resulted in those unhappy differences which led to their separation, and ultimately to his removal from Sheffield. And while his friends mourned his failings, even his opponents were ever ready to testify to his pre-eminent ability. But it was as the founder of the People's College that he established his claim to grateful remembrance. While Government and the various sections of the church were squabbling over the question of education, and doing nothing for it, he, boldly and single-handed, entered upon the task of "seeing how far the education of the youth of both sexes of the middle and working classes could be carried on compatibly with their engagements in trade." His ability would not have availed him in this work unless it had been accompanied by that indomitable perseverance which sustained him through such labours as but few men could undergo. * * He was thoroughly adapted to the work he had undertaken. Completely master of his task he gained the confidence of his students; and dull indeed must they have been not to have taken knowledge in some of the varied forms in which he presented it to them. He sought to develop the minds of his students and teach them to think, that being according to his idea the ultimate object—in fact education. None but those who had the good fortune to be his students can fully appreciate his excellences as principal of the College. If at times they found in him the imperiousness of a despot, they also found in him the kindness of a friend and the tenderness of a parent. Ever ready to communicate, it was his delight to teach, and he loved those who sat at his feet for instruction. Mr. Bayley never sought to influence the religious views of his students to his own ideas of the truth. Always reverent of sacred things, he held the domain of conscience too sacred for human interference. Mr. Bayley was a man of many faults, but to us they appear greatly diminished by the time he has been removed from Sheffield; while his excellencies, which were likewise many and best worth remembrance, are present with us. He impressed his spirit on some of the rising youths of Sheffield, and the benefit of his labours will be felt through all time. They will be no less effective because not seen, nor less real though unacknowledged.

JOHNSON: It was in 1836 that Mr. Bayley came to Sheffield, from Louth, Lincolnshire, and in 1846 that he left for a chapel in Ratcliffe Highway, London. Thence he went to Hereford, where he had been about two years at the time of his death. He was the author of "Nature considered as a Revelation," "History of Louth," "Lectures on the Early History of the Christian Church," and other books. For some years prior to his death he had been engaged on a life of Thomas Wentworth, Earl of Strafford, for which he had made most extensive researches among the State papers, the records of the Wentworth family, and similar sources.

EVERARD: There are some other points in the history of Howard street Chapel that I should like to mention. You can get a list of its ministers from the ordinary sources of information. The fourth, the Rev. J. Reece (1797) was a very amiable and exemplary Christian man, characterised by a singular simplicity and originality in his preaching. Montgomery related how he heard him preach a funeral sermon, which produced a great impression on his mind. After four years' ministry he died, January 8, 1801, universally respected; and a handsome subscription was raised to make provision for his widow and children. The next minister was the Rev. Samuel Barnard, and he was succeeded by the Rev. James Mather, a very energetic preacher and useful man, who regarded it as one special part of his ministerial duty to endeavour to neutralise, and, if possible, to extirpate from the minds of his flock, the "hyper-Calvinistic" views which his immediate predecessor had promulgated and instilled. In this he was to a great extent successful. Mr. Mather removed from Sheffield to Birmingham in 1827, and died in London in 1840. He was the father of the Rev. Dr. Robert Cotton Mather, who was for nearly forty years a Missionary in India, where he acquired a high reputation as an oriental linguist. He has lately returned to his native country, and is at present engaged in writing a "Commentary" on the New Testament, in the Hindustáne language. Mr. Mather was, in 1830, succeeded in the pulpit of Howard street Chapel by the Rev. Thomas Rawson Taylor, a young man of exemplary piety and distinguished talents. To the great grief and disappointment of that church, and of others in the town, he had scarcely entered on his ministerial duties before his health entirely broke down. He resigned, and afterwards became the classical tutor, for a short time, of Airedale College. He was a poet of no mean promise. His "Memoirs and Select Remains," including his Poems, were published, and a second edition being required, Montgomery wrote for it an introductory preface. He died of consumption, in March, 1835, in the 26th year of his age. Then came the Rev. Joseph Fox, of Hull, the Rev. Robert Slater Bayley, and so we get to modern times.

WRAGG : Near to the premises of Messrs. John Sellers and Sons, partly occupied by Mr. Richard Elliott, in Arundel street, were the works of the Messrs. Laycock, manufacturers of hair seating. Their father was a journeyman to Mr. Wildsmith, in Bridge street, a carpet weaver, and then hair weaver. Mr. Laycock left him and began for himself. His family was noted for its industry, and success was the result. Mr. Laycock gave up business in favour of his sons, and retired into Gell street, to the house now occupied by Mr. George Deakin, and died at a great age in 1836. On his right and on his left he could see the residences of two of his sons, one at the corner of Leavy greave, and the other at the corner of Glossop road. The mayor of Sheffield in 1865, Mr. W. E. Laycock, of Stumperlow grange and Portobello works, was one of his grandsons. On the opposite side to Messrs. Laycock, in Arundel street, and further on, were the works of Mr. Dewsnap, whose son, Mr. Thomas Dewsnap, of Clarke House, died in 1864, leaving a remarkable will.

EVERARD : I forget its provisions ?

TWISS : After various charitable and other bequests, he left all his real and leasehold estates, and all the residue of his personal estates, to his executors, declaring it to be his earnest wish and desire that they should devote the whole of it to building and endowing churches, chapels, and schools, or to any other charitable purposes. Up to the present time Mr. Dewsnap's " earnest desire" has not been gratified.

WRAGG : The Dewsnaps were pressers. A few years ago, for a short time resided at 91, Thomas Longworth, the brother of the celebrated Mrs. Yelverton. Just beyond Mr. Cowlishaw's was Mr. Stones, presser, father of the late Mr. Frederick Stones, edge-tool manufacturer. On the site of the School of Art were the silver shops of Messrs. Smith and Hoult. I think one of the partners resided in the house now occupied by Dr. J. C. Hall. At the other side was Mr. Spurr, the cutler, who left Church street. It is now Messrs. Bradburys, silversmiths. At the end of Arundel street are the works of the late Thomas Ellin. He came out of the country as apprentice to a person of the name of Oldale, married his master's daughter, and was in partnership with his mother-in-law in one of the lanes near Howard street Chapel. Mr. Ellin attended to business, and as the result business attended to him ; but his brother-in-law fell into poverty and obscurity, and his grandchildren are now table-knife hafters. In Sycamore street died Mr. Francis Chambers, who previously kept a public-house in Water lane. Some of his customers were Charles and Matthew Shirtcliffe, William Gray, and John Milner. William Gray will be remembered in connection with Broad lane, as the great jumper and a boot and shoe maker. Of John Milner, it was said that he was the best spring-knife cutler in the town, and as a debater he was considered unequalled in argument. On some occasion he was examined before a select committee of the House of Commons. These were accustomed to meet at Mr. Chambers's to discuss and argue.

LEONARD : Here is the Theatre Royal, with its "spirited" profile of Shakspeare and some dramatic symbols in the pediment. That was executed by " a poor wandering tramp," named Renilowe.

LEIGHTON : In the days of the South Devon Militia, of whom we talked once before, Messrs. Manley and Robertson were the lessees of the Theatre. " Oh, rare Jemmy Robertson," what a favourite were you, the darling and delight of the gods of the gallery; your appearance was at all times welcome. The orchestra consisted of Charles Clegg and his son, "Old Foster," "Billy Taylor" and his son, and others whose names I have forgotten. On the opening night they knew well who was behind them and what was expected from them. On the first flourish of their fiddles, previous to the drawing up of the curtain, the cry was for "Poor Jack"— "There's a sweet little cherub sits smiling aloft, to keep watch o'er the life of poor Jack." There was great enthusiasm, the pit rising as one man to do homage to the song and to Dibden, its writer. It was the custom then to have a professional singer, who sang between the play and the farce, and such songs were sung as tended to elevate the public taste—not Nigger melodies. The first song I heard on the stage was "He was famed for deeds of daring."

TWISS : The boards of our Theatre, humble as they are, have been trodden by distinguished feet—Mrs. Siddons, and her brother Kemble (who was the lessee for several seasons), and Charles Kean, and the elder Macready and his son.

LEONARD : The present state of Tudor place is very melancholy. Grimy black walls, whose monotony is increased by tattered shreds of flaming posting bills, stare at the once considerable residence of old Henry Tudor, while its ancient adornments of wreathed flowers contemplate with an aspect of profound melancholy the deep puddles, the chaotic boulders, the piles of stones, the layers of timber, and general waste-heap look that have invaded the sacred precincts of its once charming garden. The parade ground of the Artillery Volunteers, and the other buildings that intervene between Tudor place and Arundel street, have usurped the place of the flower beds and fruit trees of Henry Tudor, and the syca-mores that surrounded his domain have their memory perpetuated in the adjoining street, once Sycamore hill, that breathes a fragrance of anything but bright flowers and green trees. There lived Henry Tudor, head of the firm of Tudor Leader and Nicholson, one of the first, if not the first, that engaged in the manufacture of the then newly-invented process of silver-plating. The business had begun somewhat before 1758, in the manufacture of snuff boxes, and it developed into the silver-plating trade. There is a tradition that it was in one of the garrets of Tudor house that the accidental discovery of the possibility of coating copper with silver was discovered, on the site now occupied by the manufactory of Messrs. Round and Son; and it was only as late as

May, 1865, that the last portion of the old buildings was pulled down. In doing this a considerable quantity of scrap metal was found, hidden away in the roof, the unremoved booty of some unknown thief.

EVERARD: I have seen a memorandum left by one who at a later period was a member of the firm, which speaks of Henry Tudor and Thomas Leader as two silversmiths who came from London. They had a sleeping partner, a medical gentleman, named Sherburn, and, says the writer, he resided in Tudor House, the two working partners living in the house adjoining, which was taken down when the Free Library was built.

LEONARD: If Mr. Tudor did not live in the house called by his name at first, he did soon afterwards, and Daniel Leader, who, having been apprenticed to the firm as "box-maker," *i. c.* snuff box, in 1762, and afterwards became a partner, lived in the now demolished house adjoining, which too had a fruitful garden.

TWISS: Mr. Tudor was a man of wealth, and he must have had some taste, for he was one of our earliest local patrons of the fine arts. I fear, however, he may have been deceived, as plenty of other people have been, in the genuineness of his purchases, for Chantrey had no very lofty opinion of them. His friend, Mr. T. A. Ward, seems to have written to ask his friendly opinion, and Chantrey replied—"There are only three pictures in Tudor's collection which I can recommend you to purchase. The first is one of the pictures which I cleaned—the binding of Christ, by Old Franks: it is one of the best pictures of that master, worth twenty guineas. The second is an Italian picture; subject—figures and architecture, and has a good effect. I don't know the artist: it may be worth about fifteen guineas. The third is a head by Wright, of Derby; Mr. Tudor gave twelve guineas for it, which I conceive to be its full value. The Guido, Watteaus, Wouvermans, &c.—as they are pleased to call them—are, in my opinion, *very* indifferent imitations of those masters: I advise you by all means *not* to purchase."* That was in 1808.

LEONARD: Henry Tudor was a stately gentleman, of the old school, rather dogmatic, and—

LEIGHTON: Very proud. He had the character of being the proudest man in Sheffield, and he went by the name of

---

* Memorials of Chantrey, 85.

"My Lord Harry Tudor." There was a notion that he believed himself to be descended from the Royal Tudors.

LEONARD : He was certainly proud of his name, for finding that another Tudor had set up in Sheffield in the person of a journeyman comb-maker, he was greatly offended. Remonstrance being of no avail, for the comb-maker held himself to have as good right to the name as the silver-plater, he was offered a pecuniary inducement to change his patronymic. This, however, was rejected, and "Lord Harry" had to endure the presence of a second Richmond in the field. Mr. Tudor was twice married, first to Elizabeth Dodworth, 6th June, 1758, who died 8th June, 1781 ; and secondly, to Elizabeth Rimington, whom he married 6th January, 1783, and who died 22nd March, 1800. By his second marriage he had six children—two sons, Henry and George, and four daughters. Harriet became the wife of Rowland Hodgson, and Charlotte the wife of Mr. B. Fernell, solicitor, of Chesterfield.

LEIGHTON : Mr. Fernell lived afterwards in the White House, Bramall lane, and it is said that for amusement he sometimes went to blow the bellows at Bramall's file works. George Tudor, who was as proud as his father, was articled to Mr. B. J. Wake, solicitor. He visited the United States, and published a book on the subject.

LEONARD : The firm we have been talking about had its romances as well as its more prosaic trade. Thomas Leader, one of the dashing young men of the time, no sooner came of age than he improved the occasion by eloping with the daughter of John Henfrey, scissor smith, who lived in the house that stands askew at the top of Eyre street. The runaway couple were married at Gretna Green on the 2nd December, 1791. Mr. Henfrey was Master Cutler the next year. He built for himself a country mansion at Highfield, and being asked by his friends if he was not afraid of going home over Sheffield Moor after dark, he replied that he took good care always to get home by daylight.

EVERARD : In one of our former conversations we heard what Sheffield Moor was like in those days.

LEONARD : We catch a glimpse, too, of Daniel Leader in the remembrance of him, possessed by an old gentleman, Mr. William Ash,* who has recently completed his ninety-second year, and who sees some resemblance to him in one of his

---

* While the proof of this sheet is yet in the Editor's hands, the announcement of Mr. Ash's death, in his 93rd year (Oct. 10, 1874), meets his eye. Mr. Ash's recollections are referred to on pp. 40, 56, 62, 66, 153.

great-grandsons. Mr. Ash remembers Daniel Leader as he used to see him in his knee-breeches, long waistcoat, large cuffed coat, ribbed worsted stockings, and large buckles on his shoes, at the famous hostelry of the Three Stags, in Carver street, kept by Mrs. Wilson. There, with his old chum, Quaker Abraham Wigram, Daniel Leader, who is described as " a little stiff man, built like an oak," was wont to discuss local matters, and drink his pint of home brewed, in the days when our venerable friend of to-day was a youth, eating his bread and cheese, and adapting his palate to the flavour of the Sheffield ale. Abraham Wigram was a bit of a poet, and somewhat of a wit, and when old Bishop, the factor from Sharrow lane, was buried, he made some verses descriptive of his screwing habits, and moralising on his end.

LEIGHTON: Entering Norfolk street from Arundel street we have on our left, back to back with the Theatre Royal, the Assembly Rooms, and on the right a tinner's shop, once the building to which Mr. Wreaks removed the Post Office, in 1828. But the inconvenience of this situation was too great, and a move was made to the Commercial Buildings in High street, now occupied by Messrs. Levy.

TWISS: And would you actually pass over the Assembly Rooms, the scene of the most notable feature in the social life of Sheffield a century ago, with that bare mention? " From the year 1773," Hunter tells us, " the assemblies were held in two rooms of the Boys' Charity School, where the company enjoyed conversation or the mazy dance by light, not of wax, which beamed from sconces of tin." The rooms of which we are now speaking were built in 1762, and the Town Council became tenants of them in 1846. In that year (November 28) the *Independent* published some very interesting documents relating to these gatherings, which I happen to know were contributed by the most competent pen. These comprised lists of subscribers, with an attempt at identifying the persons whose names appeared ; a list of a few of the earlier Queens ; the terms of admission and the rules. These contain much curious information, but they are too long to inflict upon you now.

LEONARD: A different and perhaps older set of rules was published in the *Sheffield Times* of December 27th, 1851.

EVERARD: Opposite us is Nether Chapel—the new Nether Chapel we old men should call it, since it supplanted the old building we remember so well. Amongst the seceders from the " Upper Chapel," and one who took a great interest in and was a large subscriber to the building of the Old Nether Chapel, in 1715, was a Mr. John Smith. On the authority of Mr. Hunter's "Gens Sylvestrinæ," we learn that *this* Mr. Smith was born at Bell House, August 28th, 1684, and was baptised at Ecclesfield. He was apprenticed to John Winter, a considerable manufacturer in Sheffield, was admitted to the freedom of the Cutlers' Company in 1705, and became the Master Cutler in 1722. He was deeply engaged in the efforts of the Cutlers' Company to obtain powers to make the Don a navigable river by which Sheffield might be connected with the Humber. On that occasion the interests of the town were committed into his hands ; and he went to London and so far brought over members of both Houses of Parliament to approve and vote for the design, that the object was attained in 1726. Mr. Smith was a person of a remarkably religious spirit. He died November 15th, 1753, at the age of sixty-nine, and was buried in the chapel yard. He was the great grand-father of the late Mr. Ebenezer Smith, who married a daughter of the Rev. John Harmer, the minister of Nether Chapel, and was the father of Harmer, Joshua, F. E. and Sydney Smith, now amongst us. Some years ago a curious old relic, in the form of a scrap of writing, came into my hands, which afforded a vivid glimpse of the state of feeling entertained by the Nonconformists of that day with regard to Popery. It is in the form of an announcement made by the clerk officiating at the Nether Chapel, (Jeremiah Marshall by name,) on Sunday, the 4th November, 1750, informing the congregation that a public service would be held on the next day in the chapel on a special occasion. The Rev. John Pye, the uncle of the late Rev. John Pye Smith, was at that time the minister. The following is a copy of the notice in question :—" Please to take notice, that to-morrow will be the return of the 5th of November. There will be a Sermon preached here in commemoration of two remarkable deliverances in our favour, both as Protestants and Englishmen. The one was the Powder Plot, in the reign of King James the First, 1605, now 145 years ago ; a plot that could be contrived by none but the Devil and his younger brother, the Pope of Rome, and his accursed crew. The other was the 'Revolution' in the person of the renowned Prince of Orange, 1688, now 62 years ago. He, as an in-strument under God, delivered us from Popery and Slavery ; and the memory of the great William the III. will be sweet and valuable to every true Briton while the world endures." From what I happen to know, I have little doubt that a worthy ancestor of mine (one of the seceders from the Upper Chapel) would relish and endorse the good old clerk's announcement, and duly attend, with his family, the appointed service. Although I should not like to undertake to defend every word of Mr. Jeremiah Marshall's trenchant phraseology, yet I do admire the spirit of sturdy Protestantism and love of civil and religious liberty, that it expresses.

LEONARD : I was reading, the other day, in the *Sheffield Mercury*, of May 12, 1827, a long account of the foundation stone laying on the previous Monday, May 7. It gives in full the "oration" pronounced by the Rev. Thomas Smith on the occasion, which is interesting as containing a sketch of the history of the chapel and of his predecessors in the ministry. The inscription was as follows :—

The Lower Chapel
built 1715;
Re-built by Public Subscription
1827.
THOMAS SMITH, A.M., Minister.
WILLIAM PARKER, ⎫
JAMES BARTON, ⎬ Deacons.
DAVID HASLEHURST, ⎭
WATSON, PRITCHARD and WATSON, of York, Architects.

Below, this inscription, with a few verbal alterations, was repeated in Latin. On a roll of parchment, enclosed in a bottle and deposited under the stone, was the following history : "The Nether Chapel having stood 112 years had become inconvenient to the congregation ; and is therefore re-built by public subscription at an expense of about £4000, including £700 paid for additional land. A considerable part of this sum has been raised by weekly contributions since April, 1821, chiefly collected by ——" "Here," says the *Mercury*, "follows a list of twenty-one names, but we forbear inserting them from motives of delicacy." Reading the report now we can only regret that the newspaper, in having such a tender respect for the modesty of the collectors, deprives us of a useful bit of town-lore.

TWISS : We can get the names of the successive ministers from Hunter and other sources, but no one ever thinks of recording the deacons' names. Yet such a list would suggest many memories to old Sheffield dissenters.

EVERARD : A reminiscence I have of the opening of Nether Chapel in 1828, enables me to give you a glimpse of one who possesses a fair claim to rank among the Old Sheffield Worthies—the Rev. William Thorpe. He took part in the opening services, and that was his last appearance in his native town, since his death followed not very long after. I have often thought that there could scarcely be a more majestic and dignified appearance in the pulpit, or a nobler specimen of popular pulpit eloquence. William Thorpe was born at Masbro'. His father was the subject of a remarkable conversion.* Assembled with some boon companions one evening at the public-house, the conversation led to the agreement that each of them should take a text at random from the Bible, and try which could best imitate the preaching of the Rev. Charles Wesley, who had been lately visiting the neighbourhood. Three of his companions had successively ridiculed all things sacred, when it came to John Thorpe's turn. He mounted the table, opened the Bible, and his eye fell on the text — "Except ye repent ye shall all likewise perish." He was sobered in a moment. The impression made upon him was profound, and he proceeded to deliver a solemn and earnest discourse to the no small chagrin of his auditors. He was accustomed to say afterwards, "If ever I preached in my life, by the assistance of God, it was at that time." Having finished, he left the room without another word, and from that hour was a changed man. At first he joined the Methodists and was one of their preachers, but afterwards he became the minister of the Independent chapel at Masbro'. He died there, November 8th, 1776, aged 46, whereupon his widow removed to Sheffield with the children, and she became on intimate terms with my grandmother and family. My father described her as a stout, noble-looking woman; with bright dark eyes, a Roman nose, and hair of raven gloss and blackness. William was very much like his mother, inheriting her features and expression; and, as he advanced in manhood, assumed a similar portly form and dignified mien. At a suitable age he was apprenticed to the "silver-plated" business with a firm, the exact name of which I have forgotten, but of which Mr. Morton, the late Thomas Dunn's maternal grandfather, was a principal partner. William was a very lively youth, full of fun and practical joke; but, at the same time, was clever, intelligent, and well-informed; a great reader, more especially of history, and possessing a memory of an extraordinary kind. On one occasion he was ordered to make a teapot according to the size and pattern of an old one that had been sent with special directions from the owner that the new was not to differ in any respect from the

---

* Evangelical Magazine, February, 1794.

old. Young Thorpe carried out the instructions to the letter, rubbing off the plate and bruising exactly as the old one was bruised. Many of Thorpe's fellow workmen were imbued with the extreme views of Jacobinism, and at their instance he challenged Mr. Macready, the father of the great tragedian, who was at that time the lessee and manager of the Sheffield Theatre, to a public discussion on the causes and principles of the French Revolution. This Mr. Macready accepted ; and the meeting took place in the Freemasons' Lodge, in Paradise square (recently Mr. Hebblethwaite's school-room), which was crowded to excess. The late Mr. William Ibbitt's father belonged to the same trade, and was present on that occasion. According to his account William had quite the mastery over his opponent, and at the end the meeting, by a large majority, voted the youthful champion of political freedom the victor. The Rev. Jehoiada Brewer was at that time the minister of the Queen street Chapel; and he held similar political views. William Thorpe was happily brought under his influence, and became a decidedly religious character. At length he entered on the regular discharge of the duties of the Christian ministry, though without passing through the process of an academical training. The first place in which William Thorpe was located was as the pastor of the Independent Church at Shelley, a Yorkshire village, whence, after about a year, he went to Chester. In 1796, he became the minister of Netherfield Chapel, Penistone. In 1800 he removed to London, and thence to Bristol, where he remained to the end of his life. On the memorable occasion of the opening services of the new Nether Chapel, in the month of August, 1828, the chapel was crowded to excess. The preacher was a tall, big man, and very corpulent, but without anything heavy or vulgar about the form and expression of the face. On the contrary, his features, rising above a remarkable double chin, were finely and even delicately formed, more especially the nose and mouth. His high forehead was bald, and what portion of hair he had was of a dark colour, with a touch of grey on his short, slight whiskers, His nose was somewhat of the Roman type ; his eyes were black and piercing ; with a small mouth and arched eyebrows. His voice was remarkable for its compass and power, and was apt to swell into thunder tones as he denounced, in awful terms, the doom of the impenitent ; or become modulated into accents of the most persuasive tenderness, in urging sinners to repent and believe in the Saviour. The subject was the Christian doctrine of the Atonement. This he treated in his own peculiar style, and with a fulness of illustration, and a clearness and force of argument that I never heard exceeded ; nor, indeed, so much matter on that subject compressed within the limits of a single sermon. It is true he preached for above an hour and a half, but the attention of the people was riveted from first to last. The impression produced on the minds of his hearers by this discourse was very great. Himself the son of the Rev. John Thorpe, he was the father of another Independent minister of the same name, who was for some years the minister of Mount Zion Chapel.

LEIGHTON : Chapel walk, between Nether Chapel and the Wesleyan Chapel below (built in 1780), formerly came into Norfolk street by a series of steps. They were removed at the same time as those in Virgins' walk and East parade, descending into Campo lane, by a person named Marriott, a filesmith, who had the control of the highways.

WRAGG : Chapel walk is one of our old thoroughfares. It formerly contained, with their backs to it, some very old frame houses, built of lath and plaster. In George street, the Mechanics' Institution was commenced in 1832, and conducted on the premises of the late Messrs. Pickslay, now the site of the offices of Messrs. Broomhead, Wightman and Moore, the solicitors. This was the first attempt made in the town for the labouring classes to receive instruction in evenings, after their daily toil.

LEONARD : You spoke once before of Harwood and Thomas, who were on the site of the Sheffield Banking Company's premises.

WRAGG : At the lower corner of Change alley were the Messrs. Deakin, merchants, one of whom founded the charity that bears his name. At the other corner, until recently, were the Messrs. Woodcock, the brushmakers, who must have been people of taste, as some very valuable pictures were sold at their sale. It almost looked as if they had studied the science of astronomy. Opposite, in Norfolk street, are the Messrs. Rodgers, the cutlers, who, as formerly noticed, came from Hawley croft. I have heard it stated that originally they came from Stannington. Near, in Milk street, is Mr. Bowling's school, celebrated as being kept by the late Mr. J. H. Abraham, who, besides having the best school in the town, was of a mechanical turn of mind, for in 1822 he invented a magnetic apparatus for the protection of persons employed in dry grinding.

TWISS : A testimonial was presented to him in that year, " in token of respect for his talents, and in acknowledgment of his services to an afflicted class of workmen by his ingenious invention ;" and he also received the gold medal of the Society of Arts for the same invention.

JOHNSON : Like many other things that are theoretically sound, the magnetic apparatus was practically useless. The great complaint against it was, I believe, that it was speedily choked with the fragments of metal attracted, and then the respiration of the workman was distressingly hindered.

WRAGG : Messrs. Sansom, in Norfolk street (now Harrison Brothers and Howson), had a table-blade forger, named Muscroft, who was a man of great ingenuity. He had been a collier. He made and repaired clocks, some of which I have seen, and I believe he contrived a small gas apparatus. I think I could almost positively say that General Grainger, one of the confederate officers in the United States rebellion, was born in the Park, and was the son of one of Mr. Muscroft's daughters.

LEONARD : The public-house at the bottom of the street, now the Norfolk Arms, was, John Wilson tells us in a note to Mather's song of "Shout 'em down's barn," called " The Hullett," or Owl, and about the end of the last century it was kept by Mr. Michael Waterhouse. Its pseudonym was " Shout 'em down's," and it was a favourite rendezvous for recruiting parties.

EVERARD : At No. 14, Norfolk street, Chantrey had apartments during the recess of the Royal Academy in 1804, when he solicited the patronage of the ladies and gentlemen of Sheffield in sculpture and portrait painting. " As models from life are not generally attempted in the country," his advertisement said, " F. C. hopes to meet the liberal sentiments of an impartial public."

LEONARD : Chantrey, too, was a frequent visitor at another house in this street, that which is now occupied by Miss Barry, dressmaker, then the residence of Mr. Sterndale, surgeon, who had married Mary Handley, of whom we spoke when talking of Angel street. In his Memorials of Chantrey, Mr. Holland tells that Chantrey and Mrs. Sterndale (who was a local authoress) once met at a party at Mr. Revell's, in Norfolk street, and during the evening, a violent thunderstorm came on. Mrs. Sterndale and Chantrey disappeared in succession from the drawing room and were found taking refuge in the cellar, whither the lady had fled because of a constitutional dread of lightning.

JOHNSON : We have previously spoken of Chantrey's early sculptures. I am told that the figures which stand on either side of the entrance door of the Infirmary are the work of his chisel.

EVERARD : Histories of the Upper Chapel, or of St. Paul's Church, do not come within the scope of our conversations, since we long ago agreed that we would avoid as much as possible details that may be found in " Hunter."

LEIGHTON : Yet we should not omit any small touches that are beneath the dignity of his history. In connection with St. Paul's for instance, why should we not call to mind the name of " Dr. Inkbottle," whose large letters so long adorned or rather marred the alcove of the Pinstone street entrance? "Dr. Inkbottle" was a medical gentleman, named Frith, and he obtained his nick-name thus—Having been present at a public dinner, at the Tontine, he so far forgot himself as to carry away a bottle, supposing it to contain wine. It proved, however, to be simply a bottle of ink, and the mistake becoming known he was popularly christened " Dr. Inkbottle." He was surgeon to the " Blues," and lived in Norfolk row. He afterwards lived and died in Surrey street. Alderman Carr was apprenticed to him.

LEONARD : As to Mr. Everard's remark, it is to be observed that Hunter's notices of the Upper Chapel ministers are so brief, through " considerations which to many persons will be obvious," that it is well to add to them whenever we can. Of the Rev. Joseph Evans, for instance, his particular friend and whom he enthusiastically admired, Mr. Hunter's published account is very meagre, although he left a more extended MS. notice. From this I glean the following facts : Mr. Evans was born in April, 1728, his father being Mr. Roger Evans, a Manchester tradesman, and his mother the daughter of an eminent minister, the Rev. Josh. Dawson, of Morley. His maternal grandfather was one of the divines ejected by the Act of Uniformity, 1662. Mr. Evans studied under Dr. David Jennings, who kept a flourishing academy in London for the bringing up of young persons for the ministry, and elicited the warmest commendation from his tutor, as expressed in a letter to Dr. Doddridge. But Mr. Evans dissented from the orthodox Calvinistic tenets, which involved the loss of support from Coward's fund and removal

S

from the academy. Thereupon he succeeded the Rev. Mr. Barber as pastor of a small congregation at Burntwood, in Essex, and after a few years became assistant to Dr. Eaton, High Pavement Meeting, Nottingham. After four years he was invited, on the death of the Rev. Thomas Haynes, to the Upper Chapel, Sheffield, and he settled there in 1759. He married, on the 29th July, 1762, Susanna, eldest of the three daughters of his predecessor, Mr. Haynes. For nearly forty years he presided over the Sheffield congregation, and one at Fulwood, in conjunction with the Rev. John Dickenson for half that period, and the Rev. Benjamin Naylor for the latter half. In November, 1798, he resigned the pastoral office, and he died on the last day of the year 1803. The *Iris* of the 5th January, 1804, contained a brief obituary notice from the pen of " his worthy late coadjutor," and another, fuller and more accurate, appeared in the *Monthly Magazine* for February of the same year. I have confined myself in this epitome to the bare facts, omitting the affectionate and eulogistic language which Mr. Hunter employed.

WRAGG : On the side of the street opposite Upper Chapel, were the warehouse and town residence of Mr. Bustard Greaves, of Page Hall. The warehouse is occupied by Mr. Hay, the spirit merchant, and the site of the house is now the Savings' Bank.

LEIGHTON : Concerning the same premises and the same firm, it has been related how a young man, named Wood-head, became a partner of Mr. Greaves's. He was appren-ticed to Mr. Greaves, and being sharp and steady he was offered a partnership, after he came of age, if he could find £1000. Having no money of his own he went to one of the Rimingtons, an old friend of his employer, and told his story. Mr. Rimington, with a generosity so unexplained that I fancy some essential point may have been omitted from the narra-tive, advanced £1000, wishing young Woodhead every suc-cess, and telling him that if he failed the repayment of the loan would never be asked for. Mr. Woodhead became a wealthy man, built himself a mansion at Highfield, and lived to a good old age. It is said that manufacturers liked to do business with the Woodheads, who were factors. So long as the article was good no objection was raised to the price.

WRAGG: In Norfolk street were the warehouse and works of Blonk, Silcock and Co.—in the gates next to No. 143. Their shops extended to Norfolk lane and are now turned into tene-ments. At the top of the street, next to the Turkish Baths, are the Messrs. Barlow, whose family have been in the scissor trade for more than a century.

EVERARD: In the house now occupied by the Turkish Baths, at the corner of Charles street, died, unmarried, George Eadon, one of the sons of John Eadon, the master of the Free Writing school.

TWISS: In Union street was the second Methodist Chapel erected in the town, put up after the first in Pinstone lane had been destroyed by a mob. But that was long ago—about the middle of the last century.

WRAGG: At the top of Porter street, or as it used to be called, Ladies' walk, was Mr. Hutchinson, the coachmaker, who, as I mentioned once before, was so tall that he had a gig made expressly for himself, with a recess for his legs. His family, in Norfolk street, had been many years in the wheelwright and carriage business. He was the father of the late Mr. William Hutchinson, of the firm of Naylor, Vickers and Hutchinson.

LEIGHTON: A stroll down Ladies' walk would, at one time, have taken us into a colony of pleasant gardens. Down there was the famous file factory of Mr. Daniel Bramall, who, in 1816, built Sheaf House, afterwards the residence of Mr. George Younge. His name has been given to the street.

LEONARD: Chantrey adorned that house and took portraits of a large number of the Bramalls, and as at that other file-smith's in Shemeld croft—Nicholas Jackson's—so here, at the file-smith's in Bramall lane, he had an *affaire-de-cœur* with one of the daughters—Mary.

WRAGG: The factory was close to what is now the Cricket ground; 50 or 60 years ago these were the largest file works in the neighbourhood. In 1805, Mr. Daniel Bramall obtained a verdict of £2000 damages against a Birmingham file maker for violating his mark. Now, I believe, it is quite valueless.

EVERARD: Since we have wandered away from the town, suppose we get back to it by another route, taking in Little Sheffield and the Moor?

JOHNSON: Good. I have no doubt Little Sheffield may produce some interesting gossip, since the manufactory of George Jeeves and Son, brush-makers, was situated there. It has been said that there probably never was any one about whom so many amusing stories were told as Mr. George Jeeves, and the following have been related:—He had, besides his own workmen, a large number of apprentices, and he would station himself at his gates at six o'clock in the

morning and pull the ears of any lads who were late. One
of these lads was very lazy and troublesome to his master.
Old Jeeves used to keep a six-and-sixpenny whip for the purpose of correction, and Jack S—— got a large share of this
kind of attention. While under punishment he would loudly
promise to do better, but would quickly relapse into his old
listless ways. He was a great trouble to his employer, who was
really a good master to good servants. The lad often caused
his master to swear, of which he would bitterly repent afterwards, and he has been heard to say to the tiresome apprentice, " Thah makes me run into more sin than a little." Mr.
Jeeves had a pew at St. Paul's Church, and expected his lads
to attend there, and in time. One Sunday morning, on his
way to church down the Moor, he saw George ——, an
apprentice, playing at marbles on some waste ground. He
called out in passing, " Now, thah'll be in time, lad ; thah'll
be in time." " Yes, Sir," was the reply : but he stayed too
long, and was late at church. Old Jeeves waited his opportunity, and during the prayers sidled up to the offender, and
gave his ear a tremendous wring. George, partly from pain
and partly to serve his master out, set up a yell that re-
sounded through the church. Another of these lads, not
liking to go to church, tried to annoy his master by going
very shabbily dressed; and Mr. Jeeves quite audibly remarked,
" Go thee to 't bottom, thah shabby d——l." As a proof of
his regard for the decencies of worship, he was heard to say
to another lad, " D —— you, kneel in a praying posture."

WRAGG : With some of the best stories told of Mr.
Jeeves, the Rev. Frank Parker, incumbent of Dore, is associated. Jeeves very frequently accompanied the minister to
his Sunday labours, and when, one feast Sunday, the incumbent took for his text, " It is easier for a camel to go through
the eye of a needle than for a rich man to enter the kingdom
of heaven," Mr. Jeeves rose, and turning round to the congregation with his hand lifted, exclaimed, " There, you poor
ragged devils, did you hear that ? There's good news for
you."

LEIGHTON : A good dinner used to be one of the accom-
paniments of the Dore excursions. It is said that sometimes,
if the sermon was rather too long for his taste, Mr. Jeeves
would go to the bottom of the pulpit steps and call out in a
stage whisper, " Frank, Frank, t' goose is ready, cut it short,
man." Messrs. Jeeves had some very respectable boys, and
amongst them Mr. Thomas Marshall, afterwards a butcher in

Barkerpool, well known as "Tommy Marshall," and a very excellent man ; and also Mr. Jonathan Hoyland, brush manufacturer.

LEONARD : One whose father was an apprentice of Messrs. Jeeves's tells that it was his father's duty to fetch home Mrs. Jeeves when she had been out to visit her friends. At that time the streets were miserably paved and lighted. " I remember," he says, " my father in particular referring to Pinstone street as being very bad. Instead of a channel on each side of the street as now, our grandfathers had one channel in the middle. The sides were highest, and sloped down to this channel. The whole of what is now the west end of Sheffield was in the open country, and contained nothing more than lanes or garden walks. Mrs. Jeeves used to visit at one of the few houses then existing, I believe, at Leavy Greave, and my father would be sent with a lantern to fetch her home, and a long dreary walk it was. During his apprenticeship flour was five, six, and seven shillings a stone, and wheaten bread a luxury. He paid sixteen shillings a week to an aunt for his board, but for a long time never tasted white bread, but had instead thick sour oat-cakes, often sour before they were eaten. Many a time he would have no better dinner than milk porridge. The hours of work in these 'good old times' were from six in the morning till eight at night. At that time, owing to dirt and bad drainage, it was quite a common thing for the town to be visited with fevers almost every autumn. During my father's apprenticeship a fever broke out, which was terribly fatal in Little Sheffield, particularly in Young street and Jail street. My father, his uncle, and a young cousin, all took the fever in their house, and the poor girl died. I remember walking up Mackenzie walk—a pretty country lane in those days, leading from Sheffield Moor to Sharrow—when my father showed me a place where he was walking out on beginning to recover, and saw two little children crying bitterly and calling for their father and mother, both dead of the fever. There were no weekly returns of mortality in Sheffield in those days, or it would have shown a higher rate than our worst times."

LEIGHTON : Another notable inhabitant of Little Sheffield was old Seth Cadman, the combmaker. What Sheffielder, whose recollection goes back forty years or so, does not remember him as he used to sit, with his stall of combs, near the Old Church gates ? He was something of a celebrity in his day, and was born at Sky Edge. He became the

tenant of the old house still standing at the corner of Young
street and Hodgson street, on the 23rd August, 1803. At
that time the building must have been considerably more
than fifty years old, but it presented no sign that it would one
day be the dilapidated place it is; or that it would be closed
in by streets teeming with a hard working population. The
premises were divided into house and workshop, and from
the latter there was really a charming outlook. "Old Seth"
took a lively interest in the stirring events of his time, and
kept a diary, of which the intention was better than the spelling. Its records begin with 1807, and it is now in the possession of Seth's granddaughter, Mrs. Gillott, of Egerton
street. "Evintful Times to Future Ages" is the heading of
each page, and the entries relate to all manner of events,
private, domestic, local, national and foreign. In December,
1823, "a great flood of water came into Little Sheffield. It
was one yard Ighe in our house in Young street, did great
damige. Largest ever noung." Seth Cadman died in 1832,
aged 77. In the words of a "sampler," worked by a granddaughter, "He was followed to his grave by upwards of sixty
children, grandchildren, and great-grandchildren." His son,
Seth Cadman, died in 1849, at the age of 67, the third Seth
having died two months before, aged 26. One of the sisters
of the latter had married Mr. Gillott, and a second Mr. Crossland, spring-knife cutler, who, twenty years ago, emigrated
to America and settled in Buffalo. There he fell ill and was
in great distress, but his wife, who had had some training as
a dress-maker and was a woman of much energy, sold a
watch, and with the proceeds bought materials which she
made up into a baby's dress. That was the beginning of a
prosperous career, for the dress being displayed and sold,
other orders followed, and now she is the head of a large
establishment, and drives her carriage. Two brothers, who
continued the comb-making trade in the old house until
about ten years ago, also went out to Buffalo, and were started
in business by their sister as stationers and news agents.

LEONARD: You should not forget to add that posterity
owes a debt of gratitude to old Seth, as the first to manufacture here the small-tooth comb.

EVERARD: In those days, from Little Sheffield to the
Sugar House, at the bottom of Coalpit lane, there was scarcely
a house. It was then Sheffield Moor in reality, where tall
Mr. Hutchinson used to break in and train carriage horses.

WRAGG: The old house of Mr. Kirkby, in Button lane,

would be one of the few in the neighbourhood. It is dated 1705, and part of it is now occupied as the " Blacksmith's Cottage" public-house. Miserable shops have been built in front of part of it.

LEIGHTON : Sheffield Moor originally was not much better than a swamp, through which a path was made by two embankments being thrown up, between which was a deep ditch. The present road was made at great cost by filling up this ditch. But we have mentioned these things before.

LEONARD : The Moor has been described as " a wild common, adorned with gorse bushes and foxgloves, and possessing a bowling green."

WRAGG: The Woodman public-house on the Moor is one of the oldest dwelling-houses in the neighbourhood.

LEONARD : I think the " Rose and Crown," at Highfields, is still older. It is worth any one's while to go and look at it. I am told that there is a bedstead in one room that has never been taken down for nearly eighty years, and if it were removed now the ceiling would come down too, for it is supported by the bedstead.

EVERARD : Rather an uncomfortable place to sleep in. As we pass Bright street, Fitzwilliam street and Rockingham street, let us notice them as illustrations of the origin of our street names. They at once indicate the ownership of the soil by the house of Wentworth. The last Marquis of Rockingham married the daughter of the last Ecclesall Bright, and so came into possession of the property. As he died without issue it descended to his nephew, Earl Fitzwilliam. It is said that the Marquis, when taunted with marrying a woman of no blood, replied, that " if she had no blood she had plenty of suet."

JOHNSON: In my own recollection, about 40 years ago, the whole of the district comprising Devonshire, Hanover, Fitzwilliam, Broomhall, and other streets, has been laid out. Division street then extended no further than Canning street, and the houses on the Sheffield side of this dingy little street were open to the fields. In going to school at Western bank there was scarcely a house beyond the Bee Hive. Convent walk was a pleasant country lane, and on the left-hand side was what we called the Old Orchard, being an orchard only just broken up. In passing Mrs. Bayley's house, now the Public Hospital, we were greatly alarmed, for the house was haunted ; at least so we were told.

LEONARD : We learn from old Seth Cadman's diary, that on the 1st July, 1825, "Part of Coalpit lane was brought to rise Sheffield Moor." I confess I don't quite know what it means, unless formerly the only exit from Coalpit lane was into Button lane.

TWISS : The late Mr. Samuel Roberts (born 1763, died 1848) speaks of having heard Mr. Whitefield preach from the top of the cask at the Sugar house.

WRAGG : It is worthy of note that the houses on the Ecclesall side of Coalpit lane are older than those on the town side. In that lane was Miss Patten, whose father was in the cutlery trade. The house is now Mr. Kent's mattress shop. Up the yard were Mr. Patten's workshops. On the site of the Primitive Methodist Chapel is a large building divided into tenements, said to have been a farm house. Below was the old chapel, built by Mr. Bennet, about 1775, for a congregation of seceders from Nether Chapel, who removed to Howard street Chapel in 1790. Another congregation of Independents removed from it in 1803 to Garden street Chapel. For eight years previous to 1814 it had been occupied by the Baptists, until they removed to Townhead street Chapel. A few people, who held baptismal notions among the various Independent churches, separated from it and formed themselves into a distinct congregation or church, and chose one from among themselves to be the minister, Mr. Downes. He was said to be the most knock-kneed man in the town, even surpassing, in that respect, Tommy Hotbread. The chief man in this movement was Mr. Bowman, the pawnbroker. There is a tablet to his memory in Townhead street Chapel, stating that he was mainly instrumental in the erection of the place. In Coalpit lane, I believe, the Newboulds had been located before they went on to Sheffield Moor, and there, too, was Philip Law, edge-tool maker, where his ancestors had been about a century. Edward Middleton, of whom I spoke once before as an amateur gardener, had the Barleycorn tavern here. If all innkeepers had carried on their business as he did, the present conflict between teetotallers and publicans would not have existed, for there would have been neither drunkards nor total abstainers. He was the brother of John Middleton, the cooper, of Vicar lane.

EVERARD : We ought not to rest satisfied without a fuller notice of Mr. Edward Bennet. He was a sugar refiner, and carried on his business at the old Sugar-house, at the bottom of Coalpit lane, or Moorhead. He was a Christian man and a diligent and energetic tradesman ; and by a course of successful industry he accumulated a considerable fortune. He was a Nonconformist, and for some years was a member of the Independent Church, at the Nether Chapel. In 1780, he, together with some of the congregation, seceded, and the Coalpit lane Chapel was built chiefly, if not altogether, at his cost. He officiated as the pastor during the eight years of his life, but without receiving any emolument for his services ; but instead thereof, the sums contributed by the congregation were laid up for the erection of a chapel, to which Mr. Bennet added £250. The chapel at Howard street was built, and the congregation removed to it, in 1790. Mr. Bennet died on November 29th, 1788, two years before the opening of the new chapel in Howard street, and he left his wealth to his nephew, Mr. George Bennet, of Sunday-school and missionary celebrity. The type of Mr. Edward Bennet's character seems to have been a somewhat original one. He was possessed of strong common sense and no ordinary shrewdness. He was of a benevolent disposition, which especially manifested itself in various acts of private charity. One of his pecularities was that he had great faith in dreams. This may be in a great measure accounted for from his personal experience of one of a very singular and advantageous kind, which proved a reality, and exerted an influence on his circumstances and position through life. This is the story:— At a certain time in the last century, in consequence of war, or some other cause, sugar became so very scarce that Mr. Bennet found it quite difficult to obtain a sufficient supply to carry on his business. One night he dreamt that a large cargo of that produce had arrived, or was just about to arrive, at Liverpool, and that he went and bought the whole lot, which was to so large an amount that he had to set his wits to work to know how to raise the money to pay for it, but that, some way or other, he did raise it and secured the bargain. The next morning his mind was so impressed with this dream, that he set out to Liverpool on the strength of it. There he found the vessel had just arrived (but, I think, only still on the river, not in port) with the sugar on board. He bargained for and purchased the entire cargo, experiencing the difficulty in raising the cash to pay for it ; but either by loan on security of the goods, or in some other way, he did raise it, and thus accomplished his purpose. This eventually proved so profitable a speculation that he ever looked upon it as a " special providence," by means of which the foundation was laid of his subsequent success, fortune, and position. Mr. Bennet, in his acts of charity, was especially kind to poor ministers in the neighbourhood. A late friend of mine, likely to be well informed in the matter, used to relate an instance of this kind that occurred as the result of an intimation received in a dream. But while correct as to the circumstances, he must have been mistaken as to the person, for he told it of the Rev. Daniel Dunkerly,* of Loxley, whereas Mr. Dunkerly only became the minister at that place in 1802, fourteen years after Mr. Bennet's death. I think it possible that the recipient of Mr. Bennet's bounty was the Rev. Josiah Rhodes, Independent Minister at Stannington from 1779 to 1785. However, to the story. The good man in question, whoever he may have been, was poor, having but a small stipend, and was often in straits ; but he was of a modest and withal independent spirit, that would silently suffer much rather than complain or ask for assistance. He was at the time referred to in a special pecuniary difficulty, and did not know which way to look for deliverance, but only to that great source from whence he had often derived help and consolation before. He, therefore, prayed earnestly. The same night Mr. Bennet dreamt that his friend was in great perplexity and distress of mind for want of money. Under the impression of this dream, the next morning he sent him, anonymously, a £10 note (I think the sum was), which just came at the nick of time, and at once delivered the good man in his hour of extremity. Suspecting that it must have come from Mr. Bennet, he called upon him and ascertained the fact. The minister then asked how he could possibly know of his distress, as he had not breathed a word to a single human being on the matter ? Mr. Bennet answered that he had not been told by anybody, but that he knew it by a means which convinced him, whether it might satisfy any one else or not, that God, even now, is not limited as to the mode in which information may be acquired when necessary for the relief of His suffering and praying people. He told him that he had dreamt in the night of the fact of his distress, though without the particulars, and in the morning had simply acted on the suggestion.

---

* The Rev. Daniel Dunkerly was succeeded, in 1821, by the Rev. David Dunkerly, no relation, who married the eldest daughter of the Rev. James Mather, and who, after a pastorate of 8 or 9 years, went to Canada, and lately died there, aged 80 years.

TWISS : There are other stories of a similar kind about Mr. Bennet, but I am sorry to say I do not accurately remember the details.

LEONARD : There is an admirable story told of a Coalpit lane file manufacturer, who was in business here about the middle of last century, in partnership with his brother William —Master Cutler in 1771—while yet communication between Sheffield and London was in its infancy. Enoch Trickett was a genuine broad " Old Shevvielder." His shirt sleeves rolled up, wearing a leather apron whose bib was up to his throat, without neckerchief, he was not to be distinguished from his workmen. When the commercial spirit extended itself in the town, Enoch said he would go to " Lunnon" and see if he could sell some files and obtain orders, thinking he should get better prices there than in Sheffield. He went into a merchant's warehouse, and asked if they were in want of any files, producing his patterns, which they examined. They asked prices, and what discount was allowed. " Discount," he says, " What's that ? Oi ne'er heard tell on it afore." They explained that by making them an allowance of so much per cent., he would get their order, and upon the receipt of the goods they would remit him the money in payment. " Way, oi've telled yo t'proice on 'em, an' beloike oi'st expect t'brass for 'em." Further explanations only resulted in the reply, " Soa yo wanten me to gi yo so much money to buy t'foiles ?" The terms on which they would give him a good order were explained, but Enoch's patience was exhausted, and, " lapping" up his files, he said, " Nay, lad, nay ; oi can sell 'em for moor nor that at Breetmoor's onny toime, and tak t' brass hoam wi' me when ween 'livered." It is currently reported that Enoch never again tried his hand as a commercial traveller. When umbrellas first came into vogue in Sheffield, Enoch's brother got one. " See thee, see thee," said Enoch, " ahr Bill has getten a waukin stick wi' petticots on."

EVERARD : The father of Mr. George Hadfield, ex-M.P. for Sheffield, was one of the first to introduce the use of the umbrella into Sheffield. I have heard the late Mr. Samuel Hadfield say, that as boys he and his brother were so ashamed of it that they would not walk the same way to chapel with him on rainy Sundays.

LEIGHTON : That is almost as good as the reception accorded to the first pair of those new-fangled garments called trousers which found their way to the town. It was reserved for Mr. Marriott (Marriott and Atkinson) to introduce these garments, and when he revealed himself to his astonished townsmen in them, after a visit to London, he was greeted with the exclamation—" Why, lad, thou's getten breeches wi' chimbley poipes on 'em. Where didst get 'em ?" The ridicule was so merciless that Mr. Marriott thought it prudent to have these garments put away in a drawer until more enlightened times dawned. But, one day, when he was at work, some of his frolicsome friends went to Mrs. Marriott, and, by professing they had her " Mester's" authority, got possession of the " breeches with chimney pipes" and pawned them. So when Mr. Marriott wanted to pay his next visit to London he found out the joke that had been played him.

LEONARD : There are several claimants to the honour of having first introduced umbrellas into the town—Mr. Samuel Newbould and Mr. Holy (who are said to have brought them from Ireland), and Mr. John Greaves, merchant, of Fargate. The residence of Mr. Greaves stood where Mr. Proctor, draper, is now—a dingy old house, where he was succeeded by his son, who, as his epitaph in the Parish Church has it, was " the last survivor of a numerous and respectable family." The umbrella of Mr. Greaves the elder is still in existence, and is in the possession of his descendant, Miss Law, of Western bank. The tradition is that he brought it to Sheffield about the year 1742. He was born about 1708, and died 6th March, 1779. The ribs of the umbrella are jointed in the middle, so that they and the cover attached to them double back ; and the upper part of the stick being proportionately short, the whole when folded is only about 14 inches in length, though the bulk is considerable. The idea evidently was to construct an umbrella that could be put into the capacious pockets of those days. When it had to be hoisted there was a jointed stick to fit into the upper part, thus making the whole of a suitable length.

JOHNSON : The writer on Sheffield as it was forty years ago, from whom I have previously quoted, says that at that period " The whole of Fargate from Orchard street corner to Balm green, and on the opposite side also, consisted of small tumble-down, two-story houses, which must have been some of the oldest in Sheffield. Our fathers were not so particular as to the look of their houses as their children are. My father had a good business in Fargate, but on his marriage took a house in Rockingham lane, a little above Button lane, as a sort of country house."

LEIGHTON : There was formerly an obstruction in the thoroughfare from Barker pool into Division street. It was at the corner of Blind lane (Holly street), and it consisted of an old building that used to project into the road. It was at length taken down, and butcher Marshall built "Pool place," the row of shops extending from Blind lane to the fire brigade station. The building was old and dilapidated, and it was used as a meeting-house by some religious body on Sundays, and for other purposes on week-days. This was about the year 1811.

WRAGG : On a part of the site of the new Albert Hall were the residence and retail steel shop of the late Ebenezer Elliott, the poet; and lower down resided Mr. Foster, who died in 1846, aged 70. He was about the last survivor of the musicians that composed the local band.

LEONARD : It was at 61, Burgess street, that Ebenezer Elliott set up as an iron and steel merchant when he came to Sheffield in 1821, having been unsuccessful in business at Rotherham. His house adjoined his warehouse. He began with £100 of borrowed money, with which he bought a stock of iron, and he was wont to tell with glee how his success was such that this "tippled right over its head"—in other words, produced double the amount he gave for it. At one time so successful were his operations that, as he told Mr. Howitt, he used to sit in his chair and make £20 a day without even seeing the iron he sold. His warehouse was a dingy place. He had only one chair to offer to visitors—which had no bottom and only three legs. It was a favourite joke of his to liken this crazy chair to the British Constitution. In 1833, Elliott removed to Gibraltar street.

LEIGHTON : Burgess street is also to be remembered as the locality where the founder of the firm which afterwards built Sheaf works was established. Mr. William Greaves commenced his career as a resident in Burgess street, about the year 1775, his premises being near the top. In the first year of the present century the business was carried on by Wm. Greaves and Sons, in Cheney square.

EVERARD : We must not pass without a mention the site of the beginning of Sheffield's Water Works, when springs were found to be no longer adequate. Although its history is so well known that we need not dwell on it, suffer me to remark that in its later days it was a square walled-in pool, and that it was allowed to remain until, instead of a benefit, it had become a stagnant nuisance.

LEIGHTON : The first house erected on its site was built in 1793, by Mrs. Hannah Potter, as a public-house, with the odd sign of "Well run Dimple"—an exclamation of commendation addressed to a horse that distinguished itself on Crookes Moor racecourse.

JOHNSON : Forgive me for once more quoting James Wills, as he not only describes the old pool, but narrates an incident of some interest :—

> "The Barker's Pool, noted for nuisance indeed,
> Green over with venom, where insects did breed,
> And forming a square, with large gates in the wall,
> Where the Rev. Charles Wesley to sinners did call.
> Once when he was preaching, an officer bold
> March'd up through his audience, adorned with gold.
> Mr. Wesley perceived him with drawn sword in hand,
> And open'd his waistcoat as he saw him stand,
> Being fill'd by repentance by hearing the word.
> In those days persecution, that giant of hell,
> Stalk'd along in mad frolic ; and, strange for to tell,
> Pursued the poor Christians, abused them sore,
> Resolv'd that those people should never preach more;
> But the Wesleys and Whitfields, being fraught with pure zeal,
> Not fearing their lives, for sinners did feel;
> And the Mulberry street preaching house being too small,
> Wesley stood with his back against Barker's Pool wall."

LEONARD : Mr. Samuel Roberts gives a curious account of one of the uses to which Barker pool was put in his young days. "It was," he says, "well walled round. In the event of a fire (happily a very rare one) the water, on being let off, could be directed to most parts of the town. All the channels were then in the middle of the streets, which were generally in a very disorderly state ; manure heaps often lying in them for a week together. About once every quarter the water was let out of Barker pool, to run into all those streets into which it could be turned, for the purpose of cleansing them. The bellman gave notice of the exact time, and the favoured streets were all bustle, with a row of men, women, and children on each side of the channel, anxiously and joyfully awaiting, with mops, brooms and pails, the arrival of the cleansing flood, whose first appearance was announced by a loud continuous shout: all below was anxious expectation—all above a most amusing scene of bustling animation. Some people were throwing the water up against their houses and windows ; some raking the garbage into the kennel ; some washing their pigs ; some sweeping the pavement ; youngsters throwing water over their companions or pushing them into the wide-spread torrent. Meanwhile a constant Babel-like uproar, mixed with the barking of dogs and the grunting of pigs, was heard both above and below, till the waters, after about half an hour, had become exhausted."

LEIGHTON : As connected with the supply of water you will also remember that Mr. Roberts speaks of the supply of water brought in pipes to a receptacle in Townhead street, from which it was the business of a number of men to take it in casks, fixed on the body of a wheelbarrow, holding about fifty gallons, to all parts of the town to sell. " Water Isaac" was a well-known member of this band of barrel men. Mr. Roberts mentions too a large water reservoir belonging to Mr. Matthewman, over Mr. Winter's candlestick factory— subsequently Mr. Bardwell's auction room—for supplying the town with Crookes Moor water.

WRAGG : On the site of the houses where the Fire brigade now reside, in Balm green, there used to be some very old houses, bearing the date of erection as in the seventeenth century. In 1671, there were the following public wells : Burnt tree well, Water lane well, Workhouse well (the " pump," in Westbar, is no doubt its modern representative), Webster well, and Flint well. There were also the troughs in Water lane.

LEONARD : We have come across other sources of water supply in the course of our rambles—Bower spring, and the spring in Bailey's yard, Broomhall spring, and the rest. It is not so very many years since some of these were still used. The *Mercury*, of January 27, 1827, records that " A cast iron pump has been recently placed at the bottom of Sheffield Moor, chiefly through the exertions of the Overseers of Ecclesall Bierlow. This pump will be a great accommodation to that part of the town, they having had to procure their supply of water from an open well, which was often subject to nuisance. A reservoir has been made connected with the pump, capable of containing about 10,000 gallons, which will afford a supply for the summer months. At the head of the subscription list we see the name of Earl Fitzwilliam for £20, and that of Rowland Hodgson, Esq., for £5."

WRAGG : James Levick, the dahlia grower, was an ivory merchant in Pinstone street. He frequented Coxon's public-house, and at the election of 1836, when a Mr. Bell came down as candidate in opposition to Mr. John Parker, some one there said that he would get no one to support him. James Levick bet a guinea that he would be supported, and he won the wager by supporting him himself. I remember seeing him introduce Mr. Bell to the public from the Royal Hotel. In his rough and rugged way he said, "I beg to introduce to you Mr. John Bell." In Pinstone street resided the Withers' family, cutlers, one of whom, Benjamin Withers, was Master Cutler in 1756; a second Benjamin Withers, in 1794; and a Joseph Withers, in 1802. I believe the warehouse in Barker pool was never occupied for trade purposes, and the late Mr. Withers positively declined to let it when applied to. Lower down in Pinstone street is the shop of Mr. Turnell, the cabinet maker; on the passage over his kitchen window is a stone containing the following, "T. I. S., 1777." It was in this street that the first Methodist chapel was built, and demolished by a mob in 1743.

LEONARD: Forty years ago, there were one or two trees growing on the property of Mr. Withers, in Pinstone street. A passage leading from Fargate to New Church street was a favourite play-ground of the boys of those days, and boasted the name of " Sow Mouth." In 1825, the Town Trustees purchased some property in Pinstone lane for the purpose of widening it.

JOHNSON: Its present width makes us wonder what it must have been before. Its old name was Pinstone-croft lane, or in the vulgate, " Pincher-croft lane."

WRAGG: In New Church street resided Godfrey Fox, who has been previously noticed as occupying the Rein Deer, now the Royal Hotel, Waingate. At the corner of Cheney square resided Mr. Cheney, who was one of the first surgeons to the Infirmary, and who lived afterwards in Portobello. I think he had but one child, a daughter, who should have married Dr. Ernest, but there was some scandal and the match was broken off. This may account for the doctor spending all his life as house surgeon at the Infirmary. I would add that when a lad, he went to some one at Shire green, whose name I have forgotten, to be a fork maker.

LEONARD: The tenure of office of the modern house surgeons at the Infirmary contrasts very strangely with Dr. Ernest's 44 years' service.

WRAGG: Dr. Ernest, and old Mr. Tillotson who resided at Broomhall, were two of the last men in the town to have their hair powdered. In one of the old Sheffield directories, Cheney square is always printed China square. It looks as if the compiler fancied Cheney was a vulgarism for China.

LEIGHTON: In Fargate, near the shop of Mr. Johnson, cabinet maker, was, forty years ago, a projecting window, where a dealer in rotten-stone resided. Renwick's shop, at the corner of Orchard street, was there then, but far more modern.

JOHNSON: The upper part of Fargate, from Orchard street up to Balm green, consisted at that time, on both sides, of old tumble-down two-story houses, which must have been some of the oldest in Sheffield. I feel certain that 40 years ago there was more sociableness amongst shopkeepers than there is now. At that time they made longer days, and there was less hurry and scuffle in business. A thoroughly friendly and social set of shopkeepers occurs to my recollection in the neighbourhood of Fargate. Amongst these were William Wakefield, grocer; William Meggitt, shoemaker; Adam Renwick, basket maker; Ellis Eyre, grocer; together with the once well-known Benjamin Withers, and others. These were in the habit of indulging in daily gossip at each other's shops, and discussing the politics of the day. Retail shops were then much more gossiping places than now. But the headquarters of this kind of intelligence was the barber's shop, which almost every one frequented.

EVERARD: A Fargate shopkeeper of high respectability was Mr. Ebenezer Birks, grocer. Young Chantrey was at first sent to him, but he quickly resented being put to such uncongenial employment.

LEIGHTON: At the end of Norfolk row, opposite the old Cutlers' Arms, was the building called the old Lord's House. It formed the corner of Fargate and Norfolk row, and stood where are the shop so long occupied by Mr. Holden, watchmaker (now Mr. Rennie's, hosier), and the adjacent ones, as as far the "Old Red House." There was a double flight of steps, leading to a balcony on the level of the first floor. Mr. Rimmer, the Catholic priest, had a small room in the house, used as a chapel. The entrance was from the Norfolk row side, and there were two or three steps up to the chapel. About the time I am speaking of (1815), the building was taken down, and the land was quite open from Fargate to the Assembly Rooms in Norfolk street, and it continued open for years. Mr. Rimmer got a chapel built upon the ground, right at the back (in 1816), and that continued to be the Roman Catholic place of worship until the present St. Marie's Church was built (1846-50). We used to play on the ground, and "Old Rimmer," did not like it, and drove us off. He was a nice old gentleman—"a cheerful old chap." For a long time the ground was unfenced, but ultimately a palisade was put up

T

to keep people from the chapel, and to form a bit of a grave-ground. It was used for burying, and when the new church was built there was bother about the foundation.

WRAGG : Henry Howard, Esq., the great grandfather of the present Duke of Norfolk, resided in the Lord's House. He appears to have acted as steward to the previous Duke.

LEONARD : The lion over the door of the Assay office, in Fargate, was the work of a man named Mozley, who was employed by Ramsay, Chantrey's master.

WRAGG : The Fleur-de-lis opposite, just below the corner of Orchard street, was, sixty years ago, the residence of Mr. Jennings, who, when he retired from business, went to live at Hackenthorpe.

LEIGHTON : It has gone through many stages since then. Not many years ago it was a doctor's house.

WRAGG : On the site of the Exchange Drapery establish-ment—built as somewhat ambitious "commercial buildings"—were some very old brick shops, almost as old, I should think, as the " first brick house in Sheffield," built at the end of Pepper alley, according to the Rev. Edwin Goodwin, about the year 1696.

EVERARD : In one of the shops opposite was William Nadin, stay-maker, of whom mention was made in connection with Bank street. He was the only stay-maker of any note in the town. In those days stays were made that would last a life-time almost.

WRAGG : In the shop now occupied by Messrs. Watson, was a grocer named Greaves, who engaged the bellman to cry down Younge and Deakin's copper tokens. When he returned for payment Mr. Greaves paid him in the same token he had just cried down ; so the bellman stood on the footpath before the door, rang his bell, and proclaimed aloud that Younge and Deakin's money was paid again.

LEONARD : And thus we complete another circuit, and find ourselves once more at the Parish Church.

CHAPTER XI.

FORTY YEARS AGO.

Present—Messrs. TWISS, LEIGHTON, EVERARD, WRAGG, LEONARD and JOHNSON.

Period—A.D. 1874.

JOHNSON: I cannot, like most of you, speak of sixty years since and upwards; I only profess to speak of forty years ago, from my own knowledge. Forty-three years ago the population of Sheffield was a little short of 92,000, as compared with 240,000 in 1871. In 1832, England, practically, was without railroads, there being only three lines opened in all England; and Sheffield had none, except her coal railways, for some years after this time. We had four coaches daily to London, four to Birmingham, four to Manchester, and five to Leeds. We had about four-and-twenty coaches in all, from and to Sheffield daily, and, supposing these averaged ten passengers per journey, there would be the astounding number of 240 persons leaving our old town every day! Hansoms and cabs were, of course, unknown; but we had hackney coaches at the one "stand" at the head of High street. To Rotherham we had a vehicle, unknown to the present generation, a kind of car, called a "Waterloo;" the race is quite extinct. I believe we wrote a good many letters in those days, but letter-writing was an expensive luxury, only to be indulged in upon the following rates:—For a place not exceeding 15 miles distance, 4d.; 30, 6d.; 50, 7d.; 80, 8d.; 120, 9d.; 170, 10d.; 230, 11d.; 300, 12d.; 400, 13d.; 500, 14d. A letter containing an enclosure was charged double, and one exceeding an ounce, but not exceeding 1¼ oz., was charged four single rates! Thus a letter to London, weighing a fraction over an ounce would be three shillings and fourpence. Without railways and penny postage, the business of to-day could not be carried on. In addition to the hackney coaches, the head of the High street was favoured by the presence of a row of second-hand shoe dealers' stalls. The shoes they sold were called Lord Mayor's. The shopkeepers naturally enough objected to these shoe-stalls being fixed opposite their shops, but they were allowed to remain there for some years after this time.

Forty years ago there were no daily papers in Sheffield, but there were four weekly. News, then, if not scarce, was dear ; and people after buying the small sheet of news, price sevenpence, passed it from one to another, and it was a customary thing for three or four tradesmen to join at a newspaper. As might be expected, at this high price the number of readers was comparatively few. Hence arose another institution that has entirely died out—what we used to call "crying-papers in the streets." These formed a means of livelihood to a good many persons, both men and women. These small slips of paper were generally extracts from the newspapers of the town. Very often they were "full, true, and particular accounts" of executions and last dying speeches ; sometimes the calendar of York Assizes ; and often, especially during a dearth of news, mere catch-pennies made to sell. I remember hearing a fellow crying one of these about some wonderful appearances in the heavens, when a whole army had been seen—fully accoutred—in the sky. Even a cricket match on the ice at Little London, when Tom Marsden stood umpire, or some doggrel on the winner of the St. Leger, would sometimes serve the purpose of these wandering newsmen ; they were not over nice, and it was always "all for the low charge of one halfpenny." I remember, at the time of what was called the "Resurrection Riot" in Eyre street, in 1835, one of these gentry allowed his imagination to run wild, and informed his townsmen that during the riot "the landlord (the late Samuel Roberts, Esq.) was present, and cried, with a loud voice, 'Burn and destroy.'" But for this the man was committed to the sessions : he had gone a little too far.

WRAGG : These flying stationers generally made their appearance after some murder, or soon after the conclusion of some remarkable trial. Their "Last Dying Speeches" were long narrow slips of paper, containing about half the matter of a modern newspaper column, and the price one halfpenny. If I mistake not, they were mostly printed in York street, by a person named Ford ; then a rival named Burgin started, up one of the Market place passages— Watson's walk, I think. Sometimes they contained woodcuts, as was the case at "Honest John's" trial. Those who knew him said it was a fair likeness, and it was certainly the best half-pennyworth I ever saw.

JOHNSON : Talking of riots, these are happily gone out of fashion. Formerly, they were too plentiful. I can just remember the riot at our first borough election. Fortunately I was kept at home on that night, but I well recollect going down the next day and seeing the devastation that had taken place. Three men and two boys were shot dead on the occasion, and another young fellow died of his wounds shortly afterwards. Then, as I have already mentioned, we had the riot in Eyre street, which took place in January, 1835. At this time, a second medical school which had been established in Eyre street, corner of Charles lane, was completely gutted, and the building set on fire. The mob got an impression that it was a place where "resurrection men" sold the bodies they stole. I recollect that a small case containing the body or skeleton of a child found on the premises, was nailed up by the mob on a house opposite, to serve as an incentive to the work of destruction. The origin of the riot was a quarrel that took place on the previous day (Sunday), between the keeper of the school and his wife. This caused a disturbance, and the place bore such an evil name that the quarrel of these two persons ended in the destruction of the building, excepting the walls, on the following day. I recollect on the Monday night a great part of the mob, crying "All in a mind for Overend's," passed my father's shop, and went along Orchard street to Mr. Wilson Overend's house and surgery, causing much alarm, but doing little mischief.

For the next ten years or so, Chartist riots, more or less serious, were quite common. On the 12th September, 1839, the Chartists held a " silent" meeting in Paradise square, which was dispersed by the soldiers and police. The Chartists reassembled in " Doctor's field," at the bottom of Duke street, Sheffield moor, where they were followed by the soldiers and police, and 36 prisoners taken. At the Town Hall, next day, which was guarded by the dragoons, and the doors kept by policemen armed with cutlasses, I saw several anxious mothers inquiring for their missing ones. Amongst the rest was the mother of a young man who has since been an influential citizen in St. George's ward. He was tried at the assizes and acquitted. A night or two after the Doctor's field meeting, hearing there was to be a Chartist meeting at Skye edge in the Park, my brother and I tried to find Skye edge, but not succeeding, met the Chartists coming away. They marched down Duke street, singing lustily a Chartist melody—

"Press forward, press forward,
There's nothing to fear,
We will have the Charter, be it ever so dear."

But, alas! on turning the corner at the bottom of Duke street, they caught sight of the helmets of the 1st Dragoons, who were coming to meet them. Instead of "pressing forward" we all "pressed" every way but that, and in two minutes not a Chartist was to be seen. The dragoons on that occasion were under no less a person than Sir Charles Napier, at that time Commander of the Northern District; and I believe the incident is referred to in his life.

LEIGHTON: Going further back than you do, I recollect that 1809 or 1810 were troublous times. Flour and other necessaries were very dear, and we used to have many riots. Jacky Blacker was a leading man. I have seen a considerable mob of people following him up High street. He had a penny loaf dipped in blood, and he carried it on a spike about the streets. I remember one riot in particular. Flour was about 7s. or 7s. 6d. per stone, and the mob broke into the flour shops and distributed the flour to the people. The constables were out and the soldiers were fetched from the Barracks, and there was martial law in the town. Tradesmen were called out of their shops at night to form part of the patrol through the streets and the districts outside the town. I recollect my father being out in this way many a time. I once saw the soldiers come from the Barracks. There was a terrible riot going on in the Market place, the mob throwing things about, when the Hussars came up with their spears, rode right up into the Market place and dispersed the people. Folks could scarcely carry on business in those days. They had to shut up the moment the rabble were coming, if they did not wish to have their windows broken. People have no idea now what sort of times those were to live in.

TWISS: I remember being fetched home from school in 1816, when there was a riot. The rioters had made a procession and marched up Angel street. Afterwards I saw the soldiers go by, with Mr. Hugh Parker at their head.

LEONARD: My old friend, to whom I have had to acknowledge my indebtedness for so much information, said to me the other day: "I have seen several riots in Sheffield, and one particularly I remember. At the bottom of Spital hill was an old building that had been occupied by Jonathan Hobson as a warehouse, and when he gave it up it was used as a store for the Volunteers. At the time I speak of there was a riot about dear bread, or something of the kind. I was in 'the Pickle,' when down came the mob to the Volunteer store. The doors were soon smashed in, and the fellows pitched out guns and all sorts of things. Most of the muskets were smashed by striking them across a low wall on the opposite side of the road, but a few were shouldered by the rioters, and they tried to march. As they were going up the Wicker, a troop of cavalry from the Barracks met them, and didn't they run! It was fine to see drums, trumpets, clothing, and all sorts of military odds and ends tumbling out of the chamber windows at the store, and the mob kicking them about, and shouting and yelling like mad things ; but the soldiers brought them to their senses very soon."

EVERARD : I, too, recollect that riot, and was also an eyewitness of it. Being in the Wicker at the time, I saw the troop of Hussars sweep down to the scene of action. It was in 1812, a dreadfully distressing time of bad trade and high prices, of which mention was made when we were speaking of the large number of able-bodied men who were employed on the new burial ground.

LEONARD : The account of the affair given in the *Iris* is that it originated with those men. They came down in a body, it says, and paraded the Market place " for no imaginable purpose than to expose a spectacle of wretchedness which should work upon the passions of the indigent manufacturers" [we do not use the word in that sense of artizans now] "and excite indignation against the provision sellers." Having marched up the Market these men set up a great shout and then returned to their occupation, leaving the crowd ready to commit any mischief. Accordingly they fell upon the stores of the potato dealers, scattering, destroying, or carrying off those vegetables, breaking windows and doing other mischief. The riot act had been read, and the mob seemed pausing as if not knowing what else to do, when a voice shouted, " All in a mind for the store-room in the Wicker ;" and there they went with the result that has been described.

EVERARD : A little later than that period another " flour riot" took place ; when I saw the rioters, armed with thick sticks and bludgeons, march up Broad lane, headed by John Blackwell, *alias* Jackey Blacker, with a drawn sword in his hand, a penny loaf dipped in blood stuck on its point, and with a large placard borne beside him, with the inscription " Bread or Blood !" This man was a tailor of very dissolute habits, and the acknowledged " king" of the " gallery" at the Theatre. For this exploit he was tried and incarcerated in York Castle ; eventually he ended his days in the Sheffield Workhouse.

LEONARD : This talk about the riots, and Mr. Johnson's reference to the Chartists, remind me of a very interesting account that was prepared nine years ago by Mr. John Taylor. It was reprinted from the newspaper in the form of a little pamphlet ; but as possibly none of you have copies, except our friend Twiss, and as conversation is not very brisk this evening, suppose I read it ?

EVERARD : By all means.

LEONARD (reads) : "The Chartist conspiracy, which culminated in the audacious attempt, in January, 1840, to give the town over to pillage, anarchy, and fire, is an event of which most of us have some recollection. The number of the conspirators and their dupes has never been accurately ascertained, but probably amounted to several hundreds, exclusive of the much larger body of the moral-force Chartists, who shrank from the wild extremes of their hot-headed leaders, and also exclusive of the armed contingents expected from Rotherham, Eckington, and other places. The programme of the Chartists, and the arrangements made for carrying it out, are matters of history. Taking a hint from the Wesleyans, the Chartists met in ' classes ' at the houses of their respective ' leaders,' scattered over the town. They had a general assembly-room in Figtree lane, and a secret council-room at a public-house at the top of Lambert street. Guns, cartridges, daggers, pikes, hand grenades, and ' cats ' were provided in considerable quantities by the leaders and members of the council ; and the equipment of the conspirators was to be completed by pillaging the gun shops of the town, when the proper time came. The ' cats ' were small spiked implements to scatter in the streets for the purpose of laming the cavalry horses, being so made that however thrown on the ground one spike pointed upwards. The conspirators were to meet in their class rooms on the night of the rising, proceed thence under the command of their leaders to a few general meeting places in the outskirts of the town, and then move in bodies to execute their atrocious designs. Some of the more daring classes were deputed to take possession of the Town Hall and the Tontine, which were to be the headquarters; others were detailed to fire the Barracks as soon as the military had been called out, and to burn other obnoxious places in the town. The rest were to fire the houses of the magistrates, their clerk, and other gentlemen of position living in the outskirts, the notion being that this would draw the authorities from the town to look after their own affairs. It was supposed that, thus deserted, the general body of the population would concede all that was asked, and that a decided success in the outset would so swell the ranks of the Chartists as to give them complete control over the town and district. The poor policemen were special objects of vengeance, all the conspirators having instructions to murder every policeman they met with.

"Though the information published at the time on all these points is full and complete, the circumstances attending the discovery and frustration of the plot, constitute an unpublished chapter in the annals of Sheffield; and the men to whom the town owes its rescue from a terrible danger are not only unrewarded, but to this day unknown to the general public as the detectors of the conspiracy. The object of my paper is not to recapitulate the facts published at the time, but to recount the yet unpublished details of this, for Sheffield, most fortunate detection.

"The instrument in the great discovery was James Allen, then the keeper of the Station inn beerhouse in Westgate, Rotherham, [and not to be confounded with James Allan, who at a later period was landlord of the Station inn in that town]. He was shrewd and intelligent, a superior workman as a stove-grate fitter, and was employed by Messrs. Yates, Haywood and Co. The man who used that instrument was not the respected chief of the Sheffield police, nor any of his subordinates, but Mr. John Bland, then, and for many years afterwards, the active and intelligent chief-constable of Rotherham. For some time before the plot was fully hatched, wild rumours spread of the intention of the Chartists to possess themselves by force of the entire neighbourhood, drive out the rich, and divide the spoil. By many the rumours were regarded as the ravings of maniacs, and utterly disbelieved. But the reports that reached Mr. Bland as to the intentions of the Chartists at Rotherham, assumed such consistency and pointed so persistently to one end, that he, happily for Sheffield and the entire neighbourhood, determined to investigate them. Unsuccessful in his first efforts, he went at length to Allen. Partly, no doubt, from fear on his own account, but mainly because, though an ardent Chartist, he shrank from the horrible measures in contemplation, Allen admitted that a Chartist organisation was being established at Rotherham, in conjunction with the more extensive organisation having its head-quarters at Sheffield ; and that the directors of the whole movement, in order to avoid the suspicion that would be likely to arise from too frequent meetings at Sheffield, occasionally came down to Rotherham and held their secret councils at his house. He added that they had begun to despair of peaceable measures ; and that though he and others strenuously opposed all resort to violence, the whole tendency of their deliberations was towards a determined physical force movement. As yet the conspiracy was a mere unshaped design. It gradually ripened, however, into a definite plot against life and property, as well as against law and order. The results of the repeated conferences were regularly reported to Mr. Bland by Allen, and the conspiracy no sooner assumed a distinct shape than Mr. Bland took Allen's report of it in writing. With Allen's consent he communicated it personally to the present Earl of Effingham, then Lord Howard, resident at the time at Barbot Hall, near Rotherham, and a West Riding magistrate. On the advice of his Lordship, Mr. Bland, and Mr. Oxley, the magistrates' clerk, privately visited Mr. Hugh Parker, then the leading Sheffield magistrate, and read the statement to him. The statement was to the effect that delegates from Huddersfield and other places had met those of Sheffield and Rotherham at Allen's house ; that they had finally resolved to carry the charter by violence ; that the delegates from a distance had guaranteed the assistance of their respective districts to Sheffield ; that the Tontine and Town Hall at Sheffield were first to be seized as head quarters ; and that the town itself was to be taken possession of as a step to ulterior measures. The houses and places of business of obnoxious persons were to be sacked and burnt, no atrocity being thought too great that could pave the way for the charter. The story was laughed at and pooh-poohed by Mr. Parker and the Sheffield authorities, who refused to believe that any scheme so wild and atrocious could possibly be entertained. Still the Chartists held their sworn councils day by day, chiefly in Figtree lane and Lambert street, Sheffield. Allen's moderation having excited their suspicion of him, they met less frequently at his house, and took him less into their secrets. He was, however, sufficiently acquainted with their designs to know that a force was to be mustered at Rotherham as well as at Sheffield, and that that force was to strike their first blow by seizing the Court House, and then sacking the residence of Mr. Henry

Walker, at Clifton, and Lord Howard, at Barbot Hall. When things had reached this pass, Mr. Bland urged Allen again and again to ascertain where the ammunition and arms were collected for the final uprising. All Allen's efforts to do this, however, were vain; he only knew that there were to be a number of such depôts, and that the Chartists, when they rose, were to be plentifully armed with 'cats,' to protect them from the cavalry. The time for the execution of the plot was evidently drawing near, but Allen was still kept ignorant of those details upon which alone the police could act in anticipation of the rising. It became clear that Allen must either go the whole hog as a Chartist or break down as an informant; and Mr. Bland, whose duty was plain—to fathom and frustrate the conspiracy at any cost—urged that a man could not possibly play the traitor in a better cause than in the frustration of so hopeless and atrocious a design. Allen at length strung himself up to the emergency, and it was arranged that he should go to the next council, declare himself a convert to the absolute necessity of the physical force movement, and offer to be ready at any time with 150 men upon a day or two days' notice. This bold course re-established Allen in the confidence of the council. It was about the beginning of January, 1840. On the Wednesday, Thursday, and Friday evenings of the same week Allen attended sworn councils. On the Friday evening, January the 10th, he reported that the crisis was to come on the following night, but that the Council of delegates were to meet at Sheffield at three o'clock on the Saturday to determine the precise hour of the rising, and the several rendezvous from which the various bands of insurgents were to start on their errands of death and destruction. The information most desired by Mr. Bland all this time was the names of the leading conspirators, their meeting places, and their arms and ammunition stores. Allen left Rotherham at one o'clock on Saturday to attend the final council meeting,—the understanding with Mr. Bland being that he was to return as quickly as practicable to Rotherham after the meeting, with the details which were so much longed for and by the possession of which alone the rising could be stopped before mischief was done. Lord Howard reached Rotherham at three o'clock, remaining with Mr. Bland in readiness to act upon a moment's notice. Anxiously they waited hour after hour until past seven o'clock, and began to be terribly afraid that Allen's pluck had failed him at the last push. Between seven and eight o'clock, however, he arrived almost breathless with haste and trembling with fear.   No wonder Allen was terrified; the ferocious character of the plot gave him little reason to hope for mercy at the hands of his old friends if it were discovered that he was the betrayer.   He must never again show his head in this part of the country, for his life would not have been worth an hour's purchase.   Faithless to his wretched comrades, Allen was true to the active and energetic officer who had so cleverly turned him into an instrument for the frustration of the conspiracy.   He had brought all the required information.   The 'classes' were to meet at their leaders' houses at ten o'clock on Saturday night ; were to carefully arm themselves ; were to repair to three or four specified points, and march thence to their appointed work, each class detailing a few of its number to empty the gun shops, in order to arm their comrades.   For a few moments the recipients of this information anxiously debated the question, 'What is to be done ?'   Evidently the great rising was to be at Sheffield.   Its authorities had been aroused from their dream of incredulity by the further information which had been communicated to them from Rotherham, after their rejection of the first statement, and by the evident stir and excitement among the Chartists.   But they were still in a great measure ignorant when and how the rising was to be effected ; and it was of the most vital consequence that the intended rising should be frustrated before it had been made, not because there was the least chance of its ultimately succeeding, but because a temporary and partial success must necessarily be attended with the most dreadful results.   The Rotherham police were not charged with the safety of Sheffield, but the conspirators were one body, and their success in the greater must have been dangerous to the lesser town. The plot was discovered, and for humanity's sake, if for no other reason, Sheffield must be made aware of the extent and nearness of its danger and the means of preventing it.   So reasoned Lord Howard, and manfully determined to be himself the messenger of mercy.   Provided with a copy of the particulars of Allen's information, he mounted his horse and galloped at full speed to Sheffield, leaving Mr. Bland to take all necessary precautions to frustrate the Rotherham contingents, which were to arm at the gun shops and assemble near Brightside at twelve o'clock, under the command of Allen, or, in his absence, of such other leader as they might choose. His Lordship reached Sheffield towards ten o'clock, and found the police authorities on the *qui vive*, though quite unprovided with definite information. The intelligence was alarming but welcome. There was no time to waste in idle fears, a few hours only remaining before the mischief would begin. A detachment of soldiers was called out immediately, and, with the aid of the civil power and the remarkably accurate information supplied from Rotherham of the full details of the conspiracy, happily succeeded in frustrating it. Holberry, the principal leader, was apprehended at his own house, No. 19, Eyre lane, before he left home to head the conspirators, considerable quantities of arms and ammunition being found in the garret of his house. Booker, Peter Foden, Thompson, and other leaders, were taken in the streets or at their own homes. The general meeting places of the conspirators were visited, and the 'classes' chased and dispersed as they arrived. All was confusion and dismay in the ranks of the baffled plotters ; they fled in all directions, throwing away or hiding their arms, quantities of which were found in the neighbourhood of the dams and Crookes moor. Thus ended, with the wounding of a few policemen and two or three innocent citizens, whom necessity had forced into the streets, a conspiracy which, but for its timely discovery, would probably have resulted in enormous mischief.

"Allen, who was at once suspected by his comrades, was kept under the care of an armed guard at Rotherham for several days, until Earl Fitzwilliam had communicated with the Home Secretary, and procured his removal from this part of the country. Government, as was their duty, offered to provide Allen with the means of emigrating and setting up in life in the colonies, but he declined to leave England. Employment was found for him at his own trade in the South of England, where he remained for some time under an assumed name. At length he was recognised by a man who had known him at Rotherham, and his removal became necessary. Government provided for him elsewhere, but he never, after leaving the southern fender manufactory, communicated with Mr. Bland, or his friends here, and his fate is unknown.

"Praises and rewards were bestowed on the Sheffield police and other officials, for their ability and zeal in the discovery and frustration of the plot. They monopolised the credit due of right to Mr. Bland in the main, and to his officers in a minor degree. Mr. Bland and his associates were tongue-tied. Though the conspiracy was defeated, Chartism was still a dangerous element in society. Lady Howard was so alarmed, that Lord Howard, yielding to her natural fears, bound Mr. Bland and his officers beforehand in a solemn promise to conceal the part he and they might take in the matter, in order to avoid the vengeance of the Chartists. Galling as must have been the knowledge that others were reaping the honours and rewards due to them, Mr. Bland and his subordinates religiously kept their promise until Lord Howard had left the neighbourhood and Chartism had died out. Sheffield officials in positions of the highest trust knew that there was some secret about the discovery, but could never fathom it. It was not until the resignation of Mr. Raynor, that the least hint was publicly given that it was to Mr. Bland, Sheffield was so much indebted in 1840."

JOHNSON : There is one little inaccuracy there—the reference to Peter Foden being captured with the rest. He had been apprehended in the early part of August for taking part in riotous meetings and processions, and he did not obtain bail until the 3rd September, when Ebenezer Elliott, the corn-law rhymer, and Mr. Wostenholm, file manufacturer, Dunfields, were his sureties. For a while he kept aloof from the meetings, but he was at last prevailed upon to attend, and although he took no active part in speaking, yet he was believed to be in the secrets of the physical force party. Peter Foden was not seen in the proceedings connected with the collapse of the conspiracy, but he was suspected of being connected in them, and a warrant was issued for his apprehension. He concealed himself in the town for some time, and at last went into Wales and stayed as long as possible in various towns. He did not surrender at the Spring Assizes, at which he was indicted for conspiracy, sedition, and riot, and the recognisances of his sureties were forfeited. At last, tired of dwelling in fear of arrest, and encouraged by the collapse of the Chartist movement, he ventured to come to Sheffield, and in order to see if the authorities would notice him, he took some commodities of his own making and hawked them in various public-houses. A good living he would have earned had he not been arrested in December, 1840, at Paul Ashley's, in Watson's walk. He was tried at York, and having been advised to plead guilty by his counsel, he was committed to Wakefield for two years. He had already been in prison three months, which was taken into consideration. He served one year and nine months after his conviction. He affected an odd demeanour in prison, but ultimately being made schoolmaster, he attained more liberty and had books to read. At one time he wanted to write a detailed account of his proceedings to his family, and he secreted bits of paper and a pen, but how to obtain ink to write was a matter of difficulty. So at last he hit upon the singular plan of writing with his own blood, and concealed the document in the neck-handkerchief of a discharged prisoner. One of his children, of the name of Feargus O'Connor, died while his father was in gaol. Foden, released from prison, went to Staleybridge, where he commenced business, and got on well; but he could not settle, and removed to Doncaster. Then he sold all off and went to St. Louis, in America, and died a few years ago. The citizens made a public funeral, and presented his wife with a framed document, setting forth the respect they had for him and his family.

JOHNSON: The sentences those men received seem to me to have been light, when the magnitude of their crime is considered—Holberry, four years' imprisonment; Thos. Booker, three years'; Wm. Booker and others, two years'; others again, one year; and a large part of these sentences was remitted.

WRAGG: Holberry's was practically imprisonment for life, since he died in York Castle, in 1842, before his sentence had expired. His body was brought to Sheffield for interment, and the funeral, on the 27th of June in that year, was the excuse for a great demonstration. Another of these men, John Clayton, also died in gaol, in 1841, but he was buried at Northallerton.

TWISS: We might have mentioned two of these people when we were speaking of the Hartshead, for Peter Foden and Julian Harney were residents of that classic neighbourhood. Harney, after he had, along with Richard Otley, escaped punishment on a charge of conspiracy, went to America.

EVERARD: We have been talking of riots, and no mention can be made of such disturbances in Sheffield without recalling that famous Norfolk street outbreak which was lamentable through two of the crowd being killed, but most memorable through its being the cause of Montgomery's second incarceration in York Castle. It occurred on the 4th of August, 1795, and the events of that day are matter of local history.

LEONARD: The mildness and indirectness of Montgomery's references to Col. Athorpe's doings on that day, show that his persecution was a piece of political hostility. How Mather scathed the colonel, nick-naming him "Beef-headed Bob,"

while he satirised the volunteers who took part in the affair
as " Ruddle-neck'd tups !'

LEIGHTON : Those first volunteers were unpopular before
that, because they were necessarily obnoxious to the prevalent Jacobinical opinions of the masses; but the affair of
that day greatly increased their unpopularity.

LEONARD : My nonogenarian friend says he remembers
these " Blues." He saw them going as far as Bolehill to
meet their guns, and they had a sort of field-day at Norton.
They were fine fellows, with their blue coats, red facings,
white waistcoats, and black leggings. Mr. Athorpe was
colonel, and Mr. Fenton, lieutenant-colonel or major. Mr.
Carver, a woollen draper in High street, a tall handsome man,
was one of the captains, and Dr. Frith, in Norfolk row, was
the surgeon.

TWISS: Here is an account of the old Sheffield Volunteers, drawn up by an officer in the corps :—

"In the year 1794, the Sheffield Volunteer corps was instituted, under the title of the Loyal Independent Sheffield
Volunteers. When first begun upwards of 150 individuals
offered to furnish themselves with arms, accoutrements, and
clothing. The furnishing of arms was objected to, and
Government agreed to find arms and accoutrements, and a
certain number of days' pay, with ammunition for the service
of the regiment. A subscription was entered into by some
of the town's gentlemen to furnish clothing for those to whom
it was inconvenient to find the whole of their own. By this
means the number was increased to about 500. In 1795, the
lady of Thomas Walker, Esq., of Rotherham, made an offer
of two iron guns to the Volunteers, but they were too unwieldly for field service. She then proposed presenting the
corps with the amount equal to their value, and two brass
six-pounder field pieces were ordered from Woolwich, and the
extra expense was paid out of the regimental stock purse.
This corps, under the management of Adjutant Ratcliffe,
Captain Goodison, Drum-Major Potts (strict disciplinarians),
and a few town's gentlemen who had served as volunteers in
the American war, acquired a character for discipline, good
conduct, and soldier-like appearance which did credit to the
town they belonged to, and it was generally allowed they were
equal to any of this description of military.

"This corps was originally instituted in the month of April,
1794, for the defence of the town and neighbourhood of Sheffield during a time of the greatest difficulty and danger. It

consisted of upwards of 490 effective men, and was disbanded on the 21st May, 1802. In 1803, on the re-commencement of hostilities, the loyal inhabitants of Sheffield were again called upon to offer their services to their country. A new corps was raised, under the title of the Sheffield Volunteer Infantry. This regiment was raised upon a different principle from the former. It was supplied with arms, accoutrements, clothing, &c., by the Government. The men and officers were obliged to attend duty a certain number of days in the year, for which they were paid after the rate of the regular militia. They were several times called up on permanent duty, and while on that duty were subject to martial law. On the 15th of August, 1805, one of the attendants at the beacon at Grenoside came between five and six o'clock in the morning to Mr. Thomas Smith, constable, to inform him the beacons were lighted, the signal that the French were landed. The drummers were immediately ordered to beat to arms, and in a very short time the whole regiment was assembled under arms. In consequence of the difficulty in preparing waggons and horses requisite for the service, a considerable time elapsed before they could march, and it was nine o'clock in the evening before they arrived at Doncaster, the first stage on their route. There they halted for refreshment and further orders, an officer having been dispatched to Beverley to General Fergusson, under whose command the regiment was to be placed. On the messenger's return, the whole turned out to be a false alarm. On the 16th, the regiment, along with several others, infantry and yeomanry, were inspected by General Hodgson, and on the 17th returned to Sheffield without loss of life or limb, every man receiving two guineas besides regular pay for his services. They were greeted by a great part of the population of the town, many of whom had been left in painful anxiety.

"It is but just to the regiment to add that so great was their alacrity and zeal on this notable event that out of near 700 men not more than 14 or 16 were absent. Of these, several were on the moors grouse shooting, and on hearing of the departure of the regiment they immediately followed to Doncaster. One officer, being in Dublin, on hearing the first report, left his business unsettled and came home to join his regiment. One had a broken leg, two others were lame, others sick. To the whole the greatest commendation was due; indeed it is correctly ascertained there was only one man absent who could possibly attend, and that was a noncommissioned officer who knew, as he says, this affair was all a hoax, and, regardless of the orders of his commanding officer, took the opportunity of a walk to Baslow a-fishing.

" The conduct of the regiment on this occasion needs no comment. On the 26th they again marched to Doncaster for fifteen days' permanent duty. On the 15th of October, being the day fixed, nearly the whole of the regiment transferred their services to local Militia under nearly the same regulations as the Regular Militia. The last permanent duty performed by this regiment was at Wakefield, in August, 1813. In April, 1816, the whole of the local Militia was suspended, the officers retaining their commissions, that, in the event of their being again wanted, they might hold their rank and seniority accordingly. The following is a list of the officers of that period. Those marked * belonged to the Volunteers of 1794 :—

* Lieutenant-Colonel Commandant F. Fenton.
* Second Lieutenant-Colonel Thomas Leader.

Major John Shore.	Captain R. Clarke.
Adjutant W. W. Darling.	,,　J. Blake.
* Quarter-Master Saml. Tompkin.	Lieutenant J. Hall.
* Surgeon John Sterndale.	,,　T. Bradbury.
Captain T. Newbould.	,,　J. Drabble.
,,　T. A. Ward.	,,　J. Yeomans.
,,　C. Pickslay.	,,　T. B. Jackson.
,,　J. Brown.	Ensign S. Young.
,,　J. Wheat.	,,　J. Binney."

The following inscription is engraved on one of the field pieces :—

" This piece of artillery, with another of equal calibre, was purchased in 1795 for the use of the regiment of Sheffield Loyal Independent Volunteers in defence of their country, then disturbed by internal commotions and threatened with foreign invasion, and through a long and perilous period passed under the successive command of Lieutenant-Colonel R. A. Athorpe, Colonel Richard Earl of Effingham, and Lieutenant-Colonel Francis Fenton, by the latter of whom, and the surviving officers and privates, in a time of profound peace, after firing a royal salute in honour of the coronation of King George the Fourth, on the 19th day of July, 1821, they were transferred to the Trustees of the estates of the town of Sheffield and to their successors for ever.

" God save the King.

"Trustees of the town at the time being Robert Turner, collector ; John Shore, Peter Brownell, John Greaves, Rowland Hodgson, Francis Fenton, Benjamin Withers, Jun., Samuel

Staniforth, Thos. Asline Ward, Vincent Hy. Eyre, Samuel Mitchell."

LEIGHTON : When the Volunteers marched northwards, on the false alarm in 1805, the well-known Dr. Browne accompanied them as far as Attercliffe Common, where he took leave of them in a speech in which he made the somewhat left-handed promise to be a husband to their wives and a father to their children during their absence. One of the Volunteers, whose name was Carnelly, used to tell how splendidly the men were regaled on the road, being called " brave fellows," and " the pillars of the nation." When they returned they expected to be treated in a similar manner ; but with the alarm had vanished the enthusiasm, and they met with but a cool reception. On remonstrance being made, and a reminder given that they had been called " pillars of the nation," the rejoinder was, " Yes, cater-pillars."

LEONARD : I recently had in my hands the original parchment documents relating to the enrolment of the Volunteers of 1803. It is an interesting collection of the autographs of our grandfathers—of such of them as could write, at least, for there are not wanting instances where a cross had to take the place of a signature.

CHAPTER XII.

MR. WILLIAM SWIFT.

Scene.—A room in Leonard's house. The chair usually occupied
by Mr. Twiss stands at its customary corner—empty. The
other friends are in their accustomed places.

Period.—The 16th of December, 1874.

L EONARD :

> " The sequel of to-day unsolders all
> The goodliest fellowship of old-world lore
> Whereof this town holds record."

LEIGHTON (pointing to the empty chair) :

> " There sat the shadow, fear'd of man,
> Who broke our fair companionship
> And spread his mantle dark and cold."

EVERARD :

> " 'Tis common ; all that live must die,
> Passing through nature to eternity."

LEIGHTON :

> " Ay, Sir, it is common."

EVERARD : Therefore, instead of further lamentations on
our friend's departure, let us take up the moral of his life,
and hope that we may be as honestly mourned.

> " The man we celebrate must find a tomb,
> And we that worship him, ignoble graves."

Who can tell the story ?

LEONARD : Mr. William Swift died on Thursday evening,
December 10, 1874, at Ash Cottage, near Staveley, where a
few weeks before he retired from his usual residence in St.
James' street, for the benefit of change of air. He had all
but completed his 56th year; having been born on the 13th
December, in 1818. "Mr. Swift was a remarkable man,
whose avocation in life as assistant distributor of stamps con-
veys no idea of the esteem in which he was held, or the extent of his erudition as a genealogist and topographer. Born
in a modest cottage near Chesterfield, of humble but respectable parents, he succeeded by his own perseverance in
amassing a store of information in his own special field of

study not equalled by any other collector; and it is not too much to say that no man knew so much of the History of the Hundred of Scarsdale, or of South Yorkshire, as he did. For many generations the Swifts have lived in Staveley and the neighbourhood, but probably none of them ever knew so much of themselves and their progenitors as did the late William Swift; who, happily, is not the last of his race, but, by his marriage with another Swift, unites, in the persons of his two sons, two branches of a genealogical tree that sprung from the common root of John Swift, of Inkersall, in Staveley parish, six generations ago.

" After passing through the ordinary curriculum of a country school, he began the active duties of life as a clerk in a lawyer's office in Chesterfield, but at the age of 18 removed to Sheffield to enter the service of the late Mr. Brown, of St. James's street, and for 38 years he has remained in the same occupation, though not under the same employer. Mr. Brown was distributor of stamps as well as a solicitor, and, finding how valuable a servant he had in Mr. Swift, he gave him the entire management of his stamp business; and some years ago, when Mr. Brown was succeeded as stamp distributor by Major Fawkes, Mr. Swift retained his old place, and in the office at the corner of St. James's row, he might be seen until the end of September, when his health broke down.

" It was not his social position that gave our late friend a name and a place in the annals of Sheffield; nor was it even the kindly good nature with which he answered all inquiries; nor the humble simplicity and piety of his private life; but his marvellous industry and care as a genealogical and topographical collector. A career less eventful than his could scarcely be imagined. He lived in a house adjoining his office, and when business was over, he much too rarely went out for fresh air and exercise. Far into the night, he would pore over manuscripts, sometimes copying old parish registers, sometimes making abstracts, or copies of documents that had been lent to him, or entering up his volumes of pedigrees. His mind was ever intent on the acquisition of genealogical facts, and whether they came under his notice in written papers, or in conversation, he carefully noted them, and systematically stored them away in the volumes to which they belonged. The desire to be accurate was with him a passion. He could not endure a false date, and smiled when he observed the vanity, that, in pedigrees, could not call a

spade a spade, but turned a cutler, a grinder, or something
humbler, into a gentleman. During the thirty-eight years
he lived in Sheffield he had been carefully accumulating
fact upon fact, and there is probably not a family in the town,
save the most recent importations, of whom he had not a
more or less complete account. He was the Old Mortality of
Sheffield, and carefully copied the gravestones in the church
and chapel yards. The parish registers were more familiar
to him than to the parish clerk. He knew the genealogical
value of wills and deeds, and had made himself master of
those old handwritings under which our forefathers have
shrouded so much valuable information. Not having enjoyed
the advantage of a classical education, he yet so far mastered
the difficulties of Latin and Norman French as to be able to
translate intelligibly such mediæval documents as were couched
in those languages ; and of late years, so vast was the fund
of information which he possessed, that he was able at once
to appreciate the value of new facts that might come under
his notice, and to see meanings in entries and items that to
an ordinary observer appeared to have no special significance.
For years past he has been the oracle to which all inquirers
into Sheffield history resorted. The antiquarian student per-
petually made use of his kindly advice and counsel ; the lawyers flocked to him regularly when any question arose affecting family history ; and to one and all he was alike ready to
tell what he knew, and in return to accept any crumbs of
information his visitors might be able to impart. In this way
his store of facts grew. Persons who had learned the value
of his information were glad to be able to offer him some return in kind, when anything came under their notice. His
fame as a collector of information spread, and from far and
near matters found their way into his hands that would not
have been entrusted to one less discreet. He was scrupulous
in preserving and returning everything that was lent to him ;
and exercised a marvellous reticence in dealing with subjects
that might have given pain to families or individuals. He
never spoke unkindly, and, though his mind was the deposi-
tory of more family secrets than that of any man in Sheffield,
we never heard of an instance where an unfair or unkind use
had been made of what he knew. Like many great collectors of information, Mr. Swift seemed to lack the aptitude
for collating, arranging, and editing his materials. He
shrank from the task of composition, fancying, very mista-
kenly, that he could not compose ; and yet we have had in

our hands fragments of his that would have been no discredit to so lucid and interesting a writer as the late Joseph Hunter. Our own columns" [it is the *Independent* from which I am quoting] "have not unfrequently contained most valuable scraps from his pen ; but he would more frequently give his information verbally, and leave others to clothe it in set words. Under the signature ' St.' he sometimes contributed to *Notes and Queries*. Several papers of his have appeared in the *Reliquary :* and he has also enriched the Chesterfield newspapers from the stores of his Derbyshire lore ; but we never heard of his publishing a book, nor ever knew a man more capable of doing so. In connection with the inquiries arising out of the bequest to the town of the property of the late Samuel Bailey, Mr. Swift rendered great service ; and the Rev. Dr. Gatty, in his preface to the new edition of Hunter's Hallamshire, thus acknowledges his obligations :—' The services of Mr. William Swift, well known for his genealogical studies, experience and accuracy, as well as for his accumulated stores of information relating to the various properties of the neighbourhood, have been especially great throughout the latter part of the work, and deserve my warmest appreciation. He has extended the pedigrees with a careful hand, and by an old deed or memorandum has often contributed what the antiquarian will value.' Among his friends might be mentioned every name of note in Sheffield; but it is enough to say that he was on intimate terms with Joseph Hunter, James Montgomery, John Holland, Samuel Mitchell, and Henry Jackson ; without particularising those who have lived to feel his loss. When the late Samuel Mitchell's papers had to be arranged for the British Museum, Mr. Swift was selected to perform the task, and very ably he discharged it. He had a pure and simple mind, inexpensive tastes and habits, and if there was a thing he erred in, it was in taking too little care of his own health. At one time he paid some attention to a garden at Steel Bank, with a view to obtain out-door exercise and recreation ; but of late that has been much neglected, and sometimes for a week together he never left St. James's street. On the occasion of the funeral of Mr. John Holland, now nearly two years ago, Mr. Swift took a severe cold, which clung to him for many months ; and over a year ago he suffered greatly from a carbuncle on the leg. During the past twelve months he has not looked well, and many times have friends given him good advice in vain. He seemed unequal to the effort of tearing himself away from his favourite

home and occupations. A short visit to the sea-side in the early
autumn did but little to restore tone to his system, and for
two months or more he has been unable to attend to business,
though up to the last few days of his life his mind retained
all its clearness. A few weeks ago, in the hope of deriving
benefit from change of air, he went on a visit to friends in
his native district of Staveley, but nature was too far exhausted
to revive, and he there gradually grew worse and passed
away, leaving many sincere friends to mourn him, and not a
single enemy to throw obloquy on his memory. His wife,
who has been the attached companion of his life, and two sons
survive, and in their bereavement it may be some small consolation to know how universally the deceased husband and
father was esteemed. Some time ago Mr. Swift purchased
for himself a family burial place in the new Cemetery at
Norton, within the confines of that county of Derby he loved
so well."

EVERARD : Let me read to you also what Dr. Gatty says
of our late friend :—" I cannot allow Mr. Swift to pass away
from us without expressing my personal regret for his departure, and my conviction also that Sheffield has lost in him
one of its most useful though least self-asserting citizens.
So far as my opinion has any value, I am certainly entitled
to speak of him, for circumstances threw me into frequent
communication with him ; and there was something so
genuine and truthful in his character that acquaintance soon
ripened into friendly regard. During the four years that my
leisure time was occupied in enlarging Mr. Hunter's 'History
of Hallamshire,' my intercourse with Mr. Swift was frequent
and intimate. I had known him long before, and regarded
him as a curiosity; and I found him a treasure, when I
needed his help. I applied to three other gentlemen for co-
operation, with whom I was also acquainted—Mr. Henry
Jackson, Mr. Samuel Mitchell, and Mr. John Holland—but
was too late, for death removed the two former before they
could render substantial aid, and the several sheets written
by good, kind John Holland were not of the slightest use to
me ; and I only name this because the contrary has been
assumed in his recent biography. Mr. Swift, on the other
hand, was a true and worthy disciple of Hunter. He cared
and knew, I believe, little of the present, while he loved and
lived in the past. Remarkably sensitive and fearful of giving
offence, he seemed scarcely to like even to talk of the living,
but of their ancestry he often knew more than they them-

selves did, and he always used his knowledge with discretion and kindness. It is as a local genealogist that Sheffield may deplore his death. Whilst I was busy over ' Hallamshire,' he passed several Sundays at my house—coming here on Saturday afternoon, and going home on the following evening. We all liked him, and there was one then present who thoroughly estimated the simplicity of his character, and the reverent spirit which was a marked feature in it. He always liked our Church Service, but the hymns were the portion that seemed to interest him most. He was a good listener, and I suspect always carried away what was worth remembering. I always felt that Pegasus was harnessed to a cart, when I saw him called away from a genealogical memorandum on his desk, or an open County History in which he had discovered some ancestral link with some South Yorkshire or Derbyshire family, and that to attend at his counter to a question of stamps or licenses. His proper place would have been the Record Office or the Heralds' College; but his scholarship being self-acquired had no warranty, and his native modesty stood in his way. From his office window in St. James's row, he kept a watchful eye on the Parish Church and churchyard, which he deeply reverenced; and he himself told me that he was the means of preserving the single stone of Norman Carving which was found in the rubble of the tower in 1867, when the new clock was fixed; also of rescuing the dial slab from destruction when it was taken down, and which Dr. Sale restored at his own cost. Let me add that he possessed that generosity of feeling which is common amongst all really scientific men; whatever he knew he was ready to impart, provided the information was sought for a good purpose, and not from vulgar or mischievous curiosity. I repeat my regret that poor Swift is no longer amongst us, and I throw this small flower of appreciation on his grave."

LEIGHTON : And so this is the grievous end of our many dialogues.

EVERARD : Yes, it is no use continuing them now. Farewell!

OMNES : Farewell!

[*Exeunt.*

CHAPTER XIII.

SELF-MADE MEN.—THE REV. DANIEL CHAPMAN AND HENRY PICKFORD.

THE account given in Chapter VI. (p. 126), of the Rev. Henry Mellon, who worked his way up from the Boys' Charity School and became a clergyman of the Church of England, ought not to stand alone, for two other prominent examples of self-made men call for notice—The Rev. Daniel Chapman and Henry Pickford, " the learned grinder." The following accounts are compiled from the statements of three different writers :—

Daniel Chapman's birth takes us back seventy-five years—to the old Sheffield of 1799. He could not have been born with a silver spoon in his mouth, for at 14 years of age you could any day see him with hands and face as black as a tinker's, at the stove-grate manufactory, Roscoe place. But although spending twelve hours every day at his employment, he found a little spare time for the pursuit of knowledge, which must have been in those days, and in those circumstances of obscurity, a pursuit under great difficulties. He obtained a little private instruction two evenings a week, and was soon pronounced by his teacher " one of the best grammarians in Sheffield." Having laid this good foundation, we find him in an evening, after the day's work is done, at one time with a Rev. Mr. Whiteley, a Unitarian minister; then with a Rev. Mr. Harrison, and subsequently with Rev. Thomas Smith, one of the Professors of Rotherham Independent College. Trade becoming very depressed, his father-in-law (through whose self-denying kindness he had been assisted to the needful funds) said, " Thou must, child, stop awhile, and then begin again ; thou knows Rome was not built in a day." " True, father," replied the boy ; " but they always kept on building, until it was finished." One evening, a gentleman was delivering a lecture in the Assembly Room, Norfolk street, and gave at the close an invitation for questions. Daniel Chapman, who was behind the audience in very humble attire, solicited the lecturer's opinion on a subject to which he had not referred. The lecturer stated that it belonged to one of the most abstruse mysteries of astronomy, and as he was unable to throw any light on it, requested the youth to give the audience the benefit of his own thoughts. These he clearly explained in a way which convinced his hearers that he was more than superficially conversant with the subject. The late James Montgomery, the poet, was present on the occasion, and having sought out the obscure youth, there commenced a friendship which only terminated with death. Daniel Chapman had arrived at the age of 20 when he met in class with the Wesleyan community. The Rev. James Everett was at that time stationed in Sheffield, and met for the quarterly renewal of tickets the class of which Mr. Chapman was a member. This was on a week evening, and earlier than the usual time, so that the minister could do double duty the same evening. Daniel was therefore obliged to appear in his working dress, and face and hands bearing evidence of the nature of his employment. On being questioned in the usual way, he related his experience in language so much superior to what his apparent condition justified, that the preacher's godly jealousy was awakened, and he mingled caution against vanity and self-conceit with his counsels, and especially against indulgence in these, under such circumstances. On the following day, Daniel sent Mr. Everett a scholarly letter. Mr. Everett's surprise may be easily conjectured. He promptly waited upon Mr. Chapman, and mutual explanations and a good understanding ever afterwards resulted. About this time we find that the Rev. Thomas Smith had introduced Mr. Chapman to Dr. Bennett, professor of theology in the Rotherham College. That was an important link in the chain of events which led to his being sent to the Edinburgh University. On one frosty morning, about nine o'clock, Daniel knocked at the back door of the Rotherham College. The servant observing his humble habiliments announced him as an Irish lad wanting to speak to her master. Mrs. Bennett came to know the lad's business, supposing he was asking charity. The reply was characteristic—" Please, Madam, be so kind as to present this note (Rev. Thomas Smith's) to Mr. Bennett." The result of that interview was that Dr. Bennett made Mr. Chapman an offer to become private tutor to his children. As, however, the pulpit was the goal of Mr. Chapman's ambition, the offer was declined, and a committee of clergymen, Independent ministers, and laymen (upon which Mr. Montgomery was very active) agreed that he should go to Edinburgh, and

so be left at perfect liberty to shape out his after course. In
the University he rose to a first-class position, and carried off
the prizes both in natural and moral philosophy, and also in
Greek. On leaving the University he became a Wesleyan
minister of good note. His discourses were full of vigour
and originality. He was emphatically an *independent* thinker.
It is reported that he was taken publicly to task by one of
his seniors at the Conference for the exuberance of his beard.
Mr. Chapman's reply to the inquisition was a clear proof that
they were dealing with a true Sheffield blade, " If the growing of my beard maketh my weak brother to offend, let him
take a pair of scissors and cut it off." His uniform kindness
was a ruling trait of character : few houses that he visited
but in them he was regarded with almost enthusiastic affection. Nor was his kindness circumscribed by the limit of his
acquaintances. An incident that occurred in the streets is
but one of many that might be mentioned. He overtook an
aged woman who obtained her living by the selling of apples.
Her too heavily-laden baskets and their contents were, by a
simple accident, upset ; immediately stepping off the pavement, he assisted with the utmost alacrity in collecting the
scattered fruit ; nor was the old woman more delighted than
he in seeing the apples restored to their proper place. He
was not a little remarkable for the singularity of his appearance. His clothes hung loosely about his person, as if
they were made for a much larger man. His white cravat
was folded in a roll and tie so loosely as to rest on his bosom,
exposing the whole of the throat. His hat sloped backwards
at a very unusual angle. His warm cloak, always worn except in very hot weather, was thrown in a slovenly manner
over his shoulders. His gait was measured and slow, and
seemed incapable of being quickened. His by-the-way remarks and conversational replies were often very remarkable.
In one of the circuits where he laboured he was obliged to
decline an invitation to preach in a London chapel; and
he was thereupon visited by two ladies, who had gone in the
hope of prevailing on him to consent. After much fruitless
entreaty, one of them said playfully but earnestly, " Mr.
Chapman, I am determined not to leave your house until
you promise to oblige us." The reply was instantaneous,
" Madam, you do me infinite honour; for you will abide with
me always." It is commonly reported of him that once he
went to a small village to preach, for which journey he took
a hired conveyance. On pulling up at the destination, where

the horse was to be housed, seeing the ostler's boy coming towards him, the following scene transpired. Mr. Chapman: "Extricate this quadruped from the vehicle, stabulate him, apportion him an adequate supply of nutritious aliment, and when the solar orb shall again illumine the eastern horizon I will reward your hospitality by the needful pecuniary advantage." Boy all this time, with eyes fixed and mouth open—now precipitates himself into the presence of his employer, with the exclamation, "Eh, Mester, there's a Frenchman wants you." The kindliness of his nature extended itself also to the lower creation. He would never himself put any living thing to death. The writer was informed the other day by a Wesleyan minister who followed him in one of his circuits, that for some weeks after he arrived at the Chapel house, a colony of cats would come every Thursday mewing to the door for something to eat. On making inquiries about this queer phenomenon, he was informed that Mr. Chapman had been in the habit of feeding them regularly for some time, on that day of the week. The studied politeness which he manifested on all occasions was shown just as much to the poor beggar who came to the door as to the visitor who came in his carriage. He was often laughed at on this account; but in him it had all the force of a deeply-rooted principle. He used to say—"All men are naturally equal in the sight of God; and as God is no respecter of persons I must not be." This noteworthy life of our fellow-townsman came to its close on the 10th November, 1857. The event which gave a decidedly beneficial character to his after life—Mr. Chapman was accustomed to relate thus: "It was the death of my father. I well remember the scene. My father died in the midst of a terrific storm of thunder and lightning; and every time the artillery of heaven exploded with a tremendous crash, which made all round the bed shudder, my dying father, like an immortal spirit winging its flight to heaven on pinions of fire, exclaimed 'Glory be to God.'"

Another writer says:—My first knowledge of Daniel Chapman was hearing of his going to purchase Latin and Greek books at the shop of Mr. Pearce, the bookseller in Gibraltar street. He was often a visitor at that large depôt of learned lore, and nothing seemed to afford him more pleasure than to be allowed, for hours together, to take down and examine the contents of the different shelves. He always came in his working dress, and almost as black as a sweep. The highflown language and correct pronunciation made use of by this swarthy son of the workshop roused the bookseller's wonderment to the highest pitch, and he began to cast glances into the future as to the probabilities of this young man's ultimate destiny.

The next time Daniel's name attracted my attention was when he came like a flaming star from the north—*i.e.*, as a distinguished student from the Metropolitan University of Scotland. At this time he was announced to preach in Carver street Chapel, and my curiosity had been too keenly awakened in bygone days not to attend ; the more so, indeed, as the young man from Roscoe place came forth in the new attire of a minister of the gospel, with the laurels of a university student. Long before the usual time the chapel was crowded to excess—not even standing room. The clock struck six ; at that moment the door behind the pulpit opened, and the Rev. Daniel Chapman was at once the object of every eye. The stillness was awful. To him the audience must either have been appaling in the extreme, or else highly stimulating ; but this would depend on the susceptibility of his mental calibre, and the preparation he felt for meeting the requirements of so trying an occasion. His appearance at this time was nervous bilious ; head, somewhat small but compact ; hair, black ; forehead, rather narrow but high ; the coronal region well developed ; the organs of the inferior sentiments being small, they would not have *force* enough to give to the intellect high emotional and thrilling power. Never shall I forget the manner, intonation, and beautiful enunciation with which he uttered the words, " The first hymn on the paper" —not to mention the exquisite style in which the hymn itself was read, so different from what we had been accustomed to hear. The time for prayer arrived. It was a splendid invocation to the Deity. He ranged through the universe, making planets and suns the mere footsteps to the throne of God— lightning, the gleam of his eye ; thunder, the voice of his displeasure ; and Christ, the all-in-all for humanity's redemption. The service went on ; the time for the sermon arrived ; the book opened, and the text read was, " On his thigh and on his vestments shall be written—King of Kings, and Lord of Lords." The utterance of these words was transcendently exquisite, and an uncommon oration was delivered. In one part of a burst of eloquence, in which he quoted, for effect, his text in Greek, an old woman, roused to the top of her wonderment and the acme of her piety by these uncommon sounds, unconsciously exclaimed, " Glory ! Hallelujah !"

Daniel having, by his classical stratagem, put the crowning stone on the good lady's emotion.

For a time Daniel Chapman was very popular with the Wesleyans; his style, ornate language, and other pecularities drew overflowing congregations. Of his mental capacities verbal memory was the salient characteristic. Every other power was made the most of by the tenacity of his memory for words. Without this aid many of his faculties would have had only a sort of common-place manifestation. He had the power—whether naturally or acquired it is hard to say—of investing thoughts at the spur of the moment in language at once verbose, rotund, or singularly unique. It almost amounted to a natural aptitude to express thoughts in ornate language. This kind of style sounds grand, startles for a time, but at length ceases to have its attractions even on the public ear. As for committing it to the press, thinking it good English composition, nothing could be further from the standard of excellence. The writer was a student at the University of Edinburgh two or three years after Daniel Chapman left it. Although four years a student at the same *alma mater*, he never heard Daniel Chapman's name mentioned till within two months of his final graduation. Conversing one evening with the celebrated Professor Wilson (the Christopher North of Blackwood) on Sheffield, her poets and her scholars, Montgomery, Elliott, and Bailey having been on the *tapis*, he suddenly turned the subject and said, "By the bye, did you know a person called Daniel Chapman, who came from your town. He attended my moral philosophy class for a session. He was a man of some genius, but was sorely disappointed at not carrying off the moral philosophy gold medal; but his style of composition was peculiar and inflated; and as there were better men against whom he had to contend, he failed necessarily in what he aimed at. I was very sorry: he was an amiable man; but I have a duty to perform, and the best men alone carry off the highest honours. At that time," continued the Professor, "it was my custom to meet the students on the Saturday morning to hear them read the most brilliant passages of their prize essays. On one of these occasions I called upon Mr. Daniel Chapman to read his essay, or portions of it. What with the gravity of his manner, the peculiar stiffness of his utterance, and the grandiloquent language in which the essay was couched, it was not long before the whole class was convulsed with laughter—and I laughed too, for I could not help it. I never had so much difficulty in restoring the students to order; and, in fact, this could not be done till I had called up another student to read his essay."

Notwithstanding all this, Daniel Chapman was a remarkable man, and for him to do what he did redounded to his infinite credit. To be able to throw aside the Sheffield slang, and attain the polish and perfection that he did, shows a power of perseverance truly Demosthenic. His enunciation, in spite of what the Scotch students might think, was highly nervous, and consequently exquisitely distinct, and his pronunciation of words, on the whole, beautiful in the extreme. The manner of his sounding the vowel I, and all words containing it, in any syllable, was worthy of all imitation, for it fell upon the ear with a peculiar fascination. With a little more of the *anime* in his composition—that which gives the motive power to all the faculties—Daniel Chapman might have become the impassioned orator, and, at will, have "Ruled the fierce Democracy." As it was, the impression he produced on all audiences was of no ordinary character.

PERSONAL RECOLLECTIONS OF MR. HENRY PICKFORD.

Henry Pickford was born in Sheffield about 1806. His father, Mr. James Pickford, was an industrious, respectable, and pious man, by trade a saw grinder. Leaving school when about thirteen years of age, Henry Pickford began to work with his father at the trade of saw grinding. From that period he was " self educated," except some little assistance rendered by the late Rev. Thos. Smith, A.M., Classical Tutor of Rotherham College, and one or two other persons. His natural taste was for the acquisition of languages. He was, I believe, in a great degree animated in these pursuits by the laudable ambition of imitating that remarkable Sheffield man of whom we have just been hearing, the late Rev. Daniel Chapman. He pursued his studies, early and late, with characteristic ardour and considerable success. One day he very much astonished the attendants of the Bible Society's depôt by applying to purchase a Chaldo-Syriac Testament. This led to inquiries which, I believe, were the means of his introduction to some of the clergy. He had been brought up at the Queen street Chapel, and was a member of Mr. Boden's church, and, for some time, his thoughts had been directed towards the work of the Christian ministry amongst the Independents. Certain circumstances, however, at length occurred that led him to examine the principles and formularies of the Established Church, and having by this means arrived at certain definite views and convictions, he joined that communion under the ministry of the late Rev. Thomas Best, M.A., at St. James's Church. He was thus led to make the acquaintance of the Rev. T. D. Atkinson, at that time the esteemed incumbent of St. Philip's. From the pen of that gentleman a short notice appeared, which, as a document written at the time, furnishes a clearer and more authentic account by a competent judge of his literary attainments than could now have been supplied from memory. The following is an extract :—

" This young man, though moving in the inferior walks of life, had, by persevering industry and diligence, attained to a considerable knowledge of various languages. The writer of this article well recollects the pleasing surprise which was created in his mind some two years since by the following circumstance, which led him to make further inquiries respecting him, and ever after to feel a lively interest about his progress and future prospects. Mr. Pickford happened to call upon him. Amongst other inquiries one was made whether he had ever read any of the Greek dramatic writers ? He replied in the negative ; but wishing to ascertain his proficiency in the reading of Greek, a request was made that he would recite a few lines from Sophocles, which was lying on the table. He did so ; not only correctly as it regarded the reading, but, after a little attention, rendered the passage into English in a manner very creditable to him. This circumstance is mentioned to show that the mind of this young man was of no ordinary kind, when, without friends, almost without assistance of any sort, and certainly without any regular or efficient education, in the midst too of a laborious daily occupation, he could attain to such a proficiency. He had acquired considerable knowledge of the Latin language. The writer has now in his possession many of his translations from various authors, several books of Juvenal, the whole of Persius, &c. To Hebrew and to several of the Oriental languages he had paid much attention. Professor Lee (of Cambridge University), who had seen some of his translations, pronounced that they did him much credit. French, Italian, German, Spanish, also obtained a share of his attention. Under such circumstances a proposition was made, and through the kindness of friends nearly brought to a suc-

x

cessful conclusion, that he should be sent to the University of Cambridge, and put in a way of honourably distinguishing himself by the fair exercise of those talents which God had bestowed upon him." One of the papers above referred to by Mr. Atkinson as having been sent to Professor Lee, consisted of a translation into one of the Oriental languages of a well-known personification of one of the four Seasons, I think " Spring," by Mrs. Barbauld.

Henry Pickford was of a very amiable and cheerful disposition. Indeed, his exuberance of spirits, united with great fluency of speech, was apt, at seasons, to explode in uncontrollable fits of mirth, fun, and laughter. Some persons were inclined to regard such outbursts as indicative and proof of real habitual levity of mind. Such an opinion would certainly be a great mistake. Such occasions were simply the outward manifestation of one of Nature's kindly gifts. In fact it acted as a safety-valve.

In July, 1830, seeing that his bodily and mental powers were kept at too great and constant a strain, I persuaded him, and he actually made arrangements, to accompany me to the Western coast, in order to enjoy what at the time he very much needed, an entire relaxation for some weeks. Unfortunately for him the saw trade, which had been dull, became brisk. His employers, therefore, pressed him very hard and earnestly to do all the work he possibly could ; and he, being anxious to get all the money he was able in prospect of the University, instead of going with me to the sea-side and inhaling the invigorating breezes of the ocean, stayed at home and exerted himself to the utmost; in one instance working all night, during a season of remarkably hot weather. He ere long found that he had to pay the penalty which physical laws exact on all, without distinction, who disregard or infringe them. That great exertion did him an irreparable injury, having eventually the effect of developing a latent tendency to consumption, so that from that time he only lived a year. Although during the succeeding months there were the usual alternations of hope and fear, cloud and sunshine, yet his earthly expectations were in reality blasted. His medical advisers were Dr. (afterwards Sir Arnold) Knight, and the late Mr. Wilson Overend; but from the first they gave to his parents but slender hopes as to his recovery.

It was my privilege to visit him during the whole course of his illness. He died in July, 1831, about 25 years of age. Amidst the eager and successful pursuit of literature he had not neglected the " one thing needful." He was a young, intelligent, and sincere Christian, and purposed devoting his talents and his life to the service of his Lord and Master. Relying on Divine mercy through the atonement and intercession of Christ, his end was peace. Respecting him nothing can be more appropriate than the lines of Mrs. Hemans :

> " The ethereal fire hath shivered
> The fragile censer in whose mould it quivered,
> Brightly, consumingly."

APPENDIX.

Samuel Scantlebury. p. 7.

Mr. Samuel Scantlebury died at Chicago, U.S., the 31st December, 1874, aged 74. He was born 1st September, 1800.

Early Bankers. p. 9.

There is still standing in the Hartshead, immediately above where the Red Lion Inn crosses the passage, a poor house occupied by a working jeweller. The door opens out of the Hartshead, and the window in the side looks out into a little yard. In the wall over this is a stone with the inscription—
H.
HASLEHURST & SON,
1783.

Mr. Hall Overend and the Resurrectionists. p. 45.

Leonard : Mr. Hall Overend was an enthusiast in the cause of surgical science, which in his day was carried on amid great disadvantages and hazards, since the law provided only for the dissection of criminals who had been hanged, and the supply was altogether inadequate for the medical schools. This gave rise to the horrible practice of employing "resurrection men" to disinter clandestinely bodies which relatives supposed had been borne to their last home. Mr. Overend established the Sheffield Medical School, and was its most zealous promoter. The duty of obtaining " subjects " rested mainly upon him, and he carried it out with characteristic vigour and success. None but a man standing so high as he did, professionally and socially, could have sustained himself against the prejudice which the suspicion of the employment of " resurrection men " brought upon him, for not only were the feelings of families grievously wounded, by fears or realities, but there existed an ever-smouldering popular indignation, which the slightest incident might any day have caused to break out in riot and outrage. Besides this, was the constant risk of the capture or injury of some of the agents employed, or the search of the premises of the

school, which might have resulted in the discovery of some
body capable of being identified. It certainly was not a subject favourable to the humour of Hood's lines, representing
the ghost of a departed wife as coming to her husband's bed-
side and saying—

> " The body-snatchers, they have come,
> And made a snatch at me ;
> It's very odd that kind of men
> Can't let a body be."

Mr. Hall Overend had not even the benefit of that rule of
political economy that occupations are highly paid in proportion to their disagreeableness and danger. Both in money and
in mental anxiety and worry, he lost largely by the war he
waged against antiquated law in the interest of science and
humanity. The students had the "subjects" for the mere
sum paid to the men who procured them, while the sacrifices
and costs of Mr. Overend himself were utterly unrequited.
There were rumours that Mr. Overend personally took part
in the lifting of bodies and their conveyance to the medical
school, and it was a popular belief that his death was
hastened by injuries received in one of these nocturnal expeditions. It was improbable enough that a gentleman over
50 years of age, whose days were intensely occupied in a most
laborious practice, could personally give up his nights to the
labours, risks, and exposure incident to body-snatching ; but
I had the opportunity lately of conversing with a surgeon, in
his student days one of the young gentlemen, of the most
respectable families in the neighbourhood, who sought the
advantage of being Mr. Overend's pupils. This gentleman
holds in unbounded honour the memory of his old master,
and on my naming to him the rumour I have mentioned, it
gave rise to a very interesting conversation, which perhaps I
had better record in its original form of dialogue.

DOCTOR : Mr. Overend did not go out, but he knew what
was done, and on almost the last occasion when we brought
in a body, he happened to be in Church street, and was in a
state of extreme perturbation lest the constables should search
the house and find it. I satisfied him at last by showing
that the body could not be identified.

LEONARD : What sort of men were employed in this work?

DOCTOR : There were two men employed, but we pupils
were active accomplices, planning the operations, keeping
watch, giving signals, drawing off the watchers, and carrying
away the bodies. When we had got a corpse in the bottom
of the gig, or dressed up in cloak, bonnet, and veil, supported

between two of us, we were not long in driving to Sheffield. Mr. Overend kept good horses, and anybody who tried to catch us after we had got off, must have looked sharp.

LEONARD : I suppose you did not often venture on the town grave yards ?

DOCTOR : No ; unless there was some special reason for it, in the singularity of a case. I remember a deformed woman who had died in childbirth. We were very anxious to examine her, and we got her. But we preferred the quiet village churchyards—most of these within 12 or 14 miles were visited at times.

LEONARD : When your men got to work on a newly-filled grave, they would soon get at the body ?

DOCTOR : Well, not always. They sometimes found obstacles put in their way, or graves made deep. I remember one case where the men had excavated, and came back to us saying there was neither body nor coffin there. We had to give it up for a time ; but we were so sure that we tried again, and we found that the sexton, when he had gone low enough, had made a sort of cave along one side of the grave, and the coffin had been pushed in there.

LEONARD : You would not like now to run such a risk as you did then ?

DOCTOR : Oh, the excitement totally overbore the risk. You will quite understand how the expeditions would arouse the adventurous spirits of young medical students, who had to plan and conduct them. The greater the difficulty the more we tried to overcome it. Most of the adventures were of our own planning.

LEONARD : How did you go about them ?

DOCTOR : We went out "prospecting," to borrow a word unknown then. When we heard of a death in one of the villages, one or two of us would go out for a country walk, with a piece of bread and cheese in our pockets, and a silver coin or two, not of the largest. We rested in a little village alehouse, and of course we must look at the church or copy curious epitaphs in the churchyard. Sextons were usually communicative. We ascertained where some poor body was to be buried in a day or two, perhaps saw the sexton at work, noted the points it was necessary to watch, marked the line of retreat, and settled the best time to come. When the time arrived, we walked to the place by different ways, and the gig came after, to diminish the risk of its being observed waiting.

LEONARD : Of course it would be a great object with you, when you had rifled a grave, to have it filled up so as to show no trace of disturbance, but you must sometimes have had to escape in a hurry.

DOCTOR : Oh, yes. I remember one very funny case. It happened in a village that had been infested by fowl-stealers, who had made the people very vigilant, and we knew several of them kept their guns in readiness loaded with slugs. All had gone right with us. The night was dark. We had got the body removed to a little distance, and the men were rapidly completing the grave, when unluckily the sky cleared and the moon shone out. A young couple had been married that day, and lived in a cottage overlooking the churchyard. The bride happened to get out of bed during the night, just too soon for us, and to look out of the window. Of course she shrieked when she saw us, and her cry brought her husband to the window. She screamed " Shoot ! shoot !" and if we had seen the husband turn from the window and come back again, we should have supposed he had got his gun, and have expected a charge of slugs. Of course we could not stay to finish the work, though we got clear off with the body. We had a narrow escape at another village where the church and the rectory were adjacent. Instead of finding all quiet at the usual time as we expected, we perceived that some of the rectory family were up. The rector had gone out to dinner, and besides the servants in the house, a man was in the out premises, waiting to assist the coachman in putting up the carriage horses. We were just ready to be off, when the carriage came up, but we had to bring away a fellow pupil, whom I had put on the rectory yard wall, where he lay to watch. Our usual mode of signalling was by throwing stones in the direction of the party to be warned, but in this case our watcher was too far off, and I had no chance but to run across the rectory lawn and bring him away. On another occasion a strict watch had been set over a grave. We got the watchers into the public-house, and so entertained them with our songs and stories that our object was accomplished quietly, and we left the watchers boasting what they would have done if the body-snatchers had dared to come there.

WRAGG : I think I can tell a story how one of the *two* professional resurrectionists once got into trouble. About the year 1830, a young man died of consumption and was buried in Bradfield churchyard, close to the east end of the church. Some one near the church hearing a gig, and the feet

of a horse pacing about, got up to learn the cause of so
unusual a noise, and saw what was going on in the churchyard.   Those in the gig made a precipitate retreat towards
Sheffield.   One man was caught in endeavouring to make
his escape from the churchyard, in which he would have
succeeded, but his course was impeded by a deep snow drift.
This man suffered twelve months' imprisonment.

CAMPO LANE.   p. 46.

Mr. Hunter, in an unpublished MS., says :—"In this
name (Campo lane) is preserved the memory of the ancient
game of camping or foot ball, which was known by this
name, camping, in the time when the Promptorium was
compiled, and is still in use in that sense in the counties of
Norfolk and Suffolk.   See the Promptorium in Mr. Way's
edition, p. 60, and the Eastern Counties Glossaries, by Moore
and Forby.   *   *   The 'Campar field' occurs several times
in the returns of their Sheffield estates by the Dukes of
Norfolk, under the Acts 1 and 10 Geo. I., compelling Roman
Catholics to register their estates with the Clerk of the Peace.
This proves that there was once a field in Sheffield appropriated to this sport, and what more probable than that it was
the open space now called Paradise square ?   Campo lane, so
called, as leading to it—in full, the Camper field lane."

CHARLES SYLVESTER.   p. 46.

See "Local Notes and Queries" (*Sheffield Independent*,
Dec. 14, 1874).

DANIEL WHEELER.   pp. 53, 54.

For further particulars of Mr. Wheeler's life, see a Note
by Mr. T. O. Hinchliffe, in "Local Notes and Queries"
(*Sheffield Independent*, July 1, 1875).   The date of Mr.
Wheeler's departure for Russia is there given as 1818, and
his return 1832.   He died in New York, June 12, 1840,
aged 69.

EARLY SHEFFIELD PRINTERS.   pp. 78, 79, 107.

The following is from Mr. Hunter's MSS. :—
"The first book I have met with, published at Sheffield,
is Bagshaw's small 12mo. De Spiritualis Pecci, &c., by Nevill

Symmons, 1708. This Mr. Simmons seems to have been of a family well known in the annals of printing as purchasers of Paradise Lost, and as printers of the works of many of the Noncon. Divines in the latter half of the 17th century. They were of Worcester and London. See in the works of Baxter, or in Baxter's Life of Sylvester, an apology for himself touching some remarks which had been illiberally cast upon him as having by an exorbitant demand for his works contributed to bring ruin upon his printer, Nevill Simmons. This Mr. Simmons seems to have settled at Sheffield in consequence of his marriage with a lady of that place. He had many children, one of them a dissenting minister of some eminence, and another who succeeded to his business, and at the time of his death was post-master in Sheffield. Many of the family are buried in the chancel of the parish church there, but Mr. Simmons the elder's name does not appear among the rest who are upon the plate. I am therefore inclined to think that he was not buried here, but that the Nevill Simmons, who died in 1722, and is buried in Wakefield churchyard, is this gentleman.

"John Garnet, who had been a soldier, began printing here 39 years ago, that year the hospital was first taken down, but never printed a newspaper. Lister set up in opposition to him ; he gave out and died at Dronfield.

"The first newspaper printed in Sheffield was called the Sheffield Weekly [Journal]. The first number was published on Tuesday, 30th April, 1754. Revel Homphrey was proprietor and printer. I know not how long it existed.

"Ward began the Sheffield [Public Advertiser in 1770.]

"In 1787, Messrs. Gales and Martin issued another weekly paper, under the title of 'the Sheffield Register.' The partnership was soon after dissolved, and the paper continued with great spirit by Mr. Gales. It became one of the prints obnoxious to Government in the darkest days of Mr. Pitt's administration, and the editor not being very careful of his conduct with respect to political affairs, found it convenient to retire to America, and thus escaped a prosecution and conviction with his friend Redhead Yorke. This was in the year 1794. Mr. Montgomery, who had been for some time his foreman, took up the paper, and published it under the title of the 'Iris,' or Sheffield Advertiser for the northern counties. He has conducted it upon the same principles on which Mr. Gales did, and once suffered imprisonment for a paragraph which appeared in it.

" Ward gave up his paper in 17[93], when another was set up, professing a line of politics opposite to those of the Register, printed by Northall under the title of the Sheffield Courant. This paper had not a long existence.

" From this time to 1807 the Iris was the only newspaper published in Sheffield. In consequence of a quarrel between the Editor and a printer in the town, 'The Sheffield Mercury' was set up in opposition to it. The first number was published by Wm. Todd, on Saturday, March 28th, 1807."

EBENEZER ELLIOTT'S MONUMENT. p. 85.

Removed for the purpose of re-erection in Weston Park, July 1st, 1875.

ANGEL STREET. p. 98.

While these sheets have been passing through the press, the whole of the property mentioned at the top of p. 98 ["where is now Mr. Carter's, shoemaker, there was an obstruction in the road. It was at the bottom of the Angel yard, and Mr. Wormall's shop is part of it"], from the Angel gateway up to Messrs. Cockayne's has been demolished to make room for the expansion of that firm. In the process of destruction the workmen, on the 30th April, 1874, laid bare the upper side wall of the shop until then occupied by Mr. Wormall, next above the Angel inn, exposing for a short time to daylight a fragment of an old Sheffield house. The front was modern, but the side wall exposed was built of rubble stone, as was the fashion in Sheffield, and was much decayed. There were several old windows, of more than ordinary size, with stone stanchions, years ago bricked up, the style of which suggested that the building was erected in the 17th century. An old chimney still remained, built with large dressed stones. Was this part of the projecting building mentioned on p. 98 as being altered by Mr. Walker ?

There is a suspicion that the first Sheffield Theatre was up the Angel Inn yard, behind the property above referred to, and now used as stabling.

HOUSES IN PORTOBELLO. p. 155.

The two houses here spoken of as "yet standing," have just been demolished (June, 1875).

MADAM FELL, p. 184.

See "Local Notes and Queries" in the *Sheffield Independent* for July 6, 1874.

MR. JOHN SPENCER. pp. 186, 190.

Mr. Spencer died at Masbro' Cottage, Masbro', November 24th, 1874, in his 84th year. He deserves to be remembered as a worthy relic of what we may almost call mediæval Sheffield. A Sheffield manufacturer of the old school, he retained knee breeches, stockings, and shoes, together with the vernacular in all its purity; but he yet had something of refinement both in language and manner. When urged to push his trade by sending out more travellers, he would reply with a confident smile—"Nay lad; we'll put in a bit better stuff if it be possible, and have a bit better workmanship, and that'll sell Spencer's files, without more travellers." Many of his quaint and shrewd sayings are commonly quoted by his old associates, workmen, and neighbours. He lived on terms of hearty familiarity with his workmen and poor neighbours, and was known among the urchins of Peacroft, for whom he always had kindly words and looks, as "Daddy Spencer." Straightforwardness, urbanity of manner, and kindness of heart were his characteristics. As a boy Mr. Spencer commenced working as a file cutter, at the early age of seven years. When he was 17 years old his uncle, who was a file manufacturer, died, leaving him the business, which he, under the guidance of his mother, carried on. Being in London when the war between this country and France was brought to a close, and being unable to obtain any orders owing to the badness of trade, Mr. Spencer determined to cross the Channel and try what he could do in France. He succeeded in gaining customers, and there are houses in France who gave Mr. Spencer orders nearly sixty years ago that still continue to do business with his sons. Mr. Spencer was a man of great industry. It was his invariable rule to manufacture a good article, and to treat his workmen with kindness, and when depression came, instead of taking advantage of the times, he kept his men on full work, and stocked the goods until there was a revival, when he soon cleared off his accumulation of stock. Having himself experienced the difficulties of travelling on horseback, carrying his patterns in saddle bags, before there were even coaches, Mr. Spencer knew fully the value of improved means of communication, and he accordingly threw himself heartily into various schemes to this end when the times were ripe. He was an active promoter of the "Humber Steam Ship Company," which, every Tuesday and Friday night, ran light boats, drawn by several horses, to Thorne, and thence by steam to Hull, London, and other places. In 1835-6, Mr. John Spencer was Master Cutler. His term of office was a very important and exciting year, abounding in joint-stock schemes of all sorts. As we had then no Mayor, the Master Cutler was by courtesy the authority to call and preside over public meetings; and the Reform Act of 1832 appointed him Returning Officer. The first bill for the Sheffield and Rotherham line (of which Mr. Spencer was a warm supporter) had been lost, and it was resolved to apply again; the North Midland scheme was brought forward, and a great effort, which many of the supporters of the Sheffield and Rotherham helped to defeat, was made by Mr. Spencer and others to secure Sheffield a station on the main line. The carrying of the line by Masbrough was followed by various schemes for improving the position of Sheffield, and prospectuses for lines to Manchester and also to Goole and Hull were issued. Mr. Spencer may, indeed, be credited with the initiation of the Sheffield and Manchester railway. He pressed the subject upon the late Mr. T. A. Ward, Mr. Deakin, and Mr. E. Smith, when it was decided that if the manufacturers of Manchester would co-operate with them they would form a company to start a railway between the two towns. Mr. Spencer immediately put himself in communication with the Sidebottoms and other influential gentlemen of Manchester, and with what success the traffic upon the railway now testifies. In the year in which Mr. Spencer was Master Cutler, the Company over which he presided, the Town Trustees, and the Church Burgesses had the honour to present an address to the Duchess of Kent, on the occasion of her visit, with the Princess Victoria, to Wentworth House; and Mr. Spencer also presided as returning officer at Mr. John Parker's re-election for the borough, on the occasion of his becoming one of the Lords of the Treasury. Mr. Spencer continued to carry on successfully the business in Pea croft until the year 1849, when he gave it up to two of his sons. On retiring from business Mr. Spencer went to live on an estate he had at Masbro', where he died.

INDEX.

LEADER AND SONS, PRINTERS, INDEPENDENT OFFICE, SHEFFIELD.

Lightning Source UK Ltd.
Milton Keynes UK
UKHW010634060820
367798UK00002B/401